Lecture Notes in Artificial Intelligence   13191

Subseries of Lecture Notes in Computer Science

Series Editors

Randy Goebel
University of Alberta, Edmonton, Canada

Wolfgang Wahlster
DFKI, Berlin, Germany

Zhi-Hua Zhou
Nanjing University, Nanjing, China

Founding Editor

Jörg Siekmann
DFKI and Saarland University, Saarbrücken, Germany

T0171846

More information about this subseries at https://link.springer.com/bookseries/1244

Nikos Katzouris · Alexander Artikis (Eds.)

Inductive Logic Programming

30th International Conference, ILP 2021
Virtual Event, October 25–27, 2021
Proceedings

 Springer

Editors
Nikos Katzouris ⓘ
National Cener for Scientific
Research Demokritos
Athens, Greece

Alexander Artikis ⓘ
University of Piraeus
Athens, Greece

ISSN 0302-9743   ISSN 1611-3349 (electronic)
Lecture Notes in Artificial Intelligence
ISBN 978-3-030-97453-4   ISBN 978-3-030-97454-1 (eBook)
https://doi.org/10.1007/978-3-030-97454-1

LNCS Sublibrary: SL7 – Artificial Intelligence

This Springer imprint is published by the registered company Springer Nature Switzerland AG
The registered company address is: Gewerbestrasse 11, 6330 Cham, Switzerland

Preface

This volume contains the accepted papers of the conference track of the 30th International Conference on Inductive Logic Programming (ILP 2021)[1]. ILP is a sub-field of machine learning, focusing on learning logical representations from relational data and structured background knowledge. The ILP conference series started in 1991. It originally focused on the induction of logic programs, but over the years it has expanded its research horizon significantly, welcoming contributions to all aspects of learning in logic, including the intersection of logical/symbolic learning with neural and statistical learning.

ILP 2021 was held online, as a virtual conference, during October 25–27, 2021. This year, for the first time, ILP was part of the 1st International Joint Conference on Learning & Reasoning (IJCLR 2021)[2], which was also held online during the same period. IJCLR 2021 consisted of four conferences/workshops related to the integration of learning and reasoning, which took place in parallel but also featured joint sessions with keynote talks, poster presentations, and panel discussions. In addition to ILP 2021, the IJCLR 2021 events were as follows: the 15th International Workshop on Neural-Symbolic Learning and Reasoning (NeSy 2021); the 10th International Workshop on Statistical Relational AI (StarAI 2021); and the 10th International Workshop on Approaches and Applications of Inductive Programming (AAIP 2021).

There were several kinds of papers submitted to ILP 2021:

1. Journal track papers submitted to IJCLR 2021's Special Issue on Learning & Reasoning. The IJCLR 2021 journal track, supported by the Machine Learning journal, solicited submissions on all topics of interest to the IJCLR 2021 events, namely ILP, NeSy, StarAI, and AAIP.
2. Regular long and short ILP conference track papers describing original work with appropriate experimental evaluation and/or a self-contained theoretical contribution. Thirteen long and three short papers were submitted to the ILP conference track. From these, ten long papers and one short paper were accepted after the first round of reviews in August 2021, while authors of the remaining papers were requested to make substantial revisions, taking into account the reviewers' comments. The revised papers went through an additional round of review during September 2021, after which they were accepted for presentation at the conference and inclusion in the ILP proceedings. All accepted long papers received an oral presentation slot at the conference, while the accepted short papers were presented as posters during IJCLR 2021's joint poster sessions.
3. Late-breaking papers, i.e. extended abstracts briefly outlining novel ideas and work in progress, of high potential interest to the ILP community but not yet qualifying for the regular papers category. Three late-breaking papers were submitted to ILP, which

---

[1] http://lr2020.iit.demokritos.gr/ilp.

[2] http://lr2020.iit.demokritos.gr/.

were presented during IJCLR 2021's joint poster sessions. Late-breaking papers are not included in these proceedings.

4. Three high-quality recently-published papers (IJCAI 2021, AIJ 2021, TPLP 2021) were submitted to ILP. These papers received an oral presentation slot at the conference but are not included in these proceedings.

In addition to the regular papers from the ILP conference track, these proceedings also include one paper submitted to the AAIP workshop[3] and two papers submitted to IJCLR 2021's general track[4]. The former paper, highly relevant to ILP, was included in these proceedings in coordination with the AAIP Program Committee chairs, Ute Schmid and Cèsar Ferri. Papers submitted to IJCLR 2021's general track were reviewed by the Program Committee of one of the participating events, on the grounds of relevance to a particular topic. The two general track papers included in this volume were reviewed (and accepted) by the ILP Program Committee.

We identified several trends in the 30th ILP, including learning in knowledge graphs, neuro-symbolic and statistical relational learning approaches, logical learning in temporal domains, and applications of ILP in biology, drug design, financial forecasting, and computer vision.

Three best paper prizes were awarded[5]:

- Best paper award (supported by Springer): Tony Ribeiro, Maxime Folschette, Morgan Magnin, and Katsumi Inoue, "Learning Any Memoryless Discrete Semantics for Dynamical Systems Represented by Logic Programs". This is a journal track paper, published in the Machine Learning journal.
- Best student paper award – journal track (supported by the Machine Learning journal): Stassa Patsantzis and Stephen H. Muggleton, "Top Program Construction and Reduction for Polynomial Time Meta-Interpretive Learning". This is a journal track paper published in the Machine Learning journal.
- Best student paper award – conference track (supported by the Machine Learning journal): Thais Luca, Aline Paes, and Gerson Zaverucha, "Mapping Across Relational Domains for Transfer Learning with Word Embeddings-based Similarity". This paper was submitted in the ILP conference track.

We would like to thank everyone who contributed to the success of ILP 2021: the members of the IJCLR Organizing Committee, the members of the ILP Program Committee, our sponsors, and everyone who attended IJCLR and ILP 2021.

January 2022   Nikos Katzouris
                                                                          Alexander Artikis

---

[3] "Programmatic policy extraction by iterative local search".

[4] "Embedding Models for Knowledge Graphs Induced by Clusters of Relations and Background Knowledge" and "Answer-Set Programs for Reasoning about Counterfactual Interventions and Responsibility Scores for Classification".

[5] http://lr2020.iit.demokritos.gr/awards.

Organization

Program Committee Chairs

Nikos Katzouris	National Center for Scientific Research "Demokritos", Greece
Alexander Artikis	University of Piraeus and National Center for Scientific Research "Demokritos", Greece

Program Committee

Elena Bellodi	University of Ferrara, Italy
Krysia Broda	Imperial College London, UK
François Bry	Ludwig Maximilian University of Munich, Germany
Rui Camacho	University of Porto, Portugal
Giuseppe Cota	University of Ferrara, Italy
Andrew Cropper	University of Oxford, UK
James Cussens	University of Bristol, UK
Sebastijan Dumančić	Delft University of Technology, The Netherlands
Sao Deroski	Jozef Stefan Institute, Slovenia
Matthieu Exbrayat	Laboratoire d'Informatique Fondamentale d'Orléans, France
Nicola Fanizzi	University of Bari, Italy
Stefano Ferilli	University of Bari, Italy
Cesar Ferri	Universitat Politècnica de València, Spain
Nuno Fonseca	University of Porto, Portugal
Ramya Hebbalaguppe	Birla Institute of Technology and Science Pilani, India
Katsumi Inoue	Tokyo Institute of Technology, Japan
Nobuhiro Inuzuka	Nagoya Institute of Technology, Japan
Dimitar Kazakov	University of York, UK
Nicolas Lachiche	University of Strasbourg, France
Nada Lavrač	Jozef Stefan Institute, Slovenia
Francesca Alessandra Lisi	University of Bari, Italy
Evangelos Michelioudakis	National Center for Scientific Research "Demokritos", Greece
Stephen Muggleton	Imperial College London, UK
Aline Paes	Universidade Federal Fluminense, Brazil
Stassa Patsantzis	Imperial College London, UK

Jan Ramon	Inria, France
Fabrizio Riguzzi	University of Ferrara, Italy
Alessandra Russo	Imperial College London, UK
Vítor Santos Costa	University of Porto, Portugal
Alireza Tamaddoni-Nezhad	University of Surrey, UK
Tomoyuki Uchida	Hiroshima City University, Japan
Christel Vrain	Laboratoire d'Informatique Fondamentale d'Orléans, France
Stefan Wrobel	Fraunhofer IAIS and University of Bonn, Germany
Gerson Zaverucha	Federal University of Rio de Janeiro, Brazil
Filip Železný	Czech Technical University, Czech Republic
Riccardo Zese	University of Ferrara, Italy
Gustav Šourek	Czech Technical University in Prague, Czech Republic

Sponsors

We gratefully thank all the organizations and institutions that supported ILP 2021:

- The Artificial Intelligence journal
- The TAILOR project[6] and its Connectivity Fund.
- The Institute of Informatics & Telecommunications at the National Center for Scientific Research "Demokritos" in Athens, Greece.
- Springer
- The Machine Learning journal.

---

[6] https://tailor-network.eu/.

Contents

Embedding Models for Knowledge Graphs Induced by Clusters of Relations and Background Knowledge

Claudia d'Amato[1,2(⊠)], Nicola Flavio Quatraro[1], and Nicola Fanizzi[1,2]

[1] Dipartimento di Informatica – Università degli Studi di Bari Aldo Moro, Bari, Italy
n.quatraro@studenti.uniba.it
[2] Centro Interdipartimentale Logica e Applicazioni – Università degli Studi di Bari Aldo Moro,
Bari, Italy
{claudia.damato,nicola.fanizzi}@uniba.it

Abstract. Embedding models have been successfully exploited for predictive tasks on Knowledge Graphs (KGs). We propose TRANSROWL-HRS, which aims at making KG embeddings more semantically aware by exploiting the intended semantics in the KG. The method exploits schema axioms to encode knowledge that is observed as well as derived by reasoning. More knowledge is further exploited by relying on a successive hierarchical clustering process applied to relations, to make use of the several semantic meanings that the very same relation may have. An experimental evaluation on *link prediction* and *triple classification* tasks proves the improvement yielded by the proposed approach (coupled with different optimizers) compared to some baseline models.

1 Introduction

Knowledge Graphs (KGs) [9] are becoming increasingly important in various research and enterprise contexts. Several examples of large KGs are available, spanning from enterprise products, such as those built by Google and Amazon, to other open initiatives such as the well known DBpedia, Wikidata and YAGO. However, it is well known that KGs tend to suffer of two major problems: incompleteness and noise (e.g., see [9]). Thus, research on *knowledge graph refinement*, aiming at tackling these issues [17], has been investigated. Two tasks have gained a major attention: *Link Prediction*, focusing on predicting missing links between entities, and *Triple Classification*, that consists in assessing the correctness of a statement with respect to a KG.

Due to the need for scalable solutions, *embedding models* [3] have been widely considered, having proven their effectiveness even with very large KGs. They encode the data graph into an optimal low-dimensional space in which *graph structural information* and *graph properties* are preserved as much as possible. The various methods differ in their main building blocks [11]: the *representation space* (e.g. point-wise, complex, discrete, Gaussian, manifolds), the *encoding model* (e.g. linear, factorization, neural models) and the *scoring function* (that can be based on distance, energy, semantic matching or other criteria). The objective consists in learning embeddings such that the score of valid (positive) triples is much higher than the score of invalid triples,

© Springer Nature Switzerland AG 2022
N. Katzouris and A. Artikis (Eds.): ILP 2021, LNAI 13191, pp. 1–16, 2022.
https://doi.org/10.1007/978-3-030-97454-1_1

regarded as a sort of negative examples. However, KGs mostly encode positive assertions (examples) whilst negative constraints are more rarely found [1]. As positive-only learning settings may be tricky and prone to over-generalization, negative examples (invalid triples) have to be sought for, either by randomly *corrupting* true/observed triples or having them derived from additional special assumptions, such as the *local-closed world assumption*, which may conflict with the intended semantics of the data collection. In both cases, incorrect negative information may be generated and then used for training the embedding models. Hence alternative solutions are being investigated [1].

Even more so, existing learning methods often overlook the rich prior knowledge that already comes with the KGs, and is expressed through schema-level representations (ontologies) which call for *semantic embedding methods*, as argued in [4]. Some proposals for exploiting external *background knowledge* (BK) have been made, but often unnaturally resorting to external representations (e.g. Datalog clauses or fuzzy rules). Adopting a BK expressed as axioms in rich representations like RDFS and OWL new models have recently been proposed (e.g., see [15]).

In this work, we aim at extending a promising recent model, TRANSROWL [5], adopting a finer-grained treatment of the relationships in the BK. Specifically, inspired by the model dubbed HRS (*Hierarchical Relation Structure*) [21], the aim is to further empower the solution by taking into account the several sub-interpretations that each relationship may have. This has been shown to improve base models like TRANSE [2] and TRANSH [18]. We focus on the application of this idea to enhance TRANSROWL, and its base model TRANSR [12], with the final goal of setting up a general framework for KG embedding empowered by a larger usage of the available BK. The resulting variant is dubbed TRANSROWL-HRS. The proposed solution takes also advantage of an informed corruption process that leverages on reasoning and is able to limit the amount of false negatives introduced by an unconstrained random corruption process.

It is important to remark that, in principle, the proposed approach could be applied to more complex KG embedding methods. In this work we intended to show the feasibility of the approach, starting with well established models before moving on towards more sophisticated ones, which would require an additional formalization. The proposed solution is actually able to improve the effectiveness compared to the original models as proved through an experimentation on standard datasets focusing on link prediction and triple classification tasks.

The paper is organized as follows: basics on KG embedding models that are functional to our method definition are presented in Sect. 2; the formalization of our solution is illustrated in Sect. 3; the experimental evaluation is provided in Sect. 4; related work is discussed in Sect. 5; conclusions and future research directions are delineated in Sect. 6.

2   Basics on KGs and Embedding Models

In what follows, we shall assume familiarity with the standard representation and reasoning frameworks RDF, RDFS and OWL, as we will consider graphs made up of triples $\langle s, p, o \rangle$ of *RDF terms*, respectively the *subject*, the *predicate*, and the *object*, s.t. $s \in U \cup B$ where U is a set of URIs and B is a set of blank nodes, $p \in U$ and $o \in U \cup B \cup L$ where L stands for a set of *literals*. Given an RDF graph G, we denote with $\mathcal{E}_G$ the set of all entities occurring as subjects or objects in G, and with $\mathcal{R}_G$ the set of all predicates occurring in G.

Several KG embedding models have been proposed [3], as learned *distributed representations* (or *embeddings*) for each entity and predicate in a KG, considering different representation spaces (e.g. point-wise, complex, discrete, Gaussian, manifold). We will adopt vectors of real numbers: given a KG G, each entity $x \in \mathcal{E}_G$ is represented by a continuous *embedding vector* $\mathbf{e}_x \in \mathbb{R}^k$, where $k \in \mathbb{N}$ is user-defined. Similarly, each predicate $p \in \mathcal{R}_G$ is associated to a *scoring function* $f_p : \mathbb{R}^k \times \mathbb{R}^k \to \mathbb{R}$. For each pair of entities $s, o \in \mathcal{E}_G$, the score $f_p(\mathbf{e}_s, \mathbf{e}_o)$ measures the *confidence* that the statement $\langle s, p, o \rangle$ holds true.

In the following, we recall the basics of models that will be successively extended.

TRANSR: In this model each entity $x \in \mathcal{E}_G$ is represented by an embedding vector $\mathbf{e}_x \in \mathbb{R}^k$, and each predicate $p \in \mathcal{R}_G$ is represented by a *rotation operation* $\mathbf{e}_p \in \mathbb{R}^k$. The score of a triple $\langle s, p, o \rangle$ is given by the similarity (negative L_1 or L_2 distance) of the rotated subject embedding to the object embedding $\mathbf{e}_o$ preliminarily projected into the d-dimensional space of the relational embeddings via a suitable matrix $\mathbf{M} \in \mathbb{R}^{k \times d}$:

$$f_p'(\mathbf{e}_s, \mathbf{e}_o) = -\|(\mathbf{M}\mathbf{e}_s + \mathbf{e}_p) - \mathbf{M}\mathbf{e}_o\|_{\{1,2\}}. \tag{1}$$

The learning method is a *stochastic optimization process* that iteratively updates the distributed representations by increasing the score of the observed triples in G, contained in a given set Δ, while decreasing the score of unobserved triples in Δ', standing as negative examples. The latter are generated by means of a random *corruption process* which replaces either the subject or the object of observed triples with other entities in G. Formally, given $t \in \Delta$ and the set $\mathcal{C}_G(t)$ of all triples derived by corrupting t:

$$\Delta' = \bigcup_{\langle s,p,o \rangle \in \Delta} \mathcal{C}_G(\langle s,p,o \rangle) = \bigcup_{\langle s,p,o \rangle \in \Delta} \{\langle \tilde{s}, p, o \rangle \mid \tilde{s} \in \mathcal{E}_G\} \cup \{\langle s, p, \tilde{o} \rangle \mid \tilde{o} \in \mathcal{E}_G\}.$$

The embedding of all entities and predicates in G is learned by minimizing a *margin-based ranking loss*. Formally, let $\theta \in \Theta$ denote a configuration for all entity and predicate embeddings, i.e. the *model parameters* in the parameters space Θ. The optimal model parameters $\hat{\theta} \in \Theta$ are learned by solving the following constrained optimization problem with a specific loss functional:

$$\min_{\theta \in \Theta} \sum_{\substack{\langle s,p,o \rangle \in \Delta \\ \langle \tilde{s},p,\tilde{o} \rangle \in \Delta'}} \left[\gamma + f_p'(\mathbf{e}_s, \mathbf{e}_o) - f_p'(\mathbf{e}_{\tilde{s}}, \mathbf{e}_{\tilde{o}}) \right]_+ \text{ subject to: } \|\mathbf{e}_x\| = 1, \forall x \in \mathcal{E}_G \tag{2}$$

where $[c]_+ = \max\{0, c\}$, and $\gamma \geq 0$ is the *margin*. It enforces higher scores for observed triples w.r.t. unobserved triples, with constraints preventing trivial solutions.

TRANSROWL: This model [5] extends TRANSR by injecting more BK in the learning process. This is obtained by introducing constraints, corresponding to BK axioms, that influence the way embedding vectors are learned. Corrupted triples, that represent negative instances, are generated by a reasoner (exploiting the axioms on domain, range, disjointWith, functionalProperty). The resulting loss function is reported below:

$$L = \sum_{\substack{\langle h,r,t \rangle \in \Delta \\ \langle h',r,t' \rangle \in \Delta'}} [\gamma + f'_r(h,t) - f'_r(h',t')]_+ + \lambda_1 \sum_{\substack{\langle t,q,h \rangle \in \Delta_{\text{inverseOf}} \\ \langle t',q,h' \rangle \in \Delta'_{\text{inverseOf}}}} [\gamma + f'_q(t,h) - f'_q(t',h')]_+$$

$$+ \lambda_2 \sum_{\substack{\langle h,s,t \rangle \in \Delta_{\text{equivProperty}} \\ \langle h',s,t' \rangle \in \Delta'_{\text{equivProperty}}}} [\gamma + f'_s(h,t) - f'_s(h',t')]_+ + \lambda_3 \sum_{\substack{\langle h,\text{typeOf},l \rangle \in \Delta \cup \Delta_{\text{equivClass}} \\ \langle h',\text{typeOf},l' \rangle \in \Delta' \cup \Delta'_{\text{equivClass}}}} [\gamma + f'_{\text{typeOf}}(h,l) - f'_{\text{typeOf}}(h',l')]_+$$

$$+ \lambda_4 \sum_{\substack{\langle t,\text{subClassOf},p \rangle \in \Delta_{\text{subClass}} \\ \langle t',\text{subClassOf},p' \rangle \in \Delta'_{\text{subClass}}}} [(\gamma - \beta) + f'(t,p) - f'(t',p')]_+$$

where $q \equiv r^-$, $s \equiv r$ (properties), $l \equiv t$ and $t \sqsubseteq p$ (classes) and the triple sets Δ_π, $\pi \in \{\text{inverseOf, equivProperty, equivClass, subClass}\}$, contain additional triples generated by *reasoning* on these properties and $f'(h,p) = \|\mathbf{e}_h - \mathbf{e}_p\|$ considering the embedding vectors coming from TRANSR. The different formulation for the case of subClassOf is motivated by the fact that it encodes the additional constraint $f'_{\text{typeOf}}(e,p) > f'_{\text{typeOf}}(e,h)$ where e is an instance, h subClassOf p and $f'_{\text{typeOf}}(e,p)$ is as for the original formulation in Eq. 1. A further term, β, is required to determine the direction of the inequality to be obtained for the score values associated to subclass entities (one w.r.t. the other). The parameters $\lambda_1, \ldots, \lambda_4$ weigh the influence of each term during the learning phase.

An alternative formulation of the model, dubbed TRANSROWL^R, has been also proposed in [5], grounded on the exploitation of *axiom-based regularization*, in which the constraints that represent the related properties of the entities and relations are explicitly expressed in the loss function:

$$L = \sum_{\substack{\langle h,r,t \rangle \in \Delta \\ \langle h',r',t' \rangle \in \Delta'}} [\gamma + f'_r(h,t) - f'_r(h',t')]_+ + \lambda_1 \sum_{r \equiv q^- \in \mathcal{T}_{\text{inverseOf}}} \|r + q\| + \lambda_2 \sum_{r \equiv q^- \in \mathcal{T}_{\text{inverseOf}}} \|\mathbf{M}_r - \mathbf{M}_q\|$$

$$+ \lambda_3 \sum_{r \equiv p \in \mathcal{T}_{\text{equivProp}}} \|r - p\| + \lambda_4 \sum_{r \equiv p \in \mathcal{T}_{\text{equivProp}}} \|\mathbf{M}_r - \mathbf{M}_p\|$$

$$+ \lambda_5 \sum_{e' \equiv e'' \in \mathcal{T}_{\text{equivClass}}} \|e' - e''\| + \lambda_6 \sum_{s' \sqsubseteq s'' \in \mathcal{T}_{\text{subClass}}} \|1 - \beta - (s' - s'')\|$$

where $\mathcal{T}_{\text{inverseOf}} = \{r_1 \equiv q_1^-, r_2 \equiv q_2^-, \ldots, r_n \equiv q_n^-\}$, and $\mathcal{T}_{\text{equivProp}} = \{r_1 \equiv p_1, r_2 \equiv p_2, \ldots, r_n \equiv p_n\}$ are, resp., the sets of inverse and equivalent properties, while $\mathcal{T}_{\text{equivClass}} = \{e'_1 \equiv e''_1, e'_2 \equiv e''_2, \ldots, e'_n \equiv e''_n\}$ and $\mathcal{T}_{\text{subClass}} = \{s'_1 \sqsubseteq s''_1, s'_2 \sqsubseteq s''_2, \ldots, s'_n \sqsubseteq s''_n\}$ are, resp., the sets of equivalent classes and subclasses. Parameters $\lambda_1, \ldots, \lambda_6$ determine the weights associated to each constraint. An additional term is required for inverseOf and equivProp triples to favor the equality of their projection matrices. This is for having the same scores to the triples in their respective sets, that is the score of $\langle h,r,t \rangle$ and $\langle h,p,t \rangle$ should be equal if axiom $\langle r, \text{equivProp}, p \rangle$ holds.

3   TRANSROWL-HRS

The proposed model TRANSROWL-HRS aims at making KG embeddings more semantically aware. This is obtained by extending TRANSROWL so to take into account the subtleties in the meaning of each relation. We first motivate the choice for this research direction, hence we present the formalization and discuss on its training phase.

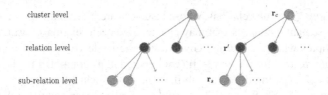

Fig. 1. Hierarchical structure for the relations in HRS [21]

3.1 TRANSROWL and Relation Hierarchies

Most translational models, including TRANSR, do not have substantial variation in the representation of the relations, whereas each relation may be associated to different meanings [19]. To this purpose, a specific *Hierarchical Relation Structure* (HRS) has been proposed [21] as a more complex model for the semantics of the relations, that was proven to improve basic models like TRANSE and TRANSH. Following this idea, we propose TRANSROWL-HRS extending TRANSROWL with a finer grained usage of the BK via a more complex treatment of the embeddings for relationships. The focus is on a three-level hierarchical structure, as also depicted in Fig. 1:

- *Relation clusters*: sets of semantically similar properties. For example the similarity of read and study may be derived from their sharing the domain and range, resp. Person and Book (or some of their super-classes). The aim is training semantically similar relations collectively, so that properties with fewer triples available would benefit from being fitted together with others with more triples in the KG;
- *Relations*: standard notion of relation as a predicate connecting subjects to objects;
- *Sub-relations*: given any relation, *sub-relations* can be defined in terms of its various interpretations. As an example, one may consider partOf: it may assume different meanings that refer, resp., to the mereological relation or to the association based on the geographic location, as in the triples ⟨CPU, partOf$_1$, Computer⟩ and ⟨Vatican, partOf$_2$, Italy⟩.

3.2 Model Formalization

Distinctions in the partitioning levels are reflected in the embeddings as follows: given a relation r and its embedding $\mathbf{r} \in \mathbb{R}^d$, the latter is defined by the linear combination of three further embedding vectors, namely $\mathbf{r} = \mathbf{r}_c + \mathbf{r}' + \mathbf{r}_s$ where $\mathbf{r}_c \in \mathbb{R}^d$ represents the cluster r belongs to, $\mathbf{r}' \in \mathbb{R}^d$ relation embedding for r and $\mathbf{r}_s \in \mathbb{R}^d$ representing the sub-relation related to the considered triple. Clusters of relations and sub-relations are determined through a clustering algorithm on the grounds of the metric of the embedding space for the relations, indicated with $\mathbf{r}_1, \mathbf{r}_2, \mathbf{r}_3, \ldots, \mathbf{r}_{|\mathcal{R}|}$. Specifically:

- *Clusters of relations*: The set of n_c clusters of relations, indicated with $\mathcal{C} = \{C_1, C_2, \ldots, C_{n_c}\}$, is found by a suitable algorithm, such as K-MEANS, running on the relations vectors $\mathbf{r}_i$ initialized by TRANSE.

– *Sub-relations:* The sub-relations, whose instances are indicated with $\hat{r}_i$, are sets representing semantic nuances that may characterize each relation r_i w.r.t. its context, i.e. the triples where it appears. Given a generic triple $\langle h, r, t \rangle$, the corresponding sub-relation results from $\hat{r} = t - h$ (with embeddings computed by TRANSE). So, for each $\langle h_i, r, t_i \rangle$, the different sub-relations $\hat{r}_i$ associated to r can be computed. The grouping $S_1^r, S_2^r, S_3^r, \ldots, S_{n_r}^r$ of sub-relations is organized through the clustering algorithm, where n_r is the number of sub-relations of r.

Moving from the HRS score function: $f_r(h, t) = \|h + r_c + r' + r_s - t\|_n$ the TRANSROWL-HRS score function is obtained by replacing the embedding vector for the relation with the linear combinations of the terms coming from the hierarchical structure, that is:

$$f_r'(h, t) = \|\mathbf{h}_r + \mathbf{r}_c + \mathbf{r}' + \mathbf{r}_s - \mathbf{t}_r\|_n \tag{3}$$

$$f'(h, t) = \|\mathbf{h}_r - \mathbf{t}_r\|_n \tag{4}$$

where n indicates the norm (L_1 or L_2) and $f'(h, t)$ is the score function that considers the subClassOf-axioms. Similarly to TRANSR, the projections of h and t to the vector space of r are computed via the matrix $\mathbf{M}_r$: $\mathbf{h}_r = \mathbf{h}\mathbf{M}_r$ and $\mathbf{t}_r = \mathbf{t}\mathbf{M}_r$ (see Sect. 2).

3.3 Training the Model

The formalization of the TRANSROWL-HRS loss function moves from the one defined for HRS [21] whilst requiring additional formulation due to different base models adopted (TRANSROWL for TRANSROWL-HRS and TRANSE for the case of HRS).

In HRS the adopted loss function is a combination of two terms: $L_{\text{Tot}} = L_{\text{B}} + L_{\text{HRS}}$, where L_{B} is the loss of the base-model HRS is applied to (that is TRANSE), taking into account that it must also consider the clusters the relations belong to, indicated by $\mathcal{C} = \{C_1, C_2, ..., C_{n_c}\}$. The term L_{HRS} manages the influence that each embedding vector among $\mathbf{r}_c$, $\mathbf{r}'$, $\mathbf{r}_e$ has in the definition of the embedding associated to $\mathbf{r}$. This is formalized considering the linear combination of each group of embeddings in the hierarchical structure of the relations, with a different specific weight:

$$L_{\text{HRS}} = \lambda_c \sum_{r_c \in \mathcal{C}} \|\mathbf{r}_c\|_2^2 + \lambda_r \sum_{r' \in \mathcal{R}} \|\mathbf{r}'\|_2^2 + \lambda_s \sum_{r_s \in \mathcal{S}} \|\mathbf{r}_s\|_2^2 \tag{5}$$

where $\mathcal{C} = \{C_1, C_2, \ldots, C_{n_c}\}$ is the set of clusters, $\mathcal{S} = \{S_1^r, S_2^r, \ldots, S_{n_r}^r \mid r \in \mathcal{R}\}$ is the set of sub-relations for each r, and λ_c, λ_r and λ_s are regularization parameters.

As for the case of TRANSROWL-HRS, the L_{HRS} term remains the same as above, whilst for the L_{B} term, the new base-model TRANSROWL needs to be taken into account, as well as the clusters the relations belong to. Hence the formulation of L_{B} for TRANSROWL-HRS will be given by the TRANSROWL loss function modified so as to consider the clusters of relations. The formulation is the following:

$$L_B = \sum_{c=1}^{n_c} \sum_{r \in C_c} \sum_{\substack{\langle h,r,t \rangle \in \Delta \\ \langle h',r',t' \rangle \in \Delta'}} [\gamma + f'_r(h,t) - f'_r(h',t')]_+ \ + \lambda_1 \sum_{c=1}^{n_c} \sum_{q \in C_c} \sum_{\substack{\langle t,q,h \rangle \in \Delta_{\text{inverseOf}} \\ \langle t',q,h' \rangle \in \Delta'_{\text{inverseOf}}}} [\gamma + f'_q(t,h) - f'_q(t',h')]_+$$

$$+ \lambda_2 \sum_{c=1}^{n_c} \sum_{s \in C_c} \sum_{\substack{\langle h,s,t \rangle \in \Delta_{\text{equivProperty}} \\ \langle h',s,t' \rangle \in \Delta'_{\text{equivProperty}}}} [\gamma + f'_s(h,t) - f'_s(h',t')]_+$$

$$+ \lambda_3 \sum_{c=1}^{n_c} \sum_{\text{typeOf} \in C_c} \sum_{\substack{\langle h,\text{typeOf},l \rangle \in \Delta_{\text{equivClass}} \\ \langle h',\text{typeOf},l' \rangle \in \Delta'_{\text{equivClass}}}} [\gamma + f'_{\text{typeOf}}(h,l) - f'_{\text{typeOf}}(h',l')]_+$$

$$+ \lambda_4 \sum_{c=1}^{n_c} \sum_{\text{typeOf} \in C_c} \sum_{\substack{\langle t,\text{subClassOf},p \rangle \in \Delta_{\text{subClass}} \\ \langle t',\text{subClassOf},p' \rangle \in \Delta'_{\text{subClass}}}} [(\gamma - \beta) + f'(t,p) - f'(t',p')]_+ \tag{6}$$

Further variants can be applied by considering: the *top-middle* and the *middle-bottom* settings. The *top-middle* focuses exclusively on the first and second level of the hierarchical structure, that is clusters of relations and relations: $\mathbf{r} = \mathbf{r}_c + \mathbf{r}'$. This affects the formalization of the L_{HRS} term in the loss function and of the score function, which is as follows:

$$L_{\text{HRS}} = \lambda_c \sum_{r_c \in \mathcal{C}} \|\mathbf{r}_c\|_2^2 + \lambda_r \sum_{r' \in \mathcal{R}} \|\mathbf{r}'\|_2^2 \tag{7}$$

$$f_r(h,t) = \|\mathbf{h}_r + \mathbf{r}_c + \mathbf{r}' - \mathbf{t}_r\|_n \tag{8}$$

The *middle-bottom* model focuses exclusively on the second and third level of the hierarchical structure $\mathbf{r} = \mathbf{r}' + \mathbf{r}_s$ (relations and sub-relations), leading to modify the formulation of the score function and L_{HRS} loss as follows:

$$L_{\text{HRS}} = \lambda_r \sum_{r' \in \mathcal{R}} \|\mathbf{r}'\|_2^2 + \lambda_s \sum_{r_s \in \mathcal{S}} \|\mathbf{r}_s\|_2^2 \tag{9}$$

$$f_r(h,t) = \|\mathbf{h}_r + \mathbf{r}' + \mathbf{r}_s - \mathbf{t}_r\|_n \tag{10}$$

Following [19], TRANSROWL-HRS adopts the *top-middle* variant as it is very likely that a KG include numerous semantically similar relations, clusters of relations then, rather than a large number of sub-relations. The single variant chosen is motivated also for controlling the complexity of the model.

Algorithm 1 reports the procedure associated to the TRANSROWL-HRS model. Preliminarily, it requires the training set S, with the related set of entities $\mathcal{E}$ and relations $\mathcal{R}$, the sets of all axioms of interest A_z, A_w used, resp., to generate further triples for the training and to generate corrupted triples, the set of clusters $\mathcal{C}$ and the dimensionality hyperparameters. The embedding vectors for entities and relations are initialized by TRANSE to avoid overfitting, as suggested in [12]; moreover the vectors associated to the clusters and the projection matrices are also initialized. The main loop iterates the following steps for a fixed number of *epochs*:

- Embedding vectors are normalized to satisfy the constraints;
- A minibatch S_{bat} of size b is sampled from S, while T_{bat} is initialized with $\emptyset$;

Algorithm 1: TRANSROWL-HRS

---

parameters:
$S = \{\langle h, r, t\rangle\}$: training set;
$\mathcal{E}, \mathcal{R}$: entity and relation sets;
$\mathcal{A}_z$: axiom sets, with $z \in \{\text{inverseOf}, \text{equivProperty}, \text{equivClass}, \text{subClassOf}\}$;
$\mathcal{C}$: cluster set;
$\mathcal{A}_w$: axiom sets, with $w \in \{\text{range}, \text{domain}, \text{functionalProperty}, \text{disjointWith}\}$;
γ: margin;
k, m: embeddings dim. for entities and relations;
$nepoch$: number of epochs;

$\mathbf{e}, \mathbf{r}' \leftarrow$ TRANSE results $\forall r' \in \mathcal{R}, \forall e \in \mathcal{E}$;   (* initialization *)
$\mathbf{r}_c \leftarrow \mathbf{0} \; \forall r_c \in \mathcal{C}$;
$\mathbf{M}_r \leftarrow \mathbf{I} \in \mathbb{R}^{k \times m} \; \forall r \in \mathcal{R}$;
while $epoch < nepoch$ **do**
    normalize $\mathbf{e}, \mathbf{r}, \mathbf{t}, \mathbf{eM}_r, \mathbf{tM}_r$ with $\mathbf{M}_r \in \mathbb{R}^{k \times d}$;
    $S_{\text{bat}} \leftarrow$ sample(S, b);
    $T_{\text{bat}} \leftarrow \emptyset$;
    for $\langle h, r, t\rangle \in S_{\text{bat}}$ **do**
        $\langle h', r, t'\rangle \leftarrow$ corrupt$(\langle h, r, t\rangle, A_w)$;
        $T_{\text{bat}} \leftarrow T_{\text{bat}} \cup \{(\langle h, r, t\rangle, \langle h', r, t'\rangle)\}$;
        switch r **do**
            case $r \in \mathcal{A}_{\text{inverseOf}}$ **do**
                $\langle t', q, h'\rangle \leftarrow$ corrupt$(\langle t, q, h\rangle, A_w)$;
                $T_{\text{bat}} \leftarrow T_{\text{bat}} \cup \{(\langle t, q, h\rangle, \langle t', q, h'\rangle)\}$;
            end
            case $r \in \mathcal{A}_{\text{equivProperty}}$ **do**
                $\langle h', s, t'\rangle \leftarrow$ corrupt$(\langle h, s, t\rangle, A_w)$;
                $T_{\text{bat}} \leftarrow T_{\text{bat}} \cup \{(\langle h, s, t\rangle, \langle h', s, t'\rangle)\}$;
            end
            case $r = \text{typeOf}$ **and** $t \in \mathcal{A}_{\text{equivClass}}$ **do**
                $\langle h', r, t'\rangle \leftarrow$ corrupt$(\langle h, r, t\rangle, A_w)$;
                $T_{\text{bat}} \leftarrow T_{\text{bat}} \cup \{(\langle h, r, l\rangle, \langle h', r, l'\rangle)\}$;
            end
            case $r = \text{typeOf}$ **and** $t \in \mathcal{A}_{\text{subClassOf}}$ **do**
                $\langle t', r, p'\rangle \leftarrow$ corrupt$(\langle t, \text{subClassOf}, p\rangle, A_w)$;
                $T_{\text{bat}} \leftarrow T_{\text{bat}} \cup \{(\langle t, \text{subClassOf}, p\rangle, \langle t', \text{subClassOf}, p'\rangle)\}$;
            end
        end
    end
    $g_t \leftarrow \sum_{((h,r,t),(h',r,t')) \in T_{\text{bat}}} \nabla L_{\text{Tot}}$;   (* gradient *)
    $\Delta_t \leftarrow -\eta g_t$;   (* update *)
    $epoch \leftarrow epoch + 1$;
end

- For each $\langle h, r, t\rangle \in S_{\text{bat}}$, a corrupted $\langle h', r, t'\rangle$ is produced[1] exploiting the axioms in A_w and the entities/relation in the triple; the pair of triples is added to T_{bat}.
- Analyzing r, all the applicable cases are considered (inclusively) w.r.t. the properties of the axioms in A_z, hence new pairs of positive and negative triples are generated and added to T_{bat};
- Lastly, the gradient g_t and updates are computed based on the triple pairs in T_{bat}, and the embedding parameters are updated by the optimizer of choice.

---

[1] A standard corruption strategy can be employed: `unif` generates negative triples by sampling a pair of entities for subject and object from $\mathcal{E}_G$, assigning uniform probabilities to the possible replacements; `bern` assigns Bernoulli distributed chances based on the type of property/mapping (1-to-1, 1-to-N, N-to-N).

The algorithm terminates when the fixed number of epochs, *nepoch*, is reached.
Three variants will be considered depending on the optimizer employed.

4 Empirical Evaluation

In this section we illustrate the experimental evaluation of TRANSROWL-HRS compared to TRANSR, TRANSROWL, TRANSROWL^R as baselines. Note that TRANSE was only used for the embeddings initialization (see Sect. 3.3) and not in the comparison as it has been shown [5] that the considered baselines are able to outperform it.

We tested the performance of the models on the tasks of *Link Prediction*, together with *Type Prediction* (that, given typeOf-triple for a subject, verifies if the model can correctly predict a class the individual belongs to) and *Triple Classification*, i.e. the ability to classify new triples as true or false. Overall the runtimes for the various models were on average comparable, with a slight overhead required by the clustering method. Further details are publicly available in the project documentation[2].

4.1 Experiment Setup

Datasets. The models were tested on four datasets drawn from well known KGs, that have been considered for experiments in related works [6, 13].

- *DBpedia*: data extracted from Wikipedia. It includes 320 classes and 1650 properties. We considered two datasets extracted to ensure axioms to test the models, namely axioms on domain, range, disjointWith, functionalProperty, equivalentClass, equivalentProperty, inverseOf, subClassOf, in the two variants: *DBpedia100K*[3] [6], containing about 100K entities, 321 relations in 600K triples; *DBpedia15K*[4] [13], containing about 12.8K entities and 278 relations in 180K triples.
- *DBPediaYAGO*: YAGO[5] is a KG with knowledge coming from different sources e.g. *WordNet, GeoNames, Wikipedia*, including 350K+ classes, 10M entities, 120M assertions [17]. It has been used to extend *DBpedia15K*, resulting in *DBPediaYAGO* having about 290K triples, with 88K entities and 316 relations.
- *NELL*: The dataset[6] comes from a knowledge extraction system from corpora of Web pages. The resulting KG amounts to 2.810K+ assertions regarding 1.186 different relations and categories. We considered a fragment of NELL2RDF-vanilla[7] that does not contain all of the properties that can be exploited by the proposed model. The considered dataset is made up of about 150K triples, with 272 properties and 68K entities. The aim was to have a dataset with a limited set of exploitable properties, namely subClassOf, inverseOf, functionalProperty, disjointWith, range and domain. The abundance of subClassOf-triples and limited number of typeOf-triples, is meant to test the ability to compensate this partial incompleteness.

---

[2] https://github.com/Keehl-Mihael/TransROWL-HRS.
[3] https://github.com/iieir-km/ComplEx-NNE_AER/tree/master/datasets/DB100K.
[4] https://github.com/nle-ml/mmkb/tree/master/DB15K.
[5] https://yago-knowledge.org/.
[6] http://rtw.ml.cmu.edu/rtw/.
[7] http://nell-ld.telecom-st-etienne.fr/.

Each dataset was randomly partitioned into *training*, *validation* and *test* sets by selecting 70%, 10%, 20% of the triples.

Parameter Settings. All models were set up along the same procedure and parameter values, consistently with the experiments illustrated in [2, 12, 21]: learning rate: 0.001; minibatch dimension: 50; entity/relation vector dimension = 100; epochs: 1000. This choice is motivated by the fact that our first aim is to verify the possible improvements of the proposed solution over the basic models when exactly the same conditions, including the parameter values, apply. The bern strategy for the triple corruption phase was adopted, as this choice led to a better performance compared to the unif strategy in previous experimental evaluations of this class of models [12, 18].

As for the hyperparameters λ_i in the loss functions, the following values have been found: as for TRANSROWL, inverseOf $\lambda_1 = 1$; equivalentProperty $\lambda_2 = 1$; equivalent-Class $\lambda_3 = 0.1$; subClassOf $\lambda_4 = 0.01$; for TRANSROWL^R: $\lambda_1 = \lambda_2 = \lambda_3 = \lambda_4 = \lambda_5 = \lambda_6 = 0.1$; as for TRANSROWL-HRS: $\lambda_c = 0.00001$; $\lambda_r = 0.0001$.

Three TRANSROWL variants are considered depending on the optimizer employed: TRANSROWL-HRS (that uses SGD), TRANSROWL-HRS Momentum and TRANSROWL-HRS AdaGrad.

4.2   Link Prediction

Following the standard procedures we focus on predicting individuals in given incomplete triples, specifically triples $\langle h, r, t \rangle$, with $h, t \in \mathcal{E}_G$ and $r \in \mathcal{R}_G$, corresponding to the patterns $\langle ?, r, t \rangle, \langle h, r, ? \rangle$. The typical metrics considered for this task are *Mean Rank* (the lower the better) and *H@10* (the higher the better). The *Raw* and *Filtered* variants are considered, the latter filtering off the corrupted triples generated for training the model. For a more specific insight, we measured separately the performance considering all properties but typeOf, and then typeOf only, which allows to focus separately on *Type Prediction* problems with the classes in the KGs. As mentioned in Sect. 3.3, following the approach adopted by the baseline methods, the embeddings were initialized by a first run of TRANSE, and the models were trained for a fixed number of epochs.

The complete outcomes of the link prediction experiments are illustrated in Table 1. Considering preliminarily the link prediction problems (no typeOf), we found that TRANSROWL-HRS adopting the AdaGrad optimizer had the best performance on almost all of the datasets and measures with some exceptions. As regards the case of *DBpediaYAGO* dataset, the TRANSR was able to do slightly better, in terms of the H@10 metric, than the new model which is a very close runner-up. A more difficult testbed was represented by the *NELL* dataset on which TRANSR had a slightly better performance also in terms of MR. The reason for this decay was due to the limited number of properties that can be exploited by the proposed model (as discussed in Sect. 4.1) as well as a limited number of relations compared to the much larger number of entities.

As for the results on the type prediction problems (typeOf columns), TRANSROWL-HRS with AdaGrad proved as the best model on *DBpediaYAGO* and *NELL* (in terms of H@10), whereas TRANSROWL-HRS with Momentum showed a better performance on *DBpedia15K*. This proves our intuition (see Sect. 4.1) that the

Table 1. Link Prediction results (MR = Mean Rank and H@10 = Hits@10)

| | DBpedia15K | | | | | | | |
| | no typeOf | | | | typeOf | | | |
model	MR (raw)	H@10 (raw)	MR (flt.)	H@10 (flt.)	MR (raw)	H@10 (raw)	MR (flt.)	H@10 (flt.)
TRANSR	600.12	60.67	586.83	63.57	504.13	85.01	13.96	95.50
TRANSROWL	606.73	60.59	593.45	63.48	484.04	**85.18**	**13.53**	96.54
TRANSROWL^R	607.43	60.71	594.13	63.65	497.40	85.12	16.50	96.24
TRANSROWL-HRS	600.08	60.62	586.83	63.43	485.08	85.17	14.96	96.61
TRANSROWL-HRS Momentum	605.23	60.48	591.95	63.40	**472.22**	85.12	14.59	**96.85**
TRANSROWL-HRS AdaGrad	**579.47**	**61.18**	**566.21**	**64.00**	506.06	85.01	25.72	94.77

| | DBpedia100K | | | | | | | |
| | no typeOf | | | | typeOf | | | |
model	MR (raw)	H@10 (raw)	MR (flt.)	H@10 (flt.)	MR (raw)	H@10 (raw)	MR (flt.)	H@10 (flt.)
TRANSR	2142.10	53.17	2112.42	55.96	**1957.42**	92.04	**1480.26**	92.25
TRANSROWL	2147.56	53.24	2117.87	56.03	1961.75	**92.29**	1503.87	**92.43**
TRANSROWL^R	2121.52	53.08	2091.81	55.95	1971.98	92.24	1511.07	**92.43**
TRANSROWL-HRS	2127.12	52.90	2097.58	55.62	1957.96	92.09	1503.34	92.23
TRANSROWL-HRS Momentum	2126.35	52.88	2096.84	55.58	1970.28	92.16	1526.95	92.31
TRANSROWL-HRS AdaGrad	**2087.74**	**53.47**	**2058.10**	**56.25**	1960.09	92.10	1519.92	92.23

| | DBpediaYAGO | | | | | | | |
| | no typeOf | | | | typeOf | | | |
model	MR (raw)	H@10 (raw)	MR (flt.)	H@10 (flt.)	MR (raw)	H@10 (raw)	MR (flt.)	H@10 (flt.)
TRANSR	7271.50	**44.64**	7239.09	**46.07**	844.51	81.98	348.65	88.99
TRANSROWL	7209.02	44.45	7176.64	45.84	868.27	82.81	373.90	91.17
TRANSROWL^R	7226.55	44.13	7194.21	45.52	845.42	81.71	352.16	88.77
TRANSROWL-HRS	7189.25	44.42	7156.92	45.68	705.91	82.96	213.18	90.98
TRANSROWL-HRS Momentum	7144.80	44.26	7112.47	45.59	731.13	82.82	241.69	92.59
TRANSROWL-HRS AdaGrad	**7104.88**	44.61	**7072.72**	45.92	**642.92**	**84.85**	**176.32**	**95.20**

| | NELL | | | | | | | |
| | no typeOf | | | | typeOf | | | |
model	MR (raw)	H@10 (raw)	MR (flt.)	H@10 (flt.)	MR (raw)	H@10 (raw)	MR (flt.)	H@10 (flt.)
TRANSR	**6891.20**	**47.40**	**6681.76**	**55.93**	2315.08	79.94	2140.16	80.50
TRANSROWL	7136.77	46.72	6929.10	55.40	2334.50	80.00	2161.67	80.56
TRANSROWL^R	7339.53	46.09	7132.22	54.15	**2310.11**	79.52	**2138.99**	80.21
TRANSROWL-HRS	7203.32	46.83	6996.17	55.34	2397.16	79.95	2223.64	80.44
TRANSROWL-HRS Momentum	7144.77	46.87	6936.06	55.29	2373.70	79.29	2201.06	79.85
TRANSROWL-HRS AdaGrad	7153.78	46.67	6949.22	55.26	2903.37	**80.35**	2730.42	**80.80**

abundance of subClassOf-triples in *NELL*, even if with a limited number of typeOf-triples, allows the method to compensate this partial incompleteness and improve the performances whilst this does not happen for the more general link prediction problem (results analyzed above) where, similarly to TRANSROWL and TRANSROWL^R, TRANSROWL-HRS resulted to suffer more of the missing axioms in the KG that are considered in the formalization of the model. In the case of *DBpedia100K*, TRANSR and TRANSROWL got slightly better scores, proving the new model not bing able to improve the baselines on type prediction problems on larger and complete datasets.

4.3   Triple Classification

Triple Classification focuses on discerning correct from incorrect triples. The evaluation measures the ability to predict whether a triple is positive or negative, i.e. it represents a true or false fact w.r.t. the KG. To make this decision, a threshold s_r is to be determined for each $r \in \mathcal{R}_G$, so to maximize the *False Positive Rate* (FPR), then test triples are deemed as positive when their score is greater than s_r, and negative otherwise [14, 18]. The value for s_r was estimated considering a random sample of r-triples selected from the training set. They represent the triples that the model has learned to deem as true; for each sampled triple the score value is computed and the threshold s_r is determined by the minimum value. The ability of the model to correctly classify triples is evaluated considering the thresholds obtained per single relation; this unavoidably increases the chance of predicting as true, triples that are actually false, thus it allows to better evaluate the model robustness on the classification of typeOf-triples.

Analogously to the previous experiments, the performance indices were determined separating the cases of typeOf-triples from those involving the other properties. This allows to better focus on the performance of the model on this relation between individuals and classes. The negative triples required for the tests, were generated by reasoning on range and domain axioms for the experiment excluding typeOf, while reasoning on disjointWith axioms were exploited to get false typeOf-triples. The experimental setting was analogous to the first part (see Sect. 4.1). Table 2 reports the complete results for each dataset in terms of *accuracy*, *precision*, *recall*, and *false positive rate*.

Focusing preliminarily on the experiments with non-typeOf relations, we observe a general similarity of the performance of the base and new models on the three *DBpedia*-based datasets with some difference on recall, which allows a little margin in favor of the best scoring model. The results observed for the experiments with *NELL* show a more contrasted outcome where a slightly higher recall yields a higher accuracy, whereas the better precision showed by TRANSROWL-HRS AdaGrad is also reflected in a lower FPR. Again this more sparse (incomplete) dataset turned out to be the most difficult testbed in the experiments, especially for methods relying on a rich BK.

Considering the experiments regarding typeOf, in the case of *DBpedia15K*, TRANSROWL-HRS Momentum was the most accurate one also because of a high precision and recall (TRANSROWL^R showed a slightly higher precision but also a much lower recall). TRANSROWL-HRS AdaGrad also had a high recall but precision dropped as testified by the high FPR. Difference in performance was even less sensible in the case of the *DBpedia100K*. The performance on *DBPediaYAGO* was sensibly better for the new models, especially in favor of TRANSROWL-HRS AdaGrad. This happened also for the experiments on *NELL* but mostly in favor TRANSROWL-HRS Momentum in this case. Again this dataset presented a particularly hard problems because of its incompleteness as testified by the low precision rates (and high FPR).

Table 2. Triple Classification results (Accuracy, Precision, Recall and FP Rate)

	DBpedia15K							
	no typeOf				typeOf			
model	Acc.	P	R	FPR	Acc.	P	R	FPR
TRANSR	**0.641**	**0.998**	**0.364**	0.001	0.972	0.966	0.946	0.378
TRANSROWL	0.631	0.997	0.347	0.002	0.962	**0.999**	0.882	**0.006**
TRANSROWL^R	0.628	**0.998**	0.342	0.001	0.981	0.969	0.972	0.523
TRANSROWL-HRS	0.634	0.995	0.353	0.002	0.985	0.994	0.961	0.135
TRANSROWL-HRS Momentum	0.628	0.997	0.342	**0.001**	**0.988**	0.997	0.966	0.074
TRANSROWL-HRS AdaGrad	0.629	**0.998**	0.343	**0.001**	0.977	0.954	**0.978**	0.682
	DBpedia100K							
	no typeOf				typeOf			
model	Acc.	P	R	FPR	Acc.	P	R	FPR
TRANSR	0.711	0.998	0.313	0.001	0.976	0.884	0.800	**0.344**
TRANSROWL	0.705	**0.998**	0.300	**0.001**	**0.987**	**0.940**	0.895	0.353
TRANSROWL^R	0.704	0.998	0.298	0.001	0.981	0.872	0.890	0.543
TRANSROWL-HRS	**0.714**	0.998	0.320	0.001	0.979	0.900	0.832	0.353
TRANSROWL-HRS Momentum	0.709	0.997	0.310	0.001	0.985	0.874	**0.945**	0.711
TRANSROWL-HRS AdaGrad	0.693	**0.998**	0.270	**0.001**	0.977	0.885	0.816	0.367
	DBpediaYAGO							
	no typeOf				typeOf			
model	Acc.	P	R	FPR	Acc.	P	R	FPR
TRANSR	0.644	0.964	0.300	0.016	0.844	0.946	0.247	0.018
TRANSROWL	**0.649**	0.968	**0.307**	0.014	0.905	0.973	0.547	0.032
TRANSROWL^R	0.636	**0.981**	0.277	**0.007**	0.854	0.953	0.299	0.020
TRANSROWL-HRS	0.643	0.966	0.296	0.015	0.873	0.967	0.386	0.021
TRANSROWL-HRS Momentum	0.645	0.974	0.299	0.011	0.873	0.981	0.381	**0.012**
TRANSROWL-HRS AdaGrad	0.647	0.975	0.302	0.011	**0.950**	**0.986**	**0.765**	0.043
	NELL							
	no typeOf				typeOf			
model	Acc.	P	R	FPR	Acc.	P	R	FPR
TRANSR	**0.758**	0.843	**0.636**	0.245	0.803	0.389	0.519	0.630
TRANSROWL	0.744	0.835	0.608	0.234	0.763	0.334	0.560	0.717
TRANSROWL^R	0.739	0.845	0.587	0.207	0.760	0.337	0.598	0.745
TRANSROWL-HRS	0.735	0.818	0.603	0.252	0.748	0.330	0.633	0.778
TRANSROWL-HRS Momentum	0.741	0.810	0.628	0.284	**0.823**	**0.421**	0.437	**0.516**
TRANSROWL-HRS AdaGrad	0.740	**0.847**	0.585	**0.202**	0.667	0.269	**0.692**	0.859

5 Related Work

The exploitation of hierarchies of relations in embedding methods has received increasing attention in the last few years, resulting as a promising approach particularly for link prediction tasks.

In [20], the *Hierarchy-Aware Knowledge Graph Embedding* (HAKE) model is proposed, showing the ability to learn complex semantic hierarchies. However, no use of the BK is considered. Similarly, in [10] a data-driven method for automatically discovering the distinct semantics associated with high-level relations in KGs and deriving an optimal number of sub-relations has been proposed, where vector embedding of entities and relations are preliminarily computed.

Additionally, various embedding approaches have been proposed that can leverage different forms of prior knowledge to learn better representations exploited for KG refinement tasks. Generally entities and relations are embedded into latent vectors with little exploitation of the rich information of the available relational structure. In [7] a method for jointly embedding KGs and logical rules has been proposed, where triples and rules are represented in a unified framework. Triples are represented as atomic formulae while rules are represented using t-norm fuzzy logics. A common loss over both representations is defined which is minimized to learn the embeddings. The specific forms of BK required, and the gap from the standard semantics of the KGs, constitute the main drawback. In [16] a solution based on adversarial training is proposed that exploits Datalog clauses to encode assumptions which are used to regularize neural link predictors. An inconsistency loss is derived that measures the degree of violation of such assumptions on a set of adversarial examples. A specific form of BK is required and a special assumption (*local CWA*) is to be made when reasoning with it. The availability of such clauses and the assumptions on their semantics represent the main limitations.

A common shortcoming of the related methods is that BK is often not embedded in a principled way. In [8], investigating the compatibility between ontological knowledge and different types of embeddings, they show that popular methods are not capable of modeling even very simple types of rules, hence they are not able to learn the underlying dependencies. Then a general framework is introduced in which relations are modeled as convex regions which exactly represent ontologies expressed by a specific form of rules, that preserve the semantics of the input ontology.

6   Conclusions and Future Work

An approach to learning embedding models has been proposed, that is based on exploiting the available prior knowledge (schema axioms) in both the training and the triple corruption process. A more complex model for the semantics of the relations is formalized as a three-level hierarchical structure for a fine-grained representation of their semantics. The resulting model TRANSROWL-HRS has been experimentally evaluated showing the improvements w.r.t. the baseline methods, particularly for link and type prediction tasks. Interestingly, the model was able to outperform the baseline models on almost all tasks, when missing axioms and limited typeOf assertions were available (the case of the *NELL* dataset, adopted for assessing the ability of the model to cope with challenging knowledge configurations, resulted hard for the baseline models), thus showing that the abundance of subClassOf-triples, even if with a limited number of typeOf-triples, allows the method to compensate this partial incompleteness and improve the performance.

Nevertheless, some shortcomings also emerged, particularly for the case of type prediction and triple classification tasks (the case involving all but typeOf relationships) when more comprehensive datasets have been considered. This suggests that a more complex hierarchical structure mostly has a value added when limited axioms are available whilst it does not play a significant role when all axioms and a sufficient number of triples can be found, thus opening a valuable research direction to be pursued.

We are currently working on the application of the presented approach to more complex embedding models which could be suitable for our purposes. We also intend to extend our solution by exploiting further schema-axioms. Furthermore, we are planning to reuse the collected additional knowledge for building and providing explanations for the answers to queries obtained exploiting the embedding models.

References

1. Arnaout, H., Razniewski, S., Weikum, G.: Enriching knowledge bases with interesting negative statements. In: AKBC 2020 (2020). https://doi.org/10.24432/C5101K
2. Bordes, A., Usunier, N., Garcia-Duran, A., Weston, J., Yakhnenko, O.: Translating embeddings for modeling multi-relational data. In: NIPS 2013. Curran Assoc., Inc. (2013)
3. Cai, H., Zheng, V.W., Chang, K.: A comprehensive survey of graph embedding: problems, techniques, and applications. IEEE Trans. Knowl. Data Eng. **30**(09), 1616–1637 (2018). https://doi.org/10.1109/TKDE.2018.2807452
4. d'Amato, C.: Machine learning for the semantic web: Lessons learnt and next research directions. Semant. Web **11**(1), 195–203 (2020). https://doi.org/10.3233/SW-200388
5. d'Amato, C., Quatraro, N.F., Fanizzi, N.: Injecting background knowledge into embedding models for predictive tasks on knowledge graphs. In: Verborgh, R., et al. (eds.) ESWC 2021. LNCS, vol. 12731, pp. 441–457. Springer, Cham (2021). https://doi.org/10.1007/978-3-030-77385-4_26
6. Ding, B., Wang, Q., Wang, B., Guo, L.: Improving knowledge graph embedding using simple constraints. In: ACL 2018, vol. 1, pp. 110–121. ACL (2018). https://doi.org/10.18653/v1/P18-1011
7. Guo, S., Wang, Q., Wang, L., Wang, B., Guo, L.: Jointly embedding knowledge graphs and logical rules. In: EMNLP 2016. ACL (2016). https://doi.org/10.18653/v1/D16-1019
8. Gutiérrez-Basulto, V., Schockaert, S.: From knowledge graph embedding to ontology embedding? an analysis of the compatibility between vector space representations and rules. In: Thielscher, M., et al. (eds.) KR 2018, pp. 379–388. AAAI Press (2018)
9. Hogan, A., et al.: Knowledge graphs (2020). arXiv:2003.02320
10. Jain, N., Krestel, R.: Learning fine-grained semantics for multi-relational data. In: ISWC 2020 Demos and Industry Tracks. CEUR Workshop Proceedings, vol. 2721, pp. 124–129. CEUR-WS.org (2020). http://ceur-ws.org/Vol-2721/paper529.pdf
11. Ji, S., Pan, S., Cambria, E., Marttinen, P., Yu, P.S.: A survey on knowledge graphs: Representation, acquisition and applications (2020). arXiv:2002.00388
12. Lin, Y., Liu, Z., Sun, M., Liu, Y., Zhu, X.: Learning entity and relation embeddings for knowledge graph completion. In: AAAI 2015, pp. 2181–2187. AAAI Press (2015)
13. Liu, Y., Li, H., Garcia-Duran, A., Niepert, M., Onoro-Rubio, D., Rosenblum, D.S.: MMKG: multi-modal knowledge graphs. In: Hitzler, P., et al. (eds.) ESWC 2019. LNCS, vol. 11503, pp. 459–474. Springer, Cham (2019). https://doi.org/10.1007/978-3-030-21348-0_30
14. Lv, X., Hou, L., Li, J., Liu, Z.: Differentiating concepts and instances for knowledge graph embedding. In: EMNLP 2018, pp. 1971–1979. ACL (2018). https://doi.org/10.18653/v1/D18-1222

15. Minervini, P., Costabello, L., Muñoz, E., Nováček, V., Vandenbussche, P.-Y.: Regularizing knowledge graph embeddings via equivalence and inversion axioms. In: Ceci, M., Hollmén, J., Todorovski, L., Vens, C., Džeroski, S. (eds.) ECML PKDD 2017. LNCS (LNAI), vol. 10534, pp. 668–683. Springer, Cham (2017). https://doi.org/10.1007/978-3-319-71249-9_40
16. Minervini, P., Demeester, T., Rocktäschel, T., Riedel, S.: Adversarial sets for regularising neural link predictors. In: UAI 2017. AUAI Press (2017)
17. Paulheim, H.: Knowledge graph refinement: a survey of approaches and evaluation methods. Semant. Web **8**, 489–508 (2016). https://doi.org/10.3233/SW-160218
18. Wang, Z., Zhang, J., Feng, J., Chen, Z.: Knowledge graph embedding by translating on hyperplanes. In: AAAI 2014, pp. 1112–1119. AAAI Press (2014)
19. Yang, B., Yih, W., He, X., Gao, J., Deng, L.: Embedding entities and relations for learning and inference in knowledge bases. In: ICLR 2015 (2015). arXiv:1412.6575
20. Zhang, Z., Cai, J., Zhang, Y., Wang, J.: Learning hierarchy-aware knowledge graph embeddings for link prediction. In: AAAI 2020, vol. 34, pp. 3065–3072 (2020). https://doi.org/10.1609/aaai.v34i03.5701
21. Zhang, Z., Zhuang, F., Qu, M., Lin, F., He, Q.: Knowledge graph embedding with hierarchical relation structure. In: EMNLP 2018, pp. 3198–3207. ACL (2018). https://doi.org/10.18653/v1/d18-1358

Automatic Conjecturing of P-Recursions Using Lifted Inference

Jáchym Barvínek[1]([⊠]), Timothy van Bremen[2], Yuyi Wang[3], Filip Železný[1], and Ondřej Kuželka[1]

[1] Czech Technical University in Prague, Prague, Czech Republic
barvijac@fel.cvut.cz
[2] KU Leuven, Leuven, Belgium
[3] ETH Zurich, Zurich, Switzerland

Abstract. Recent progress in lifted inference algorithms has made it possible to solve many non-trivial counting tasks from enumerative combinatorics in an automated fashion, by casting them as first-order model counting problems. Algorithms for this problem typically output a single number, which is the number of models of the first-order logic sentence in question on a given domain. However, in the combinatorics setting, we are more interested in obtaining a mathematical formula that holds for any given structure size. In this paper, we show that one can use lifted inference algorithms to conjecture linear recurrences with polynomial coefficients, one such class of formulas of interest.

Keywords: Lifted inference · Weighted Model Counting · Conjectures

1 Introduction

In this paper we study the connections between enumerative combinatorics and *first order model counting* (FOMC), which is the problem of computing the number of models of a given first-order logic sentence. In enumerative combinatorics, one is typically interested in counting structures that satisfy some given properties; these structures can be graphs, sets, functions etc. Many enumerative combinatorics problems can be equivalently stated as FOMC problems. For instance, the problem of counting all labeled graphs on n vertices can be equivalently seen as counting the number of models of the sentence $(\forall x : \neg e(x, x)) \land (\forall x \forall y : e(x, y) \Rightarrow e(y, x))$ on the domain $\Delta = \{1, 2, \ldots, n\}$.

The main appeal of FOMC for enumerative combinatorics is the availability of a growing body of results identifying tractable classes of FOMC problems. In a seminal result, Van den Broeck [14] and Van den Broeck, Meert and Darwiche [15] proved that computing FOMC for any sentence in the two-variable fragment of first-order logic, $\mathbf{FO}^2$, can be done in time polynomial in the size of the domain. Subsequently, Beame, Van den Broeck, Gribkoff and Suciu [1], showed that, in general, this is not the case for the three-variable fragment. However, this does not mean that there are no tractable classes of FOMC problems

© Springer Nature Switzerland AG 2022
N. Katzouris and A. Artikis (Eds.): ILP 2021, LNAI 13191, pp. 17–25, 2022.
https://doi.org/10.1007/978-3-030-97454-1_2

beyond $\mathbf{FO}^2$. Two tractable fragments, called $\mathbf{S}^2\mathbf{FO}^2$ and $\mathbf{S}^2\mathbf{RU}$, were identified in [9]. Later, Kuusisto and Lutz [10] extended the tractability results for $\mathbf{FO}^2$ by allowing the addition of a single functionality constraint, which has been recently further generalized by Kuželka [11] into the two variable fragment of first-order logic with counting quantifiers $\exists^{=k}$, $\exists^{\geq k}$ and $\exists^{\leq k}$, also known as the $\mathbf{C}^2$ fragment [8]. The latter fragment already allows expressing counting problems over non-trivial structures such as k-regular graphs.

One shortcoming of FOMC for applications in enumerative combinatorics is the fact that, when we run a FOMC algorithm on some problem, it always gives us a single number for the given domain size. However, for enumerative combinatorics, we would prefer a more analytic solution. For instance, consider the $\mathbf{C}^2$ sentence $(\forall x \exists^{=1} y : F(x, y)) \wedge (\forall y \exists^{=1} x : F(x, y))$, which asserts that the relation F is a permutation. Computing the FOMC of this sentence on domains of sizes 1, 2, 3, 4 gives us the results 1, 2, 6, 24, which we know are factorials of the domain sizes. Hence, ideally we would want to obtain a general solution of the form $n!$, or at least $a_n = n \cdot a_{n-1}$, $a_0 = 1$. The latter expression is a recurrence equation. It turns out that for many counting problems studied in combinatorics, there exist such linear recurrences with coefficients that are polynomials in n (i.e. in the domain size). In this paper we test whether one can use lifted algorithms for FOMC to conjecture such recurrent equations. We show that we are able to rediscover recurrent equations for a diverse collection of counting problems expressible in $\mathbf{C}^2$ and even conjecture new ones, such as for problems of counting the number of 2-regular-2-colored labelled graphs and 2-regular-3-colored labelled graphs for which no known recurrence exists. In particular, one of the sequences for these problems appears in the *The On-Line Encyclopedia of Integer Sequences* (OEIS[1]) but its recurrence does not and, for the other one, OEIS does not even contain the sequence. Although there have been previous works on automatic conjecture making in mathematics, e.g. works of Colton and his colleagues [4,5] in number theory, our work is, to our best knowledge, the first that allows one to automatically generate enumerative-combinatorics conjectures about combinatorial structures specified declaratively in a fragment of first-order logic. The key component that allows this approach to work are lifted inference algorithms [11,14,15] without which we would not even be able to get data for generating the conjectures.

2   Background

In this section, we give some background on first-order logic, the FOMC problem and P-recursive sequences.

2.1   First-Order Logic and Model Counting

We deal with the function-free, finite domain fragment of first-order logic. An *atom* of arity k takes the form $P(x_1, \ldots, x_k)$, where P/k comes from a vocabulary

---

[1] https://oeis.org.

of *predicates* (also called *relations*), and each argument x_i is a logical variable from a vocabulary of variables. A *literal* is an atom or its negation. A *formula* is formed by connecting one or more literals together using conjunction or disjunction. A formula may optionally be surrounded by one or more quantifiers of the form $\exists x$ or $\forall x$, where x is a logical variable. A logical variable in a formula is said to be *free* if it is not bound by any quantifier. A formula with no free variables is called a *sentence*. We follow the usual semantics of first-order logic.

In this paper we restrict ourselves to the two-variable fragment of first-order logic with counting quantifiers, which is usually referred to as the $\mathbf{C}^2$ fragment [8]. This fragment is obtained by restricting the allowed sentences to contain only two variables (w.l.o.g. we can assume that these variables are x and y) and allowing quantifiers $\exists^{=k}$, $\exists^{\leq k}$, $\exists^{\geq k}$ together with the standard $\forall$ and $\exists$ quantifiers. The quantifiers $\exists^{=k}$, $\exists^{\leq k}$, $\exists^{\geq k}$ stand for *exist exactly k, exist at most k* and *exist at least k*, respectively.

Example 1. A function $f : \Delta \rightarrow \Delta$ is called an involution if $f(f(x)) = x$ for all $x \in \Delta$. If we want to encode involutions in $\mathbf{C}^2$, we use the sentence: $\Psi = (\forall x \exists^{=1} y : f(x,y)) \wedge (\forall x \forall y : f(x,y) \Rightarrow f(y,x))$. Here, the first conjunct uses the counting quantifier $\exists^{=1}$ to force the relation f to be a function (i.e. to have exactly one value y for every value of x) and the second conjunct forces it to be involutive.

Below, we define first-order model counting.

Definition 1 (First-order model count). *The first-order model count (FOMC) of a sentence ϕ over a domain of size n is defined as:*

$$\mathsf{FOMC}(\phi, n) = |\mathsf{models}_n(\phi)|$$

where $\mathsf{models}_n(\phi)$ *denotes the set of all models of ϕ over the domain $\Delta = \{1, \ldots, n\}$. We call the sequence of numbers $a_n = \mathsf{FOMC}(\phi, n)$ the FOMC sequence of ϕ.*

Example 2. Consider the sentence $\Psi = \forall x \exists^{=1} y : f(x,y) \wedge \forall y \exists^{=1} x : f(x,y)$. What is the FOMC of this sentence over the domain $\Delta = \{1, 2\}$? To answer this question, we can enumerate the models of Ψ which in this case are $\{f(1,1), f(2,2)\}$ and $\{f(1,2), f(2,1)\}$, so the answer is that FOMC is 2 in this case. In general, since we know the models of Ψ correspond to permutations, we also know the answer must be $n!$ when $|\Delta| = n$ even without enumerating all models explicitly.

Lifted inference [7,12–14] studies ways to compute the FOMC much faster than by direct enumeration of models.[2] An important notion from the lifted

---

[2] Most algorithmic results in the lifted inference literature are presented for weighted first-order model counting (WFOMC), but for the combinatorics applications that we consider in this paper, it will be mostly sufficient to restrict our attention to FOMC even though there is, in fact, WFOMC under the hood of the algorithms that we use for FOMC—this is because existing algorithms use weights to compute FOMC with existential quantifiers [15] and with counting quantifiers [11].

inference literature is that of *domain liftability* [14], which we define below for the case of FOMC.

Definition 2 (Domain liftability). *An algorithm for computing FOMC in a fragment of first-order logic is said to be domain-lifted if it runs in time polynomial in the size of the domain for any fixed sentence from this fragment (the polynomial may depend on the sentence). A fragment of first-order logic is said to be domain-liftable if such a domain-lifted algorithm exists for it.*

In this paper we rely on the following result asserting the tractability of computing the FOMC for sentences from the $\mathbf{C}^2$ fragment of first-order logic [11], which builds on previous works of Van den Broeck [14], Van den Broeck, Meert and Darwiche [15] and Kuusisto and Lutz [10].

Theorem 1 (Kuželka, 2021 [11]). *The fragment of first-order logic limited to two variables with counting quantifiers, $\mathbf{C}^2$, is domain-liftable.*

2.2 P-Recursive Sequences

In this paper we are interested in finding *P-recursive relations* for FOMC sequences. First, we briefly introduce P-recursivity.

Definition 3. *A sequence of integers $\{a_n\}_{n=0}^{\infty}$ is called P-recursive if there exists $k \in \mathbb{N}$ and polynomials p_i for each $i = 0, ..., k$ with integer-valued coefficients such that for each $n > k$ it holds:*

$$\sum_{i=0}^{k} p_i(n) a_{n-i} = 0. \tag{1}$$

Here, we call the number k to be the order *of the sequence and maximum degree[3] $d \geq 0$ of the polynomials p_i to be the* degree *of the sequence. Furthermore, we denote with $c_{i,j}$ the coefficient of p_i at the $j-th$ power. This way, we can rewrite (1) in more detail as:*

$$\sum_{i=0}^{k} \sum_{j=0}^{d} a_{n-i} c_{i,j} n^j = 0. \tag{2}$$

Example 3. The Fibonacci sequence is P-recursive with $d = 0, k = 2, p_0(n) = -1, p_1(n) = p_2(n) = 1$.

Example 4. The sequence of factorials $n!$ is P-recursive with $d = 1, k = 1, p_0(n) = -1, p_1(n) = n$.

---

[3] It is convenient to consider the zero polynomial to have degree 0 and a single coefficient 0.

P-recursive sequences are of interest because the recurrence relations offer a straightforward and computationally inexpensive way to represent and evaluate the sequence terms, and perform other computations. See, for example, [6] for more details.

We will call the closed form expression of the form $a_{n+1} = f(a_n)$ derivable from (1) for some P-recursive sequence $\{a_n\}_{n=0}^{\infty}$ the *P-recursive relation* corresponding to the sequence. In this paper we will be trying to conjecture such relations automatically.

3 Approach

In this paper we take a pragmatic approach for conjecturing P-recursive relations. We assume that we are given a sentence in $\mathbf{C}^2$, encoding the combinatorial structures that we want to count. For instance, to count functions from Δ to Δ, the $\mathbf{C}^2$ sentence would be $\forall x \exists^{=1} y : F(x, y)$. We use an FOMC algorithm[4] to generate a sequence of numbers. We generate as many terms of this sequence as computationally tractable or up to 50 when the recurrence is already known and more is not needed. We then input the computed sequence terms into the method described below, which itself determines the number of samples from the sequence required to learn a conjecture. The conjecture, if found, is validated against the remaining terms not sampled to conjecture the equation. Success of the method does not constitute a proof that the equations we find are correct, or even that the sequence is P-recursive, but it allows us to be reasonably confident about them as conjectures. Of course, our confidence in them depends on the length of the validation sequence. Failure of the method to find a conjecture indicates that the sequence is either not P-recursive, or it is P-recursive with such a high order and/or degree that the input sequence provides insufficient information to reconstruct the recurrence equation.

3.1 Conjecturing Recurrence Relations

Our method resembles the one described in [2], but is simpler and adapted to our specific use case. Suppose we have the first l terms of a sequence $(a_0, ..., a_{l-1})$, and we are trying to conjecture a P-recursive relation for given values of the metaparameters k, d. From Eq. (2), we can directly obtain a system of $l - k$ linear equations with unknowns $c_{i,j}$. The right hand side of each equation is zero, so we can view the problem as looking for the kernel of a certain matrix M depending on $k, d, \{a_n\}_{n=0}^{l-1}$ and implicitly defined by Eq. (2). Specifically, the system of equations obtained is equivalent to the matrix equation $\mathbf{M} \cdot \mathbf{c} = \mathbf{0}$ with:

$$\mathbf{M}_{i,j} = a_{i+k-(j \mod (k+1))} (i+k)^{\lfloor \frac{j}{k+1} \rfloor} \tag{3}$$

$$\mathbf{c}_j = c_{\lfloor \frac{j}{k+1} \rfloor, j \mod (k+1)} \tag{4}$$

---

[4] The implementation that we use is based on the algorithm described in [11]. This algorithm needs access to an $\mathbf{FO}^2$ weighted FOMC oracle, for which we use our own optimized version [3] of the algorithm described in [1, Appendix C].

for $i = 0, \ldots, l-1-k$ and $j = 0, \ldots, (k+1)(d+1)-1$. (This is mostly reindexing resulting from flattening the table $c_{i,j}$ from (2) into the vector $\mathbf{c}$. See how the quotients $\left\lfloor \frac{j}{k+1} \right\rfloor$ correspond to i's in (2) and the remainders $j \mod (k+1)$ correspond to j's, and the $i+k$ here corresponds to n in (2).)

Note, that for a P-recursive sequence defined by polynomials p_i, we can generate a linear space of equivalent representations: certainly, we can multiply each of the polynomials p_i in (1) by another fixed nonzero polynomial to obtain a different representation of the same sequence. In general sometimes even different linearly independent vectors of $c_{i,j}$ can describe equivalent representations.

Example 5. Consider the sequence $a_n = n^4$. It can be verified that for $k = d = 2$ any triple of polynomials $(p_0, p_1, p_2) \in \text{span}\{(-5n^2 + 14n - 10, -32n - 32, 5n^2 - 6n+2), (-40n^2 + 101n - 65, 40n^2 + 48n + 112, 11n - 7)\}$ gives a valid P-recursive formula for this sequence. Our method unambiguously identifies this linear space when provided $\{n^4\}_{n=0}^8$.

Now, we consider the nullspace of the matrix $\mathbf{M}^{k,d}(\{a_n\}_{n=0}^{l-1})$, which we denote as $\ker \mathbf{M}^{k,d}(\{a_n\}_{n=0}^{l-1})$, to describe a P-recursivity conjecture for a sequence starting with $\{a_n\}_{n=0}^{l-1}$ if the following property holds: There exists a number $l^* < l$, such that

$$\ker \mathbf{M}^{k,d}(\{a_n\}_{n=0}^{l^*-2}) \neq \ker \mathbf{M}^{k,d}(\{a_n\}_{n=0}^{l^*-1}) \tag{5}$$

but for each $l', l^* < l' \leq l$ it holds that:

$$\ker \mathbf{M}^{k,d}(\{a_n\}_{n=0}^{l'-1}) = \ker \mathbf{M}^{k,d}(\{a_n\}_{n=0}^{l^*-1}) \neq \{\mathbf{0}\}. \tag{6}$$

This could equivalently be rephrased in machine learning terminology as follows: We consider the kernel to be a conjecture if it correctly predicts all the following sequence terms after l^* but is not unambiguously learnable from less than l^* samples. The difference $l - l^*$ is a measure of the strength of corroborating evidence for the conjecture following from the extra sequence terms available and can be seen as an analogue of the size of validation set in machine learning. Note that to construct the polynomials p_i from the kernel, we can take any linear combination of its basis vectors. In practice, the dimension of this space is often 1.

To find the metaparameters k, d we used a simple grid-search iterating over the pairs $(k, d) \in \{0, \ldots l-1\}^2$ in the order of increasing $k + d$. If no conjecture can be found this way, the algorithm exits with a failure status.

Example 6. Suppose we are given the five term sequence $\{a_n\}_{n=0}^4 = (1, 1, 2, 6, 24)$ and $k = d = 1$. The corresponding matrix is:

$$\mathbf{M} = \begin{pmatrix} a_2 & a_1 & 1a_2 & 1a_1 \\ a_3 & a_2 & 2a_3 & 2a_2 \\ a_4 & a_3 & 3a_4 & 3a_3 \\ a_5 & a_4 & 4a_5 & 4a_4 \end{pmatrix} = \begin{pmatrix} 1 & 1 & 1 & 1 \\ 2 & 1 & 4 & 2 \\ 6 & 2 & 18 & 6 \\ 24 & 6 & 96 & 24 \end{pmatrix} \tag{7}$$

The kernel has dimension one and is $\ker \mathbf{M} = \mathrm{span}\{(-1, 0, 0, 1)\}$. This would be the same if we dropped the last term of the sequence, but different if we dropped the last two. This is equivalent to dropping the bottom row(s) of $\mathbf{M}$. Therefore $l^* = 4$. We can use this basis vector to write a recurrence relation:

$$(-1 \cdot n^0 + 0 \cdot n^1)a_n + (0 \cdot n^0 + 1 \cdot n)a_{n-1} = 0 \tag{8}$$

which makes the conjectured sequence $a_n = na_{n-1} = n!$, whose correctness can be validated by the sample a_4 not needed to obtain this result.

Table 1. Examples of applying our conjecturing method to some FOMC sequences of properties in $\mathbf{C}^2$. The "Known" column indicates whether a P-recurrence formula could be found in OEIS or other sources. For the sequences marked as "No", we consider the conjectured recurrence relation to be a novel discovery (to the best of our knowledge). The sequences marked as "Yes" were correctly rediscovered by our automated method. The l^* column is the minimum number of samples required to learn the sequence in the sense defined in Sect. 3. The l column is the actual number of sequence terms we were able to compute within the total time shown in the last column.

Property	OEIS ID	k	d	Known	l^*	l	Time
P-recursive relation conjectured							a_0, a_1, a_2, a_3
Permutations	A000142	1	1	Yes	4	50	1 h 3 min
$a_n = na_{n-1}$							1, 1, 2, 6
Derangements	A000166	2	1	Yes	7	50	12 min
$a_n = (n-1)(a_{n-2} + a_{n-1})$							1, 0, 1, 2
Involutions	A000085	2	1	Yes	7	50	4 min
$a_n = a_{n-1} + (n-1)a_{n-2}$							1, 1, 2, 4
1-regular graphs (involutive derangements)	A001147	1	1	Yes	4	50	1 h 5 min
$a_n = (2n-1)a_{n-1}$. Here we use $n = 2|\Delta|$ as the property is trivially unsatisfiable for odd $|\Delta|$.							1, 1, 3, 155
2-regular graphs	A001205	3	2	Yes	14	50	6 min
$2a_n = (n-1)(2a_{n-1} + (n-2)a_{n-3})$							1, 0, 0, 1
2-regular ∩ 2-colored graphs	A054479	2	2	No	15	32	17 h 50 min
$a_n = 2(n-1)(2n-1)((2n-3)a_{n-2} + a_{n-1})$. Also using $n = 2|\Delta|$.							1, 0, 6, 120
2-regular ∩ 3-colored graphs	N/A	4	3	No	23	31	11 h 40 min
$a_n = (n-1)(a_{n-1} + (n-2)(2a_{n-2} + 3a_{n-3} + 6(n-3)a_{n-4}))$							1, 0, 0, 6
2-colored graphs	A047863	–	–	–	–	400	9 min
Does not appear to be P-recursive.							1, 2, 6, 26
3-colored graphs	A191371	–	–	–	–	400	20 min
Does not appear to be P-recursive.							1, 3, 15, 123

4   Experiments

We computed the FOMC sequences for several logical properties and attempted to compute as many terms as possible in reasonable time. We then used those sequences to find a conjecture about P-recursivity. For some of the properties, a P-recursive relation is already known and our algorithm merely reproduces it. However, for two of those properties, the algorithm conjectured a relation for which we found no such relation on OEIS. The FOMC sequences were computed using our own implementation as explained in Sect. 3, and ran on a single 3.7GHz Intel i5-9600KF processor core with up to 32 GiB memory available. This was computationally the most difficult part.

The code for finding the recurrence relation was implemented in Mathematica 12 [16]. This process was usually quick and found a solution within seconds if it existed with low degree and order. For sequences which do not seem to be P-recursive, this is comparably slower as the grid search is attempting many high-valued metaparameter candidates. The results are summarised in Table 1.

Since we were using the Mathematica software, we noticed that some of the recurrences could automatically be converted to closed-forms. For example, for the 1-regularity, we obtained the formula[5] $a_n = 2^n \pi^{-\frac{1}{2}} \Gamma(\frac{1}{2} + n)$. We got similar symbolic solutions also for permutations and derangements. For the rest of the problems, Mathematica was not able to find a solution of the recurrences in terms of standard special functions. Methods for solving recurrence equations could thus be used to extend our pipeline with closed forms at output where available.

5 Conclusions

In this short paper we proposed a methodology for generating conjectures about P-recursivity of combinatorial sequences using techniques from lifted inference. We demonstrated the potential of the approach by showing that we can rediscover non-trivial recurrence relations from the literature, as well as conjecture new ones. It is likely that these conjectures could be proven by an expert enumerative combinatorialist. In the future, we want to move from conjecturing the recurrences to proving them algorithmically, thus, if we exaggerate a bit, making an *automatic enumerative combinatorialist*.

Acknowledgements. JB and OK were supported by the Czech Science Foundation project "Generative Relational Models" (20-19104Y). JB was also supported by a donation from X-Order Lab. TvB was supported by the Research Foundation – Flanders (G095917N). FZ was supported by the Czech Science Foundation project 20-29260S.

References

1. Beame, P., Van den Broeck, G., Gribkoff, E., Suciu, D.: Symmetric weighted first-order model counting. In: PODS, pp. 313–328. ACM (2015)
2. Berthomieu, J., Faugère, J.C.: Guessing linear recurrence relations of sequence tuples and p-recursive sequences with linear algebra. In: Proceedings of the ACM on International Symposium on Symbolic and Algebraic Computation, pp. 95–102 (2016)

---

[5] Here, the expression obtained from Mathematica was originally expressed using the Pochhammer symbol which we rewrote using the gamma function.

3. van Bremen, T., Kuzelka, O.: Faster lifting for two-variable logic using cell graphs. In: Proceedings of the Thirty-Seventh Conference on Uncertainty in Artificial Intelligence, UAI 2021, pp. 1393–1402 (2021)
4. Colton, S.: Automated conjecture making in number theory using HR, otter and maple. J. Symb. Comput. **39**(5), 593–615 (2005)
5. Colton, S., Bundy, A., Walsh, T.: Automatic invention of integer sequences. In: Proceedings of the Seventeenth National Conference on Artificial Intelligence and Twelfth Conference on on Innovative Applications of Artificial Intelligence, 30 July–3 August 2000, Austin, Texas, USA, pp. 558–563 (2000)
6. Flajolet, P., Sedgewick, R.: Analytic Combinatorics. Cambridge University Press, Cambridge (2009)
7. Gogate, V., Domingos, P.M.: Probabilistic Theorem Proving. In: UAI, pp. 256–265. AUAI Press (2011)
8. Grädel, E., Kolaitis, P.G., Vardi, M.Y.: On the decision problem for two-variable first-order logic. Bull. Symb. Log. **3**(1), 53–69 (1997)
9. Kazemi, S.M., Kimmig, A., Van den Broeck, G., Poole, D.: New liftable classes for first-order probabilistic inference. In: NIPS, pp. 3117–3125 (2016)
10. Kuusisto, A., Lutz, C.: Weighted model counting beyond two-variable logic. In: LICS, pp. 619–628. ACM (2018)
11. Kuzelka, O.: Weighted first-order model counting in the two-variable fragment with counting quantifiers. J. Artif. Intell. Res. **70**, 1281–1307 (2021)
12. Poole, D.: First-order probabilistic inference. In: IJCAI, pp. 985–991. Morgan Kaufmann (2003)
13. de Salvo Braz, R., Amir, E., Roth, D.: Lifted first-order probabilistic inference. In: IJCAI, pp. 1319–1325. Professional Book Center (2005)
14. Van den Broeck, G.: On the completeness of first-order knowledge compilation for lifted probabilistic inference. In: NIPS, pp. 1386–1394 (2011)
15. Van den Broeck, G., Meert, W., Darwiche, A.: Skolemization for weighted first-order model counting. In: KR. AAAI Press (2014)
16. Wolfram Research Inc: Mathematica, Version 12.2 (2020). https://www.wolfram.com/mathematica, champaign, IL (2020)

Machine Learning of Microbial Interactions Using Abductive ILP and Hypothesis Frequency/Compression Estimation

Didac Barroso-Bergada[1](✉), Alireza Tamaddoni-Nezhad[2](✉),
Stephen H. Muggleton[3](✉), Corinne Vacher[4](✉), Nika Galic[5](✉),
and David A. Bohan[1](✉)

[1] Agroécologie, AgroSup Dijon, INRAE, Université de Bourgogne Franche -Comté,
Dijon, France
{didac.barroso-bergada,david.bohan}@inrae.fr
[2] University of Surrey, Guildford GU2 7XH, UK
a.tamaddoni-nezhad@surrey.ac.uk
[3] Imperial College London, South Kensington, London SW7 2AZ, UK
s.muggleton@imperlal.ac.uk
[4] INRAE, Univ. Bordeaux, BIOGECO, Pessac, France
corinne.vacher@inrae.fr
[5] Syngenta Crop Protection LLC, Greensboro, NC, USA
Nika.Galic@syngenta.com

Abstract. Interaction between species in microbial communities plays an important role in the functioning of all ecosystems, from cropland soils to human gut microbiota. Many statistical approaches have been proposed to infer these interactions from microbial abundance information. However, these statistical approaches have no general mechanisms for incorporating existing ecological knowledge in the inference process. We propose an Abductive/Inductive Logic Programming (A/ILP) framework to infer microbial interactions from microbial abundance data, by including logical descriptions of different types of interaction as background knowledge in the learning. This framework also includes a new mechanism for estimating the probability of each interaction based on the frequency and compression of hypotheses computed during the abduction process. This is then used to identify real interactions using a bootstrapping, re-sampling procedure. We evaluate our proposed framework on simulated data previously used to benchmark statistical interaction inference tools. Our approach has comparable accuracy to SparCC, which is one of the state-of-the-art statistical interaction inference algorithms, but with the the advantage of including ecological background knowledge. Our proposed framework opens up the opportunity of inferring ecological interaction information from diverse ecosystems that currently cannot be studied using other methods.

© Springer Nature Switzerland AG 2022
N. Katzouris and A. Artikis (Eds.): ILP 2021, LNAI 13191, pp. 26–40, 2022.
https://doi.org/10.1007/978-3-030-97454-1_3

Keywords: Abductive/Inductive Logic Programming (A/ILP) ·
Interaction Network Inference · Machine learning of ecological
networks · Hypothesis Frequency Estimation (HFE)

1 Introduction

Networks of interactions between species of microbes are believed to drive many
of the biological functions that determine effects as diverse as soil health, crop
growth, and plant and human disease. Next generation sequencing of DNA samples taken from microbial communities can produce lists of those species present
and metrics for their abundance, by treating the number of each sequence type
in the sample either as absolute or relative counts. Inferring networks from these
data could yield important results, improving our ability to manage these systems and issues [19]. For example, learning interactions of competition or predation of a disease-causing microbial agent could be used to identify species for
biological control, and the chemistry that is involved could lead to the development of new drugs [10]. Current approaches to reconstructing ecological networks of interaction between microbial species use statistical learning to infer
the presence of an interaction via correlation. Human experts subsequently interpret whether the correlation indicates an interaction between the two correlated
microbial species, such as competition or predation.

Abductive/Inductive Logic Programming (A/ILP) was previously used to
automatically generate plausible and testable food webs from ecological census
data [17]. The approach in Tamaddoni-Nezhad et al. (2012) [17] also included a
probabilistic approach, called Hypothesis Frequency Estimation (HFE) for estimating probabilities of hypothetical trophic links based on their frequency of
occurrence when randomly sampling the hypothesis space. Through a review of
the literature, it was found that many of the learned trophic links are corrob-
orated by the literature. In particular, links ascribed with high probability by
machine learning are shown to correspond well with those having multiple references in the literature. In some cases novel, high probability links were suggested,
some of which were subsequently tested and confirmed in empirical studies [18].

In this paper we extend the A/ILP and HFE approaches in Tamaddoni-
Nezhad et al. (2012) [17] for the purpose of learning microbial interactions.
We will describe the existing context on interaction inference, detail the A/ILP
based inference method and evaluate this method with a benchmark dataset.
We also compare our results with SparCC, which is a state-of-the-art statistical
interaction inference algorithm.

2 Background and Related Work

Microbial ecologists have clear criteria for interactions between species that can
readily be transcribed into logical statements. In effect, past or ongoing interactions between two microbial species will have led to changes in the abundance of
one or both species. Conceptually, therefore, two species might have undergone

Table 1. Type of interactions in function of the changes in abundance [3].

Type of interaction	Effect on Specie1 abundance	Effect on Specie2 abundance	Nature of interaction
Mutualism	Up	Up	Mutual benefits of the species
Competition	Down	Down	Species have negative effect on each other
Predation/Parasitism	Up	Down	Parasite develops at the expense of the host
Commensalism	Up	Null	Specie1 benefits while Specie2 is not affected
Amensalism	Down	Null	Specie2 has a negative effect on Specie1, but Specie2 is not affected

or might be undergoing an interaction if there is some pattern to the changes of the two species across a data-set. Thus, if one of the species always increases or decreases in abundance in the presence of the other, microbial ecologists might hypothesize an interaction between the two species. The ecological mechanisms of these interactions, along with their expected changes in abundance of the two species, have previously been described in Derocles et al. (2018) [3] as shown in Table 1.

In this paper we extend the A/ILP approach in Tamaddoni-Nezhad et al. (2012) [17] with logical statements for putative microbial interactions included as background knowledge, to infer ecological interactions directly, with less or even without the intervention of humans at the interpretation step. This direct approach would be particularly valuable for reconstructing microbial networks in previously unstudied ecosystems where human knowledge for interpretation may effectively be non-existent (Fig. 1).

In this paper we also extend the Hypothesis Frequency Estimation (HFE) approach introduced in Tamaddoni-Nezhad et al. (2012) [17]. Microbial ecologists rely on statistical probability estimates, typically at the conventional 5% significance level, to evaluate the importance of a correlational link between any two microbial species [15]. Most ILP approaches, including HFE rely on coverage based measures such as 'compression' for selecting hypotheses.

The problem we try to address here is whether compression can be evaluated within a statistical framework that meets the needs of microbial ecologists, to a degree that might be sufficient to convince them of the statistical importance and veracity of any learned interaction. In particular, we explore an extension of HFE where both the frequency and the compression of the hypotheses are considered within an statistical framework.

Benchmarking statistical learning approaches for inferring correlational links have used simulated data-sets. For example, Weiss et al. (2016) [21] produced simulated microbial data-sets to benchmark the ability of different statistical methods, such as SparCC [7] and CoNet [6], to detect different interaction types via correlation. In this paper we use the method of Weiss et al. [21] to simulate ecological-like replicated data-sets of interactions, of given interaction strengths. We then use ILP to evaluate the presence of the simulated interactions, as a

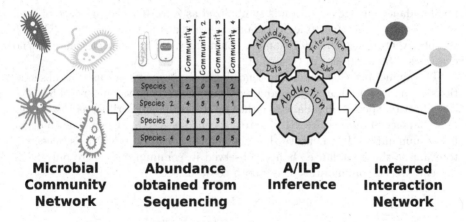

Microbial Community Network   **Abundance obtained from Sequencing**   **A/ILP Inference**   **Inferred Interaction Network**

Fig. 1. Description of the interaction inference process. Microbial communities are shaped by the interaction between their members. DNA sequencing together with bioinformatic processes allow to estimate the abundance of the different microbes present in the communities. Using the abundance information from different communities as training examples, and the rules of interaction as background knowledge, it is possible to infer an interaction network that generalizes the interactions between microbes.

known set of expectations. Our specific goals are to: determine the most sensitive parameter of compression for recovering an interaction, given a discrete number of permutations; and, evaluate the probabilistic significance of the compression parameter using a form of bootstrapping.

3   Methods

3.1   Logical Description of Microbial Interactions

A microbial interaction can be defined as a conserved effect on the abundance of one microbial species caused by the presence of another microbial species. Thus, the aim of the abductive procedure is to infer interactions, following ecological theory to explain the observed changes in the abundance of the species. To do this, the first step is to reflect the abundance changes between communities of each species using logical statements, following the form: abundance(C1, C2, S1, Dir). Here C1 and C2 symbolize two different community samples where species S1 is present and Dir the change in direction of abundance. To calculate the change in direction, the abundances of a species in the two different samples are compared using a Pearson Chi-square test. The test uses the total, summed abundance of all species in a community as the total population and checks the independence of the abundances of the species between the two samples. Where the species counts are found to be independent an abundance change is deemed to exist. An increase is symbolized as an up ($\uparrow$) and a decrease as a down ($\downarrow$). Where the species abundances are not independent between the two samples, a no abundance change condition is symbolized as zero (0). The presence of each species is also converted to logical clauses with the structure: presence (C1, S2, yes/no) where C1 refers to a sample community, S2 to a species and yes/no describes if S2 is present in C1 or not.

The abundance change and presence logical statements are used as observations in an abduction process conducted using the A/ILP system Progol 5.0 [12]. The effect on species abundances, either up or down, is described as the change in abundance of one species, S1, due to a second species, S2, when they co-occur in a community, C2. To ensure that the change is caused by S2 it is necessary to evaluate the abundance changes observed in communities where only S2 is present, C1, to communities where both co-occur, C2.

$$abundance(C1, C2, S1, up) : -$$
$$presence(C2, S2, yes),$$
$$presence(C1, S2, no),$$
$$effect\_up(S2, S1).$$

$$(1)$$

$$abundance(C1, C2, S1, down) : -$$
$$presence(C2, S2, yes),$$
$$presence(C1, S2, no),$$
$$effect\_down(S2, S1).$$

Progol5.0 uses a standard covering algorithm to conduct the abduction process where each observation is generalised using a multi-predicate search. This search is carried out over all the predicates associated with 'modeh' declarations, or abducible predicates, effect_up and effect_down. These two abducible predicates limit the possible variations in abundance that a species can experience due to the effect of another species. The search for the best hypotheses is guided by an evaluation function called 'compression' which is defined as follows:

$$f = p - (c + n) \tag{2}$$

where p is the number of observations (training examples) correctly explained by the hypothesis (positive examples), n is the number incorrectly explained (negative examples) and c is the length of the hypothesis (in this study, always 1 because the hypothesis is a single fact).

At the end of the abduction process, a list of ground hypotheses with the form effect_up/down(S2,S1) is returned, each hypothesis being supported by a compression value f. Implementations of A/ILP usually consider hypotheses with positive compression values. However, compression also offers a quantitative measure of information that can be used to discriminate between true and false interactions. For this purpose, first it is necessary to normalize compression values to a common scale. This is because while some species may not be present in all communities due their different random distribution. It is also possible that negative interactions reduce the abundance of a species to zero. Hence, each species will experience uneven combinations of abundance change mechanisms that require normalization. The normalization is performed using the logarithmic co-occurrence/occurrence ratio of the interacting species.

For an interaction between S1 and S2 to exist, there must be a consistent and constant effect, either up or down, on at least one of the species over all communities. Hence, we use the probabilistic estimator I supporting the interaction between S2 and S1 as defined below:

$$I_{S2,S1} = |f_{up}(S2, S1) - f_{down}(S2, S1)| \tag{3}$$

Compression is dependent on the order in which abundance clauses used as observations are supplied, due to the predicate search process that uses observations as seeds. To obtain reliable compression values, it is necessary to perform the inference several times, permuting randomly the order of examples to obtain different sampling of the hypothesis space. The permutation process will produce a set of possible effects and a corresponding compression value for each pair of species. Effects can be present in all the samples of the hypothesis space or just one part. Thus, it is necessary to define an approach to use the output of the abduction process, after sampling the hypothesis space, as a probabilistic measure. The HFE approach [17] estimates probabilities for hypothetical links in ecological networks, based on their frequency of occurrence when randomly sampling the hypothesis space. In this approach, the compression value was not taken into account to obtain a probabilistic measure of interaction. We propose a different method here that extends HFE to compute a probabilistic estimator I from the values of compression values f. In place of using the frequency of hypotheses with positive compression over all re-samples, here a function $func$ is applied to the f values to obtain an estimator I which summarizes the information contained in all the samples.

$$I_{S2,S1} = |func(f_{up}(S2, S1)_{1,...,n}) - func(f_{down}(S2, S1)_{1,...,m})| \tag{4}$$

In the experiments in this paper, we examined the following $func$ functions to obtain the estimator, I:

- **Frequency** = HFE is computed for each effect.
- **Independent permutations** = Where there is more than one compression value in a permutation, the sum is computed. Maximum values for each interaction among all permutations are retained.
- **Maximum** = Compression values from all permutations are pooled. Then, maximum compression is selected for each effect.
- **Sum** = Compression values from all permutations are pooled. Then, compression is summed for each effect.

3.2 Bootstrapping

Having a probabilistic measure of the likelihood of an interaction is critical for ecologists to interpret the networks resulting from interaction inference. This should allow the selection of those interactions that are realistic and might then be tested in cost- and time-expensive laboratory experiments. The most intuitive selection method would establish a threshold for the estimator value. However, most of the ecological systems where A/ILP interaction inference could help are poorly described and there are no references to guide selection of such a threshold [15].

It is a common assumption that the interaction networks shaping microbial communities are sparse. This means that the number of interactions of each species is only a small fraction of the total set of interactions that are possible. Thus, where the estimator value of the observed interactions, I, is greater than the values of non existing interactions, it is possible to assess the statistical significance of an interaction using a bootstrapping procedure. Statistical bootstrapping is a method of re-sampling a dataset to create new simulated datasets [4]. Let d be all the compression values for effect up and effect down, involving at least one of the potential interacting species S1 and S2, the real final estimator value, I_0, is obtained by applying Eq. 4 to n compression values that support an effect up of S2 on S1 and m compression values that supports and effect down of S2 on S1. The bootstrapping procedure re-samples compression values in d to obtain two new sets of values d^{up*} and d^{down*} of n and m lengths, respectively. Then, an alternative estimator value I_a is obtained applying Eq. 4 to d^{up*} and d^{down*}. If the re-sampling process is repeated B times, a pseudo p-value can be computed for the potential interaction between S1 and S2 averaging the simulated values I_a that are bigger than I_0 [11].

$$I_0 = |func(f_{up}(S2, S1)_{1,...,n}) - func(f_{down}(S2, S1)_{1,...,m})|$$
$$I_a = |func(d_{1,...,n}^{*up}) - func(d_{1,...,m}^{*down})|$$
$$p-value = \sum_{b=1}^{B} \{(I_{a_b} \geq I_0)\}/B \tag{5}$$

3.3 Simulated Data-Sets

The aim of ILP based network inference is to use logical descriptions of interactions to detect and classify those interactions between species as a function of the ecological mechanism that drives them. Hence, a simulation model to generate test-datasets should follow the different ecological mechanisms that they are simulating [5]. Information required for network inference is structured in tables, where each row contains the information for a species and each column contains the information for a microbial community. Each cell summarizes the count of individuals of each species in each community (abundance). Weiss et al. (2016) [21] proposed a simulation model to create computer-generated tables including the effects of ecological-like, linear interactions. The model uses the log-normal distribution to simulate the abundance of non-interacting species in a set of microbial communities or samples. The log-normal distribution has been shown to appropriately model the abundance distributions of microbial communities [16]. Interactions are then introduced by modifying the abundance of species in accordance with the different ecological mechanisms [5]. For any two species, say S1 and S2, the abundance modifications only happen in communities where the species co-occur. The abundance modification is based on the effect that S2 has on S1. If the effect is positive, the abundance of S1 increases as a function of the abundance of S2, modulated by a strength of the interaction. If the effect is negative, the abundance of S1 is decreased following a similar mechanism. In the case that the interaction affects both species, their abundance is modified in parallel.

Using the method proposed in Weiss et al. (2016) [21] we generated three tables containing the abundances of 16 pairs of interacting species in 100 communities. The tables were simulated using interactions of different strength values (2, 3 and 5), and four different ecological mechanisms: amensalism, commensalism, competition and mutualism [3].

3.4 Compositionality and Bias

Modern sequencing technologies allow us to recover information about microbial communities from samples of environmental DNA. As noted in Sect. 1, the number of times that a DNA sequence from a species is 'read' in a sample can be used as a measure of abundance or count. A sequencer can only read a limited number of sequences in a sample, and these are shared amongst species, imposing a compositional bias on the data [9]. Thus, to generate ecological-like microbial tables it is necessary to re-introduce compositionality into the simulated data-sets. To do this, we normalized the sequencing depth as probabilities in a multinomial distribution and then sampled the distribution to obtain the simulated counts across a common sequencing depth.

4 Experimental Evaluation

The performance of the A/ILP based microbial inference (Fig. 2) is evaluated using the computer-generated datasets. First, it is tested the number of samples of the hypothesis space and the different functions used to obtain the I statistic. Then the best setting found in the first experiment is used to asses the performance of the bootstrapping procedure compared with a threshold for I and SparCC. The simulated data and the code used to perform the experimental evaluation have been included in a public repository[1].

4.1 Experiment 1

Null Hypothesis 1: Using the estimator I as defined in (4) using different functions does not lead to higher accuracy over the frequency-based approach HFE for predicting microbial interactions.

---

[1] https://github.com/didacb/Machine-learning-of-microbial-interaction.

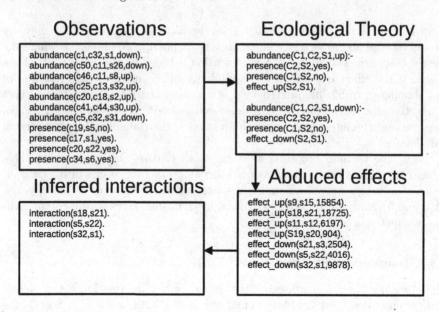

Fig. 2. Summary of the inference process of microbial interactions using A/ILP

Materials and Methods: The three computer-generated tables described in Sect. 2.1, computed using the methodology of Weiss et al. (2016) [21], are used to test the performance of functions used to obtain the estimators. 100 abductions of possible effects are performed for each table. The observations produced from the tables are randomly permuted at each execution. The logical description of effect is used as background knowledge. Then the estimators are obtained using the different functions described previously.

Since the interactions that drive the abundances of the computer-generated tables are known, it is possible to treat interaction inference as a classification problem. Interactions can be classified between existing and non existing and the estimator values obtained using the different functions are the classification accuracy. Thus, the area under the curve (AUC) of the true positive rate against the false positive rate (ROC curve) can be used as a measure of performance. AUC is computed for all functions at n permutations = 1, 5, 10, 25 and 50. An ANOVA test is performed together with a Tuckey's range test to asses the significance of differences of AUC values between all functions.

Results and Discussion: AUC values for the different methodologies to obtain estimators and number of permutations are displayed in Fig. 3. As expected, values of AUC increase as the number of permutations used for the inference increases. These stabilize at around n = 50 permutations. AUC values are similar where the strength of interaction is reduced, being significantly lower at the highest strength. This can be explained by the low performance of the logical model in describing the specific case of a negative interaction reducing the abun-

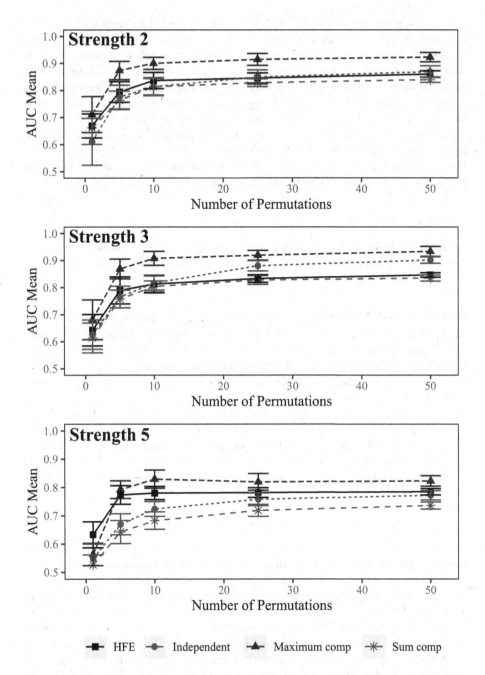

Fig. 3. Area under the ROC curve values (AUC) obtained using different number of permutations. Each plot shows the AUCs obtained inferring interactions of different strengths. Each line represents a method used to obtain the estimators. Error bars show the standard deviation of the means.

dance of a given species to 0, the likelihood of which increases with stronger interactions. This ecological process, called exclusion, greatly reduces the co-occurrence between species and, as a consequence, the information available to infer an interaction. Maximum compression used to obtain I is the metric that gives the highest values of AUC, for any given number of permutations and inter-action strengths. HFE, Sum and independent permutations have similar AUC values at strength 2 and 5 while the independent permutation method performs best at strength 3. The ANOVA shows that all functions have significantly different AUC values, except independent permutations and HFE at strength 2. Consequently, the null hypothesis can be rejected because the method using the maximum compression values to obtain I performs better than HFE in all cases.

4.2 Experiment 2

Null Hypothesis 2: The bootstrapping procedure described in Sec 3.2 leads to lower accuracy compared to the optimal threshold and other statistical methods for interaction inference.

Materials and Methods: The Bootstrapping procedure is conducted using the three computer generated tables used in the preceding experiment. The pro-cedure uses the maximum compression to obtain the I estimator. Two different bootstrapping techniques are evaluated: ordinary and strata. Ordinary boot-strapping performs the bootstrapping independently on all compression values while the strata method constrains the bootstrapping to compression values by effect. Interactions with p value < 0.05 are considered to exist. Bootstrapping accuracy is compared with the accuracy of prediction using an optimal thresh-old for I estimator. The optimal threshold metric is obtained automatically from the ROC curves of the preceding test using the pROC R package best threshold method [14]. To have a reference for comparing the performance of A/ILP infer-ring interactions, the interaction inference was also performed using SparCC [7], a widely used statistical inference tool. The process was performed using the FastSpar 1.0 implementation [20] with default parameters.

Results and Discussion: Accuracy measures are displayed in Table 2. Ordi-nary bootstrap presents better accuracy than strata bootstrap at strength = 2 and 3, while strata performs better at strength = 5. However, ordinary bootstrap allows the detection of a larger number of true positives in contrast to strata. We believe this to be the better option to use for detecting interactions, therefore. In all cases bootstrap accuracy is higher than the optimal threshold accuracy. Bootstrapped A/ILP sensitivity values are significantly lower than SparCC at all strengths. However, the specificity values are slightly higher. Thus, SparCC has a greater number of false positives, while A/ILP generates a higher number of false negatives. This produces similar accuracy measures for SparCC and boot-strapped A/ILP, independent of the interaction strength. We therefore reject the null hypothesis.

Table 2. Performance of estimator bootstrapping compared with optimal threshold obtained from the ROC curve and SparCC. The three datsets used for the interaction inference have 16 real interactions over 496 possible interactions.

Strength 2				
	Optimal threshold	Ordinary Bootstrap	Strata Bootstrap	SparCC
Total	40	13	3	26
TP	13	9	2	12
FP	27	4	1	14
TN	453	476	479	466
FN	3	7	14	4
Sensitivity	0.812	0.562	0.125	0.75
Specificity	0.944	0.992	0.998	0.971
Accuracy	0.94	0.978	0.97	0.964

Strength 3				
	Optimal threshold	Ordinary Bootstrap	Strata Bootstrap	SparCC
Total	69	7	2	31
TP	14	6	1	11
FP	55	10	1	20
TN	425	479	479	460
FN	2	10	15	5
Sensitivity	0.875	0.375	0.062	0.688
Specificity	0.885	0.998	0.998	0.958
Accuracy	0.885	0.978	0.968	0.95

Strength 5				
	Optimal threshold	Ordinary Bootstrap	Strata Bootstrap	SparCC
Total	50	27	4	40
TP	12	10	3	13
FP	38	17	1	27
TN	442	463	479	453
FN	4	6	13	3
Sensitivity	0.75	0.625	0.188	0.812
Specificity	0.921	0.965	0.998	0.944
Accuracy	0.915	0.954	0.972	0.94

5   Discussion and Conclusion

This work proposes a framework to infer ecological-like microbial interactions that allows us to use abundance information and descriptions of interactions as logic statements for obtaining a probabilistic measure of the significance of a given interaction, based on compression values. By using logical descriptions of interactions, microbial ecologists can apply their knowledge not only to the interpretation of results but also to the inference process itself.

Tamaddoni-Nezhad et al. (2013) [18] showed how the introduction of ecological expertise (in the form of background knowledge) to the interaction inference can lead to interesting results for invertebrate food webs, and we believe that the work presented here will facilitate similar results for microbial networks.

Interactions between species can be driven by different mechanisms, thus it is necessary to obtain a common quantitative measure of these interactions for appropriate ecological interpretation. Statistical relation learning (SRL) has been used to obtain quantitative measures using ILP-like representations and inference [8]. However, most of the cases where SRL has been used requires probabilistic data, where each observation has an associated probability. However, the observations obtained from NGS data are purely deterministic; a species is either present or not in a given community, and its abundance in this community is also an invariable number. Other authors have proposed different methods to perform probabilistic approaches to deterministic data, such as using a binary matrix obtained from a deterministic process to obtain a support vector machine [1]. The idea of using compression as a probabilistic estimation was also used by Bryant et al. (2001) [2] in their implementation of ASE-Progol. ASE-Progol uses compression to select between contradictory candidate hypothesis. Tamaddoni-Nezhad et al. (2012) [17] developed the Hypothesis Frequency Estimation approach for sampling and estimating the probability of abductive hypotheses. We extended this idea to use the value of compression as a measure for estimating the likelihood of any given interaction. To do this, it is necessary to sample the hypothesis space enough times to ensure that the distribution of compression values obtained for each interaction is representative of all the possible values. Our first experiment showed that a re-sampling of 50 times is enough in a setting involving 32 species and 50 communities, given that the AUC values obtained using a larger sampling were not significantly different. This experiment also showed that retaining the maximum compression values among all hypothesis space samples has greater accuracy than using the HFE, or the other numeric metrics of compression tested, independent of the strength of interactions. This is consistent with the predicate search algorithm of Progol5.0 which selects the hypothesis with the maximum compression from all possible hypotheses [13]. Lastly, it is important to note that the AUC values decreased in all cases where the interactions were strong enough to cause exclusion [3]. In future applications of A/ILP-based interaction inference, it will be important to incorporate logical rules describing exclusion in the learning.

Bootstrapping is a statistic technique used in many areas of knowledge discovery. It has also been applied in statistical inference of interactions [7]. We showed that the bootstrapping procedure has better accuracy values than the optimal thresholds obtained using ROC curves. Thus, it is possible to use this procedure for real data, where the interactions are unknown and the ROC curves cannot be used. Even though bootstrapping offers good accuracy and specificity measures, the sensitivity of inference is insufficient to detect all true interactions. As noted previously, this is in part related to the effect of interaction-derived exclusion of one or both species. It is also due to a restrictive effect of the bootstrapping procedure. Where the bootstrapping is constrained by the effect of abundance, leading to a low number of examples, the sensitivity is low. It is expected that, in real cases where each species interacts with more than one species providing more high compression values for the bootstrapping, the sensitivity will increase.

Weiss et al. (2016) [21] used their method of generate ecological-like datasets, as described in Sect. 3.3, to benchmark many of these interaction inference tools. Comparing the results obtained by SparCC in Weiss et al. (2016) [21] and in this work, a reduction in the number of interacting species reduced specificity and increased sensitivity. However the accuracy values remained similar. A/ILP inference using bootstrap obtained accuracy measures in the same range as SparCC, using the same computer-generated data. This accuracy can be further improved by expanding the range of logical descriptions to other ecological effects and interactions, such as exclusion. Also, it makes it possible to include other sources of biological and ecological information from existing databases as background knowledge.

Our work shows that A/ILP can be used to infer ecological interactions accurately from computer-generated datasets, using an estimator obtained from compression as a numeric measure of interaction and a bootstrap procedure to detect true interactions. Hence, A/ILP interaction inference has the potential to become a valuable tool for microbial ecologists for the inference of ecological interactions.

Acknowledgements. This work was supported by the Agence Nationale de la Recherche, Grant/ Award Number: ANR-17-CE32-0011, and SYNGENTA CROP PROTECTION AG. Corinne Vacher and David A. Bohan acknowledge the support of the Learn-Biocontrol project, funded by the INRAE MEM metaprogramme, and the BCMicrobiome project funded by the Consortium Biocontrôle. Alireza Tamaddoni-Nezhad and Stephen Muggleton were supported by the EPSRC Network Plus grant on Human-Like Computing (HLC).

References

1. Amini, A., Muggleton, S.H., Lodhi, H., Sternberg, M.J.E.: A novel logic-based approach for quantitative toxicology prediction. J. Chem. Inf. Model. **47**(3), 998–1006 (2007). https://doi.org/10.1021/ci600223d
2. Bryant, C.H., Muggleton, S.H., Oliver, S.G., Kell, D.B., Reiser, P., King, R.D.: Combining inductive logic programming, active learning and robotics to discover the function of genes. Electron. Trans. Artif. Intell. **6**, 1–36 (2001)
3. Derocles, S.A., et al.: Chapter one - biomonitoring for the 21st century: integrating next-generation sequencing into ecological network analysis. In: Advances in Ecological Research, vol. 58. Academic Press (2018). https://doi.org/10.1016/bs.aecr.2017.12.001
4. Efron, B., Tibshirani, R.J.: An Introduction to the Bootstrap. No. 57 in Monographs on Statistics and Applied Probability, Chapman & Hall/CRC, Boca Raton, Florida, USA (1993)

5. Faust, K., Raes, J.: Microbial interactions: from networks to models. Nat. Rev. Microbiol. **10**, 538–550 (2012). https://doi.org/10.1038/nrmicro2832
6. Faust, K., Raes, J.: CoNet app: inference of biological association networks using Cytoscape. F1000Research **5** (2016). https://doi.org/10.12688/f1000research.9050.2
7. Friedman, J., Alm, E.J.: Inferring correlation networks from genomic survey data. PLoS Comput. Biol. **8**(9) (2012). https://doi.org/10.1371/journal.pcbi.1002687
8. Getoor, L., Taskar, B.: Introduction to Statistical Relational Learning (Adaptive Computation and Machine Learning). The MIT Press (2007)
9. Gloor, G.B., Macklaim, J.M., Pawlowsky-Glahn, V., Egozcue, J.J.: Microbiome datasets are compositional: and this is not optional. Front. Microbiol. **8**, 2224 (2017). https://doi.org/10.3389/fmicb.2017.02224
10. Golubev, W.: Antagonistic Interactions Among Yeasts. Springer, Berlin Heidelberg, Berlin, Heidelberg (2006). https://doi.org/10.1007/3-540-30985-3_10
11. Li, J., Tai, B.C., Nott, D.J.: Confidence interval for the bootstrap p-value and sample size calculation of the bootstrap test. J. Nonparametric Stat. **21**(5), 649–661 (2009). https://doi.org/10.1080/10485250902770035
12. Muggleton, S.: Inverse entailment and progol. NGCO **13**(3), 245–286 (1995). https://doi.org/10.1007/BF03037227
13. Muggleton, S.H., Bryant, C.H.: Theory Completion Using Inverse Entailment. Springer, Berlin Heidelberg (2000)
14. Robin, X., et al.: proc: an open-source package for r and s+ to analyze and compare roc curves. BMC Bioinform. **12**, 77 (2011)
15. Röttjers, L., Faust, K.: From hairballs to hypotheses–biological insights from microbial networks. FEMS Microbiol. Rev. **42**(6), 761–780 (2018). https://doi.org/10.1093/femsre/fuy030
16. Shoemaker, W.R., Locey, K.J., Lennon, J.T.: A macroecological theory of microbial biodiversity. Nat. Ecol. Evol. **1**(0107), 1–6 (2017). https://doi.org/10.1038/s41559-017-0107
17. Tamaddoni-Nezhad, A., Bohan, D., Raybould, A., Muggleton, S.H.: Machine learning a probabilistic network of ecological interactions. In: Muggleton, S.H., Tamaddoni-Nezhad, A., Lisi, F.A. (eds.) ILP 2011. LNCS (LNAI), vol. 7207, pp. 332–346. Springer, Heidelberg (2012). https://doi.org/10.1007/978-3-642-31951-8_28
18. Tamaddoni-Nezhad, A., Milani, G., Raybould, A., Muggleton, S., Bohan, D.: Construction and validation of food-webs using logic-based machine learning and text-mining. Adv. Ecol. Res. **49**, 225–289 (2013)
19. Vacher, C., et al.: Chapter one - learning ecological networks from next-generation sequencing data. In: Advances in Ecological Research, vol. 54. Academic Press (2016). https://doi.org/10.1016/bs.aecr.2015.10.004
20. Watts, S.C., Ritchie, S.C., Inouye, M., Holt, K.E.: FastSpar: rapid and scalable correlation estimation for compositional data. Bioinformatics **35**(6), 1064–1066 (08 2018). https://doi.org/10.1093/bioinformatics/bty734
21. Weiss, S., et al.: Correlation detection strategies in microbial data sets vary widely in sensitivity and precision. ISME J. **10**, 1669–1681 (2016). https://doi.org/10.1038/ismej.2015.235

Answer-Set Programs for Reasoning About Counterfactual Interventions and Responsibility Scores for Classification

Leopoldo Bertossi[1,2(✉)] and Gabriela Reyes[1]

[1] Faculty of Engineering and Sciences, Universidad Adolfo Ibáñez, Santiago, Chile
leopoldo.bertossi@uai.cl, gabreyes@alumnos.uai.cl
[2] Millennium Institute for Foundational Research on Data (IMFD), Santiago, Chile

Abstract. We describe how *answer-set programs* can be used to declaratively specify counterfactual interventions on entities under classification, and reason about them. In particular, they can be used to define and compute responsibility scores as attribution-based explanations for outcomes from classification models. The approach allows for the inclusion of domain knowledge and supports query answering. A detailed example with a naive-Bayes classifier is presented.

1 Introduction

Counterfactuals are at the very basis of the notion of *actual causality* [18]. They are hypothetical interventions (or changes) on variables that are part of a causal structural model. Counterfactuals can be used to define and assign *responsibility scores* to the variables in the model, with the purpose of quantifying their causal contribution strength to a particular outcome [12,19]. These generals notions of actual causality have been successfully applied in databases, to investigate actual causes and responsibilities for query results [2,25,26].

Numerical scores have been applied in *explainable AI*, and most prominently with machine learning models for classification [28]. Usually, feature values in entities under classification are given numerical scores, to indicate how relevant those values are for the outcome of the classification. For example, one might want to know how important is the city or the neighborhood where a client lives when a bank uses a classification algorithm to accept or reject his/her loan request. We could, for example, obtain a large responsibility score for the feature value "Bronx in New York City". As such it is a *local explanation*, for the entity at hand, and in relation to its participating feature values.

A widely used score is Shap [24], that is based on the Shapley value of coalition game theory [30]. As such, it is based on *implicit* counterfactuals and a numerical aggregation of the outcomes from classification for those different counterfactual versions of the initial entity. Accordingly, the emphasis is not on the possible counterfactuals, but on the final numerical score. However, counterfactuals are interesting *per se*. For example, we might want to know if the client, by changing

N. Katzouris and A. Artikis (Eds.): ILP 2021, LNAI 13191, pp. 41–56, 2022.
https://doi.org/10.1007/978-3-030-97454-1_4

his/her address, might turn a rejection into the acceptance of the loan request. The so generated new entity, with a new address and a new label, is a *counterfactual version* of the original entity.

In [5] the x-Resp score was introduced. It is defined in terms of explicit counterfactuals and responsibility as found in general actual causality. A more general version of it, the Resp score, was introduced in [3], and was compared with other scores, among them, Shap. For simplicity we will concentrate on x-Resp.

Following up our interest in counterfactuals, we propose *counterfactual intervention programs* (CIPs). They are *answer-set programs* (ASPs) [9,16] that are used to specify counterfactual versions of an initial entity, and compute the x-Resp scores for its feature values. More specifically, here we present approaches to- and results about the use of ASPs for specifying counterfactual interventions on entities under classification, and reasoning about them. In this work, we show CIPs and their use in the light of a naive-Bayes classifier. See [5] for more details and an example with a decision-tree classifier; and [6] for more examples of the use of ASPs for actual causality and responsibility.

ASP is a flexible and powerful logic programming paradigm that, as such, allows for declarative specifications and reasoning from them. The (non-monotonic) semantics of a program is given in terms of its *stable models*, i.e. special models that make the program true [15]. In our applications, the relevant counterfactual versions correspond to different models of the CIP. In our example with a naive-Bayes classifier, we use the *DLV* system [23] and its *DLV-Complex* extension [10,11] that implement the ASP semantics; the latter with set- and numerical aggregations.

CIPs can be used to specify the relevant counterfactuals, analyze different versions of them, and use them to specify and compute the x-Resp score. By using additional features of ASP, and of *DLV* in particular, for example *strong and weak program constraints*, one can specify and compute maximum-responsibility counterfactuals. The classifier can be specified directly in the CIP, or can be invoked as an external predicate [5]. The latter case could be that of a *black-box classifier* [31], to which Shap and x-Resp can be applied.

CIPs are very flexible in that one can easily add *domain knowledge* or *domain semantics*, in such a way that certain counterfactuals are not considered, or others are privileged. In particular, one can specify *actionable counterfactuals*, that, in certain applications, make more sense and may lead to feasible changes of feature values for an entity to reverse a classification result [21,32]. All these changes are much more difficult to implement if we use a purely procedural approach. With CIPs, many changes of potential interest can be easily and seamlessly tried out on-the-fly, for exploration purposes.

Reasoning is enabled by query answering, for which two semantics are offered. Under the *brave semantics* one obtains as query answers those that hold in *some* model of the CIP. This can be useful to detect if there is "minimally changed" counterfactual version of the initial entity where the city is changed together with the salary. Under the *cautious semantics* one obtains answers that hold in all the models of the CIP, which could be used to identify feature values that do not change no matter what when we reverse the outcome. Query answering on ASPs offers many opportunities.

This paper is structured as follows. In Sect. 2, we introduce and discuss the problem, and provide an example. In Sect. 3 we introduce the naive-Bayes classifier we will use as a running example. In Sect. 4 we define the x-Resp score. In Sect. 5 we introduce *counterfactual intervention programs*. In Sect. 6, we discuss the use of domain knowledge and query answering. We end in Sect. 7 with some final conclusions. An extended version of this paper can be found in [7], which in its Appendix A provides the basics of answer-set programming; and in its Appendix B presents the complete program for the running example, in *DLV* code, and its output.

2   Counterfactual Interventions and Explanation Scores

We consider a finite set of features, $\mathcal{F}$, with each feature $F \in \mathcal{F}$ having a finite domain, $Dom(F)$, where F, as a function, takes its values. The features are applied to entities $\mathbf{e}$ that belong to a population $\mathcal{E}$. Actually, we identify the entity $\mathbf{e}$ with the record (or tuple) formed by the values the features take on it: $\mathbf{e} = \langle F_1(\mathbf{e}), \ldots, F_n(\mathbf{e}) \rangle$. Now, entities in $\mathcal{E}$ go through a *classifier*, C, that returns *labels* for them. We will assume the classifier is binary, e.g. the labels could be 1 or 0.

In Fig. 1, we have a classifier receiving as input an entity, $\mathbf{e}$. It returns as an output a label, $L(\mathbf{e})$, corresponding to the classification of input $\mathbf{e}$. In principle, we could see C as a black-box, in the sense that only by direct interaction with it, we have access to its input/output relation. That is, we may have no access to the mathematical classification model inside C.

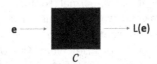

Fig. 1. A black-box classifier

The entity $\mathbf{e}$ could represent a client requesting a loan from a financial institution. The classifier of the latter, on the basis of $\mathbf{e}$'s feature values (e.g. for EdLevel, Income, Age, etc.) assigns the label 1, for rejection. An explanation may be requested by the client. Explanations like this could be expected from any kind of classifier. It could be an explicit classification model, e.g. a classification tree or a logistic regression model. In these cases, we might be in a better position to give an explanation, because we can inspect the internals of the model [31]. However, we can find ourselves in the "worst-case scenario" in which we do not have access to the internal model. That is, we are confronted to a black-box classifier, and we still have to provide explanations.

An approach to explanations that has become popular, specially in the absence of the model, assigns numerical *scores* to the feature values for an entity, trying to answer the question about which of the feature values contribute the most to the received label.

Example 1. We reuse a popular example from [27]. The set of features is $\mathcal{F} =$ {Outlook, Temperature, Humidity, Wind}, with Dom(Outlook) = {sunny, overcast, rain}, Dom(Temperature) = {high, medium, low}, Dom(Humidity) = {high, normal}, Dom(Wind) = {strong, weak}. We will always use this order for the features.

Now, assume we have a classifier, $\mathcal{C}$, that allows us to decide if we play tennis (label yes) or not (label no) under a given combination of weather features. A concrete *naive-Bayes classifier* will be given in Section 3. For example, a particular weather entity has a value for each of the features, e.g. $\mathbf{e} = ent$(rain, high, normal, weak). We want to decide about playing tennis or not under the wether conditions represented by $\mathbf{e}$.   □

Score-based methodologies are sometimes based on *counterfactual interventions*: *What would happen with the label if we change this particular value, leaving the others fixed?* Or the other way around: *What if we leave this value fixed, and change the others?* The resulting labels from these counterfactual interventions can be aggregated in different ways, leading to a score for the feature value under inspection.

Let us illustrate these questions by using the entity $\mathbf{e}$ in the preceding example. If we use the *naive-Bayes classifier* with entity $\mathbf{e}$, we obtain the label yes (c.f. Sect. 3). In order to detect and quantify the relevance (technically, the responsibility) of a feature value in $\mathbf{e} = ent$(rain, high, <u>normal</u>, weak), say, of feature Humidity (underlined), we *hypothetically intervene* its value. In this case, if we change it from normal to high, we obtain a new entity $\mathbf{e}' = ent$(rain, high, high, weak). If we input this entity $\mathbf{e}'$ into the classifier, we now obtain the label no. We say that $\mathbf{e}'$ is a *counterfactual version* of $\mathbf{e}$.

This change of label is an indication that the original feature value for Humidity is indeed relevant for the original classification. Furthermore, the fact that it is good enough to change only this individual value is an indication of its strength. If, to change the label, we also had to change other values together with that for Humidity, its strength would be lower. In Sect. 4, we revisit a particular *responsibility score*, x-Resp, which captures this intuition, and can be applied with black-box or open models.

3   A Naive-Bayes Classifier

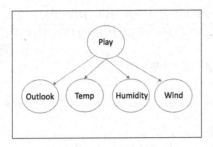

Outlook	Temperature	Humidity	Wind	Play
sunny	high	high	weak	no
sunny	high	high	strong	no
overcast	high	high	weak	yes
rain	medium	high	weak	yes
rain	low	normal	weak	yes
rain	low	normal	strong	no
overcast	low	normal	strong	yes
sunny	medium	high	weak	no
sunny	low	normal	weak	yes
rain	medium	normal	weak	yes
sunny	medium	normal	strong	yes
overcast	medium	high	strong	yes
overcast	high	normal	weak	yes
rain	medium	high	strong	no

Example 2. (Example 1 cont.) We now we build a naive-Bayes classifier for the binary variable Play, about playing tennis or not. A Bayesian network, that is the basis for this classifier, is shown right here above (left). In addition to the network structure, we have to assign probability distributions to the nodes in it. These distributions are learned from the training data in the table (right).

In this case, the features stochastically depend on the output variable Play, and are independent from each other given the output. To fully specify the network, we need the absolute distribution for the top node; and the conditional distributions for the lower nodes.

These are the distributions inferred from the frequencies in the training data:

$P(\text{Play} = \text{yes}) = \frac{9}{14}$	$P(\text{Play} = \text{no}) = \frac{5}{14}$
$P(\text{Outlook} = \text{sunny}|\text{Play} = \text{yes}) = \frac{2}{9}$	$P(\text{Outlook} = \text{sunny}|\text{Play} = \text{no}) = \frac{3}{5}$
$P(\text{Outlook} = \text{overcast}|\text{Play} = \text{yes}) = \frac{4}{9}$	$P(\text{Outlook} = \text{overcast}|\text{Play} = \text{no}) = 0$
$P(\text{Outlook} = \text{rain}|\text{Play} = \text{yes}) = \frac{3}{9}$	$P(\text{Outlook} = \text{rain}|\text{Play} = \text{no}) = \frac{2}{5}$
$P(\text{Temp} = \text{high}|\text{Play} = \text{yes}) = \frac{2}{9}$	$P(\text{Temp} = \text{high}|\text{Play} = \text{no}) = \frac{2}{5}$
$P(\text{Temp} = \text{medium}|\text{Play} = \text{yes}) = \frac{4}{9}$	$P(\text{Temp} = \text{medium}|\text{Play} = \text{no}) = \frac{2}{5}$
$P(\text{Temp} = \text{low}|\text{Play} = \text{yes}) = \frac{3}{9}$	$P(\text{Temp} = \text{low}|\text{Play} = \text{no}) = \frac{1}{5}$
$P(\text{Humidity} = \text{high}|\text{Play} = \text{yes}) = \frac{3}{9}$	$P(\text{Humidity} = \text{high}|\text{Play} = \text{no}) = \frac{4}{5}$
$P(\text{Humidity} = \text{normal}|\text{Play} = \text{yes}) = \frac{6}{9}$	$P(\text{Humidity} = \text{normal}|\text{Play} = \text{no}) = \frac{1}{5}$
$P(\text{Wind} = \text{strong}|\text{Play} = \text{yes}) = \frac{3}{9}$	$P(\text{Wind} = \text{strong}|\text{Play} = \text{no}) = \frac{3}{5}$
$P(\text{Wind} = \text{weak}|\text{Play} = \text{yes}) = \frac{6}{9}$	$P(\text{Wind} = \text{weak}|\text{Play} = \text{no}) = \frac{2}{5}$

We can use them to decide, for example, about playing or not with the following input data: Outlook = rain, Temp = high, Humidity = normal, Wind = weak. If we keep this order of the features, we are classifying the weather entity $\mathbf{e} = \langle\text{rain}, \text{high}, \text{normal}, \text{weak}\rangle$. This is done by determining the maximum probability between the two probabilities:

$$P(\text{Play} = \text{yes}|\text{Outlook} = \text{rain}, \text{Temp} = \text{high}, \text{Humidity} = \text{normal}, \text{Wind} = \text{weak}), \quad (1)$$

$$P(\text{Play} = \text{no}|\text{Outlook} = \text{rain}, \text{Temp} = \text{high}, \text{Humidity} = \text{normal}, \text{Wind} = \text{weak}). \quad (2)$$

Now, for each of the probabilities of the form $P(\mathsf{P}|\mathsf{O},\mathsf{T},\mathsf{H},\mathsf{W})$ it holds:

$$P(\mathsf{P}|\mathsf{O},\mathsf{T},\mathsf{H},\mathsf{W}) = \frac{P(\mathsf{P},\mathsf{O},\mathsf{T},\mathsf{H},\mathsf{W})}{P(\mathsf{O},\mathsf{T},\mathsf{H},\mathsf{W})} = \frac{P(\mathsf{O}|\mathsf{P})P(\mathsf{T}|\mathsf{P})P(\mathsf{H}|\mathsf{P})P(\mathsf{W}|\mathsf{P})P(\mathsf{P})}{\sum_{\mathsf{P}} P(\mathsf{O}|\mathsf{P})P(\mathsf{T}|\mathsf{P})P(\mathsf{H}|\mathsf{P})P(\mathsf{W}|\mathsf{P})P(\mathsf{P})}.$$
(3)

In particular, the numerators for (1) and (2) become, resp.:

$P(\mathsf{Outlook} = \mathsf{rain}|\mathsf{Play} = \mathsf{yes})P(\mathsf{Temp} = \mathsf{high}|\mathsf{Play} = \mathsf{yes})P(\mathsf{Humidity} = \mathsf{normal}|\mathsf{Play} = \mathsf{yes}) \times$

$$\times P(\mathsf{Wind} = \mathsf{false}|\mathsf{Play} = \mathsf{yes})P(\mathsf{Play} = \mathsf{yes}) = \frac{3}{9}\frac{2}{9}\frac{6}{9}\frac{6}{9}\frac{9}{14} = \frac{4}{189},$$
(4)

$P(\mathsf{Outlook} = \mathsf{rain}|\mathsf{Play} = \mathsf{no})P(\mathsf{Temp} = \mathsf{high}|\mathsf{Play} = \mathsf{no})P(\mathsf{Humidity} = \mathsf{normal}|\mathsf{Play} = \mathsf{no}) \times$

$$\times P(\mathsf{Wind} = \mathsf{false}|\mathsf{Play} = \mathsf{no})P(\mathsf{Play} = \mathsf{no}) = \frac{2}{5}\frac{2}{5}\frac{1}{5}\frac{2}{5}\frac{5}{14} = \frac{4}{875}.$$
(5)

The denominator for both cases is the marginal probability, i.e. $\frac{4}{189} + \frac{4}{875}$. Then, it is good enough to compare (4) and (5). Since the former is larger, the decision (or classification) becomes: $\mathsf{Play} = \mathsf{yes}$. $\square$

4   The x-Resp Score

Assume that an entity $\mathbf{e}$ has received the label 1 by the classifier $\mathcal{C}$, and we want to explain this outcome by assigning numerical scores to $\mathbf{e}$'s feature values, in such a way, that a higher score for a feature value reflects that it has been important for the outcome. We do this now using the x-Resp score, whose definition we motivate below by means of an example. The x-Resp score as defined below is not restricted to- but more suitable for binary features, i.e. that take the values true or false (or 1 and 0, resp.). The generalization in [5] is more appropriate for multi-valued features. C.f. Sect. 7 for a discussion, and [4,5] for more details.

Example 3. In Fig. 2, the black box is classifier $\mathcal{C}$. An entity $\mathbf{e}$ has gone through it obtaining label 1, shown in the first row in the figure. We want to assign a score to the feature value $\mathbf{x}$ for a feature $F \in \mathcal{F}$. We proceed, counterfactually, changing the value $\mathbf{x}$ into $\mathbf{x}'$, obtaining a counterfactual version $\mathbf{e}_1$ of $\mathbf{e}$. We classify $\mathbf{e}_1$, and we still get the outcome 1 (second row). In between, we may counterfactually change other feature values, $\mathbf{y}, \mathbf{z}$ in $\mathbf{e}$, into $\mathbf{y}', \mathbf{z}'$, but keeping $\mathbf{x}$, obtaining entity $\mathbf{e}_2$, and the outcome does not change (third row). However, if we change in $\mathbf{e}_2$, $\mathbf{x}$ into $\mathbf{x}'$, the outcome does change (fourth row).

This shows that the value $\mathbf{x}$ is relevant for the original output, but, for this outcome, it needs company, say of the feature values $\mathbf{y}, \mathbf{z}$ in $\mathbf{e}$. According to *actual causality*, we can say that the feature value $\mathbf{x}$ in $\mathbf{e}$ is an *actual cause* for the classification, that needs a *contingency set* formed by the values $\mathbf{y}, \mathbf{z}$ in $\mathbf{e}$. In this case, the contingency set has size 2. If we found a contingency set for $\mathbf{x}$ of size 1 in $\mathbf{e}$, we would consider $\mathbf{x}$ even more relevant for the output. $\square$

On this basis, we can define [4,5], for a feature value $\mathbf{x}$ in $\mathbf{e}$: (a) $\mathbf{x}$ is a *counterfactual explanation* for $L(\mathbf{e}) = 1$ if $L(\mathbf{e}\frac{\mathbf{x}}{\mathbf{x}'}) = 0$, for some $\mathbf{x}' \in Dom(F)$

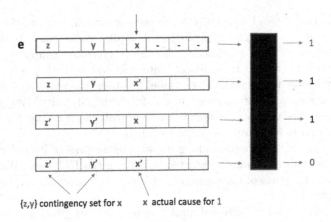

Fig. 2. Classified entity and its counterfactual versions

(the domain of feature F). (Here we use the common notation $\mathbf{e}\frac{\mathbf{x}}{\mathbf{x}'}$ for the entity obtained by replacing $\mathbf{x}$ by $\mathbf{x}'$ in $\mathbf{e}$.) (b) $\mathbf{x}$ is an *actual explanation* for $L(\mathbf{e}) = 1$ if there is a contingency set of values $\mathbf{Y}$ in e, with $\mathbf{x} \notin \mathbf{Y}$, and new values $\mathbf{Y}' \cup \{\mathbf{x}'\}$, such that $L(\mathbf{e}\frac{\mathbf{Y}}{\mathbf{Y}'}) = 1$ and $L(\mathbf{e}\frac{\mathbf{xY}}{\mathbf{x}'\mathbf{Y}'}) = 0$. We say that $\mathbf{Y}$ is *minimal* if there is no $\mathbf{Y}'$ with $\mathbf{Y}' \subsetneqq \mathbf{Y}$, that is also a contingency set for $\mathbf{x}$ in $\mathbf{e}$. Similarly, $\mathbf{Y}$ is *miminum* contingency set if it is a a minimum-size contingency set for $\mathbf{x}$ in $\mathbf{e}$.

Contingency sets may come in sizes from 0 to $n - 1$ for feature values in records of length n. Accordingly, we can define for the actual cause $\mathbf{x}$ in $\mathbf{e}$: If $\mathbf{Y}$ is a minimum contingency set for $\mathbf{x}$, x-Resp$(\mathbf{e}, \mathbf{x}) := \frac{1}{1+|\mathbf{Y}|}$; and as 0 when $\mathbf{x}$ is not an actual cause. (C.f. Sect. 7 for the Resp score that generalizes x-Resp.)

We will reserve the notion of counterfactual explanation *for (or counterfactual version of) an input entity* $\mathbf{e}$ *for any entity* $\mathbf{e}'$ *obtained from* $\mathbf{e}$ *by modifying feature values in* $\mathbf{e}$ *and that leads to a different label, i.e.* $L(\mathbf{e}) \neq L(\mathbf{e}')$. *Notice that from such an* $\mathbf{e}'$ *we can read off actual causes for* $L(\mathbf{e})$ *as feature values, and contingency sets for those actual causes. It suffices to compare* $\mathbf{e}$ *with* $\mathbf{e}'$.

In Sect. 5 we give a detailed example that illustrates these notions, and also shows the use of ASPs for the specification and computation of counterfactual versions of a given entity, and the latter's x-Resp score.

5   Counterfactual-Intervention Programs

Together with illustrating the notions introduced in Sect. 4, we will introduce, by means of an example, *Counterfactual Intervention Programs* (CIPs). The program corresponds to the naive-Bayes classifier presented in Sect. 3.

CIPs are *answer-set programs* (ASPs) that specify the counterfactual versions of a given entity, and also, if so desired, only the *maximum-responsibility* counterfactual explanations, i.e. counterfactual versions that lead to a maximum x-Resp score. (C.f. [5] for many more details and examples with *decision trees* as classifiers.).

Example 4. (Examples 1 and 2 cont.) We present now the CIP in *DLV-Complex* notation. Since the program specifies and applies counterfactual changes of attribute values, we have to indicate when an intervention is applied, when an entity may still be subject to additional interventions, and when a final version of an entity has been reached, i.e. the label has been changed. To achieve this, the program uses annotation constants o, for "original entity", do, for "do a counterfactual intervention" (a single change of feature value), tr, for "entity in transition", and s, for "stop, the label has changed".

We will explain the program along the way, as we present it, and with additional explanations as comments written directly in the *DLV* code. We will keep the most relevant parts of the program. The complete program can be found in [7, Appendix B].

The absolute and conditional probabilities will be given as facts of the *DLV* program. They are represented as percentages, because *DLV* handles operations with integer numbers. The conditional probabilities are atoms of the form p_f_c(feature value, play outcome, prob\%), with "f" suggesting the feature name, and "c", that it is a conditional probability. For example, p_h_c(normal, yes, 67) is the conditional probability (of 67%) of Humidity being normal given that Play takes value yes. Similarly, this is an absolute probability for Play: p(yes, 64).

The program has as facts also the contents of the domains. They are of the form dom_f(feature value), with "f" suggesting the feature name again, e.g. dom_h(high), for Humidity. Finally, among the facts we find the original entity that will be intervened by means of the CIP. In this case, as in Example 1, ent(e,rain,high,normal,weak,o), where constant e is an entity identifier (eid), and o is the annotation constant. This entity gets label yes, i.e. Play = yes. Through interventions, we expect the label to become no, i.e. Play = no.

Aggregation functions over sets will be needed later in the program, to build *contingency sets* (c.f. Sect. 4). So, we use *DLV-Complex* that supports this functionality. "List and Sets" has to be specified at the beginning of the program, together with the maximum integer value. This is the first part of the CIP, showing the facts: (as usual, words starting with lower case are constants; whereas with upper case, variables)

```
% DLV-COMPLEX    #include<ListAndSet>   #maxint = 100000000.
% domains:
    dom_o(sunny). dom_o(overcast). dom_o(rain). dom_t(high). dom_t(medium).
    dom_t(low). dom_h(high). dom_h(normal). dom_w(strong). dom_w(weak).
% original entity that gets label 1:
    ent(e,rain,high,normal,weak,o).
% absolute probabilities for Play (as percentage)
    p(yes, 64). p(no, 36).
% Outlook conditional probabilities (as percentage)
    p_o_c(sunny, yes, 22). p_o_c(overcast, yes, 45). p_o_c(rain, yes, 33).
    p_o_c(sunny, no, 60). p_o_c(overcast, no, 0). p_o_c(rain, no, 40).
% Temperature conditional probabilities (as percentage)
    p_t_c(high, yes, 22). p_t_c(medium, yes, 45). p_t_c(low, yes, 33).
    p_t_c(high, no, 40). p_t_c(medium, no, 40). p_t_c(low, no, 20).
```

```
% Humidity conditional probabilities (as percentage)
   p_h_c(normal, yes, 67). p_h_c(high, yes, 33).
   p_h_c(normal, no, 20). p_h_c(high, no, 80).
% Wind conditional probabilities (as percentage)
   p_w_c(strong, yes, 33). p_w_c(weak, yes, 67).
   p_w_c(strong, no, 60). p_w_c(weak, no, 40).
```

The classifier will compute posterior probabilities for Play according to Eq. (1) and (2) in Sect. 3. Next, they are compared, and the largest determines the label. As we can see from equation (3), the denominator is irrelevant for this comparison. So, we need only the numerators. They are specified by means of a predicate of the form pb_num(E,O,T,H,W,V,Fp), where the arguments stand for: eid, (values for) Outlook, Temp, Humidity, Wind and Play, resp.; and the probability as a percentage. The CIP has to specify predicate pb_num(E,O,T,H,W,V,Fp). That part of the program is not particularly interesting, and looks somewhat cumbersome due to the combination of simple arithmetical operations with probabilities. C.f. the program in [7, Appendix B].

Next, we have to specify the transition annotation constant tr, that is used in rule bodies below. It indicates that we are using an entity that is in transition. This annotation is specified as follows:

```
% transition rules: the initial entity or one affected by an intervention
   ent(E,O,T,H,W,tr) :- ent(E,O,T,H,W,o).
   ent(E,O,T,H,W,tr) :- ent(E,O,T,H,W,do).
```

Now we have to specify the classifier, or better, the classification criteria, appealing to predicate pb_num(E, O, H, W, V, Fp). More precisely, we have to compare Fp for Play value yes, denoted Fyes, with Fp for Play value no, denoted Fno. If the former is larger, we obtain label yes; otherwise label no:

```
% spec of the classifier
   cls(E,O,T,H,W,yes) :- ent(E,O,T,H,W,tr),  pb_num(E,O,T,H,W,yes,Fyes),
                    pb_num(E,O,T,H,W,no,Fno), Fyes >= Fno.
   cls(E,O,T,H,W,no)  :- ent(E,O,T,H,W,tr),  pb_num(E,O,T,H,W,yes,Fyes),
                    pb_num(E,O,T,H,W,no,Fno), Fyes < Fno.
```

Notice the use of annotation constant tr in the body, because we will be classifying entities that are in transition. Next, the CIP specifies all the one-step admissible counterfactual interventions on entities with label yes, which produces entities in transition. This disjunctive rule is the main rule.

```
% counterfactual rule: alternative single-value changes
   ent(E,Op,T,H,W,do) v ent(E,O,Tp,H,W,do) v
   ent(E,O,T,Hp,W,do) v ent(E,O,T,H,Wp,do) :- ent(E,O,T,H,W,tr),
        cls(E,O,T,H,W,yes), O != Op, T != Tp, H!= Hp, W!= Wp,
        chosen_o(O,T,H,W,Op), chosen_t(O,T,H,W,Tp), chosen_h(O,T,H,W,Hp),
        chosen_w(O,T,H,W,Wp), dom_o(Op), dom_t(Tp), dom_h(Hp), dom_w(Wp).
```

Here we are using predicates chosen, one for each of the four features. For example, chosen_h(O,T,H,W,Hp) "chooses" for each combination of values, O,T,H,W for Outlook, Temp, Humidity, and Wind, a unique (and new) value Hp for feature Humidity, and that value is taken from its domain dom_h. Through an intervention, that value Hp replaces the original value H, as one of the four possible value changes that are indicated in the rule head.

The semantics of ASPs makes only one of the possible disjuncts in the head true (unless forced otherwise by other rules in the program, which does not happen with CIPs). The chosen predicates can be specified in a generic manner [17]. Here, we skip their specification, but they can be found in [7, Appendix B].

In order to avoid going back to the original entity through counterfactual interventions, we may impose a *hard program constraint* [23]. These constraints are rules with empty head, which capture a negation. They have the effect of discarding the models where the body becomes true. In this case:

```
% not going back to initial entity
      :- ent(E,O,T,H,W,do), ent(E,O,T,H,W,o).
```

Next, we stop performing interventions when we switch the label to no, which introduces the annotation s:

```
% stop when label has been changed:
ent(E,O,T,H,W,s) :- ent(E,O,T,H,W,do), cls(E,O,T,H,W,no).
```

Finally, we introduce an extra program constraint, to avoid computing models where the original entity never changes label. Those models will not contain the original eid with annotation s:

```
% extra constraint avoiding models where label does not change
      :- ent(E,O,T,H,W,o), not entAux(E).
% auxiliary predicate to avoid unsafe negation right above
      entAux(E) :- ent(E,O,T,H,W,s).
```

The rest of the program uses counterfactual interventions to collect individual changes (next rules), sets of them, cardinalities of those sets, etc.

```
% collecting changed values for each feature:
expl(E,outlook,O)   :- ent(E,O,T,H,W,o), ent(E,Op,Tp,Hp,Wp,s), O != Op.
expl(E,temp,T)      :- ent(E,O,T,H,W,o), ent(E,Op,Tp,Hp,Wp,s), T != Tp.
expl(E,humidity,H)  :- ent(E,O,T,H,W,o), ent(E,Op,Tp,Hp,Wp,s), H != Hp.
expl(E,wind,W)      :- ent(E,O,T,H,W,o), ent(E,Op,Tp,Hp,Wp,s), W != Wp.
```

With them, we will obtain, for example, the atom expl(e,humidity,normal) in some of the models of the program, because there is a counterfactual entity that changes normal humidity into high (c.f. Sect. 2). The atom indicates that original value normal for humidity is part of an explanation for entity e. Contingency sets for a feature value are obtained with the rules below. Since we keep everywhere the eid, it is good enough to collect the names of the features whose values are changed. For this we use predicate cont(E,U,S). Here, U is a feature (with changed value), S is the *set of all* feature names whose values are changed together with that for U. These sets are build using the built-in set functions of *DLV-Complex*. Similarly with the built-in set membership check.

```
% building  contingency sets
  cause(E,U)        :- expl(E,U,X).
  cauCont(E,U,I)    :- expl(E,U,X), expl(E,I,Z), U != I.
  preCont(E,U,{I})  :- cauCont(E,U,I).
  preCont(E,U,#union(Co,{I})) :- cauCont(E,U,I), preCont(E,U,Co),
                                 not #member(I,Co).
  cont(E,U,Co)      :- preCont(E,U,Co), not HoleIn(E,U,Co).
  HoleIn(E,U,Co)    :- preCont(E,U,Co), cauCont(E,U,I), not #member(I,Co).
  tmpCont(E,U)      :- cont(E,U,Co), not #card(Co,0).
  cont(E,U,{})      :- cause(E,U), not tmpCont(E,U).
```

The construction is such that one keeps adding contingency features, using pre-contingency sets, until there is nothing else to add. In this way the contingency sets contain all the features that have to be changed with the one at hand U. For example, in one of the models we will find the atom cont(e,humidity,{}), meaning that a change of the humidity value alone, i.e. with empty contingency set, suffices to switch the label. Each counterfactual version of entity e will be represented by a model of the program. Due to model minimality, the associated set of changes of feature values that accompany a counterfactual change of feature value, say x in e, will correspond to a *minimal*, but not necessarily minimum, contingency set **Y** for x in e (c.f. Sect. 4).

The generation of contingency sets is now useful for the computation of the inverse of the x-Resp score. For this we can use the built-in set-cardinality operation #card(S,M) of *DLV-Complex*. Here, M is the cardinality of set S. The score will be the result of adding 1 to the cardinality M of a contingency set S:

```
% computing the inverse of x-Resp
  invResp(E,U,R) :- cont(E,U,S), #card(S,M), R = M+1, #int(R).
```

For each counterfactual version of e, as represented by a model of the program, we will obtain a *local* x-Resp score. So, a particular feature value, U, may have several local x-Resp scores in different models of the program. For example, in the model corresponding to the change of humidity (and nothing else) we will get the atom invResp(e,humidity,1). Finally, full explanations will be of the form fullExpl(E,U,R,S), where U is a feature name, R is its inverse x-Resp score, and S is its contingency set (of feature names).

```
% full explanations:
  fullExpl(E,U,R,S) :-  expl(E,U,X), cont(E,U,S), invResp(E,U,R).
```

Following with our ongoing example, we will get in one model the atom fullExpl(e,humidity,1,{}). Additional information, such as the new feature values that lead to the change of label can be read-off from the associated model (examples follow). The original feature values can be recovered via the eid e from the original entity.

If we run the program starting with the original entity, we obtain ten different counterfactual versions of **e**. They are represented by the ten essentially different stable models of the program, and can be read-off from the atoms with the annotation s, namely: (with value changes underlined)

1. `ent(e,rain,high, high,weak,s)`
2. `ent(e,rain,high, high, strong,s)`, `ent(e, sunny,high,normal, strong,s)`, `ent(e, sunny,high, high,weak,s)`
3. `ent(e,rain, medium, high, strong,s)`, `ent(e,rain, low, high, strong,s)`, `ent(e, sunny, low, high,weak,s)`, `ent(e, sunny, medium, high,weak,s)`;
4. `ent(e, sunny, medium, high, strong,s)`, `ent(e, sunny, low, high, strong,s)`.

Below we show only three of the obtained models (the others are found in [7, Appendix B]). In the models we show only the most relevant atoms, omitting initial facts, intermediate probabilities, and chosen-related atoms:

```
M1 {ent(e,rain,high,normal,weak,o), ent(e,rain,high,normal,weak,tr),
    cls(e,rain,high,normal,weak,yes), ent(e,rain,high,high,weak,do),
    ent(e,rain,high,high,weak,tr), cls(e,rain,high,high,weak,no),
    ent(e,rain,high,high,weak,s), expl(e,humidity,normal),
    cont(e,humidity,{}),invResp(e,humidity,1),fullExpl(e,humidity,1,{})}
M2 {ent(e,rain,high,normal,weak,o), ent(e,rain,high,high,strong,tr),
    cls(e,rain,high,high,strong,no), ent(e,rain,high,high,strong,s),
    invResp(e,humidity,2), fullExpl(e,humidity,2,{wind}),
    invResp(e,wind,2), fullExpl(e,wind,2,{humidity})}
M3 {ent(e,rain,high,normal,weak,o), ent(e,sunny,high,normal,strong,tr),
    cls(e,sunny,high,normal,strong,no),ent(e,sunny,high,normal,strong,s),
    invResp(e,outlook,2), fullExpl(e,outlook,2,{wind}), ...}
```

The first model corresponds to our running example. The second model shows that the same change of the previous model accompanied by a change for Wind also leads to a change of label. We might prefer the first model. We will take care of this next. The third model shows a different combination of changes: for Outlook accompanied by Wind. In this model, the original Outlook value has $\frac{1}{2}$ as x-Resp score.

If we are interested only in those counterfactual entities that are obtained through a minimum number of changes, and then leading to maximum responsibility scores, we can impose *weak program constraints* on the program [23]. In contrast to hard constraints, as used above, they can be violated by a model of the program. However, only those models where the number of violations is a minimum are kept. In our case, the number of value differences between the original and final entity is minimized:

```
% weak constraints to minimize number of changes
:~ ent(E,O,T,H,W,o), ent(E,Op,Tp,Hp,Wp,s), O != Op.
:~ ent(E,O,T,H,W,o), ent(E,Op,Tp,Hp,Wp,s), T != Tp.
:~ ent(E,O,T,H,W,o), ent(E,Op,Tp,Hp,Wp,s), H != Hp.
:~ ent(E,O,T,H,W,o), ent(E,Op,Tp,Hp,Wp,s), W != Wp.
```

Running the program with them, leaves only model M1 above, corresponding to the counterfactual entity $\mathbf{e}' = ent(\text{rain}, \text{high}, \text{high}, \text{weak})$. This is a maximum-responsibility counterfactual explanation.   □

6   Exploiting Domain Knowledge and Query Answering

CIPs allows for the inclusion of domain knowledge. In our example, describing a particular geographic region, it might be the case that there is never high temperature with a strong wind. Such a combination might not be allowed in counterfactuals, which could be done by imposing the program constraint:

```
:- ent(E,_,high,_,strong,tr).
```

If we run the program with this constraint, models M2 and M3 above would be discarded, so as any other where the inadmissible combination appears [8].

In another geographic region, it could be the case that there is a functional relationship between features, for example, between Temperature and Humidity: high $\mapsto$ normal, {medium, low} $\mapsto$ high. In this case, from the head of the counterfactual rule, the disjunct ent(E,O,T,Hp,W,do) could be dropped for not representing an admissible counterfactual. Instead, we could add the extra rules:

```
ent(E,O,T,normal,W,tr)  :- ent(E,O,high,H,W,tr).
ent(E,O,T,high,W,tr)    :- ent(E,O,medium,H,W,tr).
ent(E,O,T,high,W,tr)    :- ent(E,O,low,H,W,tr).
```

We can also exploit reasoning, which is enabled by query answering. Actually, the models of the program are implicitly queried, as databases (the models do not have to be returned, only the answers). Under the *cautious semantics* we obtain the answers that are true in *all* models, whereas under the *brave semantics*, the answers that are true in *some* model [23]. They can be used for different kinds of queries. The query semantics is specified when calling the program (naiveBayes.txt), so as the file containing the query (queries.txt):

```
\DLV>dlcomplex.exe -nofacts -nofdcheck -brave naiveBayes.txt queries.txt
```

If we do not use the weak constraints that minimize the responsibility, and we want the responsibility of feature Outlook, we can pose the query Q1 below under the brave semantics. The same to know if there is an explanation with less than 3 changes (Q2):

$$invResp(e,outlook,R)? \qquad \%Q1$$
$$fullExpl(E,U,R,S), R<3? \qquad \%Q2$$

Q1 returns 2, 3, and 4, then the responsibility for Outlook is $\frac{1}{2}$. Q2 returns all the full explanations with inverse score 1 or 2, e.g. e,outlook,2,{humidity}. We can also ask, under the brave semantics, if there is an intervened entity exhibiting the combination of sunny outlook with strong wind, and its label (Q3). Or perhaps, all the intervened entities that obtained label no (Q4):

$$cls(E,O,T,H,W,\_), O = sunny, W = strong? \qquad \%Q3$$
$$cls(E,O,T,H,W,no)? \qquad \%Q4$$

For Q3 we obtain, for example, `e,sunny,low,normal,strong,yes`; and for Q4, for example `e,sunny,low,high,strong`. We can ask, under the *cautions semantics*, whether the wind does not change under every counterfactual version:

```
ent(e,_,_,_,Wp,s), ent(e,_,_,_,W,o), W = Wp?          %Q5
```

We obtain the empty output, meaning Wind is indeed changed in at least one counterfactual version (i.e. stable model). In fact, the same query under the *brave semantics* returns the records where Wind remained unchanged, e.g. `rain,high,high,weak`, along with the original entity `rain,high,normal,weak`.

7   Final Remarks

Explainable data management and explainable AI (XAI) are effervescent areas of research. The relevance of explanations can only grow, as observed from- and due to the legislation and regulations that are being produced and enforced in relation to explainability, transparency and fairness of data management and AI/ML systems.

Still fundamental research is needed in relation to the notions of *explanation* and *interpretation*. An always present question is: *What is a good explanation?*. This is not a new question, and in AI (and other disciplines) it has been investigated. In particular in AI, areas such as *diagnosis* and *causality* have much to contribute. In relation to *explanations scores*, there is still a question to be answered: *What are the desired properties of an explanation score?*

Our work is about interacting with classifiers via answer-set programs. For our work it is crucial to be able to use an implementation of the ASP semantics. We have used *DLV*, with which we are more familiar. In principle, we could have used *Clingo* instead [20]. Those classifiers can be specified directly as a part of the program, as we did in our running example, or they can be invoked by a program as a external predicate [5]. From this point of view, our work *is not* about learning programs.

We have used in this paper a responsibility score that has a direct origin in *actual causality and responsibility*. When the features have many possible values, it makes sense to consider the proportions of value changes that lead to counterfactual versions of the entity at hand, and that of those that do not change the label. In this case, the responsibility score can be generalized to become an average or expected value of label differences [3,5].

There are different approaches and methodologies in relation to explanations, with causality, counterfactuals and scores being prominent approaches that have a relevant role to play. Much research is still needed on the use of *contextual, semantic and domain knowledge*. Some approaches may be more appropriate in this direction, and we argue that declarative, logic-based specifications can be successfully exploited [5]. We have seen how easy becomes adding new knowledge, which would become complicated change of code under procedural approaches.

In this work we have used answer-set programming, in which we have accommodated probabilities as arguments of predicates. Probability computation is done through basic arithmetics provided by the *DLV* system. However, it would be more natural to explore the application of probabilistic extensions of logic programming [13,14,22,29] and of ASP [1], while retaining the capability to do counterfactual analysis. In this regard, one has to take into account that the complexity of computing the x-Resp score is matched by the expressive and computational power of ASP [5].

Acknowledgments. Part of this work was funded by ANID - Millennium Science Initiative Program - Code ICN17002. Help from Jessica Zangari and Mario Alviano with information about *DLV* is very much appreciated.

References

1. Baral, C., Gelfond, M., Rushton, N.: Probabilistic reasoning with answer sets. Theor. Pract. Logic Program. **9**(1), 57–144 (2009)
2. Bertossi, L., Salimi, B.: From causes for database queries to repairs and model-based diagnosis and back. Theor. Comput. Syst. **61**(1), 191–232 (2016). https://doi.org/10.1007/s00224-016-9718-9
3. Bertossi, L., Li, J., Schleich, M., Suciu, D., Vagena, Z.: Causality-based explanation of classification outcomes. In: Proceedings of the Fourth Workshop on Data Management for End-To-End Machine Learning, DEEM@SIGMOD 2020, pp. 6:1–6:10 (2020)
4. Bertossi, L.: An ASP-based approach to counterfactual explanations for classification. In: Gutiérrez-Basulto, V., Kliegr, T., Soylu, A., Giese, M., Roman, D. (eds.) RuleML+RR 2020. LNCS, vol. 12173, pp. 70–81. Springer, Cham (2020). https://doi.org/10.1007/978-3-030-57977-7_5
5. Bertossi, L.: Declarative approaches to counterfactual explanations for classification. Theory Pract. Logic Program. (2021). https://doi.org/10.1017/S1471068421000582
6. Bertossi, L.: Score-based explanations in data management and machine learning: an answer-set programming approach to counterfactual analysis. In: Šimkus, M., Varzinczak, I. (eds.) Reasoning Web 2021. LNCS, vol. 13100, pp. 145–184. Springer, Cham (2022). https://doi.org/10.1007/978-3-030-95481-9_7
7. Bertossi, L., Reyes, G.: Answer-set programs for reasoning about counterfactual interventions and responsibility scores for classification. Extended version of this paper. arXiv Paper 2107.10159 (2021)
8. Bertossi, L., Geerts, F.: Data quality and explainable AI. ACM J. Data Inf. Qual. **12**(2), 1–9 (2020)
9. Brewka, G., Eiter, T., Truszczynski, M.: Answer set programming at a glance. Commun. ACM **54**(12), 92–103 (2011)
10. Calimeri, F., Cozza, S., Ianni, G., Leone, N.: Computable functions in ASP: theory and implementation. In: Garcia de la Banda, M., Pontelli, E. (eds.) ICLP 2008. LNCS, vol. 5366, pp. 407–424. Springer, Heidelberg (2008). https://doi.org/10.1007/978-3-540-89982-2_37
11. Calimeri, F., Cozza, S., Ianni, G., Leone, N.: An ASP system with functions, lists, and sets. In: Erdem, E., Lin, F., Schaub, T. (eds.) LPNMR 2009. LNCS (LNAI), vol. 5753, pp. 483–489. Springer, Heidelberg (2009). https://doi.org/10.1007/978-3-642-04238-6_46

12. Chockler, H., Halpern, J.: Responsibility and blame: a structural-model approach. J. Artif. Intell. Res. **22**, 93–115 (2004)
13. De Raedt, L., Kimmig, A.: Probabilistic (logic) programming concepts. Mach. Learn. **100**(1), 5–47 (2015)
14. De Raedt, L., Kersting, K., Natarajan, S., Poole, D.: Statistical Relational Artificial Intelligence. Morgan & Claypool Publishers, Synthesis Lectures on Artificial Intelligence and Machine Learning (2016)
15. Gelfond, M., Lifschitz, V.: Classical negation in logic programs and disjunctive databases. New Gener. Comput. **9**, 365–385 (1991)
16. Gelfond, M., Kahl, Y.: Knowledge Representation and Reasoning, and the Design of Intelligent Agents. Cambridge Univ, Press (2014)
17. Giannotti, F., Greco, S., Sacca, D., Zaniolo, C.: Programming with nondeterminism in deductive databases. Ann. Math. Artif. Intell. **19**(1–2), 97–125 (1997)
18. Halpern, J., Pearl, J.: Causes and explanations: a structural-model approach. part I: causes. Br. J. Philos. Sci. **56**(4), 843–887 (2005)
19. Halpern, J.Y.A.: Modification of the Halpern-Pearl definition of causality. In: Proceedings of IJCAI 2015, pp. 3022–3033 (2015)
20. Kaminski, R., Romero, J., Schaub, T., Wanko, P.: How to Build Your Own ASP-based system?! arXiv:2008.06692 (2020)
21. Karimi, A.-H., von Kügelgen, B.J., Schölkopf, B., Valera, I.: A probabilistic approach. In: Proceedings NeurIPS, Algorithmic Recourse under Imperfect Causal Knowledge (2020)
22. Kimmig, A., Demoen, B., De Raedt, L., Santos Costa, V., Rocha, R.: On the implementation of the probabilistic logic programming language ProbLog. Theor. Pract. Logic Programm. **11**(2–3), 235–262 (2011)
23. Leone, N., et al.: The DLV system for knowledge representation and reasoning. ACM Trans. Comput. Logic **7**(3), 499–562 (2006)
24. Lundberg, S., et al.: From local explanations to global understanding with explainable AI for trees. Nat. Mach. Intell. **2**(1), 2522–5839 (2020)
25. Meliou, A., Gatterbauer, W., Moore, K.F., Suciu, D. The complexity of causality and responsibility for query answers and non-answers. In: Proceedings of VLDB 2010, pp. 34–41 (2010)
26. Meliou, A., Gatterbauer, W., Halpern, J.Y., Koch, C., Moore, K.F., Suciu, D.: Causality in databases. IEEE Data Eng. Bull. **33**(3), 59–67 (2010)
27. Mitchell, T.M.: Machine Learning. McGraw-Hill, New York (1997)
28. Molnar, C.: Interpretable Machine Learning: A Guide for Making Black Box Models Explainable (2020). https://christophm.github.io/interpretable-ml-book
29. Riguzzi, F.: Foundations of Probabilistic Logic Programming. River Publ. (2018)
30. Roth, A.E. (ed.): The Shapley Value: Essays in Honor of Lloyd S. Cambridge University Press, Shapley (1988)
31. Rudin, C.: Stop explaining black box machine learning models for high stakes decisions and use interpretable models instead. Nat. Mach. Intell. **2019**(1), 206–215. Also arXiv:1811.10154 (2018)
32. Ustun, B., Spangher, A., Liu, Y.: Actionable recourse in linear classification. In: Proceedings of FAT, pp. 10–19 (2019)

Synthetic Datasets and Evaluation Tools for Inductive Neural Reasoning

Cristina Cornelio[1]([✉]) and Veronika Thost[2]

[1] Samsung AI, Cambridge, UK
c.cornelio@samsung.com
[2] IBM Research, MIT-IBM Watson AI Lab, Rüschlikon, Switzerland
vth@zurich.ibm.com

Abstract. Logical rules are a popular knowledge representation language in many domains. Recently, neural networks have been proposed to support the complex rule induction process. However, we argue that existing datasets and evaluation approaches are lacking in various dimensions; for example, different kinds of rules or dependencies between rules are neglected. Moreover, for the development of neural approaches, we need large amounts of data to learn from and adequate, approximate evaluation measures. In this paper, we provide a tool for generating diverse datasets and for evaluating neural rule learning systems, including novel performance metrics.

1 Introduction

Logical rules are a popular knowledge representation language in many domains. They represent domain knowledge, encode information that can be derived from given facts in a compact form, and allow for logical reasoning. For example, given facts *parent(ann, bob)* and *parent(bob, dan)*, the simple *Datalog* rule *grandparent(X, Z) :- parent(X, Y), parent(Y, Z)*. encodes not only the fact *grandparent(ann, dan)* but also describes its dependency on the other facts. Moreover, if the data grows and new facts are added, we can automatically derive new knowledge. Since rule formulation is complex and requires domain expertise, *rule learning* [11,25] has been an area of active research in AI for a long time, also known as *inductive logic programming* (ILP). It has recently revived with the increasing use of knowledge graphs (KGs), which can be considered as large fact collections. KGs are used in the Semantic Web, the medical domain, and companies such as Google [7] and Amazon [16]. Useful rules over these knowledge bases would obviously provide various benefits. While the development of neural ILP systems is still in its early stages, we argue that current evaluations are insufficient. We demonstrate that the reported results are questionable, especially, in terms of generalization and because the datasets are lacking in various ways.

C. Cornelio and V. Thost: Equal contribution. The work was partly conducted while C.C. was at IBM Research.

N. Katzouris and A. Artikis (Eds.): ILP 2021, LNAI 13191, pp. 57–77, 2022.
https://doi.org/10.1007/978-3-030-97454-1_5

Table 1. Overview of dataset generators for Datalog rules

Name	Rules	Facts	Predicates
Family Tree [6]	5 hand written	arbitrary	9
General Graph [6]	5 hand written	arbitrary	7
On-the-fly [15]	5 templates (1 per dataset)	max 2194	5
GraphLog [30]	no rules with same body; no rules with predicates shared among head and body	arbitrary	arbitrary
RuDaS	full Datalog expressivity	arbitrary	arbitrary

The evaluation of rule learning has changed over time. While the classical rule learning methods often focused on tricky problems in complex domains [14,24] and proved to be effective in practical applications, current evaluations can roughly be divided into three categories. (1) Some consider very small example problems with usually less than 50 facts and only few rules to be learned [10,18,27]. Often, these problems are *completely* defined, in the sense that all facts are classified as either true or false, or there are at least some negative examples given. Hence, the systems can be thoroughly evaluated based on classical measures, such as accuracy. (2) Others regard (subsets of) real KGs such as Wikidata[1] or DBpedia[2], some with millions of facts [12,13,22,33]. Since there are no rules over these KGs, the rule suggestions of the systems are usually evaluated using metrics capturing the precision and coverage of rules based on the facts contained in the KG, such as standard confidence [12]. However, since the KGs are generally incomplete, the quality of the rule suggestions is not fully captured in this way. For instance, [22] present an illustrative example rule, $gender(X, male)$:- $isCEO(X, Y), isCompany(Y)$, which might well capture the facts in many existing KGs but which is heavily biased and does not extend to the entirety of valid facts beyond them. Furthermore, we cannot assume that the few considered KGs completely capture the variety of existing domains and especially the rules in them. For example, [17] propose rules over WordNet[3] that are of very simple nature – containing only a small number of the predicates in WordNet and having only a single body atom – and very different from the ones suggested in [12] for other KGs. Also the evaluation metrics vary, especially considering the intersection between more modern and classic approaches. We will show that most of the standard information retrieval measures used in machine learning are not adequate for a logic context because they neglect important facets like the size of the Herbrand universe[4] (e.g., this may yield too high accuracy). Some other measures have been used for neural ILP such

---

[1] https://www.wikidata.org/wiki/Wikidata:Main_Page.

[2] https://wiki.dbpedia.org/.

[3] https://wordnet.princeton.edu/.

[4] We assume the reader to be familiar with first-order logic (FOL). See also Sect. 2 and Appendix A.

as mean reciprocal rank, or precision/recall@k, but they can only be applied in specific cases (i.e., if the system outputs weighted/probabilistic rules or a ranking of facts). Yet, strict logic measures are not perfect either, since they are based on the assumption that the domain is very small and human understandable. For this reason, the community should consider several metrics and define new metrics suitable for both worlds.

(3) Recent works have proposed synthetic, generated datasets but, as Table 1 shows, they are very simple and specifically restricted regarding the rules. There are well-known ILP competitions in the logic community,[5] which also provide synthetic datasets, but their evaluations are usually based only on test facts and not on rules. Further, benchmarks in the database community are related in that they cover schemata and rules. However, either their use cases and thus the kinds of rule sets considered are rather restricted (e.g., for schema mapping, there are rules from source to target schema, but the rules do not depend on each other in the sense that one is to be applied after the other [1,2]), or there is a number of fixed test scenarios [3]. Further, database data is usually curated, and the benchmarks were developed to evaluate customized algorithms.

In summary, we claim that the existing evaluation approaches are not adequate for modern ILP. In particular, recently, inductive (logical) reasoning has come into focus in the machine learning community [26,31], including neural approaches to ILP [10,18,35,36]. However, we will show that these first neuro-symbolic systems cannot compete with well-engineered purely symbolic systems such as AMIE [12] yet.[6] In order to support the development of the former, our work – in contrast to the aforementioned, more traditional ILP evaluations – focuses on more arbitrary data, on learning systems needing large amounts of data to learn from (vs. a few, fixed test sets), and on approximate solutions.

In this paper, (1) we extend the categorization of rule learning datasets beyond the numbers of constants, predicates, and facts. In particular, we propose to consider the amount/type of noise (i.e., wrong or missing facts) and (in)completeness (i.e., share of consequences of rules present in the data). (2) We present RuDaS (Synthetic Datasets for Rule Learning), a tool for generating synthetic datasets containing both facts and rules, and for evaluating neural rule learning systems, that overcomes the above mentioned shortcomings of existing works and offers complementary evaluation methods. RuDaS is parameterizable in the standard and in the new categories, and thus allows for a more fine-grained analysis of rule learning systems. (3) It also supports this analysis by computing classical and more recent metrics, including two new ones that we introduce. (4) Our experiments show that the datasets and evaluation measures provided by RuDaS help revealing the variety in the capabilities of existing ILP systems, and thus support and help researchers in developing and optimizing new, existing, and especially neural approaches. RuDaS is available at https://github.com/IBM/RuDaS.

---

[5] For example: 2016, http://ilp16.doc.ic.ac.uk/competition.

[6] A fact well-concealed in the papers, by simply ignoring symbolic competitors.

2   Rule Learning Preliminaries

We assume the reader to be familiar with basic first-order logic (FOL) concepts (e.g., inference). We consider Datalog *rules* [5]: $\alpha_0 \text{ :- } \alpha_1, \ldots, \alpha_m.$ (1) of *length* $m \geq 1$ where all *atoms* α_j, $0 \leq j \leq m$, are of the form $p(t_1, \ldots, t_n)$ with a predicate p of arity $n \geq 1$ and terms t_k, $1 \leq k \leq n$. A *term* is either a constant or a variable. α_0 is called the *head* and the conjunction $\alpha_1, \ldots, \alpha_m$ the *body* of the rule. All variables that occur in the head must occur in the body. A *fact* is an atom not containing variables.

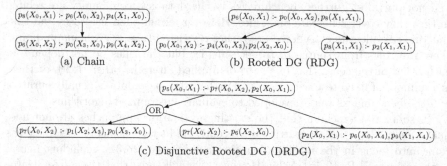

(a) Chain   (b) Rooted DG (RDG)

(c) Disjunctive Rooted DG (DRDG)

Fig. 1. Example rule structure generated for the different categories with depth 2.

Note that several classical ILP systems also consider more complex function-free Horn rules, (allowing existential quantification in the rule head or negation in the body), but most recent systems focus on datalog rules or restrictions of those [10,12,27]. In particular, most reasoning systems for KGs [22,35] consider only binary predicates and *chain rules* of form:

$$p_0(X_1, X_{m+1}) \text{ :- } p_1(X_1, X_2), \ldots, p_m(X_m, X_{m+1}) \,. \qquad (2)$$

We define the problem of *rule learning* in the most general way: given background knowledge in the form of facts, including a set of so-called *positive examples* (vs. *negative* or *counter*-examples), the goal is to learn rules that can be used to infer the positive examples from the background knowledge, based on standard FOL semantics. Intuitively, the positive examples are the consequences of the rules to be learned. As common, we do not separate the background knowledge into two types of facts but consider a single fact set as input. We recall that the *closed-world assumption* (CWA) (vs. *open world assumption* or OWA) states that all facts that are not explicitly given as true are assumed to be false.

3   RuDaS Datasets

RuDaS contains an easy-to-use generator for ILP datasets that generates datasets that vary in many dimensions and is highly parameterizable in a detailed set of metrics which can serve as a general classification scheme for ILP datasets and support evaluations. In a nutshell, we first generate a set of rules and a set of base facts, and then derive the *consequences* of the latter w.r.t. the rules. Note that, in contrast to existing approaches which are largely template-based, the RuDaS generation process includes much randomness. We also add noise and remove some facts to make it realistic, details are given below. A full description of the generation process is given in Appendix B. Each generated dataset contains the rules and the facts in files in standard Prolog format. In this section, we describe the datasets including concrete examples, which can be found in our repository.

Symbols. Our datasets are domain independent, which means that we consider synthetic names p_i for predicates, c_i for constants, and X_i for variables with $i \geq 0$. While the kinds and numbers of the symbols used is random, it can be controlled by setting the generator parameters of the number of constants/predicates and min/max arity of predicates. Observe that these numbers influence the variability and number of generated rules and facts.

Rules. RuDaS datasets contain Datalog rules [5] (see also Appendix 2) of variable structure. The generation is largely at random in terms of which predicates, variables, and constants appear in the rules; that is, in the structure of every single rule. We only require the head to contain at least one variable.

We propose four categories of set of rules depending on the dependencies between them: *Chain, Rooted Directed Graph (DG), Disjunctive Rooted DG,* and *Mixed.* Figure 1 shows a generated rule set for each category. The dependencies between the rules are represented as edges in a directed graph where the rules are the nodes. That is, an incoming edge shows that the facts inferred by the child node's rule might be used, during inference with the rule at the parent node. The node at the top is called the *root.* In the following, we use (rule) graph and DG interchangeably.

Category Chain. Each rule, except the one at the root, infers facts relevant for exactly one other rule (i.e., every node has at most one parent node) and, for each rule, there is at most one such other rule which might infer facts relevant for the rule (i.e., every node has at most one child node). However, recursive rules (where the predicate in the head occurs also in the body) represent an exception, they are relevant for themselves and for one other rule.

Category Rooted DG (RDG). It generalizes category Chain in that every rule can be relevant for several others (i.e., each node can have multiple parent nodes). Furthermore, for each rule, there may be several other rules which might infer facts relevant for the rule (i.e., a node may have several child nodes); and at least one such case exists. But, for each predicate occurring in the body of the former rule, there must be at most one other rule with this predicate in the head; that is, there are no alternative rules to derive facts relevant for a rule w.r.t. a specific body atom.

Category Disjunctive Rooted DG (DRDG). It generalizes category RDG by allowing for the latter alternative rules (represented as children of an "OR" node); and at least one such case exists.

Category Mixed. A rule graph that contains connected components of different of the above categories.

Figure 1 illustrates the differences between the categories. The numbers and categories of connected components are selected randomly by default. The shape of RuDaS rule sets can be influenced with the following parameters: number and maximal length of rules; category of connected components; min/max number of connected components; and maximal depth of rule graphs (i.e., number of rules nodes in the maximum of the shortest paths between root and leaves).

Facts. The main advantage of the RuDaS datasets, the availability of the rules, allows for classifying the facts as well. More specifically, facts can be *(ir)relevant* for inference, depending on if their predicates do (not) occur in a rule body, and they may be consequences of inferences. Such a classification of facts is impossible for all the existing datasets that do not contain rules, but allows for a better evaluation of the rule learners' capabilities (see Sect. 5).

RuDaS fact sets vary in the following parameters: dataset size (S, M, L, XL); open-world degree $n_{OW} \in [0,1]$; and amount of noise in the data n_{Noise+}, $n_{Noise-} \in [0,1]$. An S dataset contains about 50–100 facts, an M dataset about 101–1,000, an L dataset about 1,001–10,000, and an XL dataset $> 10,000$. Larger sizes are possible as well, however, since the main purpose of RuDaS is allowing the analysis of the rules learned (vs. scalability), we have not considered them so far. The open-world degree n_{OW} specifies how many of the consequences from an initial set of relevant facts, called *support* facts, are missing in the dataset (see Appendix B for more details). By noise, we mean facts that are not helpful in learning the rules either because they are not relevant for deriving the positive examples (n_{Noise+}) or because they are relevant but missing (n_{Noise-}).

Observe that our datasets are based on rules, as required for ILP, but can be applied for evaluating the closely related and very popular link prediction systems as well; specifically, auxiliary information provided with the datasets contains the missing consequences which can be used as test facts in that context.

Example Set of Datasets: RuDaS.v0. For demonstration purposes, we generated a set of datasets readily available for the community, and which we also used in our experiments (Sect. 5, for dataset details and statistics see Table 5 in Appendix C). The datasets model different possible scenarios, and mainly vary in the structures and sizes of the rule sets and in the sorts and quantities of facts. RuDaS.v0 contains 40 Chain, 78 RDG, and 78 DRDG datasets, of sizes S and M, and of depths 2 and 3, all evenly distributed. Note that each of the rules sets consists of exactly one connected component, and that we did not generate rule sets of category Mixed; Mixed datasets with connected components of possibly different categories can be easily created by combining our generated datasets. Further, we constrained both the maximal rule length and arity of atoms to two for practicality, because several existing rule learning systems require that. All the datasets were generated such that they are missing 20–40% of all consequences, 15–30% of the original support facts, and contain 10–30% facts that are irrelevant for the derivation of positive examples. Since real datasets may strongly vary in the numbers of missing consequences and noise and, in particular, since these numbers are generally unknown, we chose factors seeming reasonable to us. Also note that there is information regarding the accuracy of real fact sets such as YAGO[7] (95%) and NELL[8] (87%), that measures the amount of data correctly extracted from the Web etc. and hence corresponds to $1 - n_{\text{Noise}+}$ in our setting. Thus, our choices in this regard thus seem to be realistic. We hence simulated an open-world setting and incorporated noise. While we consider this to be the most realistic training or evaluation scenario, specific rule learning capabilities might be better evaluated in more artificial settings with either consequences or noise missing. Therefore, every dataset additionally includes files containing the incomplete set of facts without noise (i.e., $n_{\text{Noise}+} = 0$, $n_{\text{Noise-}} = 0$) and the complete fact set (i.e., $n_{\text{OW}} = 0$), with and without noise.

4   Evaluation Tools

RuDaS also contains an evaluator for comparing the rules produced by a rule learning system to the original rules in a given datase. We focus on three logic(-inspired) distances and four standard information retrieval measures that are relevant to our goal of capturing rule learning performance: 1) Herbrand distance, the traditional distance between Herbrand models; two normalized versions of the Herbrand distance 2) Herbrand accuracy (H-accuracy) and 3) Herbrand score (H-score), a new metric we propose in this paper; 4) accuracy 5) precision; 6) recall; and 7) F1-score. See Appendix A for preliminaries on Herbrand models.

Our test fact sets (both base facts and consequences) in the evaluation do not contain noise and all the consequences can be recovered by the original rules applied over the given facts. In line with that, we focus on measures that maintain the closed-world assumption, and do not consider measures that focus on the open-world aspect for evaluation (e.g., PCA in [12]). Our experiments will show that F1-score suits best the open-world evaluation over RuDaS datasets.

In what follows, $I(R, F)$ denotes the set of facts inferred by grounding the rules R over the support facts F excluding the facts in F. We denote an original rule set by $\mathcal{R}$, a learned one by $\mathcal{R}'$, and support facts by $\mathcal{F}$. Our evaluation is performed comparing two sets: 1) $I(\mathcal{R}', \mathcal{F})$ obtained by the application of the induced rules $\mathcal{R}'$ to the fact sets $\mathcal{F}$ using a forward-chaining engine (available in our tool); 2) $I(\mathcal{R}, \mathcal{F})$: the result of applying $\mathcal{R}$ to $\mathcal{F}$.[9]

Logic Measures. The *Herbrand distance* h_d between two logic programs (sets of rules), defined over the same set of constants and predicates, describes the

---

[7] https://github.com/yago-naga/yago3.

[8] http://rtw.ml.cmu.edu/rtw/overview.

[9] Note that $\mathcal{F} = \mathbb{S}'$ and $\mathbb{C}' = I(\mathcal{R}, \mathcal{F})$ given $\mathbb{S}'$ and $\mathbb{C}'$ as described in Appendix B - Output.

number of facts in which the minimal Herbrand models of the programs differ:

$$h_d(\mathcal{R}, \mathcal{R}', \mathcal{F}) := |[I(\mathcal{R}, \mathcal{F}) \cup I(\mathcal{R}', \mathcal{F})] \setminus [I(\mathcal{R}, \mathcal{F}) \cap I(\mathcal{R}', \mathcal{F})]|.$$

The *standard confidence* s_c [12] is the fraction of correctly inferred facts w.r.t. all facts that can be inferred by the learned rules capturing their precision:

$$s_c(\mathcal{R}, \mathcal{R}', \mathcal{F}) := \frac{|I(\mathcal{R}, \mathcal{F}) \cap I(\mathcal{R}', \mathcal{F})|}{|I(\mathcal{R}', \mathcal{F})|}$$

In our closed-world setting, this corresponds to the precision of a model, since it is easy to see that $|I(\mathcal{R}, \mathcal{F}) \cap I(\mathcal{R}', \mathcal{F})|$ are the number of true positive examples and $|I(\mathcal{R}', \mathcal{F})|$ corresponds to the union of true and false positive examples. The *Herbrand accuracy* h_r corresponds to the Herbrand distance normalized on the Herbrand base: $h_r(\mathcal{R}, \mathcal{R}', \mathcal{F}) := 1 - \frac{h_d}{u}$, where u is the size of the Herbrand base defined by the original program. We introduce a new metric, the *Herbrand score* (H-score) defined as:

$$\text{H-score}(\mathcal{R}, \mathcal{R}', \mathcal{F}) := \frac{|I(\mathcal{R}, \mathcal{F}) \cap I(\mathcal{R}', \mathcal{F})|}{|I(\mathcal{R}, \mathcal{F}) \cup I(\mathcal{R}', \mathcal{F})|} = 1 - \frac{h_d(\mathcal{R}, \mathcal{R}', \mathcal{F})}{|I(\mathcal{R}, \mathcal{F}) \cup I(\mathcal{R}', \mathcal{F})|}$$

H-score provides an advantage over the other metrics since it captures both how many correct facts a set of rules produces and also its completeness (how many of the facts inferred by the original rules $\mathcal{R}$ were correctly discovered), while the other measures consider these points only partially.

Note that Herbrand accuracy is not a significant measure if $\mathcal{F}$ or the Herbrand base is large, because, in these cases, it will be very high (close to 1) disregarding the quality of the rules. This happens because all the facts in $\mathcal{F}$ are considered correct predictions, also the facts in the Herbrand base that neither appear in $I(\mathcal{R}, \mathcal{F})$ nor in $I(\mathcal{R}', \mathcal{F})$.

Information Retrieval Measures. We adapted the main measures used in the machine learning evaluations to a logic context. We define: the sets of true positive examples (TP) as the cardinality $|I(\mathcal{R}, \mathcal{F}) \cap I(\mathcal{R}', \mathcal{F})|$, the set of false positive examples (FP) as the cardinality $|I(\mathcal{R}, \mathcal{F}) \setminus I(\mathcal{R}', \mathcal{F})|$; the set of false negative examples (FN) as the cardinality $|I(\mathcal{R}', \mathcal{F}) \setminus I(\mathcal{R}, \mathcal{F})|$; and the set of true negative examples (TN) as the cardinality of the difference between the Herbrand base and the union $I(\mathcal{R}, \mathcal{F}) \cup I(\mathcal{R}', \mathcal{F})$. Given these four definitions, accuracy, precision, recall, F1-score etc. can be defined as usual [28].

Note that accuracy is not a significant measure if $\mathcal{F}$ or the Herbrand base is large, for the same reason mentioned with Herbrand accuracy above. Moreover, F1-score is similar to H-score, with the difference that F1-score gives more priority to the TP examples. We believe that giving uniform priority to FN, TP, and FP is more reasonable in the context of logic; this is in line with standard logic measures like h_d. However, F1-score (compared to H-score) better suits open-world settings where some of the consequences could be missing, and thus count as FP (despite being correct). For this reason F1 would give a better estimate of the quality of the induced rules since it focuses more on the TP examples and give less priority to the generated FP examples.

We observe that, if $I(\mathcal{R}, \mathcal{F}) = I(\mathcal{R}', \mathcal{F})$, then H-score is equal to precision and both are equal to 1; and, if $I(\mathcal{R}, \mathcal{F})$ and $I(\mathcal{R}', \mathcal{F})$ are disjoint, then both are 0. The two measures coincide if $I(\mathcal{R}, \mathcal{F}) \subseteq I(\mathcal{R}', \mathcal{F})$. The main difference between the two is highlighted in the case where $I(\mathcal{R}', \mathcal{F}) \subseteq I(\mathcal{R}, \mathcal{F})$. Then, precision = 1 but H-score is < 1. We designed our new H-score this way because we want to have an H-score of 1 only if the predicted facts are exactly those produced by the original rules while precision is 1 if all predicted facts are correct.

Rule-based Measures. Several distance metrics between two sets of logic rules have been defined in the literature [8,9,21,23,29]. However, most of them strongly rely on the parse structure of the formulas and hence are more suitable for more expressive logics. For this reason, we propose a new metric, the *Rule-score (R-score)*, which is tailored to rules, in that it calculates a distance d_R between the rules that have the same head predicate and, for the latter, computes the pairwise distances d_A between the two rules' atoms. Note that, below, we consider datalog rules without constants and with only binary predicates for simplicity, but the definitions can be easily extended to non-binary atoms. An idea of how to deal with constants in addition is suggested in [9], for example.

Our distance d_A between two non-ground, binary atoms takes into account a specific mapping $\omega \in \Omega$ between their variables so that we can later lift it to rule level; Ω is the set of all possible *variable re-namings* between two sets of variables names (in our case from two rules). Given atoms $a_1 = p(X_1, X_2)$ and $a_2 = q(Y_1, Y_2)$ and such a mapping ω, $d_A(a_1, a_2, \omega) = 1$ if their predicates differ, $d_A(a_1, a_2, \omega) = 0$ if $\omega(X_1) = Y_1$ and $\omega(X_2) = Y_2$, otherwise:

$$d_A(a_1, a_2, \omega) = \frac{1}{4} \sum_{i=1}^{2} \mathbb{1}^c(\omega(X_i) = Y_i) .$$

where the *complement indicator function* $\mathbb{1}^c(e)$ of an event e is equal to 0 if the event is satisfied and 1 otherwise.

Note that d_A is based upon the main, and most used, distance metric between two *ground* atoms, the *Nienhuys-Cheng distance* [20]. In fact, it only differs from the latter in that it is defined for non-ground atoms using a variable re-naming.

Consider two rules r_1 and r_2 as follows:

$r_1: \quad p_1(A, B) :- p_2(A, A), p_3(B, B), p_4(A, B).$

$r_2: \quad p_1(X, X) :- p_2(Y, X), p_2(X, X).$

Re-namings $\omega_1 = \{A : X, B : Y\}$ and $\omega_1 = \{A : Y, B : X\}$ yield: 1) r_1 with ω_1: $p_1(X, Y) :- p_2(X, X), p_3(Y, Y), p_4(X, Y).$ and 2) r_1 with ω_2: $p_1(Y, X) :- p_2(Y, Y), p_3(X, X), p_4(Y, X).$ Let h_i and h_2 denote the head atoms of r_1 and r_2, respectively. Then, we get $d_A(h_1, h_2, \omega_1) = 0.25$ and $d_A(h_1, h_2, \omega_2) = 0.25$.

Intuitively, our distance d_R between two rules r_1 and r_2 considers matches between the rules, where a match consists of a pairing between their atoms together with a variable renaming, and takes the best match as distance (averaged over the number of atoms). More specifically, such a *pairing* for r_1 and r_2

is a set of pairs such that the first component is a body atom from r_1 and the second from r_2. It contains $\max(|b(r_1)|, |b(r_2)|)$ pairs ($|b(r_i)|$ denotes the number of atoms in the body of r_i). To represent a match, we require the atoms to have the same predicate and additionally allow for an empty placeholder atom (denoted by $-$), extending d_A such that it has maximal distance 1 to any other atom. The placeholder also accounts for the case that the rules are of different length.

For the rules of the previous example, there are two pairings:

a) $c_1 = \{(p_2(A, A), p_2(Y, X)), (p_3(B, B), -), (p_4(A, B), -)\}$;
b) $c_2 = \{(p_2(A, A), p_2(X, X)), (p_3(B, B), -), (p_4(A, B), -)\}$.

We now define the distance $d_R(r_1, r_2)$ between two rules r_1 and r_2 as:

$$\frac{1}{n_a} \min_{\omega \in \Omega} \left(d_A(h_1, h_2, \omega) + \min_{c \in \mathcal{C}} \sum_{(a_1, a_2) \in c} d_A(a_1, a_2, \omega) \right)$$

where $n_a = \max(|b(r_1)|, |b(r_2)|) + 1$ is the number of atoms of the rule with more atoms; h_i is the head atom of rule r_i; Ω is the set of all possible variable renamings between the variable names in the two rules; $\mathcal{C}$ is the set of all possible pairings for r_1 and r_2.

For the re-namings ω_1 and ω_2 and pairings c_1 and c_2 from the previous example, d_R represents the minimum of $0.25 + \sum_{(a_1, a_2) \in c_i} d_A(a_1, a_2, \omega_j)$, with the sums: 1a) $0.25 + 1 + 1 = 2.5$; 2a) $0.25 + 1 + 1 = 2.5$; 1b) $0 + 1 + 1 = 2.25$; 2b) $0.5 + 1 + 1 = 2.75$. Given that $n_a = 4$, we obtain $d_R(r_1, r_2) = 2.25/4 = 0.5625$.

Finally, our novel metric *Rule-score (R-score)* for two logic programs, the original program $\mathcal{R}$ and the induced program $\mathcal{R}'$ (rules of form (2)), is defined as:

$$\text{R-score}(\mathcal{R}, \mathcal{R}') = 1 - \frac{1}{|\mathcal{R}|} \left(\sum_{r_1 \in \mathcal{R}} \min_{r_2 \in \mathcal{R}'[hp(r_1)]} d_R(r_1, r_2) \right)$$

where the function $hp(r)$ corresponds to the head predicate of a given rule r; $\mathcal{R}[p]$ denotes the rules in $\mathcal{R}$ with head predicate p.

5   Experiments

The goal of our experiments is to demonstrate the need for a portfolio of diverse datasets for evaluating rule learning systems. As mentioned above, the existing datasets are not sufficient to comprehensively evaluate ILP methods (e.g., often fall into category Chain). Note that the purpose of our experiments is not to provide an exhaustive analysis of existing ILP systems, but to show that this kind of analysis should be part of system development, by pointing out that important aspects of rule learning that have been ignored so far may considerably impact system performance. Our evaluation does not solely focus on neuro-symbolic approaches, but includes ILP systems that are representatives for the different methodologies adopted by researchers during the years to approach the problem of rule learning. We will see that these systems represent strong baselines.

We compared the following systems (configuration details in the appendix): 1) FOIL [24], a traditional ILP system; 2) AMIE+ [12], a rule mining system; 3) Neural-LP [35]; and 4) NTP [27]. The latter are both neural approaches. AMIE+, Neural-LP, and NTP output confidence scores for the learned rules. We therefore filtered their output using a system-specific threshold, obtained using grid search over all datasets. To not disadvantage Neural-LP and NTP, which use auxiliary predicates, we ignored the facts produced on those. [10]

Table 2. Impact of different metrics, each averaged on 120 datasets with uniformly distributed categories $\in$ {CHAIN, RDG, DRDG}, sizes $\in$ {S,M}, and graph depths $\in$ {2,3}; $n_{OW} = 0.3$, $n_{Noise-} = 0.2$, $n_{Noise+} = 0.1$.

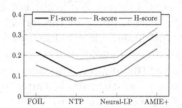

Fig. 2. Visualization shows metric similarity.

	FOIL	AMIE+	Neural-LP	NTP
H-accuracy	0.9873	0.8498	0.9850	0.9221
Accuracy	0.9872	0.8494	0.9849	0.9219
F1-score	0.2151	0.3031	0.1621	0.1125
H-score	0.1520	0.2321	0.1025	0.0728
Precision	0.5963	0.2982	0.1687	0.1021
Recall	0.2264	0.7311	0.2433	0.3921
R-score	0.2728	0.3350	0.1906	0.1811

We evaluated the systems over RuDaS.v0 (see Sect. 3 and Table 5 in the appendix) in four main experiments to understand, respectively, the variety of the performance metrics, and the impact of missing consequences, noise, rule dependencies, and dataset size. We set a time limit of 24h both for system executions and evaluations.[11] However, we did not penalize the instances that exceeded the limit since we are interested in the rules that can be learned. Generally, the runtimes varied greatly over the datasets, were often surprisingly long (AMIE, NTP can take hours; only Neural-LP usually terminated within seconds), and provide not much insight. We do not report the standard deviation since the results span over different dataset categories and sizes.

5.1 Overall Results: Comparing Different Metrics

In this experiment, we regard the overall results, reported in Table 2, in terms of the metrics introduced in Sect. 4. As expected, the results for F1-score and Herbrand score are very similar, the only difference is that F1-score is a more "optimistic" measure, giving advantage to the methods with a higher number

---

[10] Notice that NTP requires additional information in the form of rule templates, obviously representing an advantage.

[11] If a system learns very many (usually wrong) rules, the computation of measures based on a closure may become unfeasible.

of true positive examples. The results for R-score are in line with these metrics and, although translated, follow especially close the trend of H-score (see Fig. 2 for a visualization of the comparison). Hence, R-score indeed represents a valid alternative with the additional advantage of computational efficiency, since it does not require the computation of the induced facts $I(\mathcal{R}', \mathcal{F})$.

Also Herbrand accuracy and accuracy provide similar results. Observe that these two measures are not meaningful in our settings since they yield always very high performances. Note that precision and H-score are very close for AMIE+, Neural-LP, and NTP, but not for FOIL. This could be explained by the fact that the training of the former systems maximizes functions that are similar to precision, while FOIL uses heuristics to produce the rules that induce the maximum number of facts in the training set and minimum number of facts not in the training set. The great discrepancy between the two measures with FOIL means that the rules it learns do not produce many false facts but only a subset of the facts induced by the original rules. For AMIE+ instead, since precision and H-score are similar, we have that its rules produce most of the consequences of the original rules and, thanks to the good performance, they do not produce too many false facts. Considering Neural-LP and NTP the two measures are also very similar, but very low: their rules produce most of the positive examples but also a lot of false facts. We report H-score, but the R-scores we computed for comparison showed the same trends.

5.2   Impact of Missing Consequences and Noise

In this experiment, we evaluated the performance of the systems in the presence of complete information, incomplete information, and incomplete information with noise. This was performed analyzing the impact of the different parameters given in RuDaS: n_{OW}, n_{Noise+}, and n_{Noise-}. The results are reported in Table 3. The noise parameters are defines as follows (where the set memberships are intended to mean "uniformly distributed over"): *complete* datasets $n_{OW} = 0$, $n_{Noise-} = 0$, and $n_{Noise+} = 0$, *incomplete* datasets $n_{OW} \in \{0.2, 0.3, 0.4\}$, $n_{Noise-} = 0$, and $n_{Noise+} = 0$, and *incomplete + noise* datasets $n_{OW} \in \{0.2, 0.3, 0.4\}$, $n_{Noise-} \in \{0.15, 0.3\}$, and $n_{Noise+} \in \{0.2, 0.3\}$. Moreover, in order to give an impression of some of the datasets considered in existing evaluations, we included one manually created dataset, EVEN, inspired by the corresponding dataset used in [10][12], which contains complete information. We notice that FOIL shows best performance if the information is exact and complete but considerably worse performance in more noisy scenarios. This is a result of the assumptions FOIL is based upon: it assumes negative examples to be given in addition in order to guide rule learning and, in particular, missing facts to be false (see Sect. 4.1 in [24]). AMIE+ seems to perform constant on average, showing robustness to noise

---

[12] In our version, $even(X) :\!- even(Z), succ(Z, Y), succ(Y, X)$ is the only rule, and the input facts are such that we also have an accuracy of 1 if the symmetric rule $even(Z) :\!- even(X), succ(Z, Y), succ(Y, X)$ is learned (using the original fact set it would be 0). AMIE+ and Neural-LP do not support the unary predicates in EVEN.

and incomplete data in all the datasets. Neural-LP and NTP seem to be robust to noise and incomplete data but yield much worse performance generally.

5.3   Impact of Dependencies Between Rules

In this experiment, we analyze the impact of the kind of the dependencies between rules. The results are reported in Table 4. As expected, the systems perform very different depending on the datasets' rule categories. We notice that the systems perform better on the Chain datasets while only learning partially RDG and DRDG rules, meaning that the available rule learning systems are not yet able to capture complex rule set structures.

Table 3. Effect of missing consequences and noise on 144 datasets. Each H-score value is averaged on 48 datasets, with uniformly distributed categories $\in$ {RDG, DRDG}, sizes $\in$ {S,M}, and graph depths $\in$ {2,3}.

	EVEN	Compl.	Incompl.	Incompl.+Noise
FOIL	1.0	0.4053	0.1919	0.0849
AMIE+	-	0.2021	0.2098	0.2075
Neural-LP	-	0.0633	0.0692	0.0649
NTP	1.0	0.0482	0.0617	0.0574

Table 4. Impact of (1) dataset category, H-score averaged on 40 datasets; (2) dataset size and rule graph depth, H-score averaged on 30 datasets. Datasets as in Sect. 5.1.

	CHAIN	RDG	DRDG		S-2	S-3	M-2	M-3
FOIL	0.2024	0.0877	0.1633		0.2815	0.2074	0.0356	0.0934
AMIE+	0.3395	0.2275	0.1293		0.1449	0.1319	0.4392	0.2124
Neural-LP	0.1291	0.1050	0.0734		0.1155	0.0673	0.1281	0.0992
NTP	0.1239	0.0538	0.0368		0.1512	0.0432	0.0652	0.0374

Our results also confirm the system descriptions w.r.t. the rules they support. For instance, AMIE+ does not consider reflexive rules and requires rules to be connected (i.e., every atom must share an argument with each of the other atoms of the rule) and closed (all variables appear at least twice). And, by chance, the Chain datasets more often satisfy these conditions than the other datasets (this is not true in general: our generator produces comprehensive datasets that do not necessarily satisfy this property). Though, rules that are not fully supported can be recognized partially. We saw this by analyzing the rules learned by Neural-LP, which only supports chain rules of form $p_0(X_1, X_{m+1}) :\text{-} p_1(X_1, X_2), \ldots, p_m(X_m, X_{m+1})$. NTP also performs better on

Chain datasets, but the discrepancy with the other types of datasets is not substantial. This can be explained by the fact that we provided all necessary templates (for details about the system requirements see [27]). We cannot draw significant conclusions for FOIL given its unstable behaviour regarding the dataset type.

In summary, our experiments show the importance of considering datasets with different kinds of rules sets and different measures of performance to be able to fully understand the weaknesses and strengths of an ILP system.

5.4   Scalability: Impact of Dataset Size

In this experiment, we analyzed the impact of the dataset size considering four different size-depth combinations: the results for S-2, S-3, M-2, and M-3 datasets are reported in Table 4. We can observe that FOIL is not scalable, since there is a 20% performance gap from the S-dataset to the M-dataset. Although it does not seem to be influenced by the rules dependency tree depth, showing support to nested rules. AMIE+ seemingly shows constant performance and thus scalability. We can observe that there is a noticeable drop in performance if we increase the depth of the rule dependency graphs. Neural-LP and NTP are robust to noise and incomplete data but NTP is not scalable yielding good accuracy only on the very small and simple instances (S-2), while Neural-LP seems to be more scalable (we cannot see a decrease of performance, augmenting the size of the dataset) but does not support nested rules.

6   Conclusions and Future Work

In this paper, we have presented RuDaS, a system for generating datasets for rule learning and for evaluating rule learning systems. RuDaS specifically fits neural approaches that need large amounts of data to learn from. Our experiments have shown that it is important to have diverse datasets of different sizes, with several rule types, and different amounts and types of noise; and different performance metrics to fully understand the systems' strengths and, more important, weaknesses. There are various future directions such as probabilistic logics and predicate types.

A   Additional Preliminaries

Our measures are based on the concepts of Herbrand base and structure. Generally formal logic distinguishes between syntax (symbols) and its interpretation. Herbrand structures, which are used for interpretation, are however defined solely by the syntactical properties of the vocabulary. The idea is to directly take the symbols of terms as their interpretations which, for example, has proven useful in the analysis of logic programming.

The focus is on ground terms (e.g., atoms and rules), which are terms that do not contain variables.

The Herbrand base of a FOL vocabulary (of constants, predicates, etc.) is the set of all ground terms that can be formulated in the vocabulary. If the vocabulary does not contain constants, then the language is extended by adding an arbitrary new constant.

A Herbrand model interprets terms over a Herbrand base, hence it can be seen as a set of ground atoms. Let T be the set of all variable-free terms over a vocabulary V. A structure S over V and with base U is said to be a Herbrand structure iff $U = T_0$ and $c^S = c$ for every constant $c \in V$.[13]

B   Dataset Generation

In this section, we describe the generation process of the rules and facts in detail, assuming the generator parameters (also *configuration*) listed in Sect. 3 to be set.

Preprocessing. As already mentioned, most parameters are determined randomly in a preprocessing step if they are not fixed in the configuration, such as the symbols that will be used, the numbers of DGs to be generated, and their depths. However, all random selections are within the bounds given in the configuration under consideration; for instance, we ensure that the symbols chosen suffice to generate rule graphs and fact sets of selected size and that at least one graph is of the given maximal depth.

Rule Generation. According to the rule set category specified and graph depths determined, rules (nodes in the graphs) of form (2) are generated top down breadth first, for each of the rule graphs to be constructed. The generation is largely at random, that is, w.r.t. the number of child nodes of a node and which body atom they relate to; the number of atoms in a rule; and the predicates within the latter, including the choice of the *target predicate* (i.e., the predicate in the head of the root) in the very first step. RuDaS also offers the option that all graphs have the same target predicate. To allow for more derivations, we currently only consider variables as terms in head atoms; the choice of the remaining terms is based on probabilities as described in the following. Given the atoms to be considered (in terms of their number and predicates) and an arbitrary choice of head variables, we first determine a position for each of the latter in the former. Then we populate the other positions one after the other: a head variable is chosen with probability $p_h = \frac{1}{5}$; for one of the variables introduced so far, we have probability $p_v = (1 - p_h) * \frac{3}{4}$; for a constant, $p_c = (1 - p_h) * (1 - p_v) * \frac{1}{10}$; and, for a fresh variable, $p_f = (1 - p_h) * (1 - p_v) * (1 - p_c)$. While this conditional scheme might seem rather complex, we found that it works best in terms of the variety it yields; also, these probabilities can be changed easily.

Fact Generation. The fact generation is done in three phases: we first construct a set $\mathbb{D}$ of relevant facts in a closed-world setting, consisting of support facts $\mathbb{S}$ and their consequences $\mathbb{C}$, and then adapt it according to n_{OW} and $n_{\text{Noise*}}$.

---

[13] Recall that we disregard function symbols.

As it is the (natural) idea, we generate facts by instantiating the rule graphs multiple times, based on the assumption that rule learning systems need positive examples for a rule to learn that rule, and stop the generation when the requested number of facts has been generated. We actually stop later because we need to account for the fact that we subsequently will delete some of them according to n_{OW}. More specifically, we continuously iterate over all rule graphs, for each, select an arbitrary but fresh variable assignment σ, and then iterate over the graph nodes as described in the following, in a bottom-up way. First, we consider each leaf n and corresponding rule of form (2) and generate support facts $\sigma(\alpha_1), \ldots, \sigma(\alpha_m)$. Then, we infer the consequences based on the rules and all facts generated so far. For every node n on the next level and corresponding rule of form (2), we only generate those of the facts $\sigma(\alpha_1), \ldots, \sigma(\alpha_m)$ as support facts which are not among the consequences inferred previously. We then again apply inference, possibly obtaining new consequences, and continue iterating over all nodes in the graph in this way. We further diversify the process based on two integer parameters, n_{DG} and n_{Skip}: in every n_{DG}-th iteration the graph is instantiated exactly in the way described; in the other iterations, we skip the instantiation of a node with probability $1/n_{Skip}$ and, in the case of DR-DGs, only instantiate a single branch below disjunctive nodes. We implemented this diversification to have more variability in the supports facts, avoiding to have only complete paths from the leaves to the root.

In the open-world setting, we subsequently construct a set $\mathbb{D}_{OW}$ by randomly deleting consequences from $\mathbb{D}$ according to the open-world degree given: assuming $\mathbb{T} \subseteq \mathbb{C}$ to be the set of *target facts* (i.e., consequences containing the target predicate), we remove $n_{OW}\%$ from $\mathbb{C} \setminus \mathbb{T}$, and similarly $n_{OW}\%$ from $\mathbb{T}$. In this way, we ensure that the open-world degree is reflected in the target facts. Though, there is the option to have it more arbitrary by removing $n_{OW}\%$ from $\mathbb{C}$ instead of splitting the deletion into two parts.

The noise generation is split similarly. Specifically, we construct a set $\mathbb{D}_{OW+Noise}$ based on $\mathbb{D}_{OW}$ by arbitrarily removing $n_{Noise-}\%$ from $\mathbb{S}$, and by adding arbitrary fresh facts that are neither in $\mathbb{C}$ (i.e., we do not add facts we have removed in the previous step) nor contain the target predicate such that $\mathbb{D}_{OW+Noise} \setminus \mathbb{T}$ contains $n_{Noise+}\%$ of noise. In addition, we add arbitrary fresh facts on the target predicate that are not in $\mathbb{T}$ already such that subset of $\mathbb{D}_{OW+Noise}$ on that predicate finally contains $n_{Noise+}\%$ of noise.

Output. The dataset generation produces: the rules; a *training* set ($\mathbb{D}_{OW+Noise}$), which is of the requested size, and fulfills n_{OW}, n_{Noise+}, and n_{Noise-}; and custom fact sets $\mathbb{S}'$ and $\mathbb{C}'$ for our evaluation tools generated in the same way as $\mathbb{S}$ and $\mathbb{C}$. For further experiments, RuDaS also outputs $\mathbb{D}$, $\mathbb{D}_{Noise}$ (an adaptation of $\mathbb{D}$ which contains noise but all of $\mathbb{C}$), $\mathbb{D}_{OW}$, $\mathbb{S}$, and $\mathbb{C}$ (see also the end of Sect. C).

C   Statistics of RuDaS.v0

Table 5 provides statistics regarding RuDaS.v0: the generated set of datasets available to the community in our repository.

Table 5. Overview of our generated datasets, altogether 196; column # is the count of datasets described in the corresponding row. All other numbers are averages. For Chain, we have $n_{OW} = 0.3$, $n_{Noise-} = 0.2$, and $n_{Noise+} = 0.1$. For RDG and DRDG: $n_{OW} \in \{0.2, 0.3, 0.4\}$, $n_{Noise-} \in \{0.15, 0.2, 0.3\}$, and $n_{Noise+} \in \{0.1, 0.2, 0.3\}$. Note that the size bounds of our fact sets are not strict, some sizes are slightly larger than expected (e.g., 1065 for size M) because our initial generation needs to take into account that some facts, e.g., consequences, may be removed thereafter.

#	Rule type	Size	Depth	#Rules			#Facts			#Pred			#Const		
				min	avg	max	min	avg	max	min	avg	max	min	avg	max
10	CHAIN	S	2	2	2	2	51	74	95	5	7	9	31	47	71
10	CHAIN	S	3	3	3	3	49	70	97	7	8	9	31	43	64
10	CHAIN	M	2	2	2	2	168	447	908	9	10	11	97	259	460
10	CHAIN	M	3	3	3	3	120	508	958	8	10	11	52	230	374
22	RDG	S	2	3	3	3	49	84	122	6	9	11	28	50	84
12	RDG	S	3	4	5	6	56	104	172	8	10	11	41	55	75
22	RDG	M	2	3	3	3	200	646	1065	6	11	11	71	370	648
22	RDG	M	3	4	5	7	280	613	1107	10	11	11	149	297	612
22	DRDG	S	2	3	4	5	60	100	181	6	9	11	29	55	82
12	DRDG	S	3	4	7	11	58	144	573	8	10	11	34	58	89
22	DRDG	M	2	3	4	5	149	564	1027	10	11	11	88	327	621
22	DRDG	M	3	4	7	12	111	540	1126	10	11	11	70	284	680

D   Approaches to Rule Learning

Classical ILP systems such as FOIL [24] and Progol [19] usually apply exhaustive algorithms to mine rules for the given data and either require false facts as counter-examples or assume a closed world (for an overview of classical ILP systems see Table 2 in [32]). The *closed-world assumption* (CWA) (vs. *open world assumption* or OWA) states that all facts that are not explicitly given as true are assumed to be false.

Today, however, knowledge graphs with their often incomplete, noisy, heterogeneous, and, especially, large amounts of data raise new problems and require new solutions. For instance, real data most often only partially satisfies the CWA and does not contain counter-examples. Moreover, in an open world, absent facts cannot be considered as counter-examples either, since they are not regarded as false. Therefore, successor systems, with AMIE+ [12] and RDF2Rules [34] as the most prominent representatives, assume the data to be only partially complete and focus on rule learning in the sense of mining patterns that occur frequently in the data. Furthermore, they implement advanced optimization approaches that make them applicable in wider scenarios. In this way, they address already many of the issues that arise with today's knowledge graphs, still maintaining their processing exhaustive.

Recently, neural rule learning approaches have been proposed: [4, 10, 17, 22, 27, 35]. These methodologies seem a promising alternative considering that deep learning copes with vast amounts of noisy and heterogeneous data. The proposed solutions consider vector or matrix embeddings of symbols, facts and/or rules, and model inference using differentiable operations such as vector addition and matrix composition. However, they are still premature: they only learn certain kinds of rules or lack scalability (e.g., searching the entire rule space) and hence cannot compete with established rule mining systems such as AMIE+ yet, as shown in [22], for example.

E   System Configurations

All the systems have the same computational restrictions (i.e. CPU, memory, time limit, etc.). The reader can find all the details (scripts etc.) in the RuDaS GitHub repository.

FOIL

- **Paper:** Learning logical definitions from relations. Machine Learning, 5:239-266, 1990.
  https://www.semanticscholar.org/paper/Learning-logical-definitions-from-relations-Quinlan/554f3b32b956035fbfabba730c6f0300d6955dce
- **Source Code:**
  http://www.rulequest.com/Personal/ or
  http://www.cs.cmu.edu/afs/cs/project/ai-repository/ai/areas/learning/systems/foil/foil6/0.html, Version: 6
- **Running configuration:**

```
\$SYSDIR/\$SYSTEM/FOIL/./foil6 -v0 -n -m 200000
    < \$PREPROCESSINGFOLDER\$FILENAME.d
```

  -m 200000: used when the max tuples are exceeded
- **Parameter for accepting the rules:** NA – all the rules are accepted

Amie+

- **Paper:** Fast Rule Mining in Ontological Knowledge Bases with AMIE+. Luis Galárraga, Christina Teflioudi, Fabian Suchanek, Katja Hose. VLDB Journal 2015. https://suchanek.name/work/publications/vldbj2015.pdf
- **Source Code:**
  https://www.mpi-inf.mpg.de/departments/databases-and-information-systems/research/yago-naga/amie/, Version of 2015-08-26
- **Running configuration:**

```
java -jar \$SYSDIR/\$SYSTEM/amie\_plus.jar
    -mins 3 -minis 3 -minpca 0.25
    -oute \$DATA/\$SYSTEM/\$NAME/train.txt
    > \$DIR/../output/binary/\$SYSTEM/\$NAME/results.txt
```

- **Parameter for accepting the rules:** learned using grid-search $= 0.7$ – all the rules with PCA Confidence > 0.7 are accepted

Neural-LP

- **Paper:** Differentiable Learning of Logical Rules for Knowledge Base Reasoning.Fan Yang, Zhilin Yang, William W. Cohen. NIPS 2017. https://arxiv.org/abs/1702.08367
- **Source Code:**
  https://github.com/fanyangxyz/Neural-LP
- **Running configuration:**

```
python \$SYSDIR/\$SYSTEM/src/main.py
    --datadir=\$DATA/\$SYSTEM/\$NAME
    --exp\_dir=$DIR/../output/binary/$SYSTEM
    --exp\_name=\$NAME
    > \$DIR/../output/binary/\$SYSTEM/\$NAME/log.txt
```

- **Parameter for accepting the rules:** learned using grid-search $= 0.6$ – all the rules with ri-normalized prob > 0.6 are accepted

Neural-theorem prover (ntp)

- **Paper:** End-to-end Differentiable Proving. Tim Rocktaeschel and Sebastian Riedel. NIPS 2017. http://papers.nips.cc/paper/6969-end-to-end-differentiable-proving
- **Source Code:**
  https://github.com/uclmr/ntp
- **Running configuration:**

```
python \$SYSDIR/\$SYSTEM/ntp/experiments/learn.py
    \$DATA/\$SYSTEM/\$NAME/run.conf
    > \$DIR/../output/binary/\$SYSTEM/\$NAME/log.txt
```

- **Parameter for accepting the rules:** learned using grid-search $= 0.0$ – all the rules are accepted

```
{
    "data": {
        "kb": "$DATAPATH/$TRAIN.nl",
        "templates": "$DATAPATH/rules.nlt"
    },
    "meta": {
        "parent": "$SYSTEMSPATH/conf/default.conf",
        "test_graph_creation": False,
        "experiment_prefix": "$NAME",
        "test_set": "$TEST",
        "result_file": "$OUTPUTPATH/results.tsv",
        "debug": False
    },
    "training": {
        "num_epochs": 100,
        "report_interval": 10,
        "pos_per_batch": 10,
        "neg_per_pos": 1,
        "optimizer": "Adam",
        "learning_rate": 0.001,
        "sampling_scheme": "all",
        "init": None, # xavier initialization
        "clip": (-1.0, 1.0)
    },
    "model": {
```

```
"input_size": 100,
"k_max": 10,
"name": "???",
"neural_link_predictor": "ComplEx",
"12": 0.01, # 0.01 # 0.0001
"keep_prob": 0.7
    }
}
```

References

1. Alexe, B., Tan, W.C., Velegrakis, Y.: Stbenchmark: towards a benchmark for mapping systems. Proc. VLDB Endow. **1**(1), 230–244 (2008)
2. Arocena, P.C., Glavic, B., Ciucanu, R., Miller, R.J.: The ibench integration metadata generator. Proc. VLDB Endow. **9**(3) (2015)
3. Benedikt, M., et al.: Benchmarking the chase. In: Proceedings of PODS. ACM, pp. 37–52 (2017)
4. Campero, A., Pareja, A., Klinger, T., Tenenbaum, J., Riedel, S.: Logical rule induction and theory learning using neural theorem proving. CoRR abs/1809.02193 (2018)
5. Ceri, S., Gottlob, G., Tanca, L.: What you always wanted to know about datalog (and never dared to ask). In: IEEE Trans. on Knowl. and Data Eng. **1**(1), 146–166 (1989)
6. Dong, H., Mao, J., Lin, T., Wang, C., Li, L., Zhou, D.: Neural logic machines. In: Proceedings of ICLR (2019)
7. Dong, X.L., et al.: Knowledge vault: A web-scale approach to probabilistic knowledge fusion. In: Proceedings of KDD, pp. 601–610 (2014)
8. Estruch, V., Ferri, C., Hernández-Orallo, J., Ramírez-Quintana, M.J.: Distance based generalisation. In: Kramer, S., Pfahringer, B. (eds.) ILP 2005. LNCS (LNAI), vol. 3625, pp. 87–102. Springer, Heidelberg (2005). https://doi.org/10.1007/11536314_6
9. Estruch, V., Ferri, C., Hernández-Orallo, J., Ramírez-Quintana, M.J.: An integrated distance for atoms. In: Blume, M., Kobayashi, N., Vidal, G. (eds.) FLOPS 2010. LNCS, vol. 6009, pp. 150–164. Springer, Heidelberg (2010). https://doi.org/10.1007/978-3-642-12251-4_12
10. Evans, R., Grefenstette, E.: Learning explanatory rules from noisy data. J. Artif. Intell. Res. **61**, 1–64 (2018)
11. Fürnkranz, J., Gamberger, D., Lavrac, N.: Foundations of Rule Learning. Springer, Cognitive Technologies (2012)
12. Galárraga, L., Teflioudi, C., Hose, K., Suchanek, F.M.: Fast rule mining in ontological knowledge bases with AMIE+. VLDB J. **24**(6), 707–730 (2015), code available at https://www.mpi-inf.mpg.de/departments/databases-and-information-systems/research/yago-naga/amie/
13. Ho, V.T., Stepanova, D., Gad-Elrab, M.H., Kharlamov, E., Weikum, G.: Rule learning from knowledge graphs guided by embedding models. In: Vrandečić, D., et al. (eds.) ISWC 2018. LNCS, vol. 11136, pp. 72–90. Springer, Cham (2018). https://doi.org/10.1007/978-3-030-00671-6_5
14. ILP: ILP Applications and Datasets. https://www.doc.ic.ac.uk/~shm/applications.html (year na). Accessed 09 Mar 2020
15. de Jong, M., Sha, F.: Neural theorem provers do not learn rules without exploration. ArXiv abs/1906.06805 (2019)

16. Krishnan, A.: Making search easier (2018). https://blog.aboutamazon.com/innovation/making-search-easier. Accessed 03 Sept 2020
17. Minervini, P., Bosnjak, M., Rocktäschel, T., Riedel, S.: Towards neural theorem proving at scale. In: Proceedings of NAMPI (2018)
18. Minervini, P., Bošnjak, M., Rocktäschel, T., Riedel, S., Grefenstette, E.: Differentiable reasoning on large knowledge bases and natural language. In: Proceedings of AAAI Conference on Artificial Intelligence, vol. 34, no. 04, pp. 5182–5190 (2020)
19. Muggleton, S.: Inverse entailment and progol. New Gen. Comput. **13**(3&4), 245–286 (1995)
20. Nienhuys-Cheng, S., de Wolf, R.: Foundations of Inductive Logic Programming, vol. 1228. Springer (1997)
21. Nienhuys-Cheng, S.-H.: Distance between herbrand interpretations: a measure for approximations to a target concept. In: Lavrač, N., Džeroski, S. (eds.) ILP 1997. LNCS, vol. 1297, pp. 213–226. Springer, Heidelberg (1997). https://doi.org/10.1007/3540635149_50
22. Omran, P.G., Wang, K., Wang, Z.: Scalable rule learning via learning representation. In: Proceedings of IJCAI, pp. 2149–2155 (2018)
23. Preda, M.: Metrics for sets of atoms and logic programs. Ann. Univ. Craiova **33**, 67–78 (2006)
24. Quinlan, J.R.: Learning logical definitions from relations. Mach. Learn. **5**, 239–266 (1990). code available at http://www.cs.cmu.edu/afs/cs/project/ai-repository/ai/areas/learning/systems/foil/foil6/0.html
25. Raedt, L.D.: Logical and Relational Learning. Springer, Cognitive Technologies (2008)
26. Ren, H., Hu, W., Leskovec, J.: Query2box: reasoning over knowledge graphs in vector space using box embeddings. In: Proceedings of ICLR (2020)
27. Rocktäschel, T., Riedel, S.: End-to-end differentiable proving. In: Proceedings of NeurIPS, pp. 3791–3803 (2017). code available at https://github.com/uclmr/ntp
28. Russell, S., Norvig, P.: Artificial Intelligence: A Modern Approach. Prentice Hall Press (2002)
29. Seda, A.K., Lane, M.: On continuous models of computation: towards computing the distance between (logic) programs. In: Proceedings of IWFM (2003)
30. Sinha, K., Sodhani, S., Pineau, J., Hamilton, W.L.: Evaluating logical generalization in graph neural networks. ArXiv abs/2003.06560 (2020)
31. Sinha, K., Sodhani, S., Pineau, J., Hamilton, W.L.: Evaluating logical generalization in graph neural networks (2020)
32. Stepanova, D., Gad-Elrab, M.H., Ho, V.T.: Rule induction and reasoning over knowledge graphs. In: d'Amato, C., Theobald, M. (eds.) Reasoning Web 2018. LNCS, vol. 11078, pp. 142–172. Springer, Cham (2018). https://doi.org/10.1007/978-3-030-00338-8_6
33. Vaclav Zeman, T.K., Svátek, V.: Rdfrules: Making RDF rule mining easier and even more efficient. Semant-Web-J. **12**(4), 569–602 (2019)
34. Wang, Z., Li, J.: Rdf2rules: Learning rules from RDF knowledge bases by mining frequent predicate cycles. CoRR abs/1512.07734 (2015)
35. Yang, F., Yang, Z., Cohen, W.W.: Differentiable learning of logical rules for knowledge base reasoning. In: Proc. of NeurIPS, pp. 2316–2325 (2017). https://github.com/fanyangxyz/Neural-LP
36. Yang, Y., Song, L.: Learn to explain efficiently via neural logic inductive learning. In: Proceedings of ICLR (2020)

Using Domain-Knowledge to Assist Lead Discovery in Early-Stage Drug Design

Tirtharaj Dash[1]([⊠]), Ashwin Srinivasan[1], Lovekesh Vig[2], and Arijit Roy[3]

[1] Department of CSIS & APPCAIR, BITS Pilani, Goa Campus, India
tirtharaj@goa.bits-pilani.ac.in
[2] TCS Research, New Delhi, India
[3] TCS Innovation Labs (Life Sciences Division), Hyderabad, India

Abstract. We are interested in generating new small molecules which could act as inhibitors of a biological target, when there is limited prior information on target-specific inhibitors. This form of drug-design is assuming increasing importance with the advent of new disease threats for which known chemicals only provide limited information about target inhibition. In this paper, we propose the combined use of deep neural networks and Inductive Logic Programming (ILP) that allows the use of symbolic domain-knowledge (B) to explore the large space of possible molecules. Assuming molecules and their activities to be instances of random variables X and Y, the problem is to draw instances from the conditional distribution of X, given Y, B ($D_{X|Y,B}$). We decompose this into the constituent parts of obtaining the distributions $D_{X|B}$ and $D_{Y|X,B}$, and describe the design and implementation of models to approximate the distributions. The design consists of generators (to approximate $D_{X|B}$ and $D_{X|Y,B}$) and a discriminator (to approximate $D_{Y|X,B}$). We investigate our approach using the well-studied problem of inhibitors for the Janus kinase (JAK) class of proteins. We assume first that if no data on inhibitors are available for a target protein (JAK2), but a small numbers of inhibitors are known for homologous proteins (JAK1, JAK3 and TYK2). We show that the inclusion of relational domain-knowledge results in a potentially more effective generator of inhibitors than simple random sampling from the space of molecules or a generator without access to symbolic relations. The results suggest a way of combining symbolic domain-knowledge and deep generative models to constrain the exploration of the chemical space of molecules, when there is limited information on target-inhibitors. We also show how samples from the conditional generator can be used to identify potentially novel target inhibitors.

Keywords: Drug Design · Neural-Symbolic Learning · Lead Discovery

1 Introduction

Co-opting Hobbes, the development of a new drug is difficult, wasteful, costly, uncertain, and long. AI techniques have been trying to change this [1], especially in the early stages culminating in "lead discovery". Figure 1 shows the

© Springer Nature Switzerland AG 2022
N. Katzouris and A. Artikis (Eds.): ILP 2021, LNAI 13191, pp. 78–94, 2022.
https://doi.org/10.1007/978-3-030-97454-1_6

steps involved in this stage of drug-design. In the figure, library screening can be either done by actual laboratory experiments (high-throughput screening) or computationally (virtual screening). This usually results in many false-positives. Hit Confirmation refers to additional assays designed to reduce false-positives. QSAR (quantitative- or qualitative structure-activity relations) consists of models for predicting biological activity using physico-chemical properties of hits. The results of prediction can result in additional confirmatory assays for hits, and finally in one or more "lead" compounds that are taken forward for pre-clinical testing. This paper focuses on the problem of lead discovery that goes beyond the efficient identification of chemicals within the almost unlimited space of potential molecules. This space has been approximately estimated at about 10^{60} molecules. A very small fraction of these have been synthesised in research laboratories and by pharmaceutical companies. An even smaller number are available publicly: the well-known ChEMBL database [2] of drug-like chemicals consists of about 10^6 molecules. Any early-stage drug-discovery pipeline that restricts itself to in-house chemicals will clearly be self-limiting. This is especially the case if the leads sought are for targets in new diseases, for which very few "hits" may result from existing chemical libraries. While a complete (but not exhaustive) exploration of the space of 10^{60} molecules may continue to be elusive, we would nevertheless like to develop an effective way of sampling from this space.

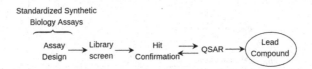

Fig. 1. Early-stage drug-design (adapted from [3]).

We would like to implement the QSAR module as a generator of new molecules, conditioned on the information provided by the hit assays, and on domain-knowledge. Our position is that inclusion of domain-knowledge allows the development of more effective conditional distributions than is possible using just the hit assays. Figure 2 is a diagrammatic representation of an ideal conditional generator of the kind we require. The difficulty of course is that none of the underlying distributions are known. In this paper, we describe a neural-symbolic implementation to construct approximations for the distributions.

2 System Design and Implementation

We implement an approximation to the ideal conditional generator using a generator-discriminator combination (see Fig. 3). We have decomposed the domain-knowledge B in Fig. 2 into constraints relevant just to the molecule-generator B_G and the knowledge relevant to the prediction of activity B_D (that

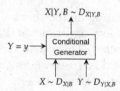

$$X|Y, B \sim D_{X|Y,B}$$

$Y = y \longrightarrow$ | Conditional Generator |

$$X \sim D_{X|B} \quad Y \sim D_{Y|X,B}$$

Fig. 2. An ideal conditional generator for instances of a random-variable denoting data (X) given a value for a random-variable denoting labels (Y) and domain-knowledge (B). Here, $Z \sim D$ denotes a random variable Z is distributed according to the distribution D. If the distributions shown are known, then a a value for X is obtainable through the use of Bayes rule, either exactly or through some form approximate inference.

is, $B = B_G \cup B_D$ and $P(X|B) = P(X|B_G)$ and $P(Y|X, B) = P(Y|X, B_D))$. The discriminator module approximates the conditional distribution $D_{Y|X,B}$, and the combination of the unconditional generator and filter approximates the distribution $D_{X|B}$. The conditional generator then constructs an approximation to $D_{X|Y,B}$. For the present, we assume the unconditional generator and discriminator are pre-trained: details will be provided below. The discriminator is a BotGNN [4]. This is a form of graph-based neural network (GNN) that uses graph-encodings of most-specific clauses (see [5]) constructed using symbolic domain-knowledge B_D.

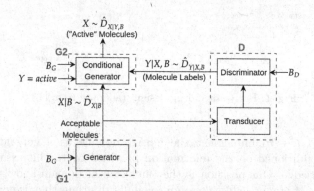

Fig. 3. Training a conditional generator for generating "active" molecules. For the present, we assume the generator (G1) and discriminator (D) have already been trained (the G1 and D modules generate acceptable molecules and their labels respectively: the $\hat{D}$'s are approximations to the corresponding true distribution). The Transducer converts the output of G1 into a form suitable for the discriminator. Actual implementations used in the paper will be described below.

The generator-discriminator combination in Fig. 3 constitutes the QSAR module in Fig. 1. An initial set of hits is used to train the discriminator. The conditional generator is trained using the initial set of hits and the filtered samples from the unconditional generator and the labels from the discriminator.

Although out of the scope of this paper, any novel molecules generated could then be synthesised, subject to hit confirmation, and the process repeated.

Generating Acceptable Molecules. The intent of module G1 is to produce an approximation to drawing samples (in our case, molecules) from $D_{X|B_G}$. We describe the actual B_G used for experiments in Sect. 3.1: for the present it is sufficient to assume that for any instance $X = x$, if $B_G \wedge X = x \models \Box$ then $Pr(x|B_G) = 0$. Here, we implement this by a simple rejection-sampler that first draws from some distribution over molecules and rejects the instances that are inconsistent with B_G.

For drawing samples of molecules, we adopt the text-generation model proposed in [6]. Our model takes SMILES representations of molecules as inputs and estimates a probability distribution over these SMILES representations. Samples of molecules are then SMILES strings drawn from this distribution.

The SMILES generation module is shown in Fig. 4. The distribution of molecules (SMILES strings) is estimated using a variational autoencoder (VAE) model. The VAE model consists of an encoder and a decoder, both based on LSTM-based RNNs [7]. This architecture forms a SMILES encoder with the Gaussian prior acting as a regulariser on the latent representation. The decoder is a special RNN model that is conditioned on the latent representation.

Fig. 4. Training a generator for acceptable molecules. Training data consists of molecules, represented as SMILES strings, drawn from a database Δ. The VAE is a model constructed using the training data and generates molecules represented by SMILES strings. B_G denotes domain-knowledge consisting of constraints on acceptable molecules. The filter acts as a rejection-sampler: only molecules consistent with B_G pass through.

The architecture of the VAE model is shown in Fig. 5. The SMILES encoding involves three primary modules: (a) embedding module: constructs an embedding for the input SMILE; (b) highway module: constructs a gated information-flow module based on highway network [8]; (c) LSTM module: responsible for dealing with sequence. The modules (b) and (c) together form the encoder module. The parameters of the Gaussian distribution is learnt via two fully-connected networks, one each for μ and σ, which are standard sub-structures involved in a VAE model. The decoder module (or the generator) consists of LSTM layers followed by a fully-connected (FC) layer. We defer the details on architecture-specific hyperparameters to Sect. 3.2. The loss function used for training our VAE model is a weighted version of the reconstruction loss and KL-divergence between VAE-constructed distribution and the Gaussian prior $\mathcal{N}(0,1)$.

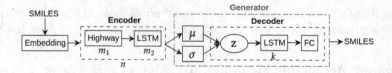

Fig. 5. Architecture of the VAE in Fig. 4. $m_{1,2}, n, k$ represent the number of blocks.

Obtaining Labels for Acceptable Molecules. The intent of module D is to produce an approximation to drawing samples (in our case, labels for molecules) from $D_{Y|X,B_D}$. We describe the actual B_D used for experiments in Sect. 3.1. The discriminator in D is a BotGNN [4], which is a form of graph neural network (GNN) constructed from data (as graphs) and background knowledge (as symbolic relations or propositions) using mode-directed inverse entailment (MDIE [5]). In this work, data consists of graph-based representations of molecules (atoms and bonds), and B_D consists of symbolic domain-relations applicable to the molecules. The goal of the discriminator is to learn a distribution over class-labels for any given molecules. Figure 6 shows the block diagram of the discriminator block.

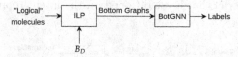

Fig. 6. Discriminator based on BotGNN. "Logical" molecules refers to a logic-based representation of molecules. Bottom-graphs are a graph-based representation of most-specific ("bottom") clauses constructed for the molecules by an ILP implementation based on mode-directed inverse entailment.

Generating Active Molecules. The intent of module G2 is to produce an approximation to drawing from $D_{X|Y,B}$. That is, we want to draw samples of molecules, given a label for the molecule and domain-knowledge B. We adopt the same architecture as the generator used for drawing from $D_{X|B_G}$ above, with a simple modification to the way the SMILES strings are provided as inputs to the model. We prefix each SMILES string with a class-label: $y = 1$ or $y = 0$ based on whether the molecule is an active or inactive inhibitor, respectively. The VAE model is also able to accommodate any data that may already be present about the target, or about related targets (it is assumed that such data will be in the form of labelled SMILES strings).

3 System Testing

Our aim is to perform a controlled experiment to assess the effect on system performance of the inclusion of high-level symbolic domain-knowledge. Specifically:

we investigate the effect on the generation of new inhibitors for the target when: (a) No domain-knowledge is available in the form of symbolic relations (but some knowledge is available in a propositional form); and (b) Some domain-knowledge is available in form of symbolic relations. We intend to test if the system is able to generate possible new inhibitors in case (a); and if the performance of the system improves in case (b).

3.1 Materials

Data. The data used are as follows. (a) ChEMBL dataset [2]: 1.9 million molecules; used to train the generator for legal molecules (G1); (b) JAK2 [9]: 4100 molecules (3700 active); used to test the conditional generator (G1) and to build the proxy model for hit confirmation (see Method section below); (c) JAK2 Homologues (JAK1, JAK3 and TYK2) [9]: 4300 molecules (3700 active); used to train the discriminator (D) and train the conditional generator (G2).

Domain-Knowledge. We use the following categories of domain-knowledge (also see Appendix A). (a) Molecular Constraints [9,10]: Logical constraints on acceptable molecules, including standard validity checks (based on molecular properties); (b) Molecular Properties [9]: Bulk-properties of molecules (propositional in nature); (c) Molecular Relations [11]: Logical statements defining ring-structures and functional groups (relational in nature).

Algorithms and Machines. We use the following software. (a) RDKit [10]: Molecular modelling software used to compute molecular properties and check for the validity of molecules; (b) Chemprop [12]: Molecular modelling software used to build a proxy model for hit confirmation; (c) Transducer: In-house software to convert representation from SMILES to logic; (d) Aleph [13]: ILP engine used to generate most-specific clauses for BotGNN; (e) BotGNN [4]: Discriminator for acceptable molecules capable of using relational and propositional domain knowledge; (f) VAE [14]: Generative deep network used for generators. We used PyTorch for the implementation of BotGNN and VAE models, and Aleph was used with YAP.

Our experimental works were distributed across two machines: (a) The discriminator (D) was built on a Dell workstation with 64 GB of main memory, 16-core Intel Xeon 3.10 GHz processors, an 8 GB NVIDIA P4000 graphics processor; (b) The generators (G1, G2) are built on an NVIDIA-DGX1 station with 32 GB Tesla V100 GPUs, 512 GB main memory, 80-core Intel Xeon 2.20 GHz processors.

3.2 Methods

We describe the procedure adopted for a controlled experiment comparing system performance in generating potential inhibitors when: (a) domain-knowledge is restricted to commonly used bulk-properties about the molecules; and (b) domain-knowledge includes information about higher-level symbolic relations consisting of ring-structures and functional groups, along with the information in (a). In either case, the method used to generate acceptable molecules (from module G1 in Fig. 3) is the same.

Let B_0 denote domain-knowledge consisting of bulk-molecular properties used in the construction of QSARs for novel inhibitors; B_1 denote the definitions in B_0 along with first-order relations defining ring-structures and functional-groups used in the construction of QSAR relations; and B_G denote the domain-knowledge consisting of constraints on acceptable molecules (see "Domain-Knowledge" in Sect. 3.1). Let Tr denote the data available on inhibitors for JAK1, JAK3 and TYK2; and Te denote the data available on inhibitors for JAK2 (see "Data" in Sect. 3.1). Let Δ denote a database of (known) legal molecules. Then:

1. Construct a generator for possible molecules given Δ (the generator in module G1 of Fig. 3) .
2. For $i = 0, 1$
   (a) Let $E_0 = \{(x, y)\}_1^{Tr}$, where x is a molecule in Tr and y is the activity label obtained based on a threshold θ on the minimum activity for active inhibition.
   (b) Let $B_D = B_i$
   (c) Construct a discriminator (for module D in Fig. 3) using E_0 and the domain-knowledge B_D (see Sect. 2);
   (d) Sample a set of possible molecules, denoted as N, from the generator constructed in Step 1;. Let $N' \subseteq N$ be the set of molecules found to be acceptable given the constraints in B_G (that is, N' is a sample from $\hat{D}_{X|B_G}$);
   (e) For each acceptable molecule x obtained in Step 2d above, let y be the label with the highest probability from the distribution $\hat{D}_{Y|X,B}$ constructed by the discriminator in Step 2c. Let $E = \{(x, y)\}_1^{N'}$
   (f) Construct the generator model (for module G2 in Fig. 3) using $E_0 \cup E$.
   (g) Sample a set of molecules, denoted as M_i, from the generator in Step 2f;
   (h) Let $M_i' \subseteq M_i$ be the molecules found to be acceptable given the constraints in B_G (that is, M_i' is a sample from $D_{Y|X,B_G}$)
3. Assess the samples $M_{0,1}$ obtained in Step 2g above for possible new inhibitors of the target, using the information in Te

The following details are relevant:

– For experiments here Δ is the ChEMBL database, consisting of approximately 1.9 million molecules. The generator also includes legality checks performed by the RDKit package, as described in Sect. 2;
– Following [9], $\theta = 6.0$. That is, all molecules with pIC50 value ≥ 6.0 are taken as "active" inhibitors;
– The discriminator in Step 2c is a BotGNN. We follow the procedure and parameters described in [4] to construct BotGNN. We use GraphSAGE [15] for the convolution block in the GNN. This is based on the results shown in [4] for including symbolic domain knowledge for graph-based data (like molecules);

- The generators in Steps 1 and 2f are based on the VAE model described earlier. The hyperparameters are as follows: vocabulary length is 100, embedding-dimension is 300, number of highway layers is 2, number of LSTM layers in the encoder is 1 with hidden size 512, and the type is bidirectional, number of LSTM layers in the decoder is 2, each with hidden size 512, dimension of latent representation ($\mathbf{z}$) is 100.
- To make our generator robust to noise and to be generalised, we also use a word-dropout technique. This technique is identical to the standard practice of dropout in deep learning except that here the tokens to the decoder are replaced by '*unknown*' tokens with certain probabilities. Here we call it the word-dropout rate and fix it at 0.5.
- The reconstruction loss coefficient is 7. We use cost-annealing [6] for the KLD-coefficient during training. We use the Adam optimizer [16] with learning rate of 0.0001; training batch-size is 256.
- In Step 2d, $|N| = 30,000$. The B_G provided here results in $|N'| = 18,000$;
- In Step 2g, $|M_0| = |M_1| = 5000$.
- The acceptable molecules $M'_{0,1}$ after testing for consistency with B_G are assessed along two dimensions:
  (a) *Activity*: In the pipeline described in Fig. 1 assessment of activity would be done by *in vitro* by hit confirmation assays. Here we use a proxy assessment for the result of the assays by using an *in silico* predictor of pIC50 values constructed from the data in Te on JAK2 inhibitors. The proxy model is constructed by a state-of-the-art activity prediction package (Chemprop [12]: details of this are in the Appendix).[1] We are interested in comparing the proportions of generated molecules predicted as "active";
  (b) *Similarity*: we want to assess how similar the molecules generated are to the set of active JAK2 inhibitors in Te.[2] A widely used measure for this is the Tanimoto (Jacquard) similarity: molecules with Tanimoto similarity >0.75 are usually taken to be similar. We are interested in the proportion of molecules generated that are similar to known target inhibitors in Te;
  Each sample of molecules M_i drawn from the conditional generator can therefore be represented by a pair (a_i, b_i) denoting the values of the proportions in (a) and (b), and (c) above. We will call this pair the "performance summary" of the set M_i;
- We compare performance summaries of sets of molecules in two ways. First, a performance summary $P_i = (a_i, b_i)$ can be compared against the performance summary $P_j = (a_j, b_j)$ in the obvious lexicographic manner. That is, P_i is better than P_j if $[(a_i > a_j)]$ or $[(a_i = a_j) \land (b_i > b_j)]$. Secondly, since all the elements of a performance summary are proportions, we are able to assess

---

[1] Such a model is only possible in the controlled experiment here. In practice, no inhibitors would be available for the target and activity values would have to be obtained by hit assays, or perhaps *in silico* docking calculations.

[2] Again, this is feasible in the controlled experiment here. In practice, we will have no inhibitors for the target, and we will have to perform this assessment on the data available for the target's homologues (Tr).

if the differences in corresponding values are statistically significant. This is done using a straightforward hypothesis test on proportions. Given an estimate p of a proportion of N instances, the distribution of proportions is approximately Normal, with mean p and s.d. $\sigma = \sqrt{\frac{p(1-p)}{N}}$. For testing the hypothesis $p_j < p_i$ at a 95% confidence level the critical value from tables of the standard normal distribution is 1.65. That is, if $p_j < 1.65\sigma$ we will say the difference is statistically significant at the 95% level of confidence.

3.3   Results

A summary of the main results obtained is in Fig. 7. The principal points in this tabulation are these: (1) The performance of the system with $B_D = B_1$ is better than with $B_D = B_0$ or simple random draw of molecules; and (2) The differences in proportions for Activity and Similarity are statistically significant at the 95% confidence level. Taken together, these results suggest that the inclusion of symbolic relations can make a significant difference to the performance of the generation of active molecules. We turn next to some questions of relevance to these results:

Qty.	$B_D = B_1$	$B_D = B_0$	Random
$\lvert M \rvert$	5000	5000	5000
$\lvert M' \rvert$	2058	2160	2877
Act	0.47 (0.01)	0.43 (0.01)	0.34 (0.01)
Sim	0.14 (0.01)	0.11 (0.01)	0.00 (0.00)

Fig. 7. Summary of system performance. $B_D = B_1$ denotes that the discriminator has access to both propositional and relational domain-knowledge; $B_D = B_0$ denotes that the discriminator has access to propositional domain-knowledge only. *Random* denotes a random draw of molecules from the unconditional molecule generator G1. M denotes the set of molecules drawn (from the conditional generator, or from the unconditional generator for *Random*). M' denotes the set of acceptable molecules generated in the sample of M molecules (acceptable molecules satisfy molecular constraints defined on molecular properties). *Act* denotes the proportion of M' that are predicted active (the proxy model predicts an pIC50 $\geq$ 6.0); *Sim* denotes the proportion of M' that are similar to active target inhibitors (Tanimoto similarity to active JAK2 inhibitors $>$ 0.75). The numbers in parentheses denote the standard deviation in the corresponding estimate.

Better Discriminators? A question arises on whether the differences in proportions would be different if we had compared against a different discriminator capable of using $B_D = B_0$. Since B_0 is essentially propositional in nature, any of the usual statistical discriminative approaches could be used. We have found replacing the BotGNN with an MLP with hyper-parameter tuning resulted in significantly worse performance than a BotGNN with $B_D = B_1$. We conjecture that similar results will be obtained with other kinds of statistical models. On the question of whether better discriminators are possible for $B_D = B_1$, we note results in [4] show BotGNNs performance to be better than techniques based on propositionalisation or a direct use of ILP. Nevertheless, better BotGNN models than the one used here may be possible. For example, we could construct an activity prediction model for the JAK2 homologues using a state-of-the-art predictor like Chemprop. The prediction of this model could be used as an additional molecular property by the BotGNN.

Better Generators? Our generators are simple language models based on variational auto-encoders. Substantial improvements in generative language models (for example, the sequence models based on attention mechanism [17,18]) suggest that the generator could be much better. In addition, the rejection-sampling approach we use to discard sample instances that fail constraints in B_G is inherently inefficient, and we suggest that the results here should be treated as a baseline. The modular design of our system-design should allow relatively easy testing of alternatives.

Related to the question of discriminators is the role of ILP in this work. ILP is used to include domain-knowledge in the construction of the BotGNN discriminator. How important was this use of ILP? A quantitative answer is difficult, but we are able to provide indirect, qualitative evidence for the utility of ILP by comparison against a recent result on the same data in [9]. That work differs from the one here in the following ways: (a) No symbolic domain-knowledge is used in the discrimination step; and (b) Substantially more computation is involved in developing the final generator–the equivalent of module G2 here–through the use of reinforcement learning (RL). The principal concern in [9] is to generate molecules similar to the active inhibitors for JAK2, and the approach results in 5% of the sampled molecules being similar. The corresponding results here are significantly higher: 14% (with $B_D = B_1$) and 11% ($B_D = B_0$). Both results were obtained with BotGNNs, without requiring the additional episodic training characteristic of RL. Therefore, we believe BotGNNs have played an important role, both in prediction and in easing computation. Since ILP is necessary for the construction of a BotGNN, their importance to the current system-design follows.[3]

Finally, we consider how samples from the conditional generator can be used to identify potential molecules for synthesis and testing in hit-confirmation assays. We propose a selection based on a combination of (predicted) activity and similarity to the existing inhibitors (when these are unavailable, we would have to rely on models constructed with the target's homologues). Using these measures, there are two surprising subsets of molecules. Molecules in S are those that are similar to JAK2 inhibitors (Tanimoto similarity >0.75), but have a low predicted activity (substantially lower than 6.0); and molecules in $\overline{S}$ are significantly different to the JAK2 inhibitors (Tanimoto similarity <0.5), but have a

---

[3] Could we have directly used ILP for constructing the discriminator? Yes, but there is substantial evidence to suggest that the use of ILP through BotGNNs results in better discriminators [4].

high predicted activity (substantially higher that 6.0).[4] For the sample in this paper, $S = \emptyset$. However, $\overline{S} \neq \emptyset$ and can provide interesting candidates for novel inhibitors. We exemplify this with a chemical assessment of 3 elements from $\overline{S}$. This is shown in Fig. 8. Molecule 1562 is identified as a possible candidate for synthesis and hit confirmation.

4   Related Work

Recent applications of AI-based methods have shown promise in transforming otherwise long and expensive drug discovery process [21,22]. The initial studies

ID	Structure	Descriptors	Assessment
551		$Act = 9.12$ $Sim = 0.15$	This molecule has very low similarity to known JAK2 inhibitors. Also none of the groups specific to JAK2 could be identified by the substructure search. Discard this molecule.
1548		$Act = 9.04$ $Sim = 0.22$	This molecule has very low similarity to known JAK2 inhibitors. Also none of the groups specific to JAK2 could be identified by the substructure search. However, the sulfonamide group commonly found in JAK family inhibitors was found to be present (highlighted)
1562		$Act = 9.49$ $Sim = 0.32$	Despite low similarity to existing JAK2 inhibitors, 1562 had one JAK2-selective subgroup and a group common to JAK inhibitors, indicating potential to act as JAK family inhibitor, but the selectivity to JAK2 cannot be confirmed. Possibly interesting new scaffold (highlighted) and worth pursuing further.

Fig. 8. A chemical assessment of possible new JAK2 inhibitors. The molecules are from the sample of molecules from the conditional generator, that are predicted to have high JAK2 activity, and are significantly dissimilar to known inhibitors. The assessment is done by one of the authors (AR), who is a computational chemist. The assessment uses structural features and functional groups identified for the JAK2 site in the literature [9,19,20].

---

[4] A good reason to consider dissimilar molecules is that it allows us to explore more diverse molecules.

were focused on exploring vast yet unexplored chemical space for a better screening library. In [23], a recurrent neural network (RNN) based generative model was trained with a large set of molecules and then fine-tuned with small sets of molecules, which are known to be active against the target. Some other works focus on drug-like property optimization, which helped in biasing the models to generate molecules with specific biological or physical properties of interest. Deep reinforcement learning has been very effective in constructing generative models that could generate novel molecules with the target properties [22,24,25]. The efficiency of these kinds of models to generate chemically valid molecules with optimized properties has improved significantly [9,24]. There are also attempts to build molecule generation models against novel target proteins, where there is a limited ligand dataset for training the model [26].

Recurrent Neural Networks (RNNs) are a popular choice for molecule generation. For example, [27] propose a bidirectional generative RNN, that learns SMILES strings in both directions allowing it to better approximate the data distribution. Attention-based sequence models such as transformers have recently been used for protein-specific molecule generation [28]. There are also generative models, for instance, masked graph modelling in [29], that attempts to learn a distribution over molecular graphs allowing it to generate novel molecule without requiring to dealing with sequences. Some generative modelling techniques for molecule generation are surveyed in [30].

Incorporating domain-knowledge into deep neural networks have shown considerable success over the years. There are several categories of domain knowledge that has been incorporated into learning, primarily referring to the way the knowledge is represented [31]. We present here a brief overview of methods that deal with domain-knowledge represented in a relational form. Possibly the earliest approach to integrating this kind of domain-knowledge is propositionalisation [32,33]. It is a technique to transform a relational representation into a propositional single-table representation where each column in the table corresponds a feature that represents a relation constructed from data and domain-knowledge. Propositionalisation is the core technique in construction of deep relational machines [34–36]: these are multi-layered perceptrons constructed from propositionalised representation of relational data and domain-knowledge. Recent studies on domain-knowledge inclusion include construction of graph neural networks (GNNs) that can learn not only from relational (graph-structured) data but also symbolic domain-knowledge. For instance, the vertex-enrichment approach in [37] constructs an enriched vertex-labelling for graph-structured data instances by treating available domain relations as hyperedges. Another approach transforms the most-specific (bottom) clauses in ILP into a bipartite graph structures [4]. These graphs are called bottom-graphs. A GNN can be learned from these bottom-graphs, thereby allowing a principled way of integrating symbolic domain-knowledge into GNNs. A recent survey presents a more elaborate discussion on various kinds of domain-knowledge and the methods of their inclusion into deep neural networks [38].

5   Concluding Remarks

Incorporating some form of domain-knowledge into AI-based scientific discovery has been emphasised strongly in [39]. A cutting-edge example of this form of scientific discovery is the Robot Scientist [3], the latest generation of which–Eve–is concerned with automating early-stage drug-design. At the heart of Eve is the development of QSAR models. To the best of our knowledge, generation of molecules is restricted to a library of known chemicals; and the use of domain-knowledge is limited to pre-defined features. In this work, we have proposed an approach that can generate novel molecules drawn from the very large space of all possible small molecules, rather than pre-defined libraries; and we use a method that allows the inclusion of relational domain-knowledge. The paper makes the following contributions: (1) We have constructed a complete end-to-end neural-symbolic system that is capable of generating active molecules that may not be in any existing database; (2) We have demonstrated usage of the system on the classic chemical problem on Janus kinase inhibitors. Importantly, working with a computational chemist, we have shown how the system can be used to discover an active molecule based on entirely new scaffolds; (3) The results reaffirm the conclusions from [4] that inclusion of relational domain knowledge through the use of ILP techniques can significantly improve the performance of deep neural networks. To the best of our knowledge, the system-design is the first-of-a-kind combination of neural generative models, techniques from Inductive Logic Programming and symbolic domain-knowledge representation for lead-discovery in early stage drug-design, and is of relevance to platforms like Eve.

Our system design is intentionally modular, to allow "plug-and-play" of discriminators and generators. Indeed, there is already evidence from the construction of language-models that the VAE-based generators we have used could be replaced by transformer-based deep networks. Thus, an immediate next step would be to replace the existing generators with pre-trained language models like GPT-2. We would also expect that molecular constraints would include both hard- and soft-constraints (unlike here, where only hard-constraints are used). This may presage a move to a probabilistic logic representation of the domain-knowledge. On discriminators, BotGNNs continue to be a good choice for inclusion of symbolic knowledge into deep networks, although, as we have pointed out, the BotGNN model could be improved by inclusion as part of domain-knowledge, results from models constructed by programs like Chemprop (the extensive use of fingerprints by such programs is essentially a form of relational information), and also the possibility of inclusion of 3-dimensional constraints (see for example, [40]). Looking beyond the goal of novel molecule generation, a promising line of research concerns the development of schedules for synthesis of new molecules. Of special interest is to consider if techniques for experiment-selection could be adopted for prioritising molecules for synthesis.

Acknowledgements. AS is a Visiting Professorial Fellow at UNSW, Sydney; and a TCS Affiliate Professor. We thank Indrajit Bhattacharya for thoughtful discussions on system-design.

A   Domain-Knowledge Used in Experiments

The domain constraints in B_G are in the form of constraints on acceptable molecules. These constraints are broadly of two kinds: (i) Those concerned with the validity of a generated SMILES string. This involves various syntax-level checks, and is done here by the RDKit molecular modelling package; (ii) Problem-specific constraints on some bulk-properties of the molecule. These are: molecular weight is in the range (200, 700), the octanol-water partition coefficients (logP) must be below 6.0, and the synthetic accessibility score (SAS) must be below 5.0. We use the scoring approach proposed in [41] to compute the SAS of a molecule based on its SMILES representation.

The domain-knowledge in B_D broadly divides into two kinds: (i) Propositional, consisting of molecular properties. These are: molecular weight, logP, SAS, number of hydrogen bond donors (HBD), number of hydrogen bond acceptor (HBA), number of rotatable bonds (NRB), number of aromatic rings (NumRings), Topological Polar Surface Area (TPSA), and quantitative estimation of drug-likeness (QED); (ii) Relational, which is a collection of logic programs (written in Prolog) defining almost 100 relations for various functional groups (such as amide, amine, ether, etc.) and various ring structures (such as aromatic, non-aromatic, etc.). The initial version of these background relations was used within DMax chemistry assistant [11]. More details on this background knowledge can be found in [4, 37].

B   Proxy Model for Predicting Hit Confirmation

A proxy for the results of hit confirmation assays is constructed using the assay results available for the target. This allows us to approximate the results of such assays on molecules for which experimental activity is not available. Of course, such a model is only possible within the controlled experimental design we have adopted, in which information on target inhibition is deliberately not used when constructing the discriminator in D and generator in G2. In practice, if such target-inhibition information is not available, then a proxy model would have to be constructed by other means (for example, using the activity of inhibitors of homologues).

We use the state-of-the-art chemical activity prediction package Chemprop.[5] We train a Chemprop model using the data consisting of JAK2 inhibitors and their pIC50 values. The parameter settings used are: `class-balance` = TRUE, and `epochs` = 100 (all other parameters were set to their default values within Chemprop). Chemprop partitions the data into 80% for training, 10% validation and 10% for test. Chemprop allows the construction of both classification and regression models. The performance of both kinds of models are tabulated below:

---

[5] It is likely that a BotGNN with access to the information in B_D along with the Chemprop prediction would result in a better proxy model. We do not explore this here.

Partition	Classification (AUC)	Regression (RMSE)
Valid	0.9472	0.6515
Test	0.8972	0.6424

The classification model is more robust, since pIC50 values are on a log-scale. We use the classification model for obtaining the results in Fig. 7, and we use the prediction of pIC50 values from the regression model as a proxy for the results of the hit-confirmation assays.

References

1. Schneider, P., et al.: Rethinking drug design in the artificial intelligence era. Nat. Rev. Drug Discov. **19**(5), 353–364 (2020)
2. Gaulton, A., et al.: The ChEMBL database in 2017. Nucleic Acids Res. **45**(D1), D945–D954 (2017)
3. Williams, K., et al.: Cheaper faster drug development validated by the repositioning of drugs against neglected tropical diseases. J. R. Soc. Interface **12**(104), 20141289 (2015)
4. Dash, T., Srinivasan, A., Baskar, A.: Inclusion of domain-knowledge into GNNs using mode-directed inverse entailment. arXiv arXiv:2105.10709 (2021)
5. Muggleton, S.: Inverse entailment and progol. New Gener. Comput. **13**(3), 245–286 (1995). https://doi.org/10.1007/BF03037227
6. Bowman, S.R., Vilnis, L., Vinyals, O., Dai, A.M., Józefowicz, R., Bengio, S.: Generating sentences from a continuous space. In: CoNLL (2016)
7. Hochreiter, S., Schmidhuber, J.: Long short-term memory. Neural Comput. **9**(8), 1735–1780 (1997)
8. Srivastava, R.K., Greff, K., Schmidhuber, J.: Highway networks. arXiv preprint arXiv:1505.00387 (2015)
9. Krishnan, S.R., Bung, N., Bulusu, G., Roy, A.: Accelerating de novo drug design against novel proteins using deep learning. J. Chem. Inf. Model. **61**(2), 621–630 (2021)
10. Landrum, G., et al.: RDKit: open-source cheminformatics (2006). https://www.rdkit.org/docs/index.html
11. Van Craenenbroeck, E., Vandecasteele, H., Dehaspe, L.: DMax's functional group and ring library (2002). https://dtai.cs.kuleuven.be/software/dmax/
12. Stokes, J.M., et al.: A deep learning approach to antibiotic discovery. Cell **180**(4), 688–702 (2020)
13. Srinivasan, A.: The aleph manual (2001). https://www.cs.ox.ac.uk/activities/programinduction/Aleph/aleph.html
14. Kingma, D.P., Welling, M.: Auto-encoding variational Bayes. In: ICLR (2014)
15. Hamilton, W.L., Ying, Z., Leskovec, J.: Inductive representation learning on large graphs. In: NIPS (2017)
16. Kingma, D.P., Ba, J.: Adam: a method for stochastic optimization. In: ICLR (2015)
17. Devlin, J., Chang, M.W., Lee, K., Toutanova, K.: BERT: pre-training of deep bidirectional transformers for language understanding. In: NAACL-HLT (2019)
18. Radford, A., Wu, J., Child, R., Luan, D., Amodei, D., Sutskever, I., et al.: Language models are unsupervised multitask learners. OpenAI Blog **1**(8), 9 (2019)

19. Dymock, B.W., See, C.S.: Inhibitors of JAK2 and JAK3: an update on the patent literature 2010–2012. Exp. Opin. Ther. Pat. **23**(4), 449–501 (2013)
20. Dymock, B.W., Yang, E.G., Chu-Farseeva, Y., Yao, L.: Selective JAK inhibitors. Fut. Med. Chem. **6**(12), 1439–1471 (2014)
21. Mak, K.K., Rao, P.M.: Artificial intelligence in drug development: present status and future prospects. Drug Disc. Today **24**(3), 773–780 (2019)
22. Popova, M., Isayev, O., Tropsha, A.: Deep reinforcement learning for de novo drug design. Sci. Adv. **4**(7), eaap7885 (2018)
23. Segler, M.H., Kogej, T., Tyrchan, C., Waller, M.P.: Generating focused molecule libraries for drug discovery with recurrent neural networks. ACS Cent. Sci. **4**(1), 120–131 (2017)
24. Born, J., Manica, M., Oskooei, A., Cadow, J., Markert, G., Martínez, M.R.: PaccMann^{RL}: de novo generation of hit-like anticancer molecules from transcriptomic data via reinforcement learning. iScience **24**(4), 102269 (2021)
25. Stahl, N., Falkman, G., Karlsson, A., Mathiason, G., Bostrom, J.: Deep reinforcement learning for multiparameter optimization in de novo drug design. J. Chem. Inf. Model. **59**(7), 621–630 (2019)
26. Bung, N., Krishnan, S.R., Bulusu, G., Roy, A.: De novo design of new chemical entities for SARS-CoV-2 using artificial intelligence. Fut. Med. Chem. **13**(6), 575–585 (2021)
27. Grisoni, F., Moret, M., Lingwood, R., Schneider, G.: Bidirectional molecule generation with recurrent neural networks. J. Chem. Inf. Model. **60**(3), 1175–1183 (2020)
28. Grechishnikova, D.: Transformer neural network for protein-specific de novo drug generation as a machine translation problem. Sci. Rep. **11**(1), 1–13 (2021)
29. Mahmood, O., Mansimov, E., Bonneau, R., Cho, K.: Masked graph modeling for molecule generation. Nat. Commun. **12**(1), 1–12 (2021)
30. Schwalbe-Koda, D., Gómez-Bombarelli, R.: Generative models for automatic chemical design. In: Schütt, K.T., Chmiela, S., von Lilienfeld, O.A., Tkatchenko, A., Tsuda, K., Müller, K.-R. (eds.) Machine Learning Meets Quantum Physics. LNP, vol. 968, pp. 445–467. Springer, Cham (2020). https://doi.org/10.1007/978-3-030-40245-7_21
31. Dash, T., Chitlangia, S., Ahuja, A., Srinivasan, A.: Incorporating domain knowledge into deep neural networks. arXiv arXiv:2103.00180 (2021)
32. Lavrač, N., Džeroski, S., Grobelnik, M.: Learning nonrecursive definitions of relations with LINUS. In: Kodratoff, Y. (ed.) EWSL 1991. LNCS, vol. 482, pp. 265–281. Springer, Heidelberg (1991). https://doi.org/10.1007/BFb0017020
33. França, M.V.M., Zaverucha, G., d'Avila Garcez, A.S.: Fast relational learning using bottom clause propositionalization with artificial neural networks. Mach. Learn. **94**(1), 81–104 (2013). https://doi.org/10.1007/s10994-013-5392-1
34. Dash, T., Srinivasan, A., Vig, L., Orhobor, O.I., King, R.D.: Large-scale assessment of deep relational machines. In: Riguzzi, F., Bellodi, E., Zese, R. (eds.) ILP 2018. LNCS (LNAI), vol. 11105, pp. 22–37. Springer, Cham (2018). https://doi.org/10.1007/978-3-319-99960-9_2
35. Lodhi, H.: Deep relational machines. In: Lee, M., Hirose, A., Hou, Z.-G., Kil, R.M. (eds.) ICONIP 2013. LNCS, vol. 8227, pp. 212–219. Springer, Heidelberg (2013). https://doi.org/10.1007/978-3-642-42042-9_27
36. Dash, T., Srinivasan, A., Joshi, R.S., Baskar, A.: Discrete stochastic search and its application to feature-selection for deep relational machines. In: Tetko, I.V., Kůrková, V., Karpov, P., Theis, F. (eds.) ICANN 2019. LNCS, vol. 11728, pp. 29–45. Springer, Cham (2019). https://doi.org/10.1007/978-3-030-30484-3_3

37. Dash, T., Srinivasan, A., Vig, L.: Incorporating symbolic domain knowledge into graph neural networks. Mach. Learn. **110**(7), 1609–1636 (2021). https://doi.org/10.1007/s10994-021-05966-z
38. Dash, T., Chitlangia, S., Ahuja, A., Srinivasan, A.: How to tell deep neural networks what we know. arXiv arXiv:2107.10295 (2021)
39. Stevens, R., Taylor, V., Nichols, J., Maccabe, A.B., Yelick, K., Brown, D.: AI for science. Technical report, Argonne National Lab. (ANL), Argonne, IL (United States) (2020)
40. Kaalia, R., Srinivasan, A., Kumar, A., Ghosh, I.: ILP-assisted de novo drug design. Mach. Learn. **103**(3), 309–341 (2016)
41. Ertl, P., Schuffenhauer, A.: Estimation of synthetic accessibility score of drug-like molecules based on molecular complexity and fragment contributions. J. Cheminform. **1**(1), 1–11 (2009)

Non-parametric Learning of Embeddings for Relational Data Using Gaifman Locality Theorem

Devendra Singh Dhami[1,2(✉)], Siwen Yan[2], Gautam Kunapuli[3],
and Sriraam Natarajan[2]

[1] Technical University of Darmstadt, Darmstadt, Germany
`devendra.dhami@cs.tu-darmstadt.de`
[2] University of Texas at Dallas, Richardson, USA
`{siwen.yan,sriraam.natarajan}@utdallas.edu`
[3] Verisk Analytics, New Jersey, USA
`gautam.kunapuli@verisk.org`

Abstract. We consider the problem of full model learning from relational data. To this effect, we construct embeddings using symbolic trees learned in a non-parametric manner. The trees are treated as a decision-list of first order rules that are then partially grounded and counted over local neighborhoods of a Gaifman graph to obtain the feature representations. We propose the first method for learning these relational features using a Gaifman graph by using relational tree distances. Our empirical evaluation on real data sets demonstrates the superiority of our approach over handcrafted rules, classical rule-learning approaches, the state-of-the-art relational learning methods and embedding methods.

Keywords: Statistical relational learning · Gaifman locality theorem · Embeddings · Relational density estimation

1 Introduction

Learning embeddings of large knowledge bases has become a necessity due to the importance of reasoning about objects, their attributes and relations in large graphs. Statistical Relational AI (StaRAI) [9,25] has the ability to learn and reason with multi-relational data in the presence of uncertainty. A scalable approach, Discriminative Gaifman Model, via *Gaifman networks* was proposed recently [23] that exploits *Gaifman's locality theorem* [8]: every first-order sentence is equivalent to a boolean combination of sentences over local entity neighborhoods of the Gaifman graph. Relational Gaifman models seek to identify locally-connected relational neighborhoods within knowledge bases for effective representation, learning and inference. While effective, discriminative Gaifman Models used relational features that were <u>hand crafted rather than learned</u>, i.e., there was *no structure learning*. Consequently, their applicability and adaptability can become severely limiting.

© Springer Nature Switzerland AG 2022
N. Katzouris and A. Artikis (Eds.): ILP 2021, LNAI 13191, pp. 95–110, 2022.
https://doi.org/10.1007/978-3-030-97454-1_7

Motivated by this limitation, we present the *first* set of approaches for relational embeddings that are guided by Gaifman locality theorem. Given that we are in a *symbolic* setting, these approaches have the distinct advantage of being both **explainable** and **interpretable**. Specifically, we propose and investigate three approaches: (1) As suggested by Niepert [23], we employ Inductive Logic Programming (ILP) to learn discriminative first-order rules. These (conjunctive) rules can then be treated as Boolean relational features. (2) Inspired by the success of random walks in deep relational models [11], we employ relational random walks (RRWs) as relational features. To this effect, we developed our own random walk implementation built on an underlying ILP engine as against a relational database as with the original work. (3) Finally, we use first-order trees learned via relational one-class classification (relOCC [14]); specifically, each path from root to leaf of a first-order trees is considered a relational feature. That is, the structure is captured by the *"relational density estimate"*, which is learned from data as a set of first-order trees. The motivation behind using a density estimation technique to learn the relational features is that *learning first order rules for positives and sampled negatives independently results in a better utilization of the search space thereby learning better discriminative features.*

Given these relational features, that can be grounded based on Gaifman's locality theorem, one could apply traditional discriminative learning algorithms such as Gradient Boosting and Logistic Regression. This allows for the embedding creation method to be decoupled from the underlying classifier.

We consider the challenging problem of structure learning to exploit the importance of local neighborhoods in knowledge graphs. Our key contributions are: (1) We present the **first method for learning relational embeddings** for reasoning over large graphs using Gaifman's locality theorem. (2) We adapt a recently developed relational learning method for constructing relational features (relOCC). (3) We adapt well-known first-order rule learners for learning local neighborhood representations (ILP, RRWs). (4) We combine these relational features with discriminative classifiers to learn discriminative Gaifman models. (5) We demonstrate that **combining the more novel first-order trees with a discriminative classifier is more effective in learning on large graphs** compared to a standard ILP learner. Specifically **our novelty lies in the fact that we are learning rules for the positive and negative instances** separately using density estimation that allows for better discrimination. An important side-effect is that these rules are **explainable** in contrast to many traditional embedding methods. (6) Our experiments reveal an important characteristic of our approach: **high recall without sacrificing precision** in both medical and imbalanced data sets.

2   Background and Related Work

Discriminative Gaifman Models: The Gaifman graph $\mathcal{G}$ of a knowledge base $\mathcal{B}$ is an **undirected graph**, where the nodes are the entities $e \in \mathcal{D}$. $\mathcal{G}$ contains edges joining two nodes only if the entities a and b corresponding to those nodes

```
TransSubstr(Pravastatin, BileSaltExportPump)
TransInhib(Simvastatin, MultidrugResistProtein1)
EnzInhib(Pravastatin, CytochromeP4502C9)
EnzSubstr(Acetaminophen, CytochromeP4502C9)
EnzInhib(Simvastatin, CytochromeP4502C9)
```

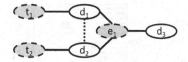

Fig. 1. An example Gaifman graph for a drug-drug interaction (DDI) knowledge base. Here, $d_1 = $ Pravastatin, $d_2 = $ Simvastatin, $d_3 = $ Acetaminophen, $t_1 = $ BileSaltExportPump, $t_2 = $ MultidrugResistProtein1 and $e_1 = $ Cytochrome P4502C9. The Gaifman graph connects entities that appear in a relationship tuple; the dotted line between d_1 and d_2 is the link we want to predict.

are present in a relation together $R(\ldots, a, \ldots, b, \ldots) \in \mathcal{B}$. $\mathcal{G}$ can be used to easily identify co-occurrences (or lack thereof) among every pair of entities in $\mathcal{B}$. Figure 1 shows a knowledge-base fragment and the corresponding Gaifman graph for a drug-drug interaction (DDI) domain. Given entities (drugs, enzymes, transporters) and their relationships, the underlying learning task is to predict if two drugs interact. The dotted line is the target, and the task is **link prediction**.

The distance $d(a, b)$ between two nodes $(a, b) \in \mathcal{G}$ is the minimum number of hops required to reach b from a. The r-neighborhood of a node $a \in \mathcal{G}$ is the set of all nodes that are at most a distance r from a in the Gaifman graph: $N_r^{\mathcal{G}}(a) = \{\bar{a} \in \mathcal{G} \mid d(a, \bar{a}) \leq r\}$. When a first-order rule $\varphi(x)$ is relativized by the neighborhood of the free variable x, the resulting first-order rule $\psi^{N_r(x)}(x)$ is called r-local. A Gaifman neighborhood can be thought of as representing second-order proximity between nodes. The interpretation is that nodes with shared neighbors are more likely to be similar and more likely to have a link between them. Discriminative Gaifman Models (DGMs, [23]) are relational models that exploit structural features of a local neighborhood. These structural features are aggregated from locally-sampled neighborhoods, and the aggregation is based on the *Gaifman locality theorem* [8] stated as: *every first-order sentence is logically equivalent to a Boolean combination of basic r-local sentences.*

For example, if querying about the drug d_1 in Fig. 1, a search within the 1-neighborhood of e_1 (say), that is $\{t_1, e_1\}$ is more relevant than searching through the complete graph, which can be significantly computationally inefficient.

Representation Learning: Learning embeddings is well-studied and can be categorized based on the underlying approaches: matrix factorization, deep learning, edge reconstruction, graph kernels and generative models [3]. In general, Gaifman models tend to scale better than many such approaches to higher-arity relations and target-query complexity owing to their local view and incorporation of count-based features as opposed to the global view of (say) neural network or factorization methods which are forced to look at the entire graph to construct effective embeddings. Recent work has also included the study of holographic embeddings [21], which measure similarity through circular correlation and hyperbolic embeddings [22], which measure similarity and construct embeddings in a hyperbolic space. While highly effective, a key drawback of these approaches is their inability to incorporate new data, often requiring training of a new model.

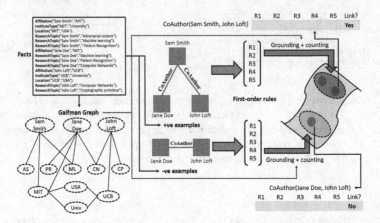

Fig. 2. An overview of learning embeddings using Gaifman locality theorem.

Relational and Structure Learning: One of the most important tasks in relational learning is that of *link prediction* which determines whether a relation (link) exists between entities based on the given relational database [27]. Structure learning has been a well-studied problem in graphical models and can be defined as the problem of identifying a graph structure to principally summarize dependencies in a data set and can be interpreted as learning probabilistic (relational) rules from data [4,13].

3   Gaifman-Guided Learning of Relational Embeddings

> **Given:** Knowledge base $\mathcal{B}$, facts F_s, and its corresponding Gaifman graph $\mathcal{G}$;
> **Output:** A discriminative model $\mathcal{M}$ that is trained for a particular link prediction task $\mathcal{T}$;
> **To-Do:** Construct a set of relational embeddings (features) Φ, and train a discriminative learner to predict $\mathcal{T}$.

We present the **first set of model learning algorithms that employs Gaifman local graphs.** Our approach, *Learning Gaifman-based relational Embeddings* (LGE), (1) constructs (explainable) rules Φ that form the base set of relational features. This is akin to structure learning in Statistical Relational AI [25] models; (2) instantiates rules (grounding) and performs counting based on task $\mathcal{T}$ to construct propositional features (embeddings) $\mathcal{F}$; and finally, (3) learns a discriminative classifier with $\mathcal{F}$. Figure 2 shows an overview of our method.

We represent predicates and constants by capitialized letters and variables by small letters. For example, in our DDI domain, Interacts(d_1, "Metformin") represents a partially grounded example where Interacts is the predicate, d_1 is a variable and "Metformin" is a constant.

Given a knowledge base $\mathcal{B}$, the Gaifman graph $\mathcal{G}$ is obtained by instantiating the entities that are connected by an edge type (relation) together in the form $R(e_1, e_2)$, that is, $relation(type_1, type_2)$. Gaifman neighborhood generation relies on three parameters: (1) r, the depth of neighborhood when counting, (2) k, the number of neighbors to sample, and (3) w, the number of neighborhoods to be generated. The relation (link) to be predicted, defined by the target predicate, forms the set of positive examples. We make the *closed-world assumption*, that is, unobserved edges in the graphs are considered to be negative examples. Hence, the negative examples are constructed by taking the Cartesian product of the entire entity set with itself and removing the examples which are present in the positive example set. Following standard ILP terminology, each relational example also has *facts* associated with it, which are the ground predicates in $\mathcal{B}$ that describe relational example, its attributes and relationships. All such facts are denoted F_s.

ILP for Rule Extraction: Our first solution is inspired by the use of an Inductive Logic Programming (ILP) style learning method. This method learns a set of discriminative Horn clauses. Specifically, we use an ILP system called WILL [29] to learn the first-order rules as features[1]. This ILP system first selects an example from the set of all examples and then finds a clause (rule) that *best covers* the examples. Ideal coverage means *all* positive examples and *no* negative examples which can easily overfit. To avoid overfitting, we obtain the *best covering* which is the most general clause that maximizes the difference between the number of positive and negative examples covered. Each *best covering* clause becomes a first-order rule in our model. The examples covered by the clause are then removed and the process is repeated till a stopping criterion (e.g., maximum of n rules) is satisfied. Some possible stopping conditions are: (1) a certain number of examples are covered by the currently extracted set of rules, or (2) we have extracted a maximum number of rules/clauses. Note that when a stopping criterion requires n rules to be extracted, it is sometimes possible to extract $m < n$ rules that cover the examples adequately. Contrarily, if the first condition is specified and the expected coverage is very high, it may require a very large number of rules to be extracted before termination. Thus, in practice, a combination of both conditions is employed. The key advantage of this method is that these rules are both *interpretable* and *explainable*.

Features via Relational Random Walks: It is easy to view a relation $R(e_1, e_2)$ as an edge between two entity type nodes $e_1 \xrightarrow{R} e_2$ in a graph. A relational random walk (RW) through a graph is a chain of such edges corresponding to a conjunction of predicates. For a random walk to be semantically sound, we should ensure that the input type (domain) of the $i + 1$-th predicate is same as output type (range) of the i-th predicate. Example RW for drug-discovery is:

```
Interacts(d0, d3) ⇐ TargetInhib(d0, t0) ∧ _TargetInhib(t0, d1)
∧TransporterSubstr(d1, t2) ∧ _TransporterInhib(t2, d3).
```

---

[1] Any ILP learner such as Aleph [26] or PROGOL [19] can be used.

This is a semantically sound random walk as it is possible to chain the second argument of each predicate to the first argument of the succeeding predicate. This random walk also contains *inverse predicates* (prefixed by an underscore, such as _Transporter). Inverse predicates are distinct from their corresponding predicates as their arguments are *reversed*. Thus, this relational random walk chains the first variable d0 in the target predicate Interacts(d0, d3) with the second variable d3. The RW chain represents a relational feature and constitutes a random local structure:

$$d0 \xrightarrow{\text{TargetInhibitor}} t0 \xrightarrow{\text{\_TargetInhibitor}} \cdots$$
$$d1 \xrightarrow{\text{TransporterSubstrate}} t2 \xrightarrow{\text{\_TransporterInhib}} d3.$$

Thus, to construct a relational random walk, only the schema describing the knowledge base is required. We adapt path-constrained random walks (PCRW, [16]) to construct relational random walks. The algorithm starts at the first entity in the target relation, and makes a walk over the (parameterized) graph to end at the second entity present in the target relation. One limitation of PCRW is that the random walks are only performed over binary relations. Consequently, we employ *our own implementation that uses a more general predicate representation that can learn with arbitrary n-ary relations*. This implementation is built on top of the WILL system [29] that we used in our first step. We constrain the length of the random walks to avoid/prevent overfitting.

Density Estimation via relOCC for Rule Learning: A common issue in many tasks, is that only the few "positive" instances of a relation are annotated due to severe class imbalance (exponentially many negatives). This is because the number of instances where the relation does not hold is very large, and annotation can be prohibitively expensive. Learning with highly imbalanced data sets requires reasoning over just the positive instances, commonly referred to as *one-class classification* (OCC). Intuitively, if we can construct a relational one-class classifier describing the positive examples, then rules characterizing this classifier are essentially features that describe positive examples. One-class classification typically requires a *distance measure* to characterize the density of the positive class. While, for standard vector and matrix data, many different distance measures exist, the issue is far more challenging for relational data, and depends on the underlying representation of the classifier.

Suppose we use an off-the-shelf learner to learn first-order trees [1] to describe each class in the data. Such first-order trees form a decision-list of logical rules (similar to ILP but with negations). These trees can then be used to compute the *relational distance* between a pair of examples x_1 and x_2, which are instances of the target predicate R(e$_1$, e$_2$) as in [14]. For a learned tree i:

$$\mathcal{RD}_i(x_1, x_2) = \begin{cases} 0, & \text{LCA}(x_1, x_2) \text{ is leaf;} \\ e^{-\lambda \cdot \text{depth}(\text{LCA}(x_1, x_2))}, & \text{otherwise,} \end{cases} \tag{1}$$

where LCA is the *least common ancestor* of examples x_1, x_2. Typically more than one tree is learned, and the one-class classifier is a weighted combination of these trees. The trees in one-class classifier are learned iteratively by updating the distance measure. Then, the overall distance function is simply the weighted combination of the individual tree-level distances: $\mathcal{CD}(x_1, x_2) = \sum_i \beta_i \mathcal{RD}_i(x_1, x_2)$ where β_i is the weight of the ith tree and $\sum_i \beta_i = 1, \beta_i \geq 0$. The non-parametric function $\mathcal{CD}(\cdot, \cdot)$ is a relational distance measure learned on the data.

The distance function can then be used to compute the density estimate for a new relational example z as a weighted combination of the distance of z from all training examples x_j, $E(z \notin \texttt{class}) = \sum_j \alpha_j \mathcal{CD}(x_j, z)$, where α_j is the weight of the labeled example x_j and $\sum \alpha_j = 1, \alpha_j \geq 0$. Note that expectation above is for $z \notin \texttt{class}$, since the likelihood of class membership of z is inversely proportional to its distance from the training examples describing that $\texttt{class}$.

We learn a tree-based distance iteratively [14] to introduce new relational features that perform one-class classification. The left-most path in each relational tree is a conjunction of predicates with no negation, that is, a clause, which can be used as a relational feature. This makes the model more tractable but any path can be used if negation can be handled. Most importantly, *this allows for an interpretation similar to a Horn clause thus making the rules both interpretable and explainable.* We present the algorithm for learning rules using relOCC and generating embeddings externally[2]. Some example rules (first 2 rules for +ve examples and rest for -ve examples) learned for DDI are:

1. EnzymeInducer(A, C), EnzymeSubstrate(B, C), EnzymeInducer(B, D), EnzymeInducer(A, D) $\implies$ Interacts(A,B)   2. EnzymeSubstrate(A, C), EnzymeSubstrate(B, C), TransporterInducer(A, D) $\implies$ Interacts(A,B)   3. EnzymeInhibitor(A, C), Enzyme(C, B), TransporterInhibitor(A, D) $\implies$ Interacts(A,B)   4. TargetAgonist(B, C), TransporterSubstrate(A, D), EnzymeSubstrate(B, E), EnzymeSubstrate(A, E) $\implies$ Interacts(A,B)

Ground Features from Relational Rules: Once extracted, relational rules are grounded and the number of satisfied groundings are aggregated . While several *feature aggregations* exist, we use *counts* as they have been previously successful in many statistical relational models [11,15]. For every predicate $\varphi \in \Phi$, the first and last entity are instantiated corresponding to the tuples satisfying the query (since it is a link prediction task, a query variable is of the type $q(e_1, e_2)$) to give a partially grounded predicate). For example, in Fig. 1, let the positive example be $Interacts(Pravastatin, Simvastatin)$. For the predicate $EnzymeInhib(d_0, t_0) \wedge \_EnzymeInhib(t_0, d_1)$, and the substitution $\{d_0/Pravastatin, d_1/Simvastatin\}$, we obtain the *partially-grounded* predicate $EnzymeInhib(Pravastatin, t_0) \wedge \_EnzymeInhib(t_0, Simvastatin)$.

Next, all the predicates that completely satisfy this partially grounded feature are obtained. The features for each query variable are then obtained as counts of the number of satisfied groundings that are also

---

[2] https://bit.ly/3jp9NA2.

present in the neighborhood of the query entities in the Gaifman graph $\mathcal{G}$. For example, in Fig. 1, if $EnzymeInhib(Pravastatin, CP4502C9) \wedge$ $\_EnzymeInhib(CP4502C9, Simvastatin)$ satisfies the given predicate, since $CP4502C9$ (CP = Cytochrome) is present in the Gaifman neighborhood of $Pravastatin$ (as well as $Simvastatin$), the count of the predicate is increased by 1. Thus, for every query variable q we obtain a propositional feature $f = [f_1, ..., f_{|\Phi|}]$ of length $|\Phi|$:

$$f_i = \begin{cases} |\psi^{N_r(q)}(q)|, & \text{if } q(e_1, e_2) \text{partially grounds } \Phi_i, \\ 0, & \text{otherwise.} \end{cases} \tag{2}$$

Recall that ψ refers to the relativized first-order formula, and consequently $\psi^{N_r(q)}(q)$ is the r-local formula for a neighborhood N of depth r. We count the number of entities in the satisfied grounded features that are also satisfied in the neighborhood structure of the Gaifman graph, thus constructing a propositionalized data set of $|pos| \times w$ +ve examples and $|neg| \times w$ -ve examples.

Learning a Discriminative Model: After learning the propositional features, any standard classifier can be used for link prediction. One could potentially use any classifier[3]. For our experiments, we employ gradient-boosting and logistic regression. The classification algorithm itself is not a key contribution of our work and as we demonstrate empirically next, any standard classifier will often suffice for learning an effective model.

Effectiveness of relOCC in Learning Structure: The motivation behind using a relational density estimation technique (relOCC) for rule learning is that *learning independently from different densities separately can potentially result in better discrimination in the learned feature space.*

The use of a relational one-class classifier [14] that classifies positive examples based on a distance metric ensures that positive examples are projected close to each other in the new feature space. Since we hypothesize that learning from the example densities separately and independently results in a better discriminative behavior, we go a step further and also learn a relational one class classifier for the negative relational examples. This results in negative examples being projected close to each other in the new feature space and further from positive examples.

An added advantage of using such a rule learning procedure to obtain the propositional examples is that the learned examples directly represent the query

Table 1. Evaluation domains and their properties.

Data set	#Entities	#Relations	#Pos	#Neg	#RW rules	#ILP rules	#relOCC rules
DDI	355	15	2832	3188	68	36	25
PPI	797	7	1915	1915	42	5	15
NELL Sports	4147	6	300	600	36	15	13
Financial NLP	650	7	186	1029	222	6	25
ICML CoAuthor	558	5	155	6498	7	15	7

---

[3] https://bit.ly/3jp9NA2.

variable. *The link prediction problem is thus reduced to a prediction problem in the new feature space.* This makes the approach independent of the learning algorithm allowing for flexibility of the use of any learning algorithm.

4 Experiments

We have made our code available at https://bit.ly/2YYHZZ4. We aim to answer the following questions: **Q1:** How do different structure learning strategies compare across diverse domains from different applications? **Q2:** How do different structure learning strategies impact performance in the presence of high class imbalance? **Q3:** What are effects of Gaifman locality parameters r, w and k? **Q4:** How does our method compare with state-of the art probabilistic ILP systems? **Q5:** How does our method compare with state-of the art relational embedding methods? **Q6:** How does our method compare with different SOTA rule learning methods including Niepert's original approach [23] of using hand-crafted rules?

Data Sets: We consider 5 *real-world relational data sets* (Table 1). **Drug-Drug Interactions (DDI)** [6] consists of 78 drugs obtained from DrugBank and the target is *interactions* between drug entities. **Protein-Protein Interactions (PPI)** [15] is obtained from Alchemy and the target is *interaction* relation between two protein entities. **NELL Sports** was generated by the Never Ending Language Learner [18] consisting of information about players and teams. The task is to predict whether a team plays a particular sport i.e. *teamplayssport*. **Financial NLP** is obtained by extracting information from *SEC Form S-1* documents and the target is to predict whether a word occurs in a given sentence i.e. the relation *sentenceContainsTarget*. **ICML Co-Author** is obtained by mining publication data from ICML 2018 and the target is the *CoAuthor* relation between persons.

Baselines (Statistical Relational Learning Methods): We compare the performance of our method with 3 state-of-the-art SRL methods. **RDN-Boost** [20] and **MLN-Boost** [13]: are SRL models that propose functional gradient boosting of relational dependency networks (RDNs) and Markov logic networks. **Tuffy** [24]: is an MLN learning and inference engine using RDBMS to obtain a solution to the scalability problems of the underlying networks.

Baselines (Relational Embedding Methods): We compare the performance of our method with 9 relational embedding methods. The first 4 methods use AmpliGraph library[4] and the last 4 use PyKEEN python package[5]. **ConvE** [5]: uses convolutions over embeddings and fully connected layers. **ComplEx** [28]: uses a latent factorization based approach for the problem of link prediction. **DistMult** [31]: learns representations of entities and relations as low-dimensional vectors and bilinear and/or linear mapping functions. **HolE** [21]: uses circular correlation of the vector representations of entities to create holographic embeddings. **SimplE** [12]: adapts the concept of Canonical Polyadic

---

[4] https://github.com/Accenture/AmpliGraph.
[5] https://github.com/pykeen/pykeen.

decomposition to learn two dependent embeddings for each entity and relation. We use the tensorflow implementation[6]. **TransE/H/R/D** [2,10,17,30]: are different translation based relational embedding methods.

Baselines (Rule Learning Methods): We compare our method to 3 rule learning methods. **Handcrafted rules (Gaifman)** [23]: consists of handwritten rules that are then simply enumerated following the Gaifman locality. **Neural LP** [32]: learns the first-order rules by ion an end-to-end differentiable model. We use author provided code[7] with #rules learned = 10. **metapath2vec** [7]: generates random walks with user defined metapaths and uses a skip-gram model to generate embeddings. We use metapath2vec in Stellargraph[8] package.

Table 2. Comparison against SRL methods for the relational domains.

Data set	Methods	Accuracy		Recall		F1		AUC-ROC		AUC-PR	
		LR	GB	LR	GB	LR	GB	LR	GB	LR	GB
DDI	RW	0.657	0.669	0.469	0.530	0.564	0.602	0.647	0.662	0.581	0.593
	ILP	0.696	0.774	0.467	0.674	0.592	0.729	0.684	0.767	0.710	0.765
	relOCC	0.860	**0.897**	0.939	**0.991**	0.864	**0.901**	0.864	**0.902**	0.797	**0.853**
	Gaifman	0.534	0.771	0.469	0.658	0.564	0.691	0.672	0.697	0.581	0.710
	MLN-Boost	0.638		0.504		0.618		0.798		0.784	
	RDN-Boost	0.755		0.662		0.718		0.828		0.831	
PPI	RW	0.700	**0.785**	0.586	0.707	0.661	0.767	0.699	**0.785**	0.651	**0.740**
	ILP	0.613	0.661	0.397	0.553	0.506	0.620	0.613	0.661	0.579	0.614
	relOCC	0.727	0.733	0.996	**0.999**	0.785	**0.789**	0.727	0.733	0.647	0.652
	Gaifman	0.608	0.652	0.382	0.524	0.499	0.606	0.613	0.654	0.591	0.619
	MLN-Boost	0.548		0.453		0.571		0.743		0.733	
	RDN-Boost	0.671		0.615		0.652		0.728		**0.740**	
NELL Sports	RW	0.783	0.822	0.414	0.569	0.569	0.689	0.696	0.762	0.565	0.594
	ILP	0.782	0.824	0.431	0.590	0.578	0.699	0.699	0.769	0.530	0.564
	relOCC	0.793	**0.833**	0.431	0.6	0.59	**0.731**	0.708	0.778	0.574	0.643
	Gaifman	0.756	0.780	0.314	0.485	0.465	0.597	0.648	0.707	0.512	0.549
	MLN-Boost	0.605		0.533		0.667		**0.894**		**0.853**	
	RDN-Boost	0.812		**0.756**		0.714		0.884		0.834	
Financial NLP	RW	0.833	0.833	0.0	0.0	0.0	0.0	0.5	0.5	0.168	0.168
	ILP	0.838	0.921	0.068	0.633	0.112	0.727	0.530	0.806	0.200	0.6023
	relOCC	0.965	0.967	0.788	0.800	0.882	0.889	0.867	0.879	0.826	0.833
	Gaifman	0.827	0.914	0.0	0.59	0.0	0.705	0.5	0.787	0.173	0.587
	MLN-Boost	0.928		0.764		0.757		**0.989**		0.807	
	RDN-Boost	**0.975**		**0.963**		**0.929**		**0.989**		**0.901**	
ICML CoAuthor	RW	0.977	0.977	0.0	0.0	0.0	0.0	0.5	0.5	0.023	0.023
	ILP	0.983	0.985	0.272	0.339	0.427	0.506	0.636	0.669	0.289	0.356
	relOCC	0.986	**0.997**	0.346	0.386	0.517	**0.557**	0.653	**0.693**	0.370	**0.40**
	Gaifman	0.981	0.984	0.100	0.327	0.174	0.493	0.529	0.664	0.127	0.343
	MLN-Boost	0.938		0.326		0.214		0.294		0.210	
	RDN-Boost	0.940		**0.434**		0.231		0.153		0.157	

---

[6] https://github.com/Mehran-k/SimplE.

[7] https://github.com/fanyangxyz/Neural-LP.

[8] https://pypi.org/project/stellargraph/.

Results: Table 1 also shows the number of relational rules learned by different techniques. Table 2 presents the results for all the relational domains (5-fold cross validation) with logistic regression (LR) and gradient boosting (GB)[9]. All experiments were run with parameter values $r = 1$, $k = 10$ and $w = 5$.

[Q1] Comparing different structure learning strategies: We compare the structure learning method by relOCC to two commonly used relational rule learning techniques, relational random walks and inductive logic programming and the results are shown in Table 2. We note that relOCC outperforms the baselines ILP and relational RWs methods across a majority of the domains. This is expected since relOCC considers the density of the positive and negative examples separately, as opposed to the other rule learning methods, allowing the features it generates to discriminate better. This answers **Q1**.

[Q2] Effect of class imbalance: Imbalanced data sets are difficult to learn from for the classical machine learning algorithms since it is assumed that the number of examples are generally equally distributed among the classes to be predicted. We consider the ICML CoAuthor (neg-to-pos ratio of 42:1) data set which is highly imbalanced and Financial NLP (neg-to-pos ratio of 6:1) data set which is relatively imbalanced; consequently, we report AUC-PR. In both domains, AUC-PR for relOCC outperforms the other structure-learning methods by a large margin. Random walk rules, in particular, cause all the examples to be classified as negative, resulting in recall and F1-scores of 0 in both domains. Thus, we can answer **Q2**: highly-imbalanced domains benefit from density-estimation-based structure learning. This also verifies our hypothesis: *learning from the example densities separately and independently results in a better discriminative behavior.*

[Q3] Effect of locality parameters: Figure 3 shows the effects of varying r (depth of neighborhoods), k (number of neighbors) and w (number of neighborhoods) on the DDI data set. Generally, k does not affect performance significantly, but increasing r causes recall report to drop sharply. This is because, with $r = 1$, entities in the query neighborhood are more tightly coupled with entities in the query variables. This parametric sensitivity analysis addresses **Q3**. Also, another important takeaway is that relOCC rules exhibit *high clinically-relevant recall (≈ 1) on medical data sets*: DDI and PPI. This has considerable implications for bioinformatics domains as recall is the most important metric; this is because a false negative (such as a misdiagnosis) results in much more serious consequences [6] than a false positive. Finally, from Fig. 3 (right), we note that varying r and k does not affect training time, as these parameters do not affect the search space. However, increasing w increases the run time since the size of the neighborhood graph to be searched increases.

---

[9] For performance of algorithms other than LR and GB see https://bit.ly/3jp9NA2.

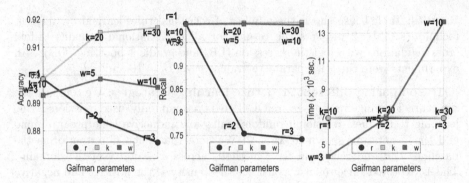

Fig. 3. (left) Accuracy, (middle) recall and (right) running time for various values of r, k and w for the DDI domain. For varying r: $w=5$ and $k=10$, for varying w: $r = 1$ and $k = 10$ and for varying k: $w = 5$ and $r = 1$.

[Q4] Comparison with PILP systems: *Our core contribution is end-to-end learning of Gaifman models that requires only data and no domain knowledge and thus we focus on comparison with a full model learning methods of MLN-Boost and RDN-Boost.* Table 2 shows that our method outperforms MLN-Boost by a significant margin and outperforms/is comparable to the performance of RDN-Boost in 4 out of 5 domains. We also note that Tuffy[10] could not effectively scale to the amount of data that we have used in our learning framework, and could not learn the structure. Instead, we tried using the ILP rules that we learned, and learned the weights. In this case as well, Tuffy could not complete training after a few hours. To put this in perspective, we sampled 10% data from all the data sets and the results for the same are presented in Fig. 4 which shows that our method is significantly better than Tuffy on both balanced and unbalanced data sets. Figure 4c shows the time taken by our method as compared to Tuffy on the sampled data set. Since Tuffy does not support structure learning i.e.

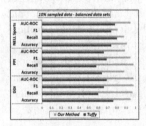

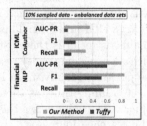

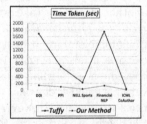

(a) Comparison of our method with Tuffy on balanced data sets.

(b) Comparison of our method with Tuffy on unbalanced data sets.

(c) Comparison of running times of our method and Tuffy.

Fig. 4. Comparison of our method and Tuffy on 10% sampled data sets.

---

[10] We also tried other systems: Alchemy, Problog, ProbCog.

rule learning, in order to keep the comparisons fair, we use the rules learned by relOCC, convert them into the Tuffy format and run the inference. Thus, for Tuffy we report only the inference time and compare it with the inference time of our method (grounding + machine learning algorithm). We are able to perform the inference far quicker than compared to Tuffy. Thus, to answer **Q4**, we outperform several SOTA probabilistic ILP methods across domains.

[Q5] Comparison with relational embedding models: To answer **Q5**, we compare against 9 state-of-the-art relational embedding methods. Table 3 shows that our method outperforms all relational embeddings by a huge margin especially in the case of imbalanced data sets i.e. Financial NLP and ICML CoAuthor. These results show the importance of constructing first order rules from the given data instead of directly using the triples since the inherent structure of the underlying graph can be captured by our method.

[Q6] Comparison with rule learning methods: Finally, to answer **Q6**, we compared against 2 state-of-the-art rule learning methods, NeuralLP and metapath2vec, and hand-written rules. For the handwritten rules, we created generic relational features as suggested by Niepert and of the form: $r(e1, e2)$; $r(e2, e1)$; $\exists x\ r(x, e)$, $\exists x\ r(e, x)$, $\exists x\ r(e1, x) \wedge r(x, e2)$, $\exists x\ r(e2, x) \wedge r(x, e1)$. These relational features are very simple, and do not cover the relational search space

Table 3. Comparison against relational embedding methods with results. We report the results for our method using relOCC rules with gradient boosting.

Data set	Metric	ConvE	ComplEx	SimplE	DistMult	HolE	TransE	TransH	TransR	TransD	relOCC
DDI	Accuracy	0.744	0.787	0.509	0.683	0.586	0.533	0.479	0.465	0.476	**0.897**
	Recall	0.931	0.832	0.051	0.988	0.922	0.522	0.662	0.802	0.793	**0.991**
	F1	0.544	0.618	0.030	0.567	0.483	0.320	0.348	0.387	0.389	**0.901**
	AUC-ROC	0.744	0.818	0.195	0.962	0.844	0.541	0.554	0.653	0.659	**0.902**
	AUC-PR	0.678	0.705	0.118	0.912	0.641	0.231	0.222	0.313	0.332	**0.853**
PPI	Accuracy	**0.747**	0.676	0.739	0.787	0.500	0.390	0.388	0.417	0.446	0.733
	Recall	0.685	0.603	0.793	0.707	0.0	0.401	0.408	0.449	0.512	**0.999**
	F1	0.729	0.650	0.752	0.768	0.0	0.397	0.400	0.435	0.480	**0.789**
	AUC-ROC	**0.829**	0.732	0.828	0.823	0.500	0.332	0.331	0.385	0.424	0.733
	AUC-PR	**0.855**	0.704	0.843	0.870	0.500	0.400	0.385	0.430	0.447	0.652
NELL Sports	Accuracy	0.667	0.629	0.548	0.607	0.756	0.544	0.530	0.470	0.448	**0.833**
	Recall	0.711	**0.733**	0.633	0.633	0.633	0.622	0.600	0.489	0.511	0.600
	F1	0.587	0.569	0.484	0.518	0.633	0.477	0.460	0.381	0.382	**0.731**
	AUC-ROC	0.743	0.762	0.620	0.694	0.745	0.589	0.571	0.456	0.489	**0.778**
	AUC-PR	0.517	0.628	0.437	0.645	0.730	0.452	0.423	0.332	0.3	**0.643**
Financial NLP	Accuracy	0.796	0.634	0.421	0.708	0.848	0.526	0.501	0.551	0.584	**0.967**
	Recall	0.963	0.472	**0.964**	0.982	0.0	0.673	0.527	0.691	0.691	0.800
	F1	0.589	0.281	0.335	0.505	0.0	0.301	0.243	0.318	0.335	**0.889**
	AUC-ROC	**0.953**	0.574	0.779	0.918	0.5	0.631	0.485	0.648	0.711	0.879
	AUC-PR	0.765	0.232	0.359	0.749	0.152	0.225	0.139	0.278	0.402	**0.833**
ICML CoAuthor	Accuracy	0.981	0.977	0.985	0.515	0.992	0.494	0.500	0.389	0.467	**0.997**
	Recall	0.636	0.85	0.200	0.964	0.0	0.909	0.836	0.727	1.0	0.386
	F1	0.020	0.030	0.007	0.032	0.0	0.029	0.027	0.020	0.031	**0.557**
	AUC-ROC	0.005	0.018	0.010	0.921	0.500	0.790	0.691	0.502	0.858	**0.693**
	AUC-PR	0.015	0.040	0.005	0.640	0.008	0.031	0.015	0.008	0.043	**0.400**

sufficiently, resulting in significantly poor performance. And hence, we created more domain-specific rules to enhance the score. For NeuralLP, the number of rules learned = 10 and for metapath2vec, the length of the learned random walk = 100, with the number of metapaths for each data set being: DDI = 3, PPI = 6, NELL Sports = 9, Financial NLP = 2 and ICML CoAuthor = 4.

It is clear from the results (Table 4) that even after enhancing the hand-crafted rules and using different rule learning methods, the rules learned by density estimation leads to much better predictive models thus answering **Q6**.

Table 4. Comparison against several rule learning strategies. We use gradient boosting for our method using relOCC rules and handwritten rules (Gaifman).

Data set	Methods	Accuracy	Recall	F1	AUC-ROC	AUC-PR
DDI	Gaifman	0.771	0.658	0.691	0.697	0.710
	Neural LP	0.632	0.777	0.470	0.741	0.404
	metapath2vec	0.717	0.767	0.717	0.768	0.696
	relOCC	**0.897**	**0.991**	**0.901**	**0.902**	**0.853**
PPI	Gaifman	0.652	0.524	0.606	0.654	0.619
	Neural LP	0.395	0.336	0.357	0.345	0.440
	metapath2vec	0.642	0.767	0.715	0.660	**0.729**
	relOCC	**0.733**	**0.999**	**0.789**	**0.733**	0.652
NELL Sports	Gaifman	0.780	0.485	0.597	0.707	0.549
	Neural LP	0.663	0.400	0.442	0.583	0.412
	metapath2vec	0.778	**0.867**	**0.765**	**0.875**	**0.850**
	relOCC	**0.833**	0.600	0.731	0.778	0.643
Financial NLP	Gaifman	0.914	0.590	0.705	0.787	0.587
	Neural LP	0.705	0.745	0.434	0.768	0.314
	metapath2vec	0.699	**0.982**	0.568	**0.927**	0.675
	relOCC	**0.967**	0.800	**0.889**	0.879	**0.833**
ICML CoAuthor	Gaifman	0.984	0.327	0.493	0.664	0.343
	Neural LP	0.718	**0.800**	0.045	0.846	0.179
	metapath2vec	0.912	**0.800**	0.333	**0.922**	0.350
	relOCC	**0.997**	0.386	**0.557**	0.693	**0.400**

5 Conclusion and Future Work

We propose the first work for full model learning for relational data using Gaifman locality theorem. In addition to exploring the viability of established structure learning methods we proposed a novel structure-learning approach based on relational density estimation. We constructs a set of rules, identify the appropriate instantiations and finally count the number of groundings per rule to obtain embeddings. We then train a discriminative classifier thus providing an effective method of doing link prediction. There are several avenues to explore such as joint learning of Gaifman models, generating explanations for a given prediction and extending Gaifman locality to hypergraphs. Another direction is employing more graph based embedding methods that can integrate with Gaifman's locality principle. Finally, evaluating on more real databases and knowledge graphs is an interesting direction.

Acknowledgments. This work is supported by the Air Force Office of Scientific Research under award number FA9550-191-0391. SN also acknowledges AFOSR award FA9550-18-1-0462. Any opinions, findings, conclusion or recommendations expressed are those of the authors and do not necessarily reflect the view of AFOSR or the US government. DSD also acknowledges ICT-48 Network of AI Research Excellence Center "TAILOR" (EU Horizon 2020, GA No 952215) and the Collaboration Lab "AI in Construction" (AICO).

References

1. Blockeel, H., De Raedt, L.: Top-down induction of first-order logical decision trees. Artif. Intell. **101**, 285–297 (1998)
2. Bordes, A., Usunier, N., Garcia-Duran, A., Weston, J., Yakhnenko, O.: Translating embeddings for modeling multi-relational data. In: NIPS (2013)
3. Cai, H., Zheng, V.W., Chang, K.C.: A comprehensive survey of graph embedding: problems, techniques, and applications. In: IEEE TKDE (2018)
4. De Campos, C.P., Zeng, Z., Ji, Q.: Structure learning of Bayesian networks using constraints. In: ICML (2009)
5. Dettmers, T., Minervini, P., Stenetorp, P., Riedel, S.: Convolutional 2D knowledge graph embeddings. In: AAAI (2018)
6. Dhami, D.S., Kunapuli, G., Das, M., Page, D., Natarajan, S.: Drug-drug interaction discovery: kernel learning from heterogeneous similarities. Smart Health **9–10**, 88–100 (2018)
7. Dong, Y., Chawla, N.V., Swami, A.: metapath2vec: scalable representation learning for heterogeneous networks. In: KDD (2017)
8. Gaifman, H.: On local and non-local properties. Stud. Logic Found. Math. **107**, 105–135 (1982)
9. Getoor, L., Taskar, B.: Intro to Statistical Relational Learning. MIT press (2007)
10. Ji, G., He, S., Xu, L., Liu, K., Zhao, J.: Knowledge graph embedding via dynamic mapping matrix. In: ACL-IJCNLP (2015)
11. Kaur, N., Kunapuli, G., Khot, T., Kersting, K., Cohen, W., Natarajan, S.: Relational restricted Boltzmann machines: a probabilistic logic learning approach. In: ILP (2017)
12. Kazemi, S.M., Poole, D.: Simple embedding for link prediction in knowledge graphs. In: NeurIPS (2018)
13. Khot, T., Natarajan, S., Kersting, K., Shavlik, J.: Learning Markov logic networks via functional gradient boosting. In: ICDM (2011)
14. Khot, T., Natarajan, S., Shavlik, J.W.: Relational one-class classification: a non-parametric approach. In: AAAI (2014)
15. Kok, S., et al.: The alchemy system for statistical relational {AI} (2009)

16. Lao, N., Cohen, W.W.: Relational retrieval using a combination of path-constrained random walks. Mach. Learn. **81**, 53–67 (2010). https://doi.org/10.1007/s10994-010-5205-8

17. Lin, Y., Liu, Z., Sun, M., Liu, Y., Zhu, X.: Learning entity and relation embeddings for knowledge graph completion. In: AAAI (2015)

18. Mitchell, T., Cohen, W., et al.: Never-ending learning. ACM Commun. **61**, 103–115 (2018)

19. Muggleton, S.: Inverse entailment and progol. New Gener. Comput. **13**, 245–286 (1995). https://doi.org/10.1007/BF03037227

20. Natarajan, S., Khot, T., Kersting, K., Gutmann, B., Shavlik, J.: Gradient-based boosting for statistical relational learning: the relational dependency network case. Mach. Learn. **100**, 75–100 (2015). https://doi.org/10.1007/s10994-015-5481-4

21. Nickel, M., Rosasco, L., Poggio, T.A., et al.: Holographic embeddings of knowledge graphs. In: AAAI (2016)

22. Nickel, M., Kiela, D.: Poincaré embeddings for learning hierarchical representations. In: NIPS (2017)

23. Niepert, M.: Discriminative Gaifman models. In: NIPS (2016)

24. Niu, F., Ré, C., Doan, A., Shavlik, J.: Tuffy: scaling up statistical inference in Markov Logic Networks using an RDBMS. In: VLDB (2011)

25. Raedt, L.D., Kersting, K., Natarajan, S., Poole, D.: Statistical Relational Artificial Intelligence: Logic, Probability, and Computation. Synthesis Lectures on AI and ML (2016)

26. Srinivasan, A.: The Aleph manual (2001)

27. Taskar, B., Wong, M.F., Abbeel, P., Koller, D.: Link prediction in relational data. In: NIPS (2004)

28. Trouillon, T., Welbl, J., Riedel, S., Gaussier, É., Bouchard, G.: Complex embeddings for simple link prediction. In: ICML (2016)

29. Walker T., et al.: ILP for bootstrapped learning: a layered approach to automating the ILP setup problem. In: ILP (2009)

30. Wang, Z., Zhang, J., Feng, J., Chen, Z.: Knowledge graph embedding by translating on hyperplanes. In: AAAI (2014)

31. Yang, B., Yih, W., He, X., Gao, J., Deng, L.: Embedding entities and relations for learning and inference in knowledge bases. In: ICLR (2015)

32. Yang, F., Yang, Z., Cohen, W.W.: Differentiable learning of logical rules for knowledge base reasoning. In: NeurIPS (2017)

Ontology Graph Embeddings and ILP
for Financial Forecasting

Can Erten[(✉)] and Dimitar Kazakov

University of York, York, UK
{can.erten,dimitar.kazakov}@york.ac.uk
http://www.cs.york.ac.uk/~kazakov

Abstract. There is a history of hybrid machine learning approaches where the result of an unsupervised learning algorithm is used to provide data annotation from which ILP can learn in the usual supervised manner [7,8]. Here we consider the task of predicting the property of cointegration between the time series of stock price of two companies, which can be used to implement a robust pair-trading strategy that can remain profitable regardless of the overall direction in which the market evolves. We start with an original FinTech ontology of relations between companies and their managers, which we have previously extracted from SEC reports, quarterly filings that are mandatory for all US companies. When combined with stock price time series, these relations have been shown to help find pairs of companies suitable to pair trading [3]. Here we use node2vec embeddings to produce clusters of companies and managers, which are then used as background predicates in addition to the relations linking companies and staff present in the ontology, and the values of the target predicate for a given time period. Progol [10] is used to learn from this mixture of predicates combining numerical with structural relations of the entities represented in the data set to reveal rules with predictive power.

Keywords: Ontologie · financial forecasting · SEC financial reports · ILP · unsupervised learning · graph embedding

1 Introduction

Financial forecasting is a broad discipline that includes the task of predicting future movements of price and volume of trade of company stock and financial products. This information can then be incorporated into profitable trading strategies. One such strategy that does not depend on the economic cycles and current market trends (bullish or bearish) is pair trading. This is a market-neutral strategy that aims to identify pairs of companies which have a predictable, stationary, long term average price when combined in a very simple portfolio in which each company is represented by a specified, optimal proportion of the total value. Maintaining this optimal proportion of each company as

© Springer Nature Switzerland AG 2022
N. Katzouris and A. Artikis (Eds.): ILP 2021, LNAI 13191, pp. 111–124, 2022.
https://doi.org/10.1007/978-3-030-97454-1_8

their prices fluctuate leads to selling the one on the rise and buying the one going down in relative terms. As the long term average is expected to be steady, this means a price trend reversal will happen over time, and the opposite trades will be made. An investor using such strategy is guaranteed to make a profit with each trade, provided the important property of stationary long term average continues to hold.

Historically, this strategy was not widely known, but has now been implemented in a number of trading tools. The suitability to pair trading of two companies is determined through a numerical test of *cointegration* [6]. With this test now available even to private individuals, the expected profit margins are thought to have shrunk, and new sources of information have been sought to forecast this desirable property in a more reliable manner. As the test is computationally costly, and the number of tests needed grows as $O(n^2)$ with the number of companies in hand, there is a lot to be gained if the number of candidate pairs could be reduced. One such potential source of information is the regular SEC reports filed by all US companies to report trades of their stock by company staff, as well as any important changes in the company management. We have used these reports, which are usually grouped and archived on a quarterly basis, to populate an ontology representing the relationships between companies and their senior managers. The result is a relatively simple knowledge graph from which we can discover that two companies share certain managers, among other things.

The idea of using non-numerical information for trading is not novel, and in fact constitutes the basis of the so called fundamental trading strategies, which look into the details of the company finances, assets, plans and the membership of their senior management. However, there is no standard, well established way to incorporate such knowledge into the day-to-day trades, and it can be argued that the short-term movements of the market have little to do with the long term viability of an investment. Nevertheless, we have considered a possible use of our ontology for this purpose, namely, we hypothesised that if two companies share directors or other senior staff that could lead to a flow of information that would make it more likely for the two companies to meet the cointegration test.

We tested this hypothesis in a previous study [3] from which it transpired that applying this criterion[1] does increase the proportion of cointegrated companies in a statistically significant way. It would be quite common to find around 5% of randomly selected company pairs to be cointegrated, while after applying this criterion their share may increase by a couple of percent or even double in some cases. Overall, such handcrafted rules bring palpable benefits, but their potential is still limited.

Since that study, we have taken our work in two directions. We have been working on the use of an in-house learner from ontologies in description logic [1] to automate the search for suitable ontology-based hypotheses. However, this article focuses on another approach, namely, the use of graph

---

[1]   modified by a parameter setting a minimum threshold on the number of shared staff.

embeddings as produced by the node2vec algorithm [4] to extract important properties of the graph nodes reflecting the content and topology of each local neighbourhood in an unsupervised way. It is common to cluster the resulting node embeddings and visualise the results in order to discover similarity between nodes. We have adopted the same approach here, using k-means clustering with a hand-selected number of clusters ($k = 20$). The cluster membership was then encoded as background knowledge of a Progol [10] learning task, where the target predicate coint(Comp1,Comp2) represented whether the prices of two companies are cointegrated or not for the period in question. In addition, we make use of background predicates showing the affiliation of managers with companies, keyperson(Company,Person), and the overall number of people connected to a company, ccon(Company,PersonCount), resp. companies connected to a person pcon(Person,CompanyCount). These are then used to define ccon2(Company,MinPersonCount) and pcon2(Person,MinCompanyCount) checking the number of connections of companies or people against the threshold value in their second attribute. We have also defined connect(Comp1,Comp2), a predicate showing whether two companies share at least one person.

In our experiment, we select a list of companies at random, split it into two, and use the first list to generate training pairs of companies (cointegrated vs non-cointegrated), while the second list is used to generate test pairs in which neither company appears in the training data. We then use Progol to learn rules which are evaluated on unseen data. The result shows that the rules we find have high predictive power and the pairs covered by them have a much higher concentration of cointegrated pairs when compared to the unprocessed test data.

2 Background

2.1 Financial Forecasting

There are clear incentives to attempt to forecast the price of financial assets. In that strife, portfolios of assets are used to reduce risk. This can be done in two ways. Diversifying the assets so they are not equally affected by adverse events and spreading the investment across more companies to reduce the relative importance of each one is one obvious approach. The other one is to use a small portfolio, of as few as two companies whose movements are inter-related in a particular way.

Correlated assets are those that tend to move together with statistical significance. The main cause for this is that companies (and markets) do not exist in isolation. They trade with each other and compete for resources and markets. Some assets are correlated because they are in the same sector (e.g. transport or entertainment), or work with the same suppliers: if there is a drop in demand for the same product, or a supplier is having problems, this will likely affect companies across the sector.

2.2 Pair Trading

Pair trading is a market neutral trading strategy enabling traders to profit from any market conditions through the use of cointegration. This is a test assessing the long term relationship between time series [6].

Two companies satisfying the statistical test for cointegration can create a portfolio which will have a stationary long term value even if the price of each company does not result in a stationary time series, provided the portfolio is regularly rebalanced to contain the same proportion of each stock. This amounts to statistical arbitrage and convergence trading strategy where the profit from the stock increasing in value is used to buy more of the stock going down in relative terms.

2.3 Securities and Exchange Commission (SEC) Reports

The U.S. Securities and Exchange Commission (SEC) is an independent agency for the United States federal government. It exists to protect investors, enforce the law against market manipulation and facilitate capital formation.[2] After the Great Depression, Congress passed Securities Act of 1934, which created SEC.

SEC requires the companies to file several different types of report on the company's activities and trades. They publish the formal specification document that every company in the United States has to provide.

The reports are mainly company statements, annual, quarterly and monthly. There are also reports to indicate an official statement or change of structure. Of particular interest to us are reports where the company needs to declare "corporate insiders," employees trading (buying or selling) more than 10% of the company's shares. Forms 3, 4 and 5 provide the framework for reporting insider trading information, where the company also discloses the title of the individual, and any important position, such as director or officer. This can be crucial information as it shows the staff member's role within the company. Their buying or selling can also be an indication of the company's financial performance.

The initial filing is on Form 3, which the insider must file within ten days of becoming an officer, director or beneficial owner. Form 4 reports changes in ownership within two business days. Form 5 is used to report any transactions that should have been reported earlier on a Form 4 as a means of deferred reporting.

SEC does not have an API, all the data is in strongly typed XML with the schema that they publish. They also provide an index file on their server for every report based on company name, period or type of report. We have built a web crawler to download the forms based on the report type and period, and we generate knowledge graphs from the downloaded data for SEC forms 3–5 to represent links between companies and people.

---

[2] https://www.investor.gov/introduction-investing/investing-basics/role-sec.

2.4   Ontologies

An ontology [9] is a structured database representing objects and their relations, known as *individuals* and *roles* in the field's parlance. Ontologies are formal representations of knowledge with well-defined semantics. An ontology allows for the grouping of individuals into classes (aka concepts). Both concepts and roles can form hierarchies, depending on the exact formalism used. The use of standard dictionaries of concepts and relevant roles not only assists the representation of domain knowledge, but also the easy integration of multiple an ontology is equivalent to a set of Description Logic (DL) axioms, which provides the semantics for query languages (such as SPARQL) and reasoners. The storage unit is a triplet with fields known as subject, predicate and object. These combine to a create a directed graph with entities represented by Unique Resource Identifiers (URI). Machine learning algorithms specialised in the use of DL to represent data and models also exist [1,9].

2.5   Node2vec Embeddings

Graph Representation Learning is a relatively new field which allows one to apply existing machine learning algorithms, such as CNN and RNN neural networks on graph data. In order to achieve that the graph need to be translated to the vector space, and represented as a tensor. The data is being converted from nodes and edges of graph information to semantic vector representations.

Node2vec is one such algorithm generating real-valued vector representations of nodes on a graph [5]. Known as embeddings, such representations make it possible to define similarity between any pair of nodes, and therefore permit the use of a range of unsupervised machine learning approaches, such as clustering. The cluster number can then be used as a label on the node, which is obtained in an unsupervised way, but can be used as background knowledge to an ILP-based supervised learning. The result is a hybrid learning approach resembling some of our earlier work [8].

3   Methodology

3.1   Data Collection

The data used is from the SEC reports, which are available to download in XML (XBRL) format. We have built an index parser to identify the available reports for a period and given type, and then built a crawler to download the actual report files. When all reports are downloaded, we apply an in-house custom parser to the XBRL (XML with metadata and schema) file in order to generate the ontology.

3.2   Data Analysis

After the data is parsed, it is stored in triplet form. This is then serialised as n-triples to be imported into an RDF graph database and our own application for analysis using the SPARQL query language [2]. A sample of the data is shown in Fig. 1.

Fig. 1. Knowledge graph sample

This can be used to construct powerful SPARQL queries to extract information from this representation, and use rich visualisation tools to see and understand the data. A sample of such data visualisations is shown on Fig. 2 and Fig. 3.

3.3   Learning and Experiment Preparation

Each experiment is prepared by our metaprogramming application generating Prolog/Progol source files. The steps that are followed each time are listed below:

- Load the serialised ontology data;
- Run a query to select companies (background information);
- Run a query to select linked people with the company information (background information);

- Split the data into a training set and a test set;
- Run the cointegration test for all pairs of companies in the report for the period in question to generate positive and negative examples;
- Run the node2vec algorithm on the data to generate node embeddings;
- Run k-means on the embeddings to obtain clusters (to be used as background knowledge);
- Generate a Progol source file from the background knowledge and target predicate examples;
- Run Progol on the data.

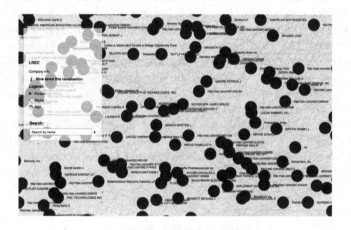

Fig. 2. Ontology visualisation (part)

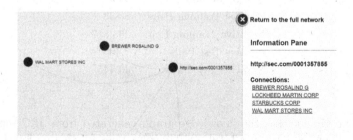

Fig. 3. Ontology visualisation of a person represented by an URI

4   Experiment Design and Results

In our experiment an ontology is generated from scratch to represent three months' worth of SEC reports. Only tabular SEC data is used, and the free form text is ignored.[3] We should clarify that at the moment, the only parts of the SEC reports that we use are related to insider trading: '*The federal securities laws require certain individuals (such as officers, directors, and those that hold more than 10% of any class of a company's securities, together we'll call, "insiders") to report purchases, sales, and holdings of their company's securities by filing Forms 3, 4, and 5.*'[4]

The result of this is a graph with nodes representing either a company or a person, and edges showing when a person is linked to a company. The algorithm node2vec [4] is then used to generate an embedding for each of the graph nodes. The embedding is a real valued vector of size set to 20. For the remaining parameters the choice was: walk_length=16, num_walks=100, workers=2. All node embeddings were then clustered using k-means with $k = 20$. (There is no link between the dimensionality of the embedding and the choice for the number of clusters.) The resulting clusters reflect the similarity between nodes as a combination of two factors, *homophily*, i.e. sharing the same neighbourhood, and *structural equivalence*, reflecting the role a node plays in the graph (e.g. a 'hub' node). The relative importance of either factor can be modified through the choice of the parameter walk_length.

With these results in hand, we carried out an experiment with the purpose of learning rules that would predicate the cointegration of two companies on their membership in a given cluster, the number of connections to a person or company, and the existence of people connected at the same time to a pair of companies.

Table 1. Dataset description

#of Training Companies	700
#of Test Companies	300
Positive Training Pairs	8,833
Negative Training Pairs	235,817
Positive Test Pairs	1,405
Negative Test Pairs	43,445

The experiment uses the knowledge graph generated from SEC reports for Q3/2017. There is data on a total of 1948 companies for this period. Of these, 1000 companies were randomly selected, and given a 70% : 30% split. All 244,650 possible pairs formed by companies in the first set were earmarked as training data, while all 44,850 pairs formed by companies in the remaining set were used as test data. As for each company we also had the time series with the

---

[3] The second author is supervising an ongoing MScRes project on extracting relations from free text at the moment of writing.

[4] https://www.investor.gov/introduction-investing/investing-basics/glossary/forms-3-4-and-5.

movement of stock prices over the entire three-month period, it was possible to apply a cointegration test to each pair of companies and label it as a positive or negative example. After some experimentation, we opted for positive-only learning for reasons of both speed and accuracy. This meant that in reality 8,833 training examples were used, all of them positive, which represented 3.61% of the 244, 650 training pairs (see Fig. 1). The background predicates and mode declarations used for learning are as follows:

```
:- modeh(1,coint(+company, +company))?
:- modeb(1,ccluster(+company,#int))?
:- modeb(1,ccon2(+company,#int))?
:- modeb(1,pcon2(+person,#int))?
:- modeb(1,connect(+company,+company))?
```

coint/2: Defines whether a pair of companies are cointegrated or not.
ccluster/2: Shows the cluster a company belongs to.
ccon2/2: The predicate succeeds if its first argument is a company with a number of connections that is equal or greater than the number in the predicate's second argument. In other words, the predicate checks that a company is connected to a certain minimum number of people. Expressed as Prolog code:

```
ccon2(Company,Threshold):-
  ccon(Company,NumberOfConnectedPeople),
  NumberOfConnectedPeople >= Threshold.
```

pcon2/2: The predicate succeeds if its first argument is a person with a number of connections that is equal or greater than the number in the predicate's second argument. In other words, the predicate checks that a person is affiliated with a certain minimum number of companies. Expressed as Prolog code:

```
pcon2(Person,Threshold):-
  pcon(Person,NumberOfConnectionsToCompanies),
  NumberOfConnectionsToCompanies >= Threshold.
```

connect/2: Defines whether a company is connected to another company via at least one key person:

```
connect(CompA,CompB):-
  keyperson(CompA,Person),
  keyperson(CompB,Person),
  CompA \= CompB.
```

We should note here that even the background predicates that define propositional properties, e.g. the cluster number, are based on relational data about connections between graph nodes, while the remaining ones express a numerical relation ('$\geq$') summarising that relational data.

The result of learning is a list of clauses of the target predicate as shown in Tables 2–3. The overall accuracy of the theory learned is 50.42% as shown

Table 2. Q3/2017 rules: results for which the χ^2 test yields $p \leq .05$ are in bold.

Rules	pos	neg	$\frac{pos}{pos+neg}$	p-value
coint(A,B) :- ccluster(B,18)	102	2327	0.04	**.0036**
coint(A,B) :- ccluster(A,3)	145	1987	0.07	**.0000**
coint(A,B) :- ccluster(B,19)	102	2690	0.04	**.0000**
coint(A,B) :- ccluster(A,2)	71	2005	0.03	.4633
coint(A,B) :- ccluster(A,0)	77	2290	0.03	.7434
coint(A,B) :- ccluster(B,16)	81	1904	0.04	**.0184**
coint(A,B) :- ccluster(A,1)	218	1956	0.10	**.0000**
coint(A,B) :- ccluster(B,17)	101	2138	0.05	**.0003**
coint(A,B) :- ccluster(B,14)	79	1473	0.05	**.0000**
coint(A,B) :- ccluster(A,13), ccluster(B,15)	10	54	0.16	**.0000**
coint(A,B) :- ccluster(A,6), ccluster(B,13)	13	100	0.12	**.0000**
coint(A,B) :- ccluster(A,7), ccluster(B,13)	15	120	0.11	**.0000**
coint(A,B) :- ccluster(A,4), ccluster(B,12)	15	114	0.12	**.0000**
coint(A,B) :- ccluster(A,5), ccluster(B,12)	5	58	0.08	**.0289**
coint(A,B) :- ccluster(A,9), ccluster(B,12)	8	53	0.13	**.0000**
coint(A,B) :- ccluster(A,8), ccluster(B,12)	3	41	0.07	.1609
coint(A,B) :- ccluster(A,12), ccluster(B,13)	10	65	0.13	**.0000**
coint(A,B) :- ccluster(A,11), ccluster(B,12)	10	112	0.08	**.0014**
coint(A,B) :- ccluster(A,10), ccluster(B,12)	3	44	0.06	.2013
coint(A,B) :- ccluster(A,7), ccluster(B,12)	14	121	0.10	**.0000**
coint(A,B) :- ccluster(A,4), ccluster(B,7)	19	238	0.07	**.0001**
coint(A,B) :- ccluster(A,7), ccluster(B,9)	8	121	0.06	**.0460**
coint(A,B) :- ccluster(A,7), ccluster(B,8)	5	115	0.04	.5163
coint(A,B) :- ccluster(A,7), ccluster(B,11)	16	123	0.12	**.0001**
coint(A,B) :- ccluster(A,7), ccluster(B,15)	4	107	0.04	.7761
coint(A,B) :- ccluster(A,7), ccluster(B,10)	8	98	0.08	**.0093**
coint(A,B) :- ccluster(A,5), ccluster(B,7)	13	112	0.10	**.0000**
coint(A,B) :- ccluster(A,6), ccluster(B,7)	23	191	0.11	**.0000**
coint(A,B) :- ccluster(A,4), ccluster(B,6)	22	143	0.13	**.0000**
coint(A,B) :- ccluster(A,4), ccluster(B,8)	5	133	0.04	.7412
coint(A,B) :- ccluster(A,4), ccluster(B,9)	6	116	0.05	.2586
coint(A,B) :- ccluster(A,4), ccluster(B,13)	18	118	0.13	**.0000**
coint(A,B) :- ccluster(A,4), ccluster(B,15)	11	105	0.09	**.0001**
coint(A,B) :- ccluster(A,4), ccluster(B,5)	14	143	0.09	**.0000**
coint(A,B) :- ccluster(A,4), ccluster(B,10)	6	101	0.06	.1425
coint(A,B) :- ccluster(A,4), ccluster(B,11)	17	124	0.12	**.0000**
coint(A,B) :- ccluster(A,5), ccluster(B,6)	9	68	0.12	**.0000**
coint(A,B) :- ccluster(A,6), ccluster(B,9)	10	95	0.10	**.0002**
coint(A,B) :- ccluster(A,6), ccluster(B,11)	9	104	0.08	**.0033**
coint(A,B) :- ccluster(A,6), ccluster(B,12)	14	101	0.12	**.0000**
coint(A,B) :- ccluster(A,6), ccluster(B,10)	10	83	0.11	**.0000**
coint(A,B) :- ccluster(A,9), ccluster(B,13)	5	61	0.08	**.0386**
coint(A,B) :- ccluster(A,11), ccluster(B,13)	13	114	0.10	**.0000**
coint(A,B) :- ccluster(A,5), ccluster(B,13)	4	63	0.06	.1830
coint(A,B) :- ccluster(A,8), ccluster(B,13)	3	45	0.06	.2155
coint(A,B) :- ccluster(A,8), ccluster(B,11)	4	40	0.09	**.0235**
coint(A,B) :- ccluster(A,8), ccluster(B,9)	2	48	0.04	.7250
coint(A,B) :- ccluster(A,8), ccluster(B,10)	1	39	0.03	.8184

Table 3. Q3/2017 rules (cont.)

Rules	pos	neg	$\frac{pos}{pos+neg}$	p-value
coint(A,B) :- ccluster(A,10), ccluster(B,13)	5	44	0.10	**.0046**
coint(A,B) :- ccluster(A,5), ccluster(B,15)	9	43	0.17	**.0000**
coint(A,B) :- ccluster(A,5), ccluster(B,10)	6	46	0.12	**.0005**
coint(A,B) :- ccluster(A,5), ccluster(B,9)	6	53	0.10	**.0020**
coint(A,B) :- ccluster(A,5), ccluster(B,11)	9	52	0.15	**.0000**
coint(A,B) :- ccluster(A,9), ccluster(B,11)	7	57	0.11	**.0003**
coint(A,B) :- ccluster(A,9), ccluster(B,15)	3	58	0.05	.4239
coint(A,B) :- ccluster(A,9), ccluster(B,10)	2	53	0.04	.8303
coint(A,B) :- ccluster(A,8), ccluster(B,15)	4	34	0.11	**.0090**
coint(A,B) :- ccluster(A,14), ccluster(B,15)	4	84	0.05	.4474
coint(A,B) :- ccluster(A,11), ccluster(B,15)	10	101	0.09	**.0004**
coint(A,B) :- ccluster(A,10), ccluster(B,11)	6	45	0.12	**.0004**
coint(A,B) :- ccluster(A,5), ccluster(B,8)	4	56	0.07	.1166
coint(A,B) :- ccluster(A,10), ccluster(B,10)	1	35	0.03	.9027
coint(A,B) :- ccluster(A,10), ccluster(B,15)	5	41	0.11	**.0026**
coint(A,B) :- ccluster(A,6), ccluster(B,15)	7	93	0.07	**.0268**
coint(A,B) :- ccluster(B,15), ccon2(A,4)	40	507	0.07	**.0000**
coint(A,B) :- ccluster(A,6), ccon2(A,2), ccon2(B,4)	26	694	0.04	.4652
coint(A,B) :- ccluster(A,7), ccluster(B,7), ccon2(B,3)	8	74	0.10	**.0006**
coint(A,B) :- ccluster(A,6), ccluster(B,6), ccon2(A,4)	0	60	0.00	.1636
coint(A,B) :- ccluster(B,13), ccon2(A,310)	4	25	0.14	**.0010**
coint(A,B) :- ccluster(A,10), ccon2(B,310)	3	7	0.30	**.0000**
coint(A,B) :- ccluster(A,13), ccluster(B,13), ccon2(A,5)	4	62	0.06	.1727
coint(A,B) :- ccluster(A,5), ccluster(B,5), ccon2(B,4)	0	34	0.00	.2944
coint(A,B) :- ccluster(A,9), ccluster(B,9), ccon2(B,2)	0	40	0.00	.2554
coint(A,B) :- ccluster(A,15), ccluster(B,15), ccon2(B,2)	0	37	0.00	.2740

Table 4. Test results

Q3/2017			
	A	¬A	Total
P	1,361	22,192	23,553
¬P	44	21,253	21,297
Total	1,405	43,445	44,850
Accuracy	50.42% ± 0.24%		
χ^2 probability	0.0000		

in Table 4, which is a very high result for such notoriously fickle data. The two classes for this binary classifications are not equally represented in the test set, as we wanted to stay faithful to the original purpose of this work, which is to eliminate negative examples from the data while preserving as many positive examples as possible. In this we succeed: 96.9% of the positive test examples are accepted by the theory, while around half of the negative examples are rejected. The resulting data sample, that is, the set of pairs accepted by the learned definition of the target predicate, contains 5.78% of positive pairs or by 85% more than the entire test set, where this percentage is 3.13%. This difference are statistically significant, and of substantial practical value, as it reduces the list of candidate cointegration pairs by half at almost no loss of 'good' pairs.

With the evaluation of the entire theory out of the way, we can look into the quality of the individual rules listed in the two tables, which also show the number of positive and negative test examples each of them covers, their precision and whether that figure is statistically different from the distribution of the entire test set. A two-tailed χ^2 test was used for that purpose.

We have grouped the rules learned by Progol by their type for ease of reading. First, we have nine rules only specifying the cluster membership of either company in the pair (see top of Table 2). Intuitively, the rules appear under-constrained, as it is unlikely that any company from a given cluster will be cointegrated with all other companies. This intuition is supported by evidence as when the rules are tested, they have large coverage but low precision (defined as the proportion of true positives in all pairs selected by the rule). Even so, some of the results show statistical significance at the $\alpha = .05$ significance level when compared with the 3.13% ratio of cointegrated pairs in the entire test set.

The second and most numerous type of rule is one that specifies the clusters each of the two companies belong to. In one case, the rule asks for the two companies to belong to the same cluster, namely, cluster 10. Most rules however specify two different clusters. Some of these rules substantially outperform the default strategy of selecting pairs at random, e.g. choosing pairs combining clusters 13 and 15 to select pairs from the unseen test data increases the proportion of cointegrated pairs 5-fold. It is tempting to find out a common denominator for all companies in each cluster, but our data does not contain additional features that can be used for that purpose. Non-systematic manual inspection of the sectors to which some of the companies belong did not show any obvious patterns either nor can we see any substantial number of connections between the two clusters when we look at the topology of the knowledge graph for the nodes in clusters 13 and 15 (Fig. 4). It is nevertheless the case that the majority of the rules do make use of the cluster labels, and most perform better than random in a statistically significant way even when their results are taken out of context, on their own. It is also to be noted that once we started using node embedding based cluster labels as background predicates, no rule based on the number of connections between the two companies in the pair has been learned, despite the positive results such rules showed in our previous research [3].

Finally, we should mention the rules setting a minimum threshold for the number of people connected to one or both companies. When the constraint appears in conjunction with the previous type of rule, the result is rules with zero positive examples covered on the test data, which suggests these rules are likely to overfit the data.

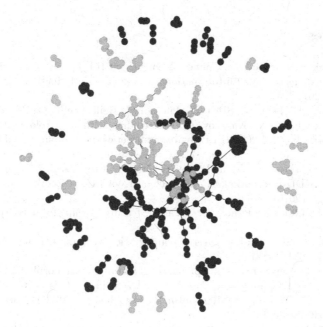

Fig. 4. Knowledge graph subset containing clusters 13 and 15 (red vs blue) (Color figure online)

5   Conclusion

The results show that the rules obtained are potentially interpretable, and that they have genuine predictive power. We conjecture that the results will further improve as we increase the data set, something we have tried to limit here to keep the complexity of the learning task under control. We shall also consider transferring the learning task on to a concurrent learner that scales up better [1]. It is important to note the hybrid nature of the approach, in which an ontology is populated with data extracted from company reports through text processing, then the embeddings for the graph nodes are generated, and clustered, all in an unsupervised manner. The cluster labels are used as background knowledge alongside other relations from the graph, and classic supervised ILP learning is applied to obtain the final results. So, we are dealing with a hybrid learning approach for two separate reasons, because it combines unsupervised with supervised learning, and as logic facts and relations are combined with the output of numerical computations based on time series. This is clearly a powerful and promising novel approach, and our future work will focus on scaling up the data set, and analysing the results with domain experts with the aim of revealing additional salient properties and relations to the range of background predicates in order to allow for ever more accurate and revealing hypotheses to be learned.

References

1. Algahtani, E., Kazakov, D.: Conner: A concurrent ILP learner in description logic. In: Proceedings of the 29th International Conference on Inductive Logic Programming (2020)
2. DuCharme, B.: Learning SPARQL, 2nd edn. O'Reilly Media (2013)
3. Erten, C., Chotai, N., Kazakov, D.: Pair trading with an ontology of SEC financial reports. In: The 2020 IEEE Symposium Series on Computational Intelligence (2020)
4. Grover, A., Leskovec, J.: node2vec: Scalable feature learning for networks. In: ACM SIGKDD International Conference on Knowledge Discovery and Data Mining (KDD) (2016)
5. Grover, A., Leskovec, J.: node2vec: scalable feature learning for networks. In: KDD (2016)
6. Johansen, S.: Statistical analysis of cointegration vectors. J. Econ. Dyn. Control 12(2), 231–254 (1988)
7. Kazakov, D.: Achievements and prospects of learning word morphology with inductive logic programming. In: Cussens, J., Džeroski, S. (eds.) LLL 1999. LNCS (LNAI), vol. 1925, pp. 89–109. Springer, Heidelberg (2000). https://doi.org/10.1007/3-540-40030-3_6
8. Kazakov, D., Manandhar, S.: Unsupervised learning of word segmentation rules with genetic algorithms and inductive logic programming. Mach. Learn. 43(1/2), 121–162 (2001). http://dblp.uni-trier.de/db/journals/ml/ml43.html#KazakovM01
9. Lehmann, J., Völker, J.: An introduction to ontology learning. Perspect. Ontol. Learn. 18, ix–xvi (2014)
10. Muggleton, S.: Inverse entailment and progol. New Gener. Comput. Spec. Issue Inductive Logic Program. 13(3–4), 245–286 (1995). http://citeseer.nj.nec.com/muggleton95inverse.html

Transfer Learning for Boosted Relational Dependency Networks Through Genetic Algorithm

Leticia Freire de Figueiredo[1]([⊠])(iD), Aline Paes[2]([⊠])(iD),
and Gerson Zaverucha[1]([⊠])(iD)

[1] Department of Systems Engineering and Computer Science,
Universidade Federal do Rio de Janeiro, Rio de Janeiro, RJ, Brazil
{lfreire,gerson}@cos.ufrj.br
[2] Institute of Computing, Universidade Federal Fluminense, Niteroi, RJ, Brazil
alinepaes@ic.uff.br

Abstract. Machine learning aims at generalizing from observations to induce models that aid decisions when new observations arrive. However, traditional machine learning methods fail at finding patterns from several objects and their relationships. Statistical relational learning goes a step further to discover patterns from relational domains and deal with data under uncertainty. Most machine learning methods, SRL included, assume the training and test data come from the same distribution. Nonetheless, in several scenarios, this assumption does not hold. Transfer learning aims at acting on scenarios like that, leveraging learned knowledge from a source task to improve the performance in a target task when data is scarce. A costly challenge associated with transfer learning in relational domains is mapping from the source and target background knowledge language. This paper proposes GROOT, a framework that applies genetic algorithm-based solutions to discover the best mapping between the source and target tasks and adapt the transferred model. GROOT relies on a set of relational dependency trees built from the source data as a starting point to build the models for the target data. Over generations, individuals carry a possible mapping. They are submitted to genetic operators that recombine subtrees and revise the initial structure tree, enabling a prune or expansion of the branches. Experimental results conducted on Cora, IMDB, UW-CSE, and NELL datasets show that GROOT reaches results better than the baselines in most cases.

Keywords: transfer learning · statistical relacional learning · genetic algorithm

1 Introduction

Machine learning algorithms aim at generalizing observations from data to find patterns that aid decision making about future observations. However, when the

Partially funded by CNPq and FAPERJ.

N. Katzouris and A. Artikis (Eds.): ILP 2021, LNAI 13191, pp. 125–139, 2022.
https://doi.org/10.1007/978-3-030-97454-1_9

patterns involve multiple objects and their relationships, traditional machine learning methods could not be enough to represent the relational interactions among data [7]. In this way, it is necessary to rely on methods that take advantage of the information that relational data could give through such interactions to generate models that show the correlations between the multiple objects [11]. *Relational learning* is a machine learning branch that englobes methods capable of dealing with relational data. Statistical relational learning combines relational learning and statistical learning with data under uncertainty [11].

Still, most relational and non-relational machine learning methods assume that the training and testing data come from the same feature space and distribution. When this assumption does not hold, it is necessary to collect more data and learn a new model from scratch, which can be expensive and, sometimes, even impossible. To tackle those situations, transfer learning between related tasks shows as a viable solution. [23] Transfer learning is a technique that leverages knowledge previously learned from a source task to boost the induction of a model to a target task, mainly when data is scarce [22]. Transfer learning has drawn the attention of relational learning for some time to improve and accelerate learning in the target domain [13,15].

However, relational learning poses an additional challenge when transferring knowledge from a source domain to a target domain since their vocabulary will probably differ. Thus, it is necessary to establish a mapping from both vocabularies so that the learned hypothesis can be used to represent the target data. In [2], giving the hypothesis in the form of a relational regression tree, the framework called TreeBoostler first finds a mapping, defining the replacement between the source and target predicates, through a constrained search space built upon their predicates. In relational setting, the predicate corresponds to a relation between arguments that correspond to the attributes of the relation. For example, if the dataset indicates that Mary is daughter of John, we can define a predicate called daughter that has the arguments Mary and John [1]. Also, the attributes are typed. In the daughter relation, the arguments can be typed as *person*.[1] For each possibility of mapping predicates and their types, the procedure verifies if it can improve an evaluation function and revise the structure, making pruning or expanding the leaves to new branches. However, finding the best mapping could be challenging when background knowledge, from the source, target, or both domains, has many predicates and types. A possible way to solve this problem is to use metaheuristics to find the best solution instead of searching almost entirely the mapping space, constrained only to a few restrictions.

This work proposes GROOT [2], a framework written in Python that receives an initial set of trees from the source domain and applies genetic algorithm-based solutions to transfer a learned hypothesis from a source domain to a target

---

[1] The types are defined into the language bias, which here follows the Aleph and Progol definitions.

[2] https://github.com/MeLL-UFF/groot: the online repository contains the GROOT code, an experiment example, besides the datasets used for the experiments contained in this paper and the results.

domain. The solutions are measured by RDN-Boost, creating a set of trees that approximate the joint probability distribution over the variables as a product of conditional distributions [19]. One solution is considered the best if it has the best area under the Precision-Recall curve (AUC PR) metric. Each individual in the genetic algorithm carries a possible mapping. The crossover between them will combine random subtrees in two different individuals and the mutation could expand or prune a branch. We experiment GROOT with four domains and find out GROOT gives a better result in some metrics but needs a long time to return the answers.

To sum up, our contributions are as follows: develop a method based on genetic algorithm to map predicates between a source task to a target task and use genetic operators to help the revision of the structure trees. The experiment are made with relational datasets to evaluate how GROOT improves the results compared with the baseline. The remainder of the paper is organized as follows: Sect. 2 introduces the necessary background to understand fundamental concepts addressed in this paper. In this section, we clarify about RDN-Boost, transfer learning, and genetic algorithm. Next, Sect. 3 brings related work showing transfer learning between relational tasks. Section 4 explains the GROOT framework, including their algorithms and inner components. Section 5 presents the results from GROOT, compared with the RDN-Boost and TreeBoostler results. The final section ends with the conclusion about the work and next steps.

2   Background Knowledge

In this section, we briefly introduce important concepts to the reader to understand the foundations of our contributions. First, we describe the RDN-Boost method. Next, we explain basic notions on transfer learning and finalize the section with genetic search and optimization.

2.1   RDN-Boost

Dependency networks (DNs) are graphical models for probabilistic interactions. A DN is a directed graph $G = (V, E)$, usually cyclic, where each node $v_i \in V$ corresponds to a random variable $X_i \in X$, where X is a set of variables enconding probabilistic relationships. Each node is also associated with a positive joint distribution approximated with a set P of conditional probability distributions that are calculated as:

$$p_i(X_i|\boldsymbol{parents(X_i)}) = p(X_i|X_1, \ldots, X_{i-1}, X_{i+1}, \ldots, X_n) = p(X_i|X \setminus X_i) \quad (1)$$

where $parents(X_i)$ denotes the set of nodes with incoming edges to X_i. Unlike Bayesian networks, the DN graph can be cyclic [10].

Relational dependency networks (RDNs) are an extension of DNs to the relational setting. A RDN models the dependencies in a directed graph G_M, like in DNs, but each node corresponds to an object in the data and an edge corresponds to a relationship among the objects. To each node in the graph, it is associated a conditional probability, given by Eq. 1 [19, 21].

Finally, *RDN-Boost* [19] considers the conditional probability distribution as a regression trees set to each predicate and, at each iteration, the idea is to maximize the likelihood of the distributions with respect to a potential function. The potential function is defined using an initial potential ψ_0 and, iteratively, adds the gradients Δ, which is the gradient of the likelihood function. In this way, the potential function is given by

$$\psi_m = \psi_0 + \Delta_1 + ... + \Delta_m \tag{2}$$

where Δ_i is the gradient at iteration i. When computing the Eq. 1, each branch is applied to determine the branches that are satisfied and their regression values are summed up to the potential function [19].

2.2 Transfer Learning

Traditionally, machine learning methods assume the train and test data come from the same distribution and feature space. However, in some scenarios, training data is scarce due to difficulties and the cost to collect them. The lack of training data may degrade the machine learning method performance [26].

A possible way to tackle the lack of training data is to transfer a learned model from a source task to the target task, allowing the use of data from different domains, distributions, and tasks. The traditional learning process of machine learning methods is to use, from scratch, the data from a target domain to train and test a task. *Transfer learning* method aims to extract knowledge from a source task and apply it to a target task, alleviating the need to train the model from scratch in the target task [23].

Transfer learning is formalized as follows. Let $\mathcal{X}$ be the feature space, $P(X)$ the marginal probability distribution over $\mathcal{X}$, and $\mathcal{D} = \{\mathcal{X}, P(X)\}$ a domain. The source domain $\mathcal{D}_s$ is defined as $\mathcal{D}_s = \{\mathcal{X}_s, P(X_s)\}$ and the target domain, $\mathcal{D}_t = \{\mathcal{X}_t, P(X_t)\}$. A task T is defined by a label space $\mathcal{Y}$ and an objective function $f(\cdot)$ that can be learned from the training data (x_i, y_i), where $x_i \in \mathcal{X}$ and $y_i \in \mathcal{Y}$. A source task is defined as $T_s = (\mathcal{Y}_s, f_s(\cdot))$ and a target domain, $T_t = (\mathcal{Y}_t, f_t(\cdot))$. With a source domain $\mathcal{D}_s$ and a source task T_s, a target domain $\mathcal{D}_t$ and a target task T_t, where $\mathcal{D}_s \neq \mathcal{D}_t$ or $T_s \neq T_t$, the goal is to learn the target function $f(\cdot)$ leveraging the knowledge from $\mathcal{D}_s$ and T_s [23, 26, 27].

2.3 Genetic Algorithm

Genetic algorithm (GA) is a population-based metaheuristic based on natural selection and the principles of genetic. The method walks in a space of candidate hypotheses to find the best candidate, defined by the objective function, called fitness [8, 17]. GA relies on a population composed of individuals. Each individual contains a feasible solution to the problem, encoded in their chromosomes with genes inside. The evaluation of the population is made by the fitness function that informs if an individual is a good or a bad candidate. Along the generations, the GA evolves the solutions using genetic operators:

1. **Selection**: selects the best individuals according to their fitness value and reallocates it to the population. One way to make the selection is the tournament selection, which selects randomly k individuals from the population and, with a probability p, selects the best.
2. **Recombination**: two parent individuals form new offsprings, recombining their genes at different points.
3. **Mutation**: an individual has one of their genes randomly modified, generating a new solution, feasible or not.

At the end of all these steps, the old population is replaced by the new population generated by the genetic operators. Also, it is possible to apply an elitist technique, where the best individual of the last generation is introduced on the current population without modifications [4,17].

3   Related Work

Previous works have already proposed novel methods for leveraging transfer learning to relational domains. In [2], the authors propose a framework called TreeBoostler to transfer a RDN-Boost model learned from a source task to a target task, searching for the best mapping between source predicates and types and target predicates and types. After finding the mapping between the source and target vocabulary, the performance of the transferred RDN-Boost is evaluated over the target data. In order to accommodate target predicates that were not mapped and adjust the learned trees to the target data, TreeBoostler employ a final revision step. Such a component selects the revision points as the places in the trees that have low probabilities for the true class. Next, from the revision points, the revision operators either expand leaves to generate new branches or prune nodes. TreeBoostler has a limitation when searching the best mapping: the source predicate can only be substituted by one and only one target predicate and the same is valid for the types. Furthermore, the search is almost complete in the sense that are only some restrictions to avoid experimenting with the whole search space of possible mappings. Depending on the size of the vocabulary, this can be a quite expensive process. Nevertheless, TreeBoostler was successfully compared to TAMAR [15] and TODTLER [9].

Our framework is similar to the introduced solution but makes use of a genetic algorithm instead of an exhaustive search. Also, GROOT allows making a map between many source predicates to many target predicates, just adding an identifier to the source predicate to turn it into a unique on. The source types can be mapped to many target types, however, the target types can only be mapped to one source type.

Metaheuristics have already been used in Inductive Logic Programming. In QG/GA [18], the authors investigate a method called Quick Generalization (QG), which implements a random-restart stochastic bottom-up search to build a consistent clause without the needing to explore the graph in detail. The genetic algorithm (GA) evolves and recombines clauses generated by the QG, that forms the population.

In [25], the authors present EDA-ILP and REDA-ILP, an ILP system based on Estimation of Distribution Algorithms (EDA), a genetic algorithm variation. Instead of using genetic operators, EDA builds a probabilistic model of solutions and sample the model to generate new solutions. Across generations, EDA-ILP evaluates the population using Bayesian networks and returns the fittest individual. In REDA-ILP, the method also applies Reduce algorithm in bottom clauses to reduce the search space. In [14], the authors propose GENSYNTH, a tool that synthesizes invented predicates, free from bias, to Datalog language problems. According to a fitness function, the tool uses steps inspired in the genetic algorithm to find interpretable programs without language bias quickly.

4   GROOT: Genetic Algorithms to Aid Transfer Learning with bOOsTsrl

The proposed framework transfers relational dependency trees learned from a source domain to a target domain. The idea is to take advantage of the built structure trees using the source domain as a starting point to learn how to solve the target task. Instead of conducting a complete search into the space of solutions, GROOT employs a genetic algorithm to find the best mapping between the predicates that optimizes the area under the Precision-Recall curve (AUC PR) value. In addition, GROOT includes genetic operators to revise the source structure to better accommodate the target examples.

4.1   Population

Along the generations, the genetic algorithm evaluates individuals in the population, where which one carries a possible solution to the problem. In GROOT, each individual is composed of chromosomes, a feasible mapping corresponding to each node in the trees, and the fitness function value. Each chromosome is a structure corresponding to one tree and each tree has alleles, corresponding to each node. In our framework, each individual has 10 chromosomes. Figure 1 depicts how the individuals are encoded in GROOT.

GROOT allows mapping many source predicates to many target predicates. To distinguish which source predicate has been replaced, a unique identifier is appended to each one of them. This is made because if the source predicate is the same always, the transfer will be made with the first mapped target predicate. The map between the predicates is made at random but restricted to predicates with the same arity and language bias. The target predicates are selected according to the arity and language bias of the source predicate and are part of the feasible substitution set. The predicates are mapped sequentially, respecting the order they appear in the trees. If there are no feasible target predicates to replace the source predicate, the source predicate is mapped to

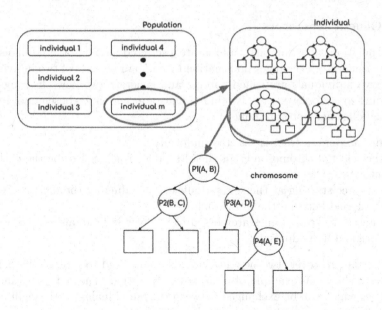

Fig. 1. Schema showing how the individuals are defined in GROOT. Each chromosome represents a tree and each allele, a predicate. The alleles carry the mapping between the source and target vocabulary.

null. For example, this case can occur when a source predicate has arity one but none of the predicates in the target background knowledge has this arity.

We assume that GROOT input includes a set of trees from the source dataset created with RDN-Boost using predicates from the source vocabulary. Each individual is a copy of this set, and each tree corresponds to a chromosome in the individual. For each predicate appearing in the nodes, GROOT verifies which predicate from the target vocabulary can be mapped for the source predicate. Using the IMDB dataset as an example, consider that a node has an atom originated from the *director(+person)* predicate template. We need to find a predicate in the target dataset with the same definition (arity equals one and person as the type of the argument). Supposing the transference IMDB → UW-CSE, we can map it either to *professor(+person)* or *student(+person)* as they have the same arity and same type. If there is no target predicate with the same arity and types, the source predicate is mapped to *null(null)*. If mapping between types is also possible, in this case, is *person → person*, we randomly choose the target predicate that can uniformly replace the source predicate. The main node in the trees already has a determined predicate, which is the predicate RDN-Boost is learning. For example, for the IMDB dataset, the main predicate is *workedunder(+person, +person)*, which will be mapped to *advisedby(+person, +person)*, in the UW-CSE dataset.

4.2   Genetic Operators

The population can recombine and mutate a selected number of individuals. The crossover operator exchanges information by combining parts of two individuals. These two individuals are called parents and generate two new offsprings [17]. According to a crossover rate, two individuals are randomly chosen and, in each one, the following steps are done:

1. a chromosome (a tree) is selected uniformly
2. in the selected chromosome, an allele (a node) is elected to be the exchange point
3. the subtree starting at the selected alleles, including all the following nodes, are swapped between the individuals
4. the unselect chromosomes are passed to the new individuals as they were in the original individuals

After the crossover, two new individuals are created to replace the parents. The Fig. 2 shows an example of a crossover operation. The red nodes indicate the alleles which will be exchanged between the individuals. On the right side of the figure, it is possible to see the final result.

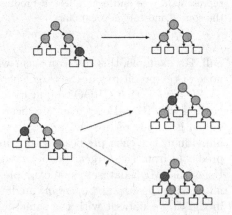

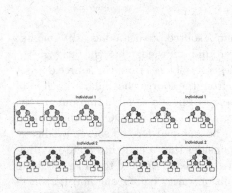

Fig. 2. Example of crossover between two individuals with 3 chromosomes. The red nodes are selected to be exchanged (Color figure online).

Fig. 3. A mutation example. Top: pruning starts from the orange node and erases all the leaves below it. Bottom: the expansion example shows the possibility to include a new node in one leaf (Color figure online).

The mutation operator selects an individual according to a mutation rate and applies small changes in their alleles. In GROOT, instead of changing the mapping, a revision structure is applied. When evaluating the individuals, a weighted variance of each node is returned as a result of the covered examples. An example is covered when a path in the hypothesis covers it. If a node has a variance higher than 2.5×10^{-3}, it is considered a revision point and could be pruned or expanded. This value is the same value used as default in TreeBoostler [2]. The decision to prune or expand is made uniformly. A chromosome can have many revision points but just one is chosen to be revised, at a generation. The expansion is made if a revision point has, at least, one leaf. The leaf is expanded with one predicate from the target domain. When pruning a node, all the leaves under the revision point are also erased and, at the place of the node, a leaf is set. In this case, it is necessary to have leaves in both branches. The Fig. 3 exemplifies how the mutation occurs in the individual. The Fig. 3 exemplifies how the mutation occurs in the individual.

4.3 Selection and Evaluation

Selection copies individuals with better fitness values to the population of individuals. A method called tournament selection is used in GROOT. The tournament selection chooses, at random, some individuals to enter into a tournament. The individual in the group with the best fitness value wins and is selected to be included in the population [4]. GROOT also applies elitism selection, where the fittest individual of the generation is guaranteed to be in the next generation. An individual is considered the fittest when it has the lowest negative AUC PR. If more individuals have the same fitness value, the one with the lowest negative conditional log-likelihood (CLL)[3] score is chosen.

After applying the genetic operators, the population is evaluated to set the fitness value for each individual. GROOT uses genetic algorithm to minimize the negative value of the AUC PR value. The individuals carry the mapping between the source and target predicates and the structure to make the transfer. The mapping and structure trees are given to RDN-Boost, which trains the model with the training dataset. The test dataset is used to evaluate how the model performs and gives as result the area under the ROC curve (AUC ROC), AUC PR, conditional log-likelihood values and others. The individual receives the AUC PR value as the fitness value.

5 Experimental Results

In this section we present the experiments devised to answer the following research questions:

– **Question 1:** Does GROOT perform better than learning from scratch?
– **Question 2:** Does GROOT perform better than another transfer learning framework?
– **Question 3:** Does GROOT reach good results in a viable time?

---

[3] Conditional log-likelihood gives the probability log of a given example be true, given the other random variables.

Table 1. Hyperparameters used in the optimization function.

	Parameters
Mutation rate	[0.1, 0.15, 0.2, 0.25, 0.3, 0.35, 0.4]
Crossover rate	[0.6, 0.65, 0.7, 0.75, 0.8, 0.85, 0.9, 0.95]
Number of individuals	[10, 30, 50]

The first question focus on verifying the benefits of transfer learning compared to learning from scratch. The second question is relative to how our framework can perform comparing with another transfer learning framework when using the same data. The final question addresses how long GROOT takes to run the entire transfer process.

Next, we present the datasets used in the experiments and, finally, the methodology used to find the parameters of the genetic algorithm and the results.

5.1 Datasets

We used the following four datasets for the experiments.

- Cora dataset [3] contains citations to Computer Science research papers. The dataset has 1295 distinct citations to 122 papers. The goal is to predict *samevenue*, which shows the relation between two venues. The dataset has 10 predicates and five types, with the number of all ground literals equals to 152100.
- IMDB dataset [16] contains five mega examples, describing four movies, their directors and the first-billed actors who appear in them. A mega example contains a connected group of facts and each one is independent of the other [16]. The main predicate is *workedunder*, indicating if two persons worked together. The dataset has six predicates, three types and 71824 ground literals.
- NELL [5] is a system that extracts information from web texts, learning to read each day better than the day before. Our experiments ran with two datasets created by the system: Finances, which predict if a company belongs to an economic sector and Sports, predicting which sports a team plays. NELL Sports dataset has eight predicates, four types and 4323, while NELL Finances has 10 predicates, five types and 51578 ground literals.
- UW-CSE dataset [16] is a dataset with mega-examples based on five Computer Science areas and lists facts about people in the academic department and their relationships. The relation *advisedby* predicts if one person is advised by another person. The dataset has 14 predicates, nine types and 16900 ground literals.

Methodology. We compared the results generated by GROOT with the performance of TreeBoostler, another framework to transfer learning between relational domains that also uses RDN-Boost to evaluate their results. We also compared with the results from models learned from scratch, produced by RDN-Boost and RDN-B-1. RDN-B-1 differs from RDN-Boost because the model learns just one tree, instead of a set of trees. GROOT starts from the trees created by RDN-Boost when learning from the source domain for each experiment. The datasets are, initially, divided in folds. For our experiments, we joined all the folds and split it into three new folds, training the model with one fold and evaluating with the remaining data, employing the same methodology used in literature [2,6,12]. Cross-validation is applied: for each of the three folds, we train five times to accommodate randomness with the current training set and test with the other folds, completing each experiment with 15 trainings. The final results are then averaged over the runs. Each training fold is divided into three sub-folds to find the hyperparameters for the genetic algorithm. On these three sub-folds, an internal cross-validation procedure is applied: one fold is selected for training and two folds for validation. Finding the best combination of parameters for the genetic algorithm is a hard task. Thus, this search uses gp_minize from Scikit-Optimize package [24] built with Scikit-Learn. The gp_minize function uses Bayesian optimization, approximating the desired function to optimize by a Gaussian process. We used 10 evaluations to get the parameters in each validation set. The RDN-Boost also has hyperparameters but we used the same as defined in TreeBoostler [2]. The best validation set gives the parameters to be used in the training fold. When training, we sample the amount of negative as been the ratio of two negatives for one positive; when testing, we used all the examples from the test dataset [20]. At the final generation, the best individual of the population is chosen to give the mapping to generate the results.

Table 2. Results for the experiment with IMDB and UW-CSE datasets, comparing with TreeBoostler, RDN-B-1 and RDN-Boost. The table shows the values for AUC ROC, AUC PR, CLL, and runtime. The first two rows show the results when learning the target dataset from scratch.

IMDB → UW-CSE

	CLL	AUC ROC	AUC PR	Time
RDN-B-1	-0.239 ± 0.000	0.796 ± 0.000	0.085 ± 0.000	2.595 ± 0.124 s
RDN-B	**-0.814 ± 0.003**	0.801 ± 0.005	0.094 ± 0.011	7.582 ± 0.457 s
TreeBoostler	-0.368 ± 0.004	0.905 ± 0.004	0.168 ± 0.014	11.152 ± 0.700 s
GROOT	-0.262 ± 0.033	**0.939 ± 0.010**	**0.336 ± 0.018**	18.3 ± 6.5 min

Results. The results are presented in Tables 2, 3, 4, and 5, with the experiments realized between the IDMB, UW-CSE, Cora and NELL datasets, reporting the mean and standard deviation results. When GROOT finds the best results for the metric, the values are shown in bold. GROOT obtains an improvement for at least one metric in most of the experiments and achieves comparable results when confronting with methods that learn from scratch, answering positively the **Question 1** and **Question 2**.

Table 3. Results for the experiment with IMDB and Cora datasets, comparing with TreeBoostler, RDN-B-1 and RDN-Boost. The table shows the values for AUC ROC, AUC PR, CLL, and runtime. The first two rows show the results when learning the target dataset from scratch.

IMDB → Cora

	CLL	AUC ROC	AUC PR	Time
RDN-B-1	-0.213 ± 0.004	0.534 ± 0.008	0.012 ± 0.000	5.9 ± 5.1 min
RDN-B	-0.500 ± 0.01	0.542 ± 0.006	0.013 ± 0.001	42.8 ± 7.6 min
TreeBoostler	-0.325 ± 0.008	0.729 ± 0.006	0.261 ± 0.022	194.0 ± 50.1 min
GROOT	-0.326 ± 0.006	0.582 ± 0.005	0.183 ± 0.010	41.0 ± 0.6 min

Table 4. Results for the experiment with IMDB and Cora datasets, comparing with TreeBoostler, RDN-B-1 and RDN-Boost. The table shows the values for AUC ROC, AUC PR, CLL, and runtime. The first two rows show the results when learning the target dataset from scratch.

Cora → IMDB

	CLL	AUC ROC	AUC PR	Time
RDN-B-1	-0.224 ± 0.000	0.843 ± 0.000	0.487 ± 0.000	2.249 ± 0.067 s
RDN-B	-0.697 ± 0.000	0.843 ± 0.000	0.487 ± 0.000	4.100 ± 0.137 s
TreeBoostler	-0.236 ± 0.000	0.958 ± 0.001	0.541 ± 0.055	9.564 ± 0.140 s
GROOT	-0.208 ± 0.015	**0.965 ± 0.012**	0.326 ± 0.176	86.4 ± 30.8 min

In Table 3, GROOT did not provide a good result. This is because the source structure trees learned from the IMDB dataset have nodes with predicates containing arity equals to one. The predicates from the Cora dataset have only predicates with arity greater or equal to two. GROOT could not deal with this problem and just replaced the source predicate with a null predicate. The null predicate is a predicate that does not exist in any of the vocabularies and indicates an absence of mapping. Instead of the previous commented table, in Table 2, the framework reaches the best result in AUC PR and AUC ROC metrics. This occurs because GROOT can map the same source predicate to different target predicates, instead of TreeBoostler that attributes only one target predicate to one source predicate.

The statistical significance was measured by a paired t-test with $p <= 0.05$. The values are considered statistically significant in the experiment IMDB → Cora in all metrics, except by the pair GROOT and TreeBoostler. In the experiment IMDB → UW-CSE, the AUC PR value is statistically significant when considering the pair GROOT with both RDN-B-1 and RDN-Boost. Although most of the experiments needed a long time to get the results, the experiment IMDB → Cora reached the worst runtime in TreeBoostler results. This occurs because the mapping between the predicates is poor, requiring a revision that almost recreates all the trees. We wanted to show this case as en example of a bad transfer scenario. Taking into account the experiment IMDB → Cora, we attribute a partial negative answer to the **Question 3**. We conclude that, besides the number of predicates and types, the quantity of ground literals also impacts the time, mainly in the revision step. However in GROOT the revision is not made in all revision points, so this is not an issue, enabling the framework to have a lower runtime.

Table 5. Results for the experiment with Nell datasets, comparing with TreeBoostler, RDN-B-1 and RDN-Boost. The table shows the values for AUC ROC, AUC PR, CLL, and runtime. The first two rows show the results when learning the target dataset from scratch.

Nell Sports → Nell Finances

	CLL	AUC ROC	AUC PR	Time
RDN-B-1	-0.178 ± 0.005	0.601 ± 0.069	0.045 ± 0.025	10.948 ± 2.003 s
RDN-B	**-0.284 ± 0.019**	0.796 ± 0.032	0.114 ± 0.027	56.401 ± 11.519 s
TreeBoostler	-0.167 ± 0.006	**0.979 ± 0.003**	0.083 ± 0.026	2.6 ± 0.8 min
GROOT	-0.197 ± 0.028	0.976 ± 0.012	**0.167 ± 0.080**	534.8 ± 219.3 min

6   Conclusion

This work proposes a framework called GROOT aiming at transfer learning between relational domains. GROOT uses a genetic algorithm to find a mapping between predicates from source and target datasets. Along with generations, each individual carries a mapping for the transfer, exchange information with other individuals, and revise their structure trees to get better performance.

The results presented an improvement, when compared with the baselines, in the value of the metrics. In most of the experiments, GROOT improves the AUC ROC values, even with the genetic algorithm optimizing the AUC PR metric. We showed from experiments that GROOT reaches better or competitive results when comparing with another transfer learning framework. This is possible because our framework provides a larger search space to make the mappings between source and target domains, allowing more combinations for the predicates replacement. Unlike TreeBoostler, GROOT allows mapping many source predicates to many target predicates and one source type to many target types. However, those enhancements are generally followed with a longer runtime than the baselines.

In future work, we intend to improve the evaluation component since the genetic algorithm evaluates, in every generation, many individuals to train and test the model. A possible solution for this problem is to rely on clever and faster inference procedures. Another improvement concerns the tree revision. In GROOT, the revision is made, at most, once in each tree, per generation. After finding the best mapping and generate the model, the resulting structure could be revised using a metaheuristic search, making prunings and expansions in the branches.

References

1. Inductive logic programming in a nutshell. In: Introduction to Statistical Relational Learning. The MIT Press (August 2007)
2. Azevedo Santos, R., Paes, A., Zaverucha, G.: Transfer learning by mapping and revising boosted relational dependency networks. Mach. Learn. **109**(7), 1435–1463 (2020). https://doi.org/10.1007/s10994-020-05871-x
3. Bilenko, M., Mooney, R.J.: Adaptive duplicate detection using learnable string similarity measures. In: Getoor, L., Senator, T.E., Domingos, P.M., Faloutsos, C. (eds.) Proceedings of the 9th ACM SIGKDD International Conference on Knowledge Discovery and Data Mining, Washington, DC, USA, 24–27 August 2003, pp. 39–48. ACM (2003)
4. Burke, E.K., Kendall, G.: Search Methodologies: Introductory Tutorials in Optimization and Decision Support Techniques, 2nd edn. Springer, Boston (2013). https://doi.org/10.1007/978-1-4614-6940-7
5. Carlson, A., Betteridge, J., Kisiel, B., Settles, B., Hruschka, E.R., Jr., Mitchell, T.M.: Toward an architecture for never-ending language learning. In: Fox, M., Poole, D. (eds.) Proceedings of the 24th AAAI Conference on Artificial Intelligence, AAAI 2010. AAAI Press (2010)
6. Davis, J., Domingos, P.M.: Deep transfer via second-order Markov logic. In: Danyluk, A.P., Bottou, L., Littman, M.L. (eds.) Proceedings of the 26th Annual International Conference on Machine Learning, ICML 2009. ACM International Conference Proceeding Series, Montreal, Quebec, Canada, 14–18 June 2009, vol. 382, pp. 217–224. ACM (2009)
7. De Raedt, L.: Logical and Relational Learning, 1st edn. Springer, Heidelberg (2008). https://doi.org/10.1007/978-3-540-68856-3
8. Gandomi, A., Yang, X.S., Talatahari, S., Alavi, A.: Metaheuristic algorithms in modeling and optimization, pp. 1–24 (12 2013)
9. Haaren, J.V., Kolobov, A., Davis, J.: TODTLER: two-order-deep transfer learning. In: Proceedings of the 29th AAAI Conference on Artificial Intelligence, AAAI 2015, pp. 3007–3015. AAAI Press (2015)
10. Heckerman, D., Chickering, D.M., Meek, C., Rounthwaite, R., Kadie, C.: Dependency networks for inference, collaborative filtering, and data visualization. J. Mach. Learn. Res. **1**, 49–75 (2001)
11. Khosravi, H., Bina, B.: A survey on statistical relational learning. In: Farzindar, A., Kešelj, V. (eds.) AI 2010. LNCS (LNAI), vol. 6085, pp. 256–268. Springer, Heidelberg (2010). https://doi.org/10.1007/978-3-642-13059-5_25
12. Kumaraswamy, R., Odom, P., Kersting, K., Leake, D., Natarajan, S.: Transfer learning via relational type matching. In: Aggarwal, C.C., Zhou, Z., Tuzhilin, A., Xiong, H., Wu, X. (eds.) 2015 IEEE International Conference on Data Mining, ICDM 2015, Atlantic City, NJ, USA, 14–17 November 2015, pp. 811–816. IEEE (2015)
13. Kumaraswamy, R., Ramanan, N., Odom, P., Natarajan, S.: Interactive transfer learning in relational domains. KI - Künstliche Intelligenz **34**(2), 181–192 (2020). https://doi.org/10.1007/s13218-020-00659-6
14. Mendelson, J., Naik, A., Raghothaman, M., Naik, M.: GenSynth: synthesizing Datalog programs without language bias. In: Proceedings of the AAAI Conference on Artificial Intelligence, vol. 35, pp. 6444–6453 (2021)
15. Mihalkova, L., Huynh, T., Mooney, R.J.: Mapping and revising Markov logic networks for transfer learning. In: Proceedings of the 22nd National Conference on Artificial Intelligence, vol. 1, pp. 608–614. AAAI Press (2007)

16. Mihalkova, L., Mooney, R.J.: Bottom-up learning of Markov logic network struc-
    ture. In: Ghahramani, Z. (ed.) Proceedings of the 24th International Conference
    Machine Learning, ICML 2007. ACM International Conference Proceeding Series,
    vol. 227, pp. 625–632. ACM (2007)
17. Mitchell, T.M.: Machine Learning. McGraw-Hill, New York (1997)
18. Muggleton, S., Tamaddoni-Nezhad, A.: QG/GA: a stochastic search for progol.
    Mach. Learn. **70**(2–3), 121–133 (2008)
19. Natarajan, S., Khot, T., Kersting, K., Gutmann, B., Shavlik, J.: Boosting relational
    dependency networks. In: Frasconi, P., Lisi, F.A. (eds.) Online Proceedings of the
    International Conference on Inductive Logic Programming 2010, pp. 1–8 (June
    2010). https://lirias.kuleuven.be/handle/123456789/283041
20. Natarajan, S., Khot, T., Kersting, K., Gutmann, B., Shavlik, J.W.: Gradient-based
    boosting for statistical relational learning: the relational dependency network case.
    Mach. Learn. **86**(1), 25–56 (2012)
21. Neville, J., Jensen, D.: Relational dependency networks. J. Mach. Learn. Res. **8**,
    653–692 (2007)
22. Olivas, E.S., Guerrero, J.D.M., Sober, M.M., Benedito, J.R.M., Lopez, A.J.S.:
    Handbook of Research on Machine Learning Applications and Trends: Algorithms,
    Methods and Techniques - 2 Volumes. Information Science Reference - Imprint of:
    IGI Publishing, Hershey, PA (2009)
23. Pan, S.J., Yang, Q.: A survey on transfer learning. IEEE Trans. Knowl. Data Eng.
    22(10), 1345–1359 (2010)
24. Pedregosa, F., et al.: Scikit-learn: machine learning in Python. J. Mach. Learn.
    Res. **12**, 2825–2830 (2011)
25. Pitangui, C.G., Zaverucha, G.: Learning theories using estimation distribution
    algorithms and (reduced) bottom clauses. In: Muggleton, S.H., Tamaddoni-Nezhad,
    A., Lisi, F.A. (eds.) ILP 2011. LNCS (LNAI), vol. 7207, pp. 286–301. Springer, Hei-
    delberg (2012). https://doi.org/10.1007/978-3-642-31951-8_25
26. Weiss, K., Khoshgoftaar, T.M., Wang, D.: A survey of transfer learning. J. Big
    Data **3**(1), 9 (2016). https://doi.org/10.1186/s40537-016-0043-6
27. Yang, Q., Zhang, Y., Dai, W., Pan, S.J.: Transfer Learning. Cambridge University
    Press (2020). https://doi.org/10.1017/9781139061773

Online Learning of Logic Based Neural Network Structures

Victor Guimarães$^{(\boxtimes)}$ ⓘ and Vítor Santos Costa ⓘ

CRACS and DCC/FCUP, Universidade do Porto, Porto, Portugal
victorguimaraes13@gmail.com, vsc@dcc.fc.up.pt

Abstract. In this paper, we present two online structure learning algorithms for NeuralLog, NeuralLog+OSLR and NeuralLog+OMIL. NeuralLog is a system that compiles first-order logic programs into neural networks. Both learning algorithms are based on Online Structure Learner by Revision (OSLR). NeuralLog+OSLR is a port of OSLR to use NeuralLog as inference engine; while NeuralLog+OMIL uses the underlying mechanism from OSLR, but with a revision operator based on Meta-Interpretive Learning. We compared both systems with OSLR and RDN-Boost on link prediction in three different datasets: Cora, UMLS and UWCSE. Our experiments showed that NeuralLog+OMIL outperforms both the compared systems on three of the four target relations from the Cora dataset and in the UMLS dataset, while both NeuralLog+OSLR and NeuralLog+OMIL outperform OSLR and RDN-Boost on the UWCSE, assuming a good initial theory is provided.

Keywords: Online Learning · Inductive Logic Programming · Meta-Interpretive Learning · Neural Network · Neural-Symbolic Learning and Reasoning · Theory Revision from Examples

1 Introduction

Neural networks have achieved a great success on a wide range of tasks [14]. However, traditional neural network models cannot take advantage of background knowledge, which may contain additional information about the examples, as well as expert knowledge. On the other hand, Inductive Logic Programming (ILP) [17] is a field of study that tries to learn first-order logic theories in order to describe a set of examples given background knowledge [17], but ILP struggles to deal with numeric features and uncertainty and noise; which are inherent characteristics of real world applications.

The field of Neural-Symbolic Learning and Reasoning tries to combine the strengths of both neural networks and logic systems, in order to obtain models that are both capable of dealing with numeric features, uncertainty and noise and can also take advantage of existing background knowledge [6].

V. Guimarães—Financed by the Portuguese funding agency, FCT - Fundação para a Ciência e a Tecnologia through Ph.D. scholarships 2020.05718.BD.

N. Katzouris and A. Artikis (Eds.): ILP 2021, LNAI 13191, pp. 140–155, 2022.
https://doi.org/10.1007/978-3-030-97454-1_10

NeuralLog is a system developed to transform a first-order logic program into a neural network. It receives as input a set of first-order clauses that are used to define the neural network model, and a set of facts that becomes weights in the neural network. Then, those weights are fine-tuned, given a set of examples [9].

Online Structure Learner by Revision (OSLR) is a theory revision algorithm that revises the logic theory to cope with the arrival of new examples [7,8]. OSLR uses a tree structure representation of the logic theory, and applies revision operators to this structure in order to improve the theory to the new examples.

In this paper, we propose two structure learning algorithms for NeuralLog: NeuralLog+OSLR, which is a ported version of the OSLR algorithm to use NeuralLog as inference engine; and NeuralLog+OMIL, which uses the same underlying theory revision mechanism used by NeuralLog+OSLR (and OSLR), but applies a new revision operator, based on the Meta-Interpretive Learning (MIL) system Metagol [18].

Metagol is a MIL system that have recently been shown to achieve good performance when learning logic theories from examples [18]. MIL systems use a higher-order logic theory in order to define the hypotheses space and the searching mechanism of first-order theories from examples. To the best of our knowledge, it is the first time MIL is applied to learn first-order logic theories online, where new examples arrive over time.

We compared our approach with the original OSLR [7] and RDN-Boost [12] for link prediction tasks in three different datasets: the Cora [21] and the UWCSE [24] datasets, which were also used on [7]; and the UMLS [13] dataset. Our experiments show that NeuralLog+OMIL outperforms OSLR and RDN-Boost on three of the four target relations from the Cora dataset and in the UMLS dataset. While NeuralLog+OSLR and NeuralLog+OMIL outperform OSLR and RDN-Boost on the UWCSE, assuming a good initial theory is provided.

The remainder of the paper is as follows: in Sect. 2, we briefly give the background knowledge in order to understand this work; in Sect. 3, we present our two structure learning algorithms for online theory revision for NeuralLog; in Sect. 4, we present the performed experiments and obtained results; in Sect. 5, we present the works related to ours; and we conclude and propose directions for future work in Sect. 6.

2   Background Knowledge

In this work, a first-order logic program is a set of Horn clauses [11]. A Horn clause has the form of $b(.) \leftarrow p_1(.) \wedge \cdots \wedge p_n(.)$. where $b(.)$ is called the head of the clause and the set of p_i represents a conjunction and is called the body of the clause. The terms between parentheses can be either constants, represented by a string starting with a lowercase letter; or variables, represented by a string starting with an upper case letter. b and p_i are predicate names, and the predicate name followed by its terms is called an atom. A literal is either an atom or the negation of an atom. First-order logic functions and negation are not considered in this work, although we will refer to the atoms in the body of a clause as literals, to distinguish them from the atom of the head. A fact is a Horn clause with empty body, where all terms are constant.

NeuralLog treats facts of a logic program as numeric matrices, and the rule inference is performed as algebraic operations in those matrices [9]. In addition, each NeuralLog fact has an associated weight that influences the final result of the rule inference. Those weights can be learned by the neural network, in order to best fit a set of examples.

Inductive Logic Programming (ILP) is a subfield of machine learning which is concerned with finding logic theories to describe a set of examples, given background knowledge [25]. Meta-Interpretive Learning (MIL) uses a higher-order logic theory, in order to define the hypotheses space of possible first-order logic theories and to learn a first-order theory from the examples [18]. In a higher-order logic, the predicate names in the rules can be variables, and the logic inference system should find the substitution of the name in order to prove the rule. Metagol [18] is a MIL system which uses a modified Prolog meta-interpreter that resolves a higher-order theory similarly to a first-order SLD-Algorithm [29].

Another approach to learn first-order logic theories is by revising an initial (partially correct) logic theory, in order to adapt it to new examples. This approach is called *theory revision from examples* [3,26]. This characteristic of starting from a (possibly empty) initial theory in order to adapt it to new examples makes theory revision a suitable candidate to be applied to online environment, where new examples are arriving over time.

3   Online Theory Revision with NeuralLog

In this section, we present the two structure learning algorithms proposed in this work. We start by presenting NeuralLog+OSLR, our implementation of OSLR. Then, we present NeuralLog+OMIL, an online implementation of MIL.

3.1   Online Structure Learner by Revision

Online Structure Learner by Revision (OSLR) [7] is a system developed to learn logic theories in an online fashion, originally based on ProPPR [28]. It relies on theory revision techniques in order to adapt an existing theory to cope with new arriving examples. In this subsection, we present NeuralLog+OSLR, our implementation of OSLR that learns theories in the NeuralLog language.

The top-level revision algorithm implemented by OSLR is as follows: when new examples arrive, they are placed into a tree structure that represents the logic theory; then, a revision is proposed to the point of the theory that has the biggest potential to bring a gain for the theory; after, the revision is evaluated against an accepting criterion; finally, the revision is either accepted or rejected and the algorithm evaluates the next revision, until no more revision points are changed from the current examples, when the algorithm waits for new examples.

NeuralLog+OSLR follows the OSLR top-level algorithm with minimal changes, in order to make it better suited for neural networks. In the remainder of this subsection, we summarize the OSLR algorithm in order to keep

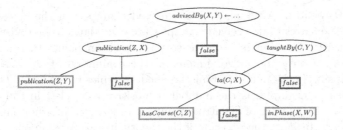

Fig. 1. Tree Structure Representation of the UWCSE Theory Example

Table 1. Theory Example for the UWCSE Dataset

$advisedBy(X, Y) \leftarrow taughtBy(C, Y) \land ta(C, X) \land hasCourse(C, Z).$
$advisedBy(X, Y) \leftarrow taughtBy(C, Y) \land ta(C, X) \land inPhase(X, W).$
$advisedBy(X, Y) \leftarrow publication(Z, X) \land publication(Z, Y).$

this work self-contained. In addition, we point out the differences between NeuralLog+OSLR and the original OSLR. However, we refer the reader to [7,8], for a more detailed explanation of OSLR.

Data Representation. Online Structure Learner by Revision (OSLR) starts by constructing a tree representation of a, possible empty, theory for each target predicate. This tree structure represents all the rules in the theory, whose head predicate is equal to the target predicate. The root of the tree represents the head of the rules for the target predicate, while the other nodes represent the literals in the body of the rules. The level immediately after the head represents the literals in the first position in the body of the rules, and there will be a node for each different literal in the first position. The next level represents the literals in the second position and so on. For each internal (non-leaf) node in the tree, a default *false* node is appended as child. The *false* nodes are always leaves.

This tree structure plays two roles: identifying the revision points on the theory; and storing the examples that shall be used to revise these points. Figure 1 shows an example of the tree representation of the theory shown in Table 1.

Each path from the root of the tree to a non-false leaf represents a rule in the theory. Rules that are a subset of another rule are not considered. The leaves represent the possible revision points and are shown as squares in Fig. 1.

When a new example arrives, it is passed through the tree to decide where it will be placed. The example starts in the root, then it is recursively passed through the nodes in the tree as described: for each node u in the children nodes of the current node v, if the (partial) rule from the root to u proves the example, we pass the example down to u. If the example is not proved by any of the children nodes of v, it is placed in the false node connected to v. This process repeats until the example reaches the leaves of the tree. If the example is proved by more than one child node, it goes to all the nodes that prove it.

Theory Revision. After placing the arrived examples in the correspondent leaves, all the leaves that received examples are candidates to be revised. OSLR uses a heuristic function in order to sort the revision points to prioritize the ones that may have the bigger impact in the evaluation of the theory. This heuristic is simply the number of misclassified examples in the leaf. The number of misclassified examples is the number of positive examples, in the case of a false leaf; or the number of negative examples, in the case of a non-false leaf.

In order to propose the revision of the theory, it uses revision operators that are applied to the revision points. There are two possible operations to revise the tree: adding new nodes to the tree; or removing nodes from the tree. OSLR applies all the possible operators to each revision point and uses the examples contained in the point in order to evaluate the revision on the theory.

Adding Node. It can be applied to both false and non-false leaves. When applied to a false leaf, the new nodes are used in order to generate a new rule that starts from the root until the parent of the false leaf. This new rule will be added to the theory in order to make the theory more generic and is an attempt to prove positive examples that fell in the false leaf. On the other hand, adding node to a non-false leaf extends the path from the root to the new leaf, thus, extending the rule and making the theory more specific, which is an attempt to avoid proving false examples in the non-false leaf. There are two algorithms to select the nodes to be added, both relying on the concept of the bottom clause [15]: the hill-climbing algorithm, which tries to add a candidate literal at a time, until certain stop criteria is met; and the relational path-finding algorithm [22], which tries to find a path between the variables of the example.

Deleting Node. It can be applied to non-false leaves or to false leaves whose parent has a single non-false child and this non-false child is also a leaf; this approach is described as *Alternative 1* in [8]. When applied to a false leaf, it deletes the literal represented by its sibling node, in an attempt to make the theory more generic, in order to prove the positive examples in the false leaf. When applied to a non-false leaf, it deletes the rule represented by the leaf, in an attempt to make the theory more specific, avoiding proving negative examples.

After applying all the possible revision operators to a given revision point, the operator that better improves the performance of the theory, given the examples in the revision point, is selected to be evaluated against the acceptance criteria, which will be described below.

The adding node operator is actually two distinct revision operators, one for the hill-climbing and another for the relational path-finding. Thus, alongside the deletion operator, they all compete among each other and the one that achieves the best result for the revision point is selected.

Accepting the Revision. Once the operator that has the biggest metric in a given revision point is selected, OSLR uses a threshold to decide if the improvement of the revised theory over the current theory is significant.

This threshold is based on the Hoeffding's bound [10] and is given by $\epsilon = \sqrt{\frac{R^2 \ln(1/\delta)}{2n}}$ where R is the size of the range of the given metric, n is the number of examples used in the evaluation and δ is a parameter defined by the user. An improvement larger than ϵ means that the probability of the revised theory to be actually better than the current theory is $1 - \delta$.

The examples used to evaluate the theories are the ones in the revision points. If the improvement of the revised theory over the current one is greater than ϵ, the revision is accepted and the examples used to evaluate it are discarded. Otherwise, the revision is discarded and the examples are unchanged. After either case, the algorithm continues to try to revise the remaining revision points, if there are any revision points left to be revised.

Clause Modifiers. In OSLR, after a revision is accepted, a feature, in the ProPPR language [28], is generated for the rule that was modified by the revision. This is the point where our implementation differs the most from the original OSLR. NeuralLog language does not support the ProPPR features, although, in some cases, they might be similar to the addition of a literal to the rule whose weight should be learned by the neural network. As such, instead of computing the features in the same way OSLR does, which would select a subset of terms in the rule to have associated weights to be learned, we create a unique weight for each rule, which is learned by the neural network and is independent of the instantiation of the terms in the rule. Our experiments using OSLR showed that the difference between this approach and the original one is minimal.

The addition of the weight is done by a clause modifier, which appends the weight to the body of the revised rules. These weights are represented in the form of a literal, with a unique constant for each rule; and this literal is marked as learnable in the NeuralLog language.

In addition to appending a literal to the rule with a unique constant, we have two more clause modifiers that are useful for the neural network construction. The first one is a clause modifier that appends a literal to the rule with a term from the head of the rule. This modifier is used to append an activation function for the rule, whose term must be the last variable in the head of the rule.

The other modifier changes the predicate name of the head of the rule to another name, by appending a suffix at the end of the name, this modifier is useful to learn a set of rules that indirectly proves the examples. For instance, suppose one wants to learn examples from the predicate $p/2$ without changing rules that have the $p/2$ predicate in the head. One could add the rule $p(X, Y) \leftarrow p_1(X, Y)$. to the background knowledge and use a clause modifier to change the head of the rules, learned from the examples, from $p/2$ to $p_1/2$. This is specially useful in the definition of neural networks, because it allows us to isolate the learned part of the theory and to add neural network components around it. For instance, the addition of biases and output functions for the target predicates.

3.2   Online Meta-Interpretive Learning

In this work, we propose a novel approach by combining the MIL hypotheses search strategy with the online learning mechanism from OSLR. We call this Online Meta-Interpretive Learning approach as NeuralLog+OMIL.

To achieve such a goal, we created a new revision operator based on the MIL search strategy used by Metagol, which proposes revisions to nodes in the OSLR tree representation. Then, we use the same NeuralLog+OSLR machinery, replacing the three original revision operators by our MIL revision operator.

In order to reuse NeuralLog+OSLR machinery we have to adapt the MIL algorithm to work with the OSLR tree structure. In Metagol, a higher-order clause, such as $P(X, Y) \leftarrow Q(X, Z) \wedge R(Z, Y)$, is directly applied to the target relation and the resolution system searches for substitutions to the higher-order variables (representing predicate names) which proves the positive examples.

Instead of applying the higher-order clauses to the input examples, NeuralLog+OMIL creates a target atom to be proved by the higher-order program, based on the revision point to which the MIL operator is applied.

In order to propose the revision of the theory, we apply each higher-order clause to solve the target atom generated by the revision point. Then, each higher-order variable of this clause is replaced by a valid predicate from the background knowledge. For each possible first-order rule, the revision point is replaced by the body of the rule and the theory is evaluated against the examples of the revision point. If the operator is applied to the false leaf, it uses the new atoms to create a new rule whose body starts with the path from the root to the parent of the false leaf node in the tree. Finally, if the first-order theory evaluation is greater than the Hoeffding's bound threshold, the algorithm returns it, otherwise, it continues to the next first-order theory, if any.

In order to give the OMIL operator more information to propose the revision, we create a different target atom, depending on the revision point.

Root Node. When the operator is applied to the false leaf of the root node, we use the predicate of the example as target atom; in this case, the operator tries to learn a rule to directly predict the examples.

Propositional Literal. When the literal has no variables, the target atom would have a special predicate, only used inside this operator, with the same variables as the head of the rule. This will inform the operator about the input and output variables of the rule.

Literal Connected to the Output. When the target literal is connected to the output, it will be the target atom. In this way, the same terms of the target literal will be used by the operator.

Literal Disconnected from the Output. When the literal is not connected to the output, the target atom will have the special predicate name, and the variables will be the input variable of the disconnected literal and the output variable of the rule. As such, the operator will be able to find a body which connects the input of the literal to the output of the rule, closing this path.

These modifications to the target atom gives the OMIL operator enough information to find meaningful rules: (1) having the information about the input and output variables of the rule, in the first two cases; (2) the information about the final part of a path in the rule, in the third case; and (3) the information about an open path and the output variable of the rule, in the last case. The use of this information will depend on the higher-order theory. However, it allows the user to define meta-rules that might: (1) create new paths, (2) replace the final part of an existing path, or (3) close an existing open path; respectively.

In order to restore the deletion behaviour from OSLR, we added two special rules to the higher-order theory: $P(X, Y) \leftarrow true.$ and $P(X, Y) \leftarrow false.$

The *true* literal is a special literal that is always true. Since the body of a rule is a conjunction (logic **AND**) of literals, the addition of a literal that is always true does not change the result of the conjunction, as such it can be removed from the rule. When the true rule is applied to a literal, the literal is replaced by the true literal, that is not added to the rule, since it will have no effect on it, thus, the application of this rule represents a literal removal. On the other hand, the *false* literal is a special literal that is always false. As such, a rule whose body includes a *false* literal will always fail to be proved, and can be removed from the theory. Thus, the application of the false rule to append a literal in the body of a rule will result in the deletion of the rule from the theory.

Applying any of these rules to a false leaf would produce no effect. For the true rule, it would generate a rule whose body is a subset of another rule, which is not allowed by the OSLR algorithm. For the false rule, it would result in an attempt of creating a new rule with the *false* literal in its body, which would be excluded and the theory would remain unchanged.

After the proposal of the modification of the theory by the operator, the clause modifiers are applied to the modified rule as usual, which will be the rule formed by the existing tree and the literal in the body of the clause generated by the higher-order theory.

4   Experiments

In order to show the capabilities of NeuralLog+OSLR and NeuralLog+OMIL, we compared them with OSLR in online learning of logic theories, for link prediction, in three distinct datasets: the Cora dataset, which is a citation matching dataset [21]; the Unified Medical Language System (UMLS), which is a medical dataset [13]; and the UWCSE dataset, which describes relations between professors and students in the University of Washington [24]. In addition, we also include the comparison with RDN-Boost [12], a system that learn Relational Dependency Networks (RDNs) [19], which was also presented in [7,8].

Link prediction is the task to find the entities related to another entity, given a relation. In this case, given a query $? - p(a, X)$, we would like to find the substitutions of X that match the positive examples, without matching the negative ones. We call p the target relation, a the input entity and the substitution of X are the output entities.

4.1   Datasets

Cora. The Cora dataset contains four target relations, *Same Author*, *Same Bib*, *Same Title* and *Same Venue*. We ran each of these relations separately.

UMLS. It is a dataset between biomedical entities. We selected the *Affects* as target relation, since it is the most frequent relation in this dataset, as it is done in [27]. Since it has no negative examples, we generated approximately 2 negative examples for each positive example, by selecting a random output entity that appears in the target relation, but is not related to the input entity, following the Local Closed World Assumption (LCWA) [5].

UWCSE. This dataset has one target relation *Advised by*, that relates the students with supervisors. The UWCSE dataset also contains ternary facts, which are not supported by NeuralLog. Thus, we converted them to binary, by concatenating two terms that always appear together in the theory. We also added two additional predicates to extract either term, given the concatenated form.

Table 2 shows the statistics of the datasets, for a total of 6 target relations. Since the number of negative examples in the UWCSE is much bigger than the positive ones, we downsample the set of negative examples to be twice as much as the number of positives ones, as it is done in [12].

Table 2. Size of the Datasets

Relation	# Positives	# Negatives
Same author	488	66
Same Bib	30,971	21,952
Same title	661	714
Same venue	2,887	4,976
Affects	1,022	–
Advised by	113	16,601

4.2   Simulating the Online Environment

In order to properly evaluate the online systems, we use these datasets to simulate an online environment by reproducing the procedure used in [7,8]. We split each target relation into $N + 1$ iterations, where iteration 0 has only the background knowledge and each of the following iterations has approximately $|E|/N$ examples, where $|E|$ is the total number of examples of each relation.

We pass each iteration, in order, to the system. When an iteration arrives, the current model is tested with it, before training. Then, the system trains on this iteration and the evaluation of each iteration is recorded. This evaluation procedure is known as *Prequential* [2]. Since RDN-Boost is designed for batch learning, we transformed each iteration of the online learning environment into a batch learning task by appending all the examples from the previous iteration to it. Then, we applied RDN-Boost to each of those tasks.

Following the procedure from [7,8], we set the number N of iterations to approximately 30 for all the target relations except the *Advised by* which was set to 91. We ran each experiment 30 times and reported the average of the area under the Precision-Recall curve as the evaluation metric. The Hoeffding's bound δ parameter was set to 10^{-3} and updated to half its value, each time a revision was accepted. OSLR only considers the number of unrelated examples to compute the Hoeffding's bound, however, we had to relax this restriction for the UMLS dataset, given the reduced number of unrelated examples.

NeuralLog systems add a weight for each rule, as well as an activation function. Also, a bias is added to the output of the target relation, which then passes through an output function. The weights and biases are parameters to be learned by the neural network. After each accepted revision, the neural network adjusts its parameters on the same set of examples used by the revision. It uses the adagrad optimization algorithm to reduce the mean squared error with L2-regularisation for 10 epochs, with a learning rate of 0.01 and the l2 $\lambda = 0.01$. For OSLR, we replaced its feature generation by another one that creates a single weight for each rule, in order to be closer related to NeuralLog, although this change did not have a big impact in the final result.

4.3   Results

We now present the results of the experiments. All pairs of systems were compared for statistical significance using two-tailored paired t-test with $p < 0.05$. There is a statistical significance between the pairs, unless stated otherwise.

Figure 2 shows the evaluation of the systems in the Cora dataset over the epochs. As can be seen, NeuralLog+OMIL outperforms both OSLR and RDN-Boost over all iterations for the *Same Author* and the *Same Venue* relations, while it underperforms OSLR and RDN-Boost on all iterations on the *Same Bib* relation. For the *Same Title* relation, NeuralLog+OMIL has a stable behaviour over the iterations, while OSLR have some ups and downs. However, OSLR is able to achieve a better result in the final iteration, where all the examples are used, and also has a better overall result, measured by the area under the curve of iterations. NeuralLog+OSLR performed worse than OSLR in all relations of the Cora dataset, but it is able to outperform RDN-Boost in all relation, except for the *Same Bib*. There was no statistical difference between NeuralLog+OMIL and OSLR, and for NeuralLog+OSLR and RDN-Boost for the area under the curve and the final result, in the *Same Author* relation. There were no statistical difference between OSLR and RDN-Boost for the area under the curve and the final result, in the *Same Bib* relation. Finally, there were no statistical difference

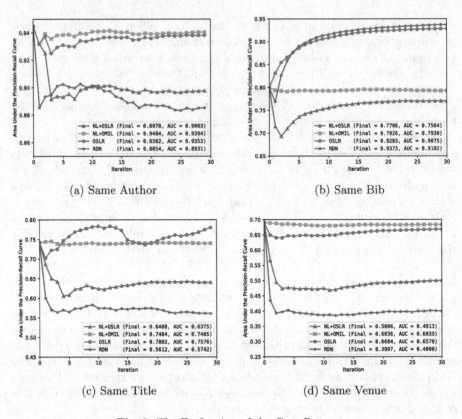

(a) Same Author   (b) Same Bib

(c) Same Title   (d) Same Venue

Fig. 2. The Evaluation of the Cora Dataset

between NeuralLog+OMIL and OSLR for the area under the curve and the final result, in the *Same Title* relation.

Figure 3 shows the results of the experiments for the UMLS and UWCSE datasets. On Fig. 3a, we can see that NeuralLog+OMIL, OSLR and RDN-Boost get better as new examples arrive, ending with an evaluation greater than NeuralLog+OSLR. However, NeuralLog+OSLR performs much better than the other systems on the initial iterations, achieving a better overall evaluation, given the area under the curve. There was no statistical difference between NeuralLog+OSLR and NeuralLog+OMIL nor between NeuralLog+OMIL and RDN-Boost, for the result of the final iteration. Also, there was no statistical difference between the area under the curve between OSLR and RDN-Boost.

In order to evaluate the impact of an initial theory, we performed three experiments with the UWCSE dataset, using a hand-crafted theory provided by Alchemy[1]. Since Alchemy supports a more complex logic language, we removed the rules whose logic feature were not supported by both OSLR and NeuralLog. Then, we used two sets of theory: a complete set, containing more rules, which

---

[1] http://alchemy.cs.washington.edu/.

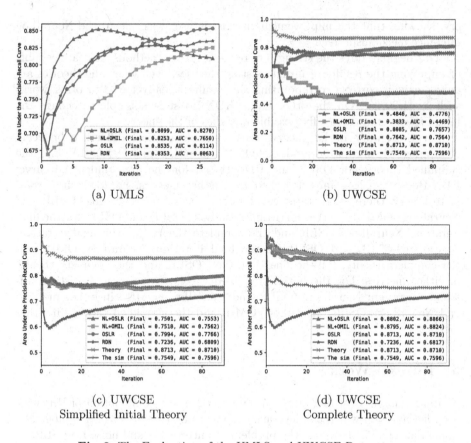

(a) UMLS

(b) UWCSE

(c) UWCSE
Simplified Initial Theory

(d) UWCSE
Complete Theory

Fig. 3. The Evaluation of the UMLS and UWCSE Datasets

are more specific; and a simplified version of this theory, containing only some generic rules from the complete set. The *Theory* lines in the figures show the result of the initial theory, while the *The sim* shows the results of the simplified theory; both theories were inferred by OSLR, without any training.

As can be seen in Figs. 3b, OSLR outperforms both NeuralLog systems and RDN-Boost, when they all start from an empty theory, however, it cannot outperform the complete theory. On the other hand, when the systems start from the simplified theory (Fig. 3c), OSLR can improve over the simplified theory, however, not yet outperforming the complete theory; while NeuralLog systems stay close to the performance of the simplified theory and RDN-Boost performed worse than the theory itself. Finally, when starting from the complete theory (Fig. 3d), both NeuralLog+OSLR and NeuralLog+OMIL are able to improve over the complete theory, with a slight advantage for NeuralLog+OSLR, while OSLR is only capable of achieving the same performance as the complete theory and RDN-Boost, again, performed worse than the theory. However, neither NeuralLog+OSLR nor NeuralLog+OMIL were able to change the complete theory, showing that the improvement in this dataset was due to the NeuralLog inference mechanism itself.

This demonstrates the strength of revision theory methods, that are capable of improving the results of initial existing theories, even when the theories are only partially correct, corroborating the results already found in other works such as [4,20,23]. On the other hand, RDN-Boost is not able to change the initial theory and cannot fix possible mistakes of the theory.

For the empty initial theory, there is no statistical difference between: NeuralLog+OSLR and NeuralLog+OMIL, in either metrics; OSLR and the simplified theory nor OSLR and RDN-Boost, for the area under the curve; RDN-Boost and the simplified theory, in either metrics. For the initial complete theory, there is no statistical difference between: NeuralLog+OSLR and NeuralLog+OMIL, in either metrics; NeuralLog+OSLR and OSLR, for the final iteration; NeuralLog+OSLR and the complete theory, for the final iteration; NeuralLog+OMIL and OSLR for the final iteration; NeuralLog+OMIL and the complete theory, for the final iteration; OSLR and the complete theory, in either metrics. For the initial simplified theory, there is no statistical difference between: NeuralLog+OSLR and NeuralLog+OMIL, in either metrics; and NeuralLog+OSLR/NeuralLog+OMIL and the simplified theory, in either metrics.

5   Related Work

Neural-Symbolic Learning and Reasoning studies the combination of ILP with deep learning [6], which can leverage deep learning the ability of handling relational data while addressing the problem of uncertainty and noise from ILP.

TensorLog [1] is a system closely related to NeuralLog. Both TensorLog and NeuralLog store logic facts in matrix form and perform logic inference through numeric operations on those matrices. However, NeuralLog differs from TensorLog in the way the neural network is built from the logic theory. Furthermore, NeuralLog is more flexible than TensorLog, mainly because it treats numeric attributes as logic terms that can be easily manipulated through logic rules. Differently from TensorLog, NeuralLog also supports rules containing free variables, which might be important for some tasks.

MIL have already been applied in Iterated Structural Gradient [27], to learn theories for ProPPR, a Stochastic Logic Programming system [16]. However, ProPPR uses an inference mechanism that cannot be easily integrated with neural networks. MIL is well suited to integrate with NeuralLog, since the higher-order theory allows the user to define a template in order to create the relational part of the network. This template can be used to append this relational part to an existing neural network.

We implemented the OSLR theory revision algorithm as our online learning mechanism [7,8]. We opted for this algorithm because it has a clear separation between the structure learning algorithm and the underneath inference mechanism, which allowed us to easily port it to work with NeuralLog. Finally, the flexibility of OSLR allowed us to implement the new MIL revision operator to apply MIL online. To the best of our knowledge, it is the first time that MIL is applied to online learning tasks.

6   Conclusion

In this paper we presented two online structure learning algorithms based on NeuralLog [9], NeuralLog+OSLR and NeuralLog+OMIL. Both learning algorithms are based on Online Structure Learner by Revision (OSLR) [7,8]. NeuralLog+OSLR is a port of OSLR, using NeuralLog as inference engine; while NeuralLog+OMIL uses the underlying mechanism from OSLR, but with a revision operator based on Meta-Interpretive Learning (MIL) [18]. We compared our proposal with OSLR [7,8] and RDN-Boost [12] on link prediction task in three different datasets: Cora [21], UMLS [13] and UWCSE [24]. Our experiments showed that NeuralLog+OMIL outperforms OSLR and RDN-Boost on three of the four target relations from the Cora dataset and in the UMLS dataset. While NeuralLog+OSLR and NeuralLog+OMIL outperformed OSLR and RDN-Boost on the UWCSE, whenever a good initial theory is provided.

As future work, we would like to experiment with NeuralLog structure learning algorithms on more datasets, including mixing the relation part of the neural network with propositional neural network models. For instance, the combination of models for natural language processing with relational tasks.

References

1. Cohen, W.W., Yang, F., Mazaitis, K.: TensorLog: a probabilistic database implemented using deep-learning infrastructure. J. Artif. Intell. Res. **67**, 285–325 (2020)
2. Dawid, A.P.: Present position and potential developments: some personal views: statistical theory: the prequential approach. J. Royal Stat. Soc. Ser. A (General) **147**(2), 278–292 (1984)
3. De Raedt, L.: Logical and Relational Learning, 1st edn. Springer-Verlag, Berlin, Heidelberg (2008)
4. Duboc, A.L., Paes, A., Zaverucha, G.: Using the bottom clause and modes declarations on FOL theory revision from examples. Mach. Learn. **76**(1), 73–107 (2009)
5. Galárraga, L.A., Teflioudi, C., Hose, K., Suchanek, F.: AMIE: association rule mining under incomplete evidence in ontological knowledge bases. In: Proceedings of the 22Nd International Conference on World Wide Web, pp. 413–422. WWW 2013. ACM, New York, NY, USA (2013). https://doi.org/10.1145/2488388.2488425
6. Garcez, A.D., et al.: Neural-symbolic learning and reasoning: contributions and challenges. In: AAAI Spring Symposium Series (2015)
7. Guimarães, V., Paes, A., Zaverucha, G.: Online probabilistic theory revision from examples with ProPPR. Mach. Learn. **108**(7), 1165–1189 (2019). https://doi.org/10.1007/s10994-019-05798-y
8. Guimarães, V.: Online Probabilistic Theory Revision from Examples: A ProPPR Approach. Master's thesis, PESC, COPPE, Federal University of Rio de Janeiro, Rio de Janeiro, RJ, Brazil (2018)

9. Guimarães, V., Costa, V.S.: Neurallog: A neural logic language (2021)

10. Hoeffding, W.: Probability inequalities for sums of bounded random variables. J. Am. Stat. Assoc. **58**(301), 13–30 (1963)

11. Horn, A.: On sentences which are true of direct unions of algebras. J. Symbol. Logic **16**(1), 14–21 (1951)

12. Khot, T., Natarajan, S., Kersting, K., Shavlik, J.: Gradient-based boosting for statistical relational learning: the Markov logic network and missing data cases. Mach. Learn. **100**(1), 75–100 (2015)

13. Kok, S., Domingos, P.: Statistical predicate invention. In: Proceedings of the 24th International Conference on Machine Learning, pp. 433–440. ICML 2007. Association for Computing Machinery, New York, NY, USA (2007)

14. LeCun, Y., Bengio, Y.: The Handbook of Brain Theory and Neural Networks. Chap. Convolutional Networks for Images, Speech, and Time Series, pp. 255–258. MIT Press, Cambridge (1998)

15. Muggleton, S.: Inverse entailment and Progol. New Gener. Comput. **13**(3), 245–286 (1995)

16. Muggleton, S.: Stochastic logic programs. In: New Generation Computing, vol. 32, pp. 254–264. Academic Press, Cambridge, EUA, January 1996

17. Muggleton, S., De Raedt, L.: Inductive logic programming: theory and methods. J. Log. Program. **19**(20), 629–679 (1994)

18. Muggleton, S.H., Lin, D., Tamaddoni-Nezhad, A.: Meta-interpretive learning of higher-order dyadic datalog: predicate invention revisited. Mach. Learn. **100**(1), 49–73 (2015). https://doi.org/10.1007/s10994-014-5471-y

19. Neville, J., Jensen, D.: Relational dependency networks. Mach. Learn. **8**(Mar), 653–692 (2007)

20. Paes, A., Zaverucha, G., Costa, V.S.: On the use of stochastic local search techniques to revise first-order logic theories from examples. Mach. Learn. **106**(2), 197–241 (2016). https://doi.org/10.1007/s10994-016-5595-3

21. Poon, H., Domingos, P.: Joint inference in information extraction. In: Proceedings of the 22Nd National Conference on Artificial Intelligence. AAAI 2007, vol. 1, pp. 913–918. AAAI Press, Vancouver, British Columbia, Canada, July 2007

22. Richards, B.L., Mooney, R.J.: Learning relations by pathfinding. In: Proceedings of the Tenth National Conference on Artificial Intelligence (AAAI-1992), pp. 50–55, San Jose, CA, July 1992

23. Richards, B.L., Mooney, R.J.: Automated refinement of first-order horn-clause domain theories. Mach. Learn. **19**(2), 95–131 (1995)

24. Richardson, M., Domingos, P.: Markov logic networks. Mach. Learn. **62**(1), 107–136 (2006)

25. Shan-Hwei Nienhuys-Cheng, R.D.W.A.: Foundations of Inductive Logic Programming. Lecture Notes in Computer Science 1228. Lecture Notes in Artificial Intelligence. Springer-Verlag, Berlin, Heidelberg, 1 edn. (1997)

26. Shapiro, E.Y.: Algorithmic Program Debugging, 1st edn. The MIT Press, Cambridge, EUA (1983)

27. Wang, W.Y., Mazaitis, K., Cohen, W.W.: Structure learning via parameter learning. In: Proceedings of the 23rd ACM International Conference on Conference on Information and Knowledge Management, pp. 1199–1208. CIKM 2014. Association for Computing Machinery, New York, NY, USA (2014)

28. Wang, W.Y., Mazaitis, K., Lao, N., Cohen, W.W.: Efficient inference and learning in a large knowledge base. Mach. Learn. **100**(1), 101–126 (2015). https://doi.org/10.1007/s10994-015-5488-x
29. Warren, D.H.D., Pereira, L.M., Pereira, F.: Prolog - the language and its implementation compared with lisp. SIGPLAN Not. **12**(8), 109–115 (1977)

Programmatic Policy Extraction
by Iterative Local Search

Rasmus Larsen[(⊠)][iD] and Mikkel Nørgaard Schmidt[iD]

Department of Applied Mathematics and Computer Science,
Technical University of Denmark, Kongens, Lyngby, Denmark
{ralars,mnsc}@dtu.dk

Abstract. Reinforcement learning policies are often represented by neural networks, but programmatic policies are preferred in some cases because they are more interpretable, amenable to formal verification, or generalize better. While efficient algorithms for learning neural policies exist, learning programmatic policies is challenging. Combining imitation-projection and dataset aggregation with a local search heuristic, we present a simple and direct approach to extracting a programmatic policy from a pretrained neural policy. After examining our local search heuristic on a programming by example problem, we demonstrate our programmatic policy extraction method on a pendulum swing-up problem. Both when trained using a hand crafted expert policy and a learned neural policy, our method discovers simple and interpretable policies that perform almost as well as the original.

Keywords: Program synthesis · Reinforcement learning · Hindley-Milner type system · Neighborhood search

1 Introduction

While neural policy representations are by far the most common in modern Reinforcement Learning (RL), other representations are worth considering. Programmatic policies provide a number of potential benefits: For example, a program might be read and understood by a human, something that generally is not possible with a neural network. Programs are also inherently compositional, which allows for not only reuse of policies in new combinations, but also compositional reasoning about their behavior.

However, learning programmatic policies is challenging. The structured, discrete space of programs does not allow for the gradient based optimization that neural policies benefit greatly from. Compared to a more standard inductive synthesis setting, programmatic policies must be evaluated in an environment that, whether simulated or real, is expensive to interact with. Several approaches exist that attempt to handle this interaction issue, such as learning a parametric environment model [6], imitating an existing policy [1,14], or evaluating fewer programs by learning to search more efficiently [2]. Furthermore, [13] extend the

© Springer Nature Switzerland AG 2022
N. Katzouris and A. Artikis (Eds.): ILP 2021, LNAI 13191, pp. 156–166, 2022.
https://doi.org/10.1007/978-3-030-97454-1_11

imitation setting by providing a framework for intertwining RL and programmatic policy imitation.

This imitation-projection framework brings us a step closer to programmatic RL, where programs can be learned gradually through interaction with the environment. Essentially, this allows similar sample efficiency when compared to policy gradient methods, since the imitation-projection step is performed offline by scoring programs according to an imitation learning objective. One could even plausibly imagine that the inductive bias in a problem-specific policy language could lead to improved learning. The framework leaves many choices open in terms of how the policy update and programmatic policy projection steps are performed, as well as in terms of defining the program space. [13] perform experiments with a specific choice of update and projection, using two tailored program spaces based on PID controllers with either decision tree regression or Bayesian optimisation over some parameters as the projection operator.

In this paper we experiment with a more general program space based on Domain Specific Languages (DSLs) implemented in a typed lambda calculus. We demonstrate a method for re-using projections by local search around a previous projection, potentially reducing the required computational effort while allowing much longer programmatic policies to be found. Since imitation-projection greatly reduces environment interaction, the presented method takes advantage of this and performs relatively large searches in program space. Demonstrating the method on the pendulum swing-up task, we show that a simple and effective programmatic policy can be found by imitating a learned neural policy.

2   Methods

Our framework is based on previous work on imitation-projected and programmatically interpretable reinforcement learning [13,14]. We extend these methods to DSLs defined in a general-purpose programming language, namely the lambda calculus with Hindley-Milner type system. Using the building block of depth-limited type-directed program search, we construct an algorithm for finding a programmatic imitation of a given control policy. In order to discover programs much larger than what the depth limit of a single search allows, the algorithm performs multiple iterations of local search.

2.1   Program Synthesis by Type-Directed Search

By choosing the lambda calculus with Hindley-Milner type system, we obtain an expressive program space, in which exhaustive search for programs of a specified type is straightforwardly defined. An especially useful feature of this program representation is that the type system can be used to reduce the search space, by filtering candidate programs that do not type check. Further filtering is possible, such as the filtering of semantically similar programs as done in MagicHaskeller [9]. In this program representation, DSLs can be defined as sets of typed functions and constants, which together represent the space of possible programs to be searched.

Algorithm 1. Depth-limited local search (typed neighborhood)

```
1    input: domain specific language 𝒟
2    input: imitation dataset Γ
3    input: initial program P
4    output: best program in typed neighborhood p*
5    function N_n^d(𝒟, P, l)    // generates the neighborhood for location l in P
6      return ∅ if d = 0
7      T = TYPE(P, l)    // type of expression at l in P
8      C = {e | e : t ∈ 𝒟 ∧ T can unify with YIELD(t)}    // everything valid from DSL
9      P' = {edit(P, l, c)) | c ∈ C}
10     // return all complete programs, recursively generate partial programs
11     return {p ∈ P' | p is complete} ∪ N_n^{d-1}(𝒟, p', l')  ∀p' ∈ {p' ∈ P' | p' is partial}
12       where l' is the location of the first hole in p'
13   end
14   p* ← ∅, v* ← ∞    // best program and imitation loss
15   foreach l ∈ set of all paths in P
16     E_l = EXPRESSION(P, l)    // expression at location
17     𝒟' = 𝒟 ∪ (E_l, TYPE(E_l))    // locally extend DSL with E_l
18     foreach p ∈ N_n^d(𝒟', P, l)
19       evaluate p on Γ and update p* and v*
20     end
21   end
```

Our starting point for program synthesis is a simple version of depth-limited type-directed search. This choice is not a given; other, more advanced program search algorithms can be used. Here, the space of all programs in a DSL is a tree, with the empty program at the root. Internal nodes are partial programs, with each branch being a candidate substitution for a hole in a partial program. Enumerating through this search tree results in generating all valid programs, according to the DSL, as the leaves of the tree.

We take advantage of the typed language to reduce the search space. Instead of yielding all syntactically valid programs, as explained above, we want to yield only well-typed programs. This type-directed search algorithm is the same as used by e.g. [2] to sample programs from a prior distribution, but instead of sampling, all programs are enumerated. To expand a node in the search tree, a typed hole (an empty program with a type annotation) in the corresponding partial program is selected for synthesis. Then, valid candidates are selected from the set of all DSL candidates by unification; the resulting context of the unification is propagated to the further expansion of child nodes, ensuring that any constraints are satisfied. All candidates that can produce the correct type are considered, even if they would need arguments applied to them first.

2.2   Typed Neighborhood

In Algorithm 1.1, the type-directed depth-limited synthesis algorithm is used to generate what we call the typed neighborhood of a given program. This construction applies the basic synthesis algorithm in multiple places of an existing program, resulting in a iterative local search method that can both add and remove subprograms in each iteration. Because of this, the algorithm can synthesize larger programs, while also benefiting from work performed in previous iterations of the search.

Algorithm 2. Iterative local programmatic policy imitation

```
1    input: oracle policy f
2    optional input: initial program p_init = ∅
3    output: imitation program p_K
4    collect N on-policy trajectories using f:
5        τ_0 = ( (s_0^0, f(s_0^0), s_1^0, f(s_1^0), ... ), ..., (s_0^N, f(s_0^N), s_1^N, f(s_1^N), ... ) )
6    create supervised dataset Γ_0 = {(s, f(s)) | s ∈ τ_0}
7    derive p_0 from Γ_0 by local search from p_init   // algorithm 1
8    for k = 1, ..., K
9        collect M on-policy trajectories using p_{k-1}:
10           τ_k = ( (s_0^0, p_{k-1}(s_0^0), s_1^0, p_{k-1}(s_1^0), ... ), ..., (s_0^M, p_{k-1}(s_0^M), s_1^M, p_{k-1}(s_1^M), ... ) )
11       create supervised dataset Γ' = {(s, f(s)) | s ∈ τ_k}
12       aggregate datasets:
13           Γ_k = Γ_{k-1} ∪ Γ'   // or Γ_k = Γ_0 ∪ Γ', which is cheaper
14       derive p_k from Γ_k by local search from p_{k-1}   // algorithm 1
15    end
```

In more detail, we use a tree edit operation to define the programs contained within a typed neighborhood. Define the edit operation $\texttt{edit}(P, l, P')$ as the program obtained by replacing the subprogram at location l in program P with the program P'. Given a typed DSL $\mathcal{D}$, containing functions, constants, and their (polymorphic) types, the neighborhood of the program P at location l is the set of programs obtained by generating all well-typed expressions P' contained in $\mathcal{D}$, written $N_n^d(\mathcal{D}, P, l)$. The definition of a location is the root-to-expression path in the abstract syntax tree (AST) of the program. Here, we use the concept of a location in a generalized manner that can encompass multiple simultaneous locations, that is, a location l can represent multiple paths in the AST that are to be simultaneously replaced using independent edit operations. The neighborhood of a program P is thus the union of the neighborhoods at all locations, $N_n^d(\mathcal{D}, P) = \bigcup_{l \in L(P)} N_n^d(\mathcal{D}, P, l)$, where the neighborhood is parameterized with a maximum depth d of the expressions generated by edit operations, and with a maximum number of simultaneous edits n.

Furthermore, the expression being edited is dynamically added as a candidate to the DSL, and for the depth evaluation this candidate counts as having a depth of 1. This allows an edit not just to replace an expression, but to also extend an expression by using it as part of the new expression, despite the result otherwise being too large (compared to the depth limit). The size of the neighborhood $|N_n^d(\mathcal{D}, P)|$ is quite sensitive to all involved parameters $\mathcal{D}$, P, n, and d, but these can be flexibly chosen based on the problem and available computational resources.

Algorithm 3. Imitation-Projected Programmatic Reinforcement Learning with Local Synthesis

```
1    input: initial policy π₀
2    optional input: initial program p₀ = ∅
3    output: trained policy π_J, program p_J
4    for j = 1,...,J
5        π_j ← UPDATE(π_{j-1})    // reinforcement learning, e.g. policy gradient
6        p_j ← PROJECT(π_j, p_init = p_{j-1})    // program synthesis by algorithm 2
7    end
```

2.3 Policy Extraction by Local Synthesis

We use the typed neighborhood to discover programs that imitate reinforcement learning policies. In this setting, input/output examples are obtained by executing an existing policy and storing the state observations together with the corresponding actions chosen by the policy in each state. Thus, the policy synthesis problem is framed as imitation learning. Like in previous policy imitation methods, an interactive dataset aggregation method such as DAgger [11] is used: Instead of imitating only on states that the expert experiences, which is called behavioral cloning, some experience from the imitation policy is periodically added to the set of states considered. This allows subsequent imitation iterations to correct mistakes that otherwise wouldn't be observed, since the expert policy never experiences these mistakes. However, unless the expert is a global optimum, it is possible that it also makes mistakes on states which are not usually observed, and for this reason it is not always a clear benefit. The iterative imitation approach using the typed neighborhood is described in Algorithm 1.2.

One purpose of this search algorithm is to fit into the full imitation-projection framework from [13]. A simple, modified version of this framework is shown in Algorithm 1.3. The difference consists of the projection step, which now also depends on the previous projection, as enabled by Algorithm 1.1. Compared to Algorithm 1.2, the main difference is that each iteration also contains an `Update` step, which optimizes the expert policy.

3 Experiments

We present three different program synthesis experiments: The first is a programming by example (PBE) task with sampled ground truth programs, demonstrating the efficacy of the local search heuristic in Algorithm 1.1. The second is a policy extraction task, testing Algorithm 1.2, where the ground truth is a hand-coded policy. In these two first experiments, the DSL used for the search contains the true program used to generate observational data. Finally, in our third experiment we examine if we can learn a simple yet effective policy by imitation from a more complicated neural network policy which is trained using an existing reinforcement learning algorithm.

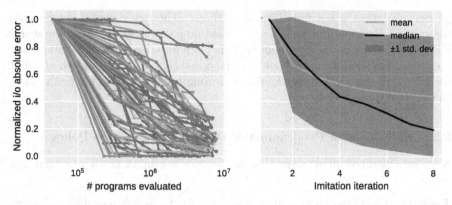

Fig. 1. Programming by example: Learn a program from input-output examples. Experiment on 100 sampled programs. Left: For each program, the absolute error (normalized wrt. first iteration) by number of programs evaluated. Right: Mean, median, and standard deviation by search iteration.

3.1   Programming by Example with Local Program Search

As a first evaluation of the method, we used a straightforward PBE task, whose purpose is to show that the described iterative local search is capable of synthesizing nontrivial programs from input-output specifications.

DSL: We defined a language containing the set of constants $\{-1, 0, 0.5, 0.8, 1, 3, 5, 6, \text{true}\}$, which are all `Floating` point numbers except `true` which is `Boolean`, and the functions with associated type signatures $\{\text{if} : \text{Bool} \Rightarrow \text{T0} \Rightarrow \text{T0} \Rightarrow \text{T0}, >$ $: \text{Float} \Rightarrow \text{Float} \Rightarrow \text{Bool}, \wedge : \text{Bool} \Rightarrow \text{Bool} \Rightarrow \text{Bool}, \oplus : \text{Bool} \Rightarrow \text{Bool} \Rightarrow \text{Bool}, - :$ $\text{Float} \Rightarrow \text{Float} \Rightarrow \text{Float}), * : \text{Float} \Rightarrow \text{Float} \Rightarrow \text{Float}, \cdot^2 : \text{Float} \Rightarrow \text{Float}\}$.

Data: The observation space (i.e. input) to these programs consists of three `Float`s, which are distinct variables that can be used just like constants. 10 sets of these numbers were randomly sampled as inputs to be used during synthesis. Ground truth programs of some length, as a simple proxy for complexity, were sampled from a weighted distribution over the DSL. In order to obtain samples that have a reasonable length, we designed a distribution on the abstract syntax of our DSL that puts more probability on higher-arity functions. Further, the probability of sampling `true` was weighted significantly down, while the probability of sampling an input variable was weighted higher. Since program length is not the best measure of complexity, samples were rejected on other criteria as well. Programs were discarded if: the length of the program (number of tokens) was less than 8, program output was constant, or an input-output equivalent program, on some randomly chosen inputs, existed within a depth 4 search of the DSL.

Results and Discussion: Results from $d = 4$ local search on 100 sampled ground truth programs can be seen in Fig. 1, which shows that for many of the programs an exact fit is found on the given inputs. Even for programs where an exact solution is not found, most of the searches show significant progress through the iterations, although a few make no progress at all. Since the search is deterministic, if no improvement is made in an iteration, further iterations will not lead to better results. It should also be noted that a single iteration of search with $d = 5$ in this setting corresponds to evaluating about as many programs as 20 iterations with $d = 4$.

3.2   Imitation of a Programmatic Pendulum Swing-Up Policy

Next we examined if we were able to discover a ground truth programmatic policy.

Task: We based the experiment on a simple, classical control problem, the pendulum swing-up task. The state space consists of the angle and angular velocity of the pendulum, and the action space is the torque applied to the base of the pendulum, normalized to the interval [-1, 1]. This two-dimensional state space allows us to easily display and visually compare policies. The simulator is discretized with a time step of 0.05s, and an episode is 200 steps long. The reward function is $r(\theta, \dot{\theta}, a) = ((\theta + \pi \; (\mathrm{mod} \; 2\pi)) - \pi)^2 + 0.1\dot{\theta} + 0.001a^2$, which results in a reward of 0 if the pendulum is perfectly balanced with no torque applied, and a reward of $-\pi^2$ when the pendulum is pointing straight down while not moving. While the state space of the pendulum task is $(\theta, \dot{\theta})$, the observation space supplied to the policies is $(\texttt{x1}, \texttt{x2}, \texttt{x3}) = (\sin \theta, \cos \theta, \dot{\theta})$.

DSL: We used a simple, pure DSL with primitives suitable for solving the RL task, containing the constants $\{-6, -1, 1, 0.5, 0.6, 8, 10\}$, and the functions $\{\texttt{if} :$ $\texttt{Bool} \Rightarrow \texttt{T0} \Rightarrow \texttt{T0} \Rightarrow \texttt{T0}, \texttt{gt} : \texttt{Float} \Rightarrow \texttt{Float} \Rightarrow \texttt{Bool}, \texttt{sub} : \texttt{Float} \Rightarrow \texttt{Float} \Rightarrow$ $\texttt{Float}, \texttt{add} : \texttt{Float} \Rightarrow \texttt{Float} \Rightarrow \texttt{Float}, \texttt{mul} : \texttt{Float} \Rightarrow \texttt{Float} \Rightarrow \texttt{Float}, \texttt{sign} :$ $\texttt{Float} \Rightarrow \texttt{Float}, \texttt{sqr} : \texttt{Float} \Rightarrow \texttt{Float}\}$.

Ground Truth: We hand crafted a ground truth policy in the DSL, capable of swinging up the pendulum from any starting state. The policy achieves an average reward of approximately -211 and a maximum of -113. This handcrafted policy is given by the program ((if ((gt x1) 0.6)) ((sub ((mul x2) -6)) x3)) (sign ((mul ((sub ((add ((mul 0.5) (sqr x3))) ((mul ten) ((sub x1) 1)))) 8)) ((mul -1) x3))).

Synthesis: At each iteration of the local search we used a search depth of $d = 4$ which was found to be enough to discover the if expression that switches between swing-up and balancing. As training data we used $N = 5$ state trajectories from the ground truth policy and $M = 2$ trajectories from the latest programmatic imitation policy. All training states were expert labelled with actions from the ground truth policy. For evaluation we simulated 100 rollouts from uniformly random states in the range $\frac{\pi}{2} \leq \theta \leq \frac{3\pi}{2}$, $-1 \leq \dot{\theta} \leq 1$, which is the pendulum below horizontal with relatively low velocity.

Results and Discussion: The results of the experiment is shown in Fig. 2 (left column). After four iterations of imitation learning a simple policy was found,

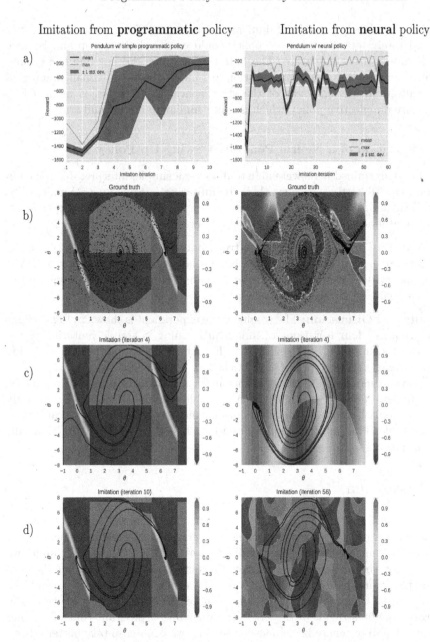

Fig. 2. Pendulum swing-up imitation learning of a programmatic policy from a ground truth programmatic (left) or neural (right) policy. Policies are visualized as a heat map; the state space is pendulum angle, θ, and angular velocity, $\dot{\theta}$, and the action is pendulum torque. The goal state is $\theta = 0$ (mod 2π), $\dot{\theta} = 0$. a) Cumulative reward of test trajectories. b) Ground truth programmatic/neural policy. Points indicate all states seen during training. c) Programmatic policy found after four iterations of imitation learning, with five test trajectories shown. d) Programmatic policy found after several more iterations, with five test trajectories shown.

capable of balancing the pendulum and swinging up from some states. After approximately ten iterations the policy could effectively swing up and balance the pendulum from any state. The imitation learning did not find the ground truth programmatic policy by iteration 10, likely due to the small number of observations in certain areas of the state space. Nonetheless, it managed to synthesize an effective policy which is quite similar to the ground truth.

3.3   Imitation of a Neural Pendulum Swing-Up Policy

Finally, we examined if we were able to discover a simple, interpretable policy in a more realistic setting, with synthesis by imitating a trained neural policy. The task, DSL, and synthesis procedure were as described in the previous experiment, with the ground truth policy as the only difference.

Ground Truth: The neural ground truth policy was found by TD3 [3], using feed-forward neural networks with 2 hidden layers of 24 neurons for both the actor and critic. Training was run for 5 million steps with a learning rate of 10^{-4} to ensure relatively good convergence.

Results and Discussion: The results of the experiment is shown in Fig. 2 (right column). After four iterations of imitation learning, a simple imitating policy capable of swinging up and balancing the pendulum is found. This imitation policy is (mul x1) (cos (exp (sign ((add x3) ((add −1) (sqr (exp x2))))))). After several more iterations, at iteration 56, a significantly more complicated programmatic policy was found which resembles the neural policy more closely but yields only a minor performance improvement, while being significantly less interpretable. This imitation policy has a length of 121 tokens, i.e. function calls plus arguments.

4   Discussion

We have presented and evaluated our method with simple experiments, and much remains to be done. As mentioned, one goal is to integrate the local search with reinforcement learning as described by Algorithm 1.3. While simple, we believe that the presented results show potential, especially through the programs that were discovered in only a few iterations. In particular, it would be interesting to evaluate this approach on more structured tasks, where neural networks might struggle with generalization while a program could be found that immediately generalizes. In such a setting, we could also take better advantage of type-directed search, with more complicated DSLs containing e.g. logic, matrix or computer vision functions potentially still remaining computationally tractable.

It should also be mentioned that local, iterated synthesis as a concept remains orthogonal to several other improvements in program synthesis; for example, enumerating or sampling programs according to a learned probability distribution as in e.g. [2] is possible, as is better filtering as in [9]. Instead of depth-limited search, it would be possible to limit the search to programs above a certain likelihood. However, it seems unclear how this distribution would be effectively learned for policies.

4.1 Related Work

Previous work on synthesizing programmatic policies at the intersection of RL and genetic programming (GP) include GPRL [6] which is based on offline GP, performed in a previously learned parametric model of the system of interest. They include a comparison with behavioral cloning, i.e., direct imitation of the actions of a trained policy. Their method performs better on the actual (simulated, but not learned) system. It is well known that behavioral cloning can lead to poor performance, e.g. [11], which could explain the observed performance gap. It seems likely that interaction with the model can overcome some of the distributional issues arising from behavioral cloning. In RL, it might be preferable to not learn a parametric model if it is used for credit assignment (i.e. policy learning) [5]. [4] proposed a method for using program repair in neural program synthesis. After neural synthesis, the resulting program might not be correct or even satisfy the input-output relation. The authors propose to learn a neural debugger that outputs so-called edits which correct potential errors in the program. The relation to this work is apparent in how we use an edit operator to define the neighborhood of a program. [8] describe a way to integrate GP, RL and simulated systems. By first synthesizing a policy using GP in the simulated system, it can later be adapted and fine-tuned through RL, allowing the policy to function on a real robot. [7] describe an imitation learning method that improves the inductive generalization by adapting the teacher distribution according to the imitating policy. The presented neighborhood search method can be considered an instance of the (Very) Large-Scale Neighborhood Search framework [10]. Deterministic versions of genetic algorithms have been considered before, such as in [12].

References

1. Bastani, O., Pu, Y., Solar-Lezama, A.: Verifiable reinforcement learning via policy extraction, May 2018. http://arxiv.org/abs/1805.08328
2. Ellis, K., Morales, L., Meyer, M.S., Solar-Lezama, A., Tenenbaum, J.B.: DREAM-CODER: bootstrapping domain-specific languages for neurally-guided Bayesian program learning. In: Neural Abstract Machines & Program Induction Workshop at NIPS (2018)
3. Fujimoto, S., van Hoof, H., Meger, D.: Addressing function approximation error in actor-critic methods, February 2018. http://arxiv.org/abs/1802.09477
4. Gupta, K., Christensen, P.E., Chen, X., Song, D.: Synthesize, execute and debug: learning to repair for neural program synthesis. In: Advances in Neural Information Processing Systems, July 2020. http://arxiv.org/abs/2007.08095
5. van Hasselt, H.P., Hessel, M., Aslanides, J.: When to use parametric models in reinforcement learning? In: Wallach, H., Larochelle, H., Beygelzimer, A., d' Alché-Buc, F., Fox, E., Garnett, R. (eds.) Advances in Neural Information Processing Systems, vol. 32. Curran Associates, Inc. (2019)

6. Hein, D., Udluft, S., Runkler, T.A.: Interpretable policies for reinforcement learning by genetic programming, December 2017. http://arxiv.org/abs/1712.04170
7. Inala, J.P., Bastani, O., Tavares, Z., Solar-Lezama, A.: Synthesizing programmatic policies that inductively generalize. In: International Conference on Learning Representations (ICLR) (2020)
8. Kamio, S., Mitsuhashi, H., Iba, H.: Integration of genetic programming and reinforcement learning for real robots. In: Cantú-Paz, E., et al. (eds.) GECCO 2003. LNCS, vol. 2723, pp. 470–482. Springer, Heidelberg (2003). https://doi.org/10.1007/3-540-45105-6_59
9. Katayama, S.: Efficient exhaustive generation of functional programs using Monte-Carlo search with iterative deepening. In: Ho, T.-B., Zhou, Z.-H. (eds.) PRICAI 2008. LNCS (LNAI), vol. 5351, pp. 199–210. Springer, Heidelberg (2008). https://doi.org/10.1007/978-3-540-89197-0_21
10. Pisinger, D., Ropke, S.: Large Neighborhood Search, pp. 399–419. Springer, US (2010). https://doi.org/10.1007/978-1-4419-1665-5_13
11. Ross, S., Gordon, G.J., Bagnell, J.A.: A reduction of imitation learning and structured prediction to No-Regret online learning, November 2010
12. Salomon, R.: The deterministic genetic algorithm: implementation details and some results. In: Proceedings of the 1999 Congress on Evolutionary Computation-CEC99 (Cat. No. 99TH8406). IEEE (2003). https://doi.org/10.1109/cec.1999.782001
13. Verma, A., Le, H., Yue, Y., Chaudhuri, S.: Imitation-projected programmatic reinforcement learning. In: Wallach, H., Larochelle, H., Beygelzimer, A., dÁlché-Buc, F., Fox, E., Garnett, R. (eds.) Advances in Neural Information Processing Systems, vol. 32, pp. 15752–15763. Curran Associates, Inc. (2019)
14. Verma, A., Murali, V., Singh, R., Kohli, P., Chaudhuri, S.: Programmatically interpretable reinforcement learning, April 2018. http://arxiv.org/abs/1804.02477

Mapping Across Relational Domains for Transfer Learning with Word Embeddings-Based Similarity

Thais Luca[1]([⊠])(iD), Aline Paes[2]([⊠])(iD), and Gerson Zaverucha[1]([⊠])(iD)

[1] Department of Systems Engineering and Computer Science,
Universidade Federal do Rio de Janeiro, Rio de Janeiro, RJ, Brazil
{tluca,gerson}@cos.ufrj.br
[2] Institute of Computing, Universidade Federal Fluminense, Niteroi, RJ, Brazil
alinepaes@ic.uff.br

Abstract. Statistical machine learning models are a concise representation of probabilistic dependencies among the attributes of an object. Most of the models assume that training and testing data come from the same distribution. Transfer learning has emerged as an essential technique to handle scenarios where such an assumption does not hold, as it relies on leveraging the knowledge acquired in one or more learning tasks as a starting point to solve a new task. Statistical Relational Learning (SRL) extends statistical learning to represent and learn from data with several objects and their relations. In this way, SRL deals with data with a rich vocabulary composed of classes, objects, their properties, and relationships. When employing transfer learning to SRL, the primary challenge is to transfer the learned structure, mapping the vocabulary from a source domain to a different target domain. To address the problem of transferring across domains, we propose TransBoostler, which uses pre-trained word embeddings to guide the mapping as the name of a predicate usually has a semantic connotation that can be mapped to a vector space model. After transferring, TransBoostler employs theory revision operators further to adapt the mapped model to the target data. In the experimental results, TransBoostler has successfully transferred trees from a source to a distinct target domain, performing equal or better than previous work but requiring less training time.

Keywords: Transfer learning · Statistical relational learning · Word embeddings

1 Introduction

In traditional machine learning methods, data is represented in a tabular format. This type of representation despises the relational structure of the data, which contains crucial information about how objects participate in relationships and

Supported by CAPES, FAPERJ, and CNPq.

N. Katzouris and A. Artikis (Eds.): ILP 2021, LNAI 13191, pp. 167–182, 2022.
https://doi.org/10.1007/978-3-030-97454-1_12

events. Most of the real-world data is relational, and exploring the structure of relational data allows finding solutions to problems of higher complexity [9].

Statistical Relational Learning (SRL) combines elements from statistical and relational modeling to relational learning aiming at representing and learning in domains with complex relational and rich probabilistic structure [11]. SRL has succeeded in many real-world applications as real data also require handling uncertainty from noise and incomplete information. Most of SRL models assume training and testing data must belong to the same feature space and have the same distribution. If those distributions differ from each other, a new model must be trained using newly collected data.

To address the existence of training and testing data from different distributions, transfer learning [33] has emerged as an important technique given that collecting new data can be a costly or even impossible task. Transfer learning has recently gained much interest from researchers due to its success in Deep Learning applications [27]. It relies on leveraging the knowledge acquired in one or more learning tasks to achieve a good initial performance for solving a new task. Furthermore, they also target at reducing the amount of time it takes to learn a model from scratch [24]. More importantly, applying transfer learning to SRL models admits training and testing domains to differ in distributions as it has successfully been verified in previous works [1,13,16]. However, relational learning differs from function-based and traditional machine learning methods since the former data has a rich vocabulary composed of classes, objects, their properties, and relationships [10]. Therefore, the challenge of applying transfer learning to SRL models is primarily how to transfer the learned structure, mapping the vocabulary from a source domain to the most appropriate objects, properties, and relations in a different target domain. TreeBoostler [1], a system that employs transfer learning to a Relational Dependency Boosting (RDN-B) framework, recursively tries to transfer nodes from source regression trees to build target regression trees. It tries every possible mapping of a source predicate and chooses the best mapping using weighted variance as the decision criterion. This approach can be costly and time-consuming. Thus, devising other more efficient mechanisms for mapping the vocabulary is vital.

In this work, we propose to use pre-trained word embeddings to guide the mapping as the name of the predicates usually have a semantic connotation that can be mapped to a Vector Space Model (VSM). The mechanism proposed here is named as TransBoostler[1]. As TreeBoostler, it also focuses on transferring Boosted Relational Dependency Networks (RDNs) but uses pre-trained word vector representations of predicates for mapping. It maps the predicates that appear in trees learned in the source domain to the most similar predicates in a target domain. Thus, there is no searching as it takes advantage of the context of embeddings to choose the best mapping. As TreeBoostler, our algorithm also includes a Theory Revision component to propose modifications in order to count on predicates from the target domain that were not mapped to any pred-

---

[1] The source code and experiments are publicy available at https://github.com/MeLL-UFF/TransBoostler.

icate from the source domain. Also, the revision component may accommodate modifications pointed out by the target training data.

We evaluated TransBoostler in real-world relational datasets training on one single fold and testing on the remaining folds to simulate the scenario of few data available. We tested mapping by similarity using three different similarity metrics. Our results demonstrate that the proposed algorithm can successfully transfer learned theories across different domains by mapping predicates using similarity. However, mapping by similarity can impair performance depending on the source and target domains.

This paper is organized as follows. Section 2 introduces necessary background. Section 3 compares our proposal to other algorithms in the literature. Section 4 presents TransBoostler and how it performs predicate mapping. Section 5 describes experimental results of TransBoostler for different datasets. Finally, Sect. 6 presents our conclusions.

2   Background Knowledge

This section presents an overview of concepts used to build the contributions of this paper, namely, functional gradient boosting to learn RDNs, transfer learning, word embeddings, and the similarity metrics we relied on to map predicates.

2.1   Functional Gradient Boosting of Relational Dependency Networks

In real-world applications, the logical structure of the data may contain crucial information about how objects interact with each other. This information about how objects participate in relationships and events can help reach conclusions about other objects allowing for solving even more complex problems [9]. Relational datasets store data across multiple tables, where each table represents different types of entities and how these entities may relate to each other.

Following first-order logic (FOL), relations are represented as logical facts while domains are represented using constants, variables and predicates. For instance, the logical fact *publication("Title", "Jane Doe")* can be used to represent the relation between a published material identified by *Title* and the person named as *Jane Doe* that wrote that material. In this case, *publication* is the name of the predicate while *Title* and *Jane Doe* are constants representing the entities of the domain. Arguments may be associated with a type. In our example, the first argument is associated with the type *title* while the second is associated with the type *person*. Since we have two arguments, we say this predicate is of arity two. Predicates can also represent properties of objects. Two examples are *actor* and *director* to distinguish if a person is an actor or a director. Both have one single argument of type *person*, so their arity is one. An atom is a predicate applied to terms. A term can be a variable, constant or function symbol applied to terms. Atoms that assert a relationship among constants are called ground atoms (e.g. *publication(title, person)*). A literal can be an atom or a negated atom. A disjunction of literals with only one positive literal is a definite clause.

Statistical Relational Learning (SRL) combines elements from statistical and probabilistic modeling to represent and learn in domains with complex relational and rich probabilistic structure [11]. SRL models are a concise representation of probabilistic dependencies among the attributes of different related objects. One of such models are the Relational Dependency Networks (RDNs) [23]. RDNs are graphical models that have the capacity of expressing and reasoning dependencies. They approximate the joint distribution of a set of random variables as a product of conditional distributions over a ground atom. RDNs consist of a set of *predicates* and *function* symbols where associated with each predicate Y_i in the domain is a conditional probability distribution $P(Y_i|\mathbf{Pa}(Y_i))$ that defines the distribution over the values of Y_i given its parents' values $\mathbf{Pa}(Y_i)$ [23].

RDN-B [22] proposes to represent each conditional probability distribution in a relational dependency network as a weighted sum of regression models. These models grow in a stage-wise optimization and, instead of representing the conditional distribution for each attribute (relation) as a single relational probability tree, they build a set of relational regression trees using gradient-based boosting. As boosting is a nonparametric approach, the number of parameters grows with the number of training episodes. Thus, interactions between random variables are introduced as needed and the large search space is not explicitly considered. RDN-B is fast and straightforward to implement. Most importantly, it enables learning structure and parameters simultaneously.

2.2   Transfer Learning

Transfer learning has emerged primarily to handle scenarios where training and testing distributions differ. Besides, as it leverages previous learned knowledge to address a new domain, it may reduce the need for huge amounts of data. As data can be easily outdated, and newly data can be expensive or impossible to collect, it may be the key to reduce re-calibration effort as a model trained in one time period can be adapted to predict data in a new time period [24,33]. Transfer learning aims at providing machine learning methods with the ability of recognizing knowledge previously learned in a source domain and apply this knowledge to a new model in a target domain. It contributes to improving performance and tends to make learning a new task less time- and data consuming, as exploiting knowledge learned from one or more previous tasks avoids learning from scratch one specific domain. For SRL models, the main challenge is how to transfer vocabulary from a source domain into a quite different target domain.

2.3   Word Embeddings

Pre-trained continuous word representations have become a great asset for Natural Language Processing (NLP) and machine learning applications [26]. Word embeddings are the most common and useful way to represent words as dense vectors of fixed length.

When it comes to word embeddings, a word is characterized by the company it keeps, such that words that appear in similar contexts must have similar meanings [6]. For instance, *student* and *professor* tend to have similar semantics since they usually appear in similar contexts. The term *embedding* is commonly used to refer to word representations generated using neural networks as the standard approach to learning these representations is to train log-bilinear models as Word2Vec [19] and fast-Text [4].

Fast-Text, the model used in this work, aims at predicting the words in the surrounding context given a target word. It relies on negative sampling and embeddings created from sub-words to tackle out-of-vocabulary words. Thus, fast-Text considers each word is represented as a bag of character n-gram. The problem of predicting context words is modeled as a set of independent binary classification tasks, where the goal is to predict the presence or absence of context words. Given a word at position t, called w_t, all context words are considered as positive examples and negative samples are chosen at random from a dictionary. For each word w in the vocabulary there are two vectors, $\mathbf{u}_{w_t}$ and $\mathbf{v}_{w_c}$, corresponding to the target word w_t and the same word acting as context word w_c, respectively. Given a dictionary of n-grams of size G, the n-grams appearing in w can be denoted by $G_w \subset \{1, \ldots, G\}$ and a vector representation $\mathbf{z}_g$ is associated to each n-gram g. Each word is represented by the sum of its n-grams representations. The score function is the sum of the dot product between $\mathbf{z}_g$ and word vector $\mathbf{v}_{w_c}$ for every n-gram g in G_w. In this way, fast-Text allows sharing the representation across words and does not ignore its internal structure.

Word embeddings are useful for operations like distance measures [26]. Here, we apply three distance measures to find a mapping between a pair of predicates:

Euclidean Distance is the simplest way to measure distance between two real-valued vectors. The distance between two vectors $\mathbf{p}, \mathbf{q} \in \mathbb{R}^n$ is given by 1.

$$d(p,q) = ||p - q||_2 \tag{1}$$

Soft Cosine Measure is a modification of the traditional cosine similarity measure as it takes into account the similarity between features (words) in the VSM [25]. It considers the cosine similarity of each pair of features to build a matrix of similarity $s_{i,j}$ which introduces new features to the VSM. Thus, the Soft Cosine similarity between two vectors $\mathbf{p}, \mathbf{q} \in \mathbb{R}^n$ is given by Eq. 2. If there is no similarity between features, $s_{ii} = 1$ and $s_{ij} = 0$ for $i \neq j$, is equivalent to the traditional cosine similarity measure.

$$soft\_cosine(p,q) = \frac{\sum \sum_{i,j}^{N} s_{i,j} p_i q_j}{\sqrt{\sum \sum_{i,j}^{N} s_{i,j} p_i p_j} \sqrt{\sum \sum_{i,j}^{N} s_{i,j} q_i q_j}} \tag{2}$$

Word Mover's Distance (WMD) also considers the semantic similarity between word pairs [14]. It considers the "travel cost" between words to obtain the minimum cumulative cost of moving a given document $\mathbf{d}$ to a document $\mathbf{d}'$. Assuming text documents are represented as normalized bag-of-words (nBOW) vectors, the similarity between individual word pairs is given by the Euclidean distance and WMD solves the linear transportation problem to obtain how costly it is to travel from one document to another.

3   Related Work

The main challenge of applying transfer learning to learn relational data is how to transfer vocabulary. LTL [13] performs type-matching to identify predicates in the target domain that are similar in their relational structure to predicates in the source domain. It performs type-based tree construction and uses theory refinement in each clause by adding or deleting predicates to try to improve its accuracy. The TAMAR [16] algorithm uses weighted pseudo- log-likelihood (WPLL) to transfer Markov Logic Networks from a source domain to a target domain. The mapping that gives the best WPLL in the target domain is used as mapping for a clause in the source domain. It also revises the structure to improve its accuracy. There are many applications of embeddings for relational tasks. TransE [5] uses embeddings of entities to represent relationships as translations in the vector space of entities and relations. Based on TransE, TransH [31] represents relations as translating operations on a hyperplane, and entities can have multiple representations accordingly to a relation. In [30], authors show evidence that embedded representations can be useful for problems poor in domain knowledge, but results depend on the embedding method used.

TreeBoostler [1] is the most closely related to our algorithm. It performs an exhaustive search by building type constraints to find adequate mappings for a source predicate in the target domain. It uses weighted variance as the decision criterion to choose the best adequate mapping. Then, to improve its accuracy, it revises those trees by pruning and expanding nodes. Our algorithm proposes a modification to TreeBoostler's mapping component. It takes advantage of the semantics of pre-trained word vectors to find mappings by similarity, followed by refining the clauses to better fit the target domain.

4   TransBoostler

Our proposed algorithm comprises the same top-level components as proposed by [1], namely, first the source boosted trees structure are transferred to a different target domain, and next the algorithm revises its trees by pruning and expanding nodes to try to better fit the new data. The main difference is how our algorithm finds adequate predicate mappings.

4.1   Transferring and Revising the Structure

As TreeBoostler, our algorithm also adopts the local mapping approach introduced by [16], which constructs the best mapping for predicates that appear in each source clause, separately and independently of how other clauses were mapped. Local mapping is generally more scalable since the number of predicates in a single clause is smaller than the total number of predicates of the source domain. It is also more flexible as mapping one part of the structure does not hold or depends on other parts.

Each path from the root to the leaf in a relational regression tree can be seen as a clause in a logic program. These paths may share the same inner nodes with different paths in the tree, so paths are not independent. As RDN-B works on a set of relational trees, these are not independent and cannot be interpreted individually. Thus, the algorithm translates just the predicates that no longer have appeared in the structure. If a predicate has already appeared in the structure, the same mapping is used.

Our proposed algorithm also uses Theory Revision [32] to repair possible faults that can prevent theories from predicting examples correctly. Only mapping the predicates is usually not enough as knowledge comes from a different distribution domain [16]. The theory revision component searches for points in the trees to adjust the initial mapped source theory to fit the target data, hence, improving its inferential capabilities.

The revision component searches for paths in trees that are responsible for bad predictions of examples and defines them as revision points. If a positive example is not covered by the theory, it means the theory is too specific and needs to be generalized, so we call it a specialization point. If theory covers negative examples, it is too general and needs to be specialized, so we call it a generalization point. These points need to be modified in order to increase accuracy, so modifications are proposed to revision points by applying revision operators. The pruning operator (generalization operator) increases coverage of examples by deleting nodes from a tree, while the expansion operator (specialization operator) decreases coverage of examples by expanding nodes in each tree. The Pruning operator is applied first to prune the tree from the bottom to the top recursively, removing nodes whose children are leaves marked as revision points. Then, the Expansion operator is applied and recursively adds nodes that give the best split in a leaf marked as a revision point.

The pruning procedure could prune an entire tree and, if this happens, the revision algorithm would have to expand nodes from an empty tree, which is the same as learning from scratch. If pruning results in a null model, deletion of all the trees, the operator is ignored as if it was never applied. Finally, the revision algorithm uses the conditional log-likelihood (CLL) to score both transferred and revised theory. If the revised theory scores better than before, it is implemented.

4.2 Mapping Component

Assuming predicates have meaningful names, TransBoostler takes advantage of the semantic of pre-trained word vectors to find a suitable mapping by similarity. TransBoostler first builds a list of pairs of predicates ordered by their similarity, computed with metrics over the embeddings of predicates. Next, it follows such an ordered list to employ the most similar mappings. Source trees are pre-trained using RDN-B, and transference starts from the root node of the first source tree and works recursively to find the best mapping for not-mapped predicates.

Text Normalization: In relational datasets, predicates can be made of one, two, or more words. Then, the first step of the transfer process is to split each predicate into its component words. We use Ekphrasis [2] with Wikipedia corpora for word segmentation. As an example, suppose we have a predicate *athleteplaysforteam*. It should be segmented into *athlete plays for team*. Also, some predicates or words can appear in shortened form, which is the case of *"ta"* that stands for *teaching assistant* and *"tempadvisedby"* that stands for *temporarily advised by*. After word segmentation, every shortened word is replaced by its full form using a pre-built dictionary. Thus, *"ta"* becomes *"teaching assistant"* and *"tempadvisedby"* becomes *"temporarily advised by"*. Lastly, WordNet lemmatizer [21] was used to turn verbs into their base form. Verbs are identified in predicates by a Part-Of-Speech Tagger (POS Tagger) tool [28].

Word-Vectors Representation: Word vectors pre-trained on Wikipedia with fast-Text Skip-gram [20] are used to represent each predicate in the VSM. The use of pre-trained word vectors is important as relational datasets have a limited vocabulary. Also, pre-trained word vectors contribute to finding more similar predicates as similar words are approximated by their contexts. If a word does not belong to the pre-trained model vocabulary, it is represented as a null vector. When applying Euclidean distance, word vectors of the same predicate are concatenated to become one single vector. We choose concatenation because it avoids information loss since we have very short sentences. Suppose two predicates *company has office* and *company ceo*. As *company has office* is a 3-dimensional vector with components $(\mathbf{x}, \mathbf{y}, \mathbf{z})$ and *company ceo* is 2-dimensional with components $(\mathbf{x}, \mathbf{w})$, we must express both in the same feature space before concatenating. Then, we create two new vectors whose components represent terms in predicates. To express *company has office*, we set its components to $(\mathbf{x}, \mathbf{y}, \mathbf{z}, \mathbf{0})$. To express *company ceo*, we set its components to $(\mathbf{x}, \mathbf{0}, \mathbf{0}, \mathbf{w})$.

Mapping by Similarity: A source predicate is mapped to a target if they have the highest similarity value in comparison with other targets. Suppose a source i and a list of predicates of the target domain $[x, y, z]$. Then, i is mapped to y if and only if $sim(i, y) > sim(i, x)$ and $sim(i, y) > sim(i, z)$, where sim is the similarity function. We only map predicates of same arity and, if there is a tie, we use alphabetical order. Every source is given the most similar predicate in the target domain. It is not permitted to have more than one distinct source predicate mapped to the same target predicate. If the algorithm cannot find a compatible mapping, the predicate is mapped to "empty".

After transfer, we can have three different scenarios as modeled by [1]: (1) the best scenario is when all literals in an inner node have a non-empty predicate mapping, which means we have the same number of literals in the transferred tree; (2) an inner node has some predicate mapped to "empty", but at least one mapped to non-empty. In this case, the ones mapped to empty are discarded; (3) an inner node that has all its literals mapped to an empty predicate, which is the worst case. Discarding all the literals results in an empty node, which affects the tree structure. Then, the algorithm discards the empty node, promotes its left child and appends its right child to the right-most path of the subtree. If the left child is a leaf, the right child is promoted. If both are leaves, it is discarded.

5   Experimental Results

In this section, we present the experiments performed to evaluate TransBoostler. We compare our results with RDN-B [22], which learns from the target dataset from scratch, and TreeBoostler [1], which is a SRL transfer learning approach.

Experiments Setup. For the trees learned by TransBoostler, we follow the same experimental setup as TreeBoostler, so we set the depth limit of trees to be 3, the number of leaves to be 8, the number of regression trees to 10, the maximum number of literals per node to 2, subsampling of negative examples is in a ratio of 2 negatives for 1 positive, and the initial potential is -1.8. Testing is done with all the negative examples. TransBoostler is evaluated with three similarity metrics: Soft Cosine, Euclidean distance, and WMD. We consider two versions of our algorithm: one only considering predicate mapping and parameter learning (TransBoostler*) and the completed version that additionally performs theory revision (TransBoostler). We compare the two versions to evaluate how revising can improve transferring. As TreeBoostler was successfully compared with other transfer methods, these results are omitted.

We used six publicly available datasets paired as in previous literature [1, 13,16,18]: (1) IMDB dataset [17] aims at predicting which actor has worked for a director by learning the *workedunder* relation. It is divided into five mega-examples [16] where each one presents information about four movies; (2) Cora [3] is a dataset of Computer Science research papers. It contains 1295 distinct citations to 122 papers and its goal is to predict if two venues represent the same conference by learning the *samevenue* relation. This dataset is divided into five mega-examples; (3) UW-CSE [12] contains information about the Department of Computer Science and Engineering at the University of Washington (UW-CSE). It consists of five mega-examples to predict if a student is advised by a professor; (4) Yeast protein [15] is a dataset obtained from MIPS Comprehensive Yeast Genome Database and contains information about proteins. The goal is to predict if a protein is associated with a class. It consists of four folds independent of each other; (5) Twitter [29] dataset consists of tweets about Belgian soccer matches divided into two independent folds. The goal is to predict the account type (club, fan, or news); and (6) NELL [7] is a machine learning system that extracts information from web texts and converts it into a probabilistic knowledge base. We consider Sports and Finances domains. Sports contains information about athletes, teams, leagues, etc. The goal is to predict which sport is played by a team. Finances contains information about economic sectors of companies, companies' CEOs, companies' country, etc. The goal is to predict if a company belongs to an economic sector. It is split randomly into three folds.

Results. Results are averaged over n runs, where, for each run, a new learned source model is used for transference. We used conditional log-likelihood (CLL), area under the ROC curve (AUC ROC), area under the PR curve (AUC PR) [8] and training time as measures to compare performance. We did not consider the time required to load the fast-Text model, as it is negligible, but we did consider time to calculate similarities between predicates.

The first experiment simulates the transfer learning scenario by learning from a reduced set of data. Following the previous literature, training is performed on one fold and testing on the remaining n−1 folds. Tables 1 and 2 present the transfer experiments for pairs IMDB and Cora, and Yeast and Twitter. Each of them was treated as source and target domains on each turn. Table 3 presents the results for IMDB → UW-CSE and NELL Sports → NELL Finances. We omitted the opposite transferring from UW-CSE to IMDB and NELL Finances to NELL Sports. The former is too easy, and the latter results in learning from scratch for TreeBoostler as it cannot find useful mappings. We measured the statistical significance between TransBoostler and the baselines using a paired t-test with $p \leq 0.05$. In tables, $\star$ indicates when TransBoostler is significantly better than TreeBoostler. $\diamond$ indicates that the difference between TransBoostler against RDN-B results is significantly better.

As can been seen from the results, TransBoostler performs comparably to baselines in all but one experiment for AUC ROC. Using pre-trained word vectors to find mappings by similarity did improve runtime for transferring pairs Yeast and Twitter. Yeast is one of the largest datasets, and TransBoostler uses far less runtime than TreeBoostler to learn it. To reduce the searching space, TreeBoostler creates type constraints during mapping, which result in some of the predicates being mapped to null. However, TransBoostler maps all source predicates, as it focuses only on similarity. Then, mapping more predicates to a target reduces revision time. As shown in Table 1, for IMDB → Cora, our algorithm is more time-consuming. Theories learned using IMDB contain three distinct predicates. Two of them have arity one, and one is of arity two. As Cora has no predicates of arity one, only the predicate of arity two is mapped. Then, it takes more time to revise the structure. TreeBoostler finds *venue* as the best mapping for *movie*, while TransBoostler using Soft Cosine, Euclidean distance and WMD, finds *haswordauthor*, *author*, and *sameauthor*, respectively. For the opposite experiment, Cora → IMDB, TransBoostler is competitive to RDN-B and finds the same mappings as TreeBoostler: *haswordvenue* is mapped to *movie*, and *haswordtitle* is mapped to *genre*. This shows mapping by similarity is cogent. As can be seen in Table 3, for NELL Sports → NELL Finances, our algorithm underperforms TreeBoostler for AUC ROC but outperforms RDN-B. In this case, TreeBoostler finds four adequate mappings and TransBoostler maps every source predicate to different targets, except when using Euclidean distance.

Table 1. Comparison between TransBoostler and baselines for IMDB and Cora datasets.

	IMDB → Cora				Cora → IMDB			
	CLL	AUC ROC	AUC PR	Run-Time(s)	CLL	AUC ROC	AUC PR	Run-Time(s)
RDN-B	−0.693	0.558	0.426	76.97	−0.075	1.000	1.000	2.89
TreeBoostler	−0.659	0.606	0.530	45.74	−0.075	0.999	0.954	4.29
TransBoostler Soft Cosine	−0.675⋆	0.599	0.464	51.18	−0.074	1.000⋆	1.000	4.36
TransBoostler Euclidean	−0.677	0.589	0.453	52.61	−0.076	0.999	0.927	4.42
TransBoostler WMD	−0.668	0.600	0.463	54.44	−0.076	0.999⋆	0.948	4.43
TreeBoostler*	−0.659	0.574	0.518	1.63	−0.115	0.982	0.888	0.95
TransBoostler* Soft Cosine	−0.699⋆	0.500	0.379	2.20	−0.306⋆◇	0.868	0.092	1.94
TransBoostler* Euclidean	−0.699⋆	0.500	0.379	2.15	−0.304⋆◇	0.868	0.092	1.90
TransBoostlter* WMD	−0.699⋆	0.500	0.379	2.23	−0.308⋆◇	0.868	0.092	1.92

Table 2. Comparison between TransBoostler and baselines for Yeast and Twitter datasets.

	Yeast → Twitter				Twitter → Yeast			
	CLL	AUC ROC	AUC PR	Run-Time(s)	CLL	AUC ROC	AUC PR	Run-Time(s)
RDN-B	−0.122	0.990	0.347	23.45	−0.253	0.926	0.230	15.55
TreeBoostler	−0.096	0.994	0.395	86.63	−0.166	0.986	0.267	34.96
TransBoostler Soft Cosine	−0.127	0.994⋆	0.382	23.38	−0.280⋆◇	0.920	0.169	20.39
TransBoostler Euclidean	−0.107	0.994	0.389	26.09	−0.282⋆◇	0.894	0.325	13.05
TransBoostler WMD	−0.107	0.994	0.374	24.55	−0.240⋆	0.953	0.282	19.64
TreeBoostler*	−0.103	0.993	0.334	7.17	−0.166	0.986	0.267	2.17
TransBoostler* Soft Cosine	−0.154	0.993	0.339	4.51	−0.336⋆◇	0.820	0.299	3.35
TransBoostler* Euclidean	−0.110	0.994	0.405	5.65	−0.336⋆◇	0.820	0.307	2.44
TransBoostlter* WMD	−0.110	0.994	0.391	4.45	−0.336⋆◇	0.820	0.304	2.51

Table 3. Comparison between TransBoostler and baselines for pairs of datasets IMDB and UW-CSE and NELL Sports and NELL Finances.

	IMDB → UW-CSE				NELL Sports → NELL Finances			
	CLL	AUC ROC	AUC PR	Run-Time(s)	CLL	AUC ROC	AUC PR	Run-Time(s)
RDN-B	−0.257	0.940	0.282	8.74	−0.323	0.692	0.062	24.86
TreeBoostler	−0.247	0.939	0.302	4.78	−0.165	0.980	0.071	124.59
TransBoostler Soft Cosine	−0.255	0.936	0.284	5.94	−0.321⋆	0.721	0.087	62.70
TransBoostler Euclidean	−0.254	0.936	0.275	6.44	−0.320⋆	0.750	0.069	54.04
TransBoostler WMD	−0.247	0.936	0.274	5.89	−0.324⋆◇	0.741◇	0.079	53.81
TreeBoostler*	−0.267	0.930	0.293	0.63	−0.315	0.979	0.068	8.85
TransBoostler* Soft Cosine	−0.385⋆◇	0.608	0.035	1.17	−0.366⋆◇	0.531	0.001	6.92
TransBoostler* Euclidean	−0.296⋆◇	0.906	0.131	1.53	−0.365⋆◇	0.558	0.002	5.88
TransBoostlter* WMD	−0.288⋆◇	0.906	0.131	1.19	−0.365⋆◇	0.540	0.002	5.66

We also compare the performance of TransBoostler for different amounts of target data. We employed traditional cross-validation methodology as training is performed on n-1 folds and testing on the remaining one. In this experiment, we incrementally increase the amount of target data. Training data is shuffled and divided into five sequence parts. As in the previous experiment, the process is done in n runs, and curves obtained by averaging the results. Experiments are presented in Figs. 1, 2, 3, 4, 5, and 6. As can been seen, TransBoostler outperforms or equates the baselines for most experiments, and results show it performs better than TreeBoostler for smaller amounts of data. The exceptions are AUC ROC and AUC PR curves presented in Fig. 1 and AUC ROC presented

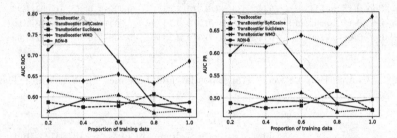

Fig. 1. Learning curves for AUC ROC (left) and AUC PR (right) for IMDB → Cora transfer experiment.

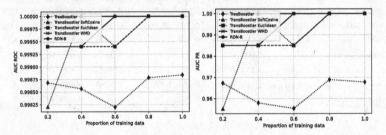

Fig. 2. Learning curves for AUC ROC (left) and AUC PR (right) for Cora → IMDB transfer experiment.

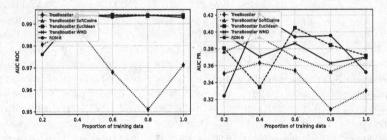

Fig. 3. Learning curves for AUC ROC (left) and AUC PR (right) for Yeast → Twitter transfer experiment.

in Fig. 6. These correspond to experiments IMDB → Cora and NELL Sports → NELL Finances, in which TransBoostler has difficulty finding best mappings. Figure 4 also shows Twitter → Yeast underperforms for AUC ROC.

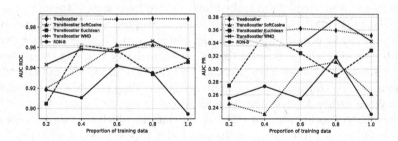

Fig. 4. Learning curves for AUC ROC (left) and AUC PR (right) for Twitter → Yeast transfer experiment.

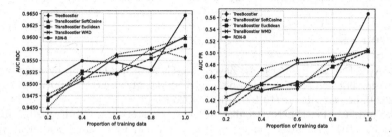

Fig. 5. Learning curves for AUC ROC (left) and AUC PR (right) for IMDB → UW-CSE transfer experiment.

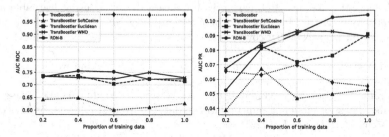

Fig. 6. Learning curves for AUC ROC (left) and AUC PR (right) for NELL Sports → NELL Finances transfer experiment.

6   Conclusions

In this paper, we presented TransBoostler, an algorithm that transfers Boosted RDNs learned from a source domain to a different target domain. TransBoostler leverages pre-trained word embeddings to find mappings between predicates by similarity. It also relies on Theory Revision to propose modifications to the mapped model by pruning and expanding nodes in order to improve its accuracy. As observed in the experimental results, modifying the mapping component to map by similarity has good performance and can be less time-consuming than a previous related transfer learning approach, depending on the pair of datasets. It remains a future investigation to understand whether or not to transfer from one domain to another and the effect of the data in which the embeddings were trained. Other possible future is to select the top-N most similar predicates to proceed with the mapping. The proposed mapping component can also be applied to different and more general relational models and testing this component to them is also an interesting future work direction.

References

1. Azevedo Santos, R., Paes, A., Zaverucha, G.: Transfer learning by mapping and revising boosted relational dependency networks. Mach. Learn. **109**(7), 1435–1463 (2020). https://doi.org/10.1007/s10994-020-05871-x
2. Baziotis, C., Pelekis, N., Doulkeridis, C.: Datastories at SemEval-2017 task 4: deep LSTM with attention for message-level and topic-based sentiment analysis. In: Proceedings of the 11th International Workshop on Semantic Evaluation (SemEval-2017), pp. 747–754. Association for Computational Linguistics, Vancouver, Canada, August 2017
3. Bilenko, M., Mooney, R.J.: Adaptive duplicate detection using learnable string similarity measures. In: Proceedings of the 9th ACM SIGKDD International Conference on Knowledge Discovery and Data Mining, pp. 39–48. KDD 2003. ACM, New York, NY, USA (2003)
4. Bojanowski, P., Grave, E., Joulin, A., Mikolov, T.: Enriching word vectors with subword information. Trans. Assoc. Comput. Linguist. **5**, 135–146 (2017)
5. Bordes, A., Usunier, N., Garcia-Duran, A., Weston, J., Yakhnenko, O.: Translating embeddings for modeling multi-relational data. In: Neural Information Processing Systems (NIPS), pp. 1–9 (2013)
6. Camacho-Collados, J., Pilehvar, M.T.: Embeddings in natural language processing. In: Proceedings of the 28th International Conference on Computational Linguistics: Tutorial Abstracts, pp. 10–15 (2020)
7. Carlson, A., Betteridge, J., Kisiel, B., Settles, B., Hruschka Jr, E.R., Mitchell, T.M.: Toward an architecture for never-ending language learning. In: AAAI, vol. 5. Atlanta (2010)
8. Davis, J., Goadrich, M.: The relationship between precision-recall and ROC curves. In: Proceedings of the 23rd International Conference on Machine Learning, pp. 233–240 (2006)
9. De Raedt, L.: Logical and Relational Learning. Springer Science & Business Media (2008). https://doi.org/10.1007/978-3-540-68856-3

10. Friedman, N., Getoor, L., Koller, D., Pfeffer, A.: Learning probabilistic relational models. In: IJCAI, vol. 99, pp. 1300–1309 (1999)
11. Getoor, L., Taskar, B.: Statistical relational learning (2007)
12. Khosravi, H., Schulte, O., Hu, J., Gao, T.: Learning compact Markov logic networks with decision trees. Mach. Learn. **89**(3), 257–277 (2012)
13. Kumaraswamy, R., Odom, P., Kersting, K., Leake, D., Natarajan, S.: Transfer learning via relational type matching. In: 2015 IEEE International Conference on Data Mining, pp. 811–816. IEEE (2015)
14. Kusner, M., Sun, Y., Kolkin, N., Weinberger, K.: From word embeddings to document distances. In: Bach, F., Blei, D. (eds.) Proceedings of the 32nd International Conference on Machine Learning, Proceedings of Machine Learning Research, vol. 37, pp. 957–966. PMLR, Lille, France, 07–09 July 2015. http://proceedings.mlr. press/v37/kusnerb15.html
15. Mewes, H.W., et al.: MIPS: a database for genomes and protein sequences. Nucleic Acids Res. **30**(1), 31–34 (2002)
16. Mihalkova, L., Huynh, T., Mooney, R.J.: Mapping and revising Markov logic networks for transfer learning. In: AAAI, vol. 7, pp. 608–614 (2007)
17. Mihalkova, L., Mooney, R.J.: Bottom-up learning of Markov logic network structure. In: Proceedings of the 24th International Conference on Machine Learning, pp. 625–632. ICML 2007. ACM, New York, NY, USA (2007)
18. Mihalkova, L., Mooney, R.J.: Transfer learning from minimal target data by mapping across relational domains. In: 21st International Joint Conference on Artificial Intelligence. Citeseer (2009)
19. Mikolov, T., Chen, K., Corrado, G., Dean, J.: Efficient estimation of word representations in vector space. arXiv preprint arXiv:1301.3781 (2013)
20. Mikolov, T., Grave, E., Bojanowski, P., Puhrsch, C., Joulin, A.: Advances in pre-training distributed word representations. In: Proceedings of the International Conference on Language Resources and Evaluation (LREC 2018) (2018)
21. Miller, G.A.: WordNet: a lexical database for English. Commun. ACM **38**(11), 39–41 (1995)
22. Natarajan, S., Khot, T., Kersting, K., Gutmann, B., Shavlik, J.: Gradient-based boosting for statistical relational learning: the relational dependency network case. Mach. Learn. **86**(1), 25–56 (2012)
23. Neville, J., Jensen, D.: Relational dependency networks. J. Mach. Learn. Res. **8**, 653–692 (2007). JMLR.org. ISSN: 1532-4435
24. Pan, S.J., Yang, Q.: A survey on transfer learning. IEEE Trans. Knowl. Data Eng. **22**(10), 1345–1359 (2009)
25. Sidorov, G., Gelbukh, A., Adorno, H.G., Pinto, D.: Soft similarity and soft cosine measure: similarity of features in vector space model. Computación y Sistemas **18** (2014)
26. Torregrossa, F., Allesiardo, R., Claveau, V., Kooli, N., Gravier, G.: A survey on training and evaluation of word embeddings. Int. J. Data Sci. Anal. **11**(2), 85–103 (2021). https://doi.org/10.1007/s41060-021-00242-8
27. Torrey, L., Shavlik, J.: Transfer learning. In: Handbook of Research on Machine Learning Applications and Trends: Algorithms, Methods, and Techniques, pp. 242–264. IGI global (2010)
28. Toutanova, K., Klein, D., Manning, C.D., Singer, Y.: Feature-rich part-of-speech tagging with a cyclic dependency network. In: Proceedings of the 2003 Conference of the North American Chapter of the Association for Computational Linguistics on Human Language Technology, vol. 1, pp. 173–180. NAACL 2003, ACl, USA (2003)

29. Van Haaren, J., Kolobov, A., Davis, J.: TODTLER: two-order-deep transfer learning. In: Proceedings of the 29th AAAI Conference on Artificial Intelligence, vol. 4, pp. 3007–3015. AAAI (2015)
30. Vig, L., Srinivasan, A., Bain, M., Verma, A.: An investigation into the role of domain-knowledge on the use of embeddings. In: Lachiche, N., Vrain, C. (eds.) ILP 2017. LNCS (LNAI), vol. 10759, pp. 169–183. Springer, Cham (2018). https://doi.org/10.1007/978-3-319-78090-0_12
31. Wang, Z., Zhang, J., Feng, J., Chen, Z.: Knowledge graph embedding by translating on hyperplanes. In: Proceedings of the AAAI Conference on Artificial Intelligence, vol. 28 (2014)
32. Wrobel, S.: First order theory refinement. Adv. Inductive Logic Programm. **32**, 14–33 (1996)
33. Yang, Q., Zhang, Y., Dai, W., Pan, S.J.: Transfer Learning. Cambridge University Press, Cambridge (2020)

A First Step Towards Even More Sparse Encodings of Probability Distributions

Florian Andreas Marwitz[(✉)][ID], Tanya Braun[ID], and Ralf Möller[ID]

Institute of Information Systems, University of Lübeck, Lübeck, Germany
florian.marwitz@student.uni-luebeck.de,
{braun,moeller}@ifis.uni-luebeck.de

Abstract. Real world scenarios can be captured with lifted probability distributions. However, distributions are usually encoded in a table or list, requiring an exponential number of values. Hence, we propose a method for extracting first-order formulas from probability distributions that require significantly less values by reducing the number of values in a distribution and then extracting, for each value, a logical formula to be further minimized. This reduction and minimization allows for increasing the sparsity in the encoding while also generalizing a given distribution. Our evaluation shows that sparsity can increase immensely by extracting a small set of short formulas while preserving core information.

Keywords: Probabilistic graphical models · Sparse encoding · Lifting

1 Introduction

Modeling real world scenarios requires dealing with uncertainties. A full joint probability distribution, factorized into local distributions for a sparse encoding, over a set of random variables (randvars) allows for modeling such scenarios. With first-order logic, we can compactly encode relationships between large sets of randvars, representing sets of indistinguishable randvars by parameterizing randvars with logical variables (logvars). However, encoding local distributions over (parameterized) randvars usually relies on the values stored in a table or list for ease of handling the encoding, with more compact encodings like algebraic decision diagrams leading to a huge overhead [5]. Thus, there is an exponential number of values to store per local distribution, also called factor or, if logvars are involved, parfactor.

Turning to first-order logic for a sparse encoding, Markov Logic Networks (MLNs) [12] use weighted first-order logic (FOL) formulas to represent a probability distribution compactly. Canonically transforming a parfactor into formulas translates each entry in the parfactor into one formula (given Boolean ranges of the randvars), which means an exponential number of formulas [15]. Therefore, this paper works towards an even more sparse encoding by reducing the number of values in a distribution, allowing for combining different entries into a single formula. Specifically, this article presents CoFE (Compact Formula Extraction),

© Springer Nature Switzerland AG 2022
N. Katzouris and A. Artikis (Eds.): ILP 2021, LNAI 13191, pp. 183–192, 2022.
https://doi.org/10.1007/978-3-030-97454-1_13

a method for extracting FOL formulas from parfactors. We test out two strategies for reducing the number of values in a parfactor, guided by an ϵ margin that caps the distance between the original distribution and the modified distribution. Our proof-of-concept evaluation shows that CoFE makes a reduction in the number of formulas possible and can even be robust against noise added to values, while keeping the error in query answers in the reduced model small.

The theoretical foundations for query answering in parfactor graphs are laid by Poole with first-order probabilistic inference [11], also introducing parfactors as a modeling formalism. Richardson and Domingos introduce MLNs as another approach to combine FOL and probabilistic graphical models [12]. There exist various query answering algorithms, exact and approximate, that work with either parfactors or MLNs, e.g., [1–3,8]. In terms of related work, there exist well-established techniques in statistics to approximate a discrete randvar with another discrete or continuous randvar. Please refer to [4] for details. However, the problem these techniques solve does not apply here as it lacks the first-order aspect of MLNs and parfactors. There exists a range of probabilistic logic learners that return a set of weighted FOL formulas, of which ProbLog [6] is a prominent representative. However, again, the problem setting does not apply as these learners have a set of (positive and negative) samples, which is not available in our case. Statistical relational learners such as the boosted tree learner [10] also focus on the problem of learning a model from a set of samples. We have a model in the form of a set of parfactors given, which we want to transform into an MLN to preserve semantics while reducing the number of formulas necessary.

The rest of this paper is structured as follows: First, we define and explore the required math. Second, we present CoFE. Third, we evaluate CoFE empirically. Last, we end with a conclusion.

2   Notations and Problem Statement

In this section, we define parfactors and MLNs. Parfactors are functions mapping argument values to real numbers called potentials. An MLN is a set of pairs of a FOL formula and a weight. Furthermore, we show the transformation of a parfactor to an MLN and define a distance for two parfactors. Definitions for parfactors are mainly based on [14] and for MLNs on [12].

Definition 1 (Parfactor model). *Let $\mathbf{R}$ be a set of randvar names, $\mathbf{L}$ a set of logical variable (logvar) names, Φ a set of factor names, and $\mathbf{D}$ a set of constants (universe). All sets are finite. Each logvar L has a domain $\mathcal{D}(L) \subseteq \mathbf{D}$. A constraint C is a tuple $(\mathcal{X}, C_{\mathcal{X}})$ of a sequence of logvars $\mathcal{X} = (X_1, \ldots, X_n)$ and a set $C_{\mathcal{X}} \subseteq \times_{i=1}^{n} \mathcal{D}(X_i)$. The symbol $\top$ for C marks that no restrictions apply, i.e., $C_{\mathcal{X}} = \times_{i=1}^{n} \mathcal{D}(X_i)$. A parameterized randvar (PRV) $R(L_1, \ldots, L_n), n \geq 0$, is a syntactical construct of a randvar $R \in \mathbf{R}$ possibly combined with logvars $L_1, \ldots, L_n \in \mathbf{L}$. If $n = 0$, the PRV is parameterless and constitutes a propositional randvar. The term $\mathcal{R}(A)$ denotes the possible values (range) of a PRV A. An event $A = a$ denotes the occurrence of PRV A with range value*

$a \in \mathcal{R}(A)$. We denote a parfactor g by $\phi(\mathcal{A})_{|C}$ with $\mathcal{A} = (A_1, \ldots, A_n)$ a sequence of PRVs, $\phi : \times_{i=1}^{n} \mathcal{R}(A_i) \mapsto \mathbb{R}^+$ a potential function with name $\phi \in \Phi$, and C a constraint on the logvars of $\mathcal{A}$. A set of parfactors forms a model $G := \{g_i\}_{i=1}^{n}$. With Z as normalizing constant, G represents the full joint distribution $P_G = \frac{1}{Z} \prod_{f \in gr(G)} f$, with $gr(G)$ referring to the groundings of G w.r.t. given constraints.

Parfactor size refers to the size of the range of the parfactor arguments $\mathcal{A}$, i.e., $|\mathcal{R}(\mathcal{A})|$. Parfactors only contain universal quantifiers. For comparing parfactors, we need to define a distance. In this paper, we use the Hellinger distance, defined for probability distributions, as it allows to have zeroes in the distribution. One could however use any distance function of their own choosing. As the potentials in a parfactor do not need to form a probability distribution, we normalize the potentials for calculating the Hellinger distance between two parfactors.

Definition 2 (Hellinger distance). Let $\phi_1(\mathcal{A})$ and $\phi_2(\mathcal{A})$ be two parfactors defined over the same PRVs $\mathcal{A}$. Let Σ_1 and Σ_2 denote the sum of the potentials of ϕ_1 and ϕ_2, respectively. The Hellinger distance is then defined as

$$H(\phi_1(\mathcal{A}), \phi_2(\mathcal{A})) = \frac{1}{\sqrt{2}} \sqrt{\sum_{a \in \mathcal{R}(\mathcal{A})} \left(\sqrt{\frac{\phi_1(a)}{\Sigma_1}} - \sqrt{\frac{\phi_2(a)}{\Sigma_2}} \right)^2}.$$

Definition 3 (MLN). An MLN M is a set of pairs (F_i, w_i), where F_i is an FOL formula and $w_i \in \mathbb{R}$. With Z as normalizing constant, M represents the full joint distribution $P_M = \bigcup_{x \in \mathcal{R}(X)} \frac{1}{Z} \exp\left(\sum_i w_i n_i(x)\right)$, where X is the set of all grounded randvars in M, w_i the weight of formula F_i, and $n_i(x)$ the number of true groundings of F_i in x.

The Problem. We can canonically transform a parfactor into an MLN by adding a formula for every potential given Boolean ranges of PRVs. For non-boolean PRVs, transforming parfactors is more elaborate. Due to the exponential function in the semantics of an MLN, the weight is the natural logarithm of the potential. Consider the parfactor $\psi(Friends(X,Y), Smokes(X), Smokes(Y))$ from the smokers dataset [3], which maps $(1, 1, 1)$ to the potential 7.39 and the remaining range value combinations to the potential 1. We add a formula for each range value combination of the three PRVs together with the natural logarithm of the potential: For $\psi(1, 1, 1) = 7.39$, we add the pair $(a \wedge b \wedge c, 2)$, with a, b, c referring to the three PRVs being set to true. For $\psi(1, 1, 0) = 1$, we add the pair $(a \wedge b \wedge \neg c, 0)$ and so on. Thus, we have as many formulas as is the parfactor size. But instead of eight formulas, we would like to extract only two:

$$0 \quad \neg friends(X, Y) \vee \neg smokes(X) \vee \neg smokes(Y) \tag{1}$$
$$2 \quad friends(X, Y) \wedge smokes(X) \wedge smokes(Y) \tag{2}$$

which we could even reduce to one formula given the MLN semantics and the fact that formulas that evaluate to false receive the weight 0.

Table 1. Reduction result for a parfactor $\phi : \{0,1\}^3 \rightarrow \mathbb{R}^+$. The last two columns show which numbers are mapped to the same one when applying the respective strategy. DBSCAN parameters are $\theta_d = 1, \theta_n = 1$. Without reduction, we need eight formulas. With quartiles, we need four formulas and two with clustering.

$a \in \{0,1\}$	$b \in \{0,1\}$	$c \in \{0,1\}$	$\phi(a,b,c)$	quartile	cluster
0	0	0	1	1	1
0	0	1	4.7	1	2
0	1	0	4.8	2	2
0	1	1	4.9	2	2
1	0	0	5	3	2
1	0	1	5.1	3	2
1	1	0	5.2	4	2
1	1	1	5.3	4	2

The smokers example showcases the power of compactly encoding a distribution with few formulas. However, the potentials are rarely distributed this nicely. Consider the example parfactor in the first four columns of Table 1. With the canonical transformation, we transform the parfactor into eight formulas. But if we reduce the number of different potentials, a single formula can encode more than one potential. If we map, for example, lines 2 to 7 to the potential 5, reducing the number of different potentials from 8 to 2, we can encode the same information in two formulas, $(\neg a \wedge \neg b \wedge \neg c, \ln 1)$ and $(a \vee b \vee c, \ln 5)$. In this example, we have an exponential reduction in the amount of extracted formulas.

3   CoFE: Compact Formula Extraction

As we argue above, directly transforming parfactors to formulas still requires an exponential number of values. Therefore, we propose CoFE for extracting compact formulas from parfactors by reducing the number of different potentials in a parfactor. The formula extraction process consists of three steps, (1) *reduction*, (2) *extraction*, and (3) *minimization*. The individual steps are explained below.

The first step is *reduction*. The goal is to reduce the amount of different numbers in a parfactor while modifying the distribution only minimally. We formalize the notion of minimal modification by considering the distance between the original and the modified version, which should be lower than a predefined maximum distance ϵ. For reduction, we test out two straight-forward strategies, based on quantiles and clustering, respectively. Investigating more complex strategies is left as future work. In the *quantile* strategy, we calculate q-quantiles and map each number belonging to a quantile to the mean of the quantile. We increase q ($q = 1, 2, 3, \ldots,$ parfactor size $- 1$) until the distance is smaller or equal to ϵ. In the worst case, we do not modify the potential function at all as all qs might yield a distance larger than ϵ. In the *clustering* strategy, we cluster the numbers in the potentials and map each number of a cluster to the mean of the cluster. For clustering, we use DBSCAN [7,13], a density-based clustering algorithm, as it does not need the amount of clusters (k) as input. It needs two other parameters, though: a threshold distance between two points to be considered neighbors (θ_d) and a minimum number of neighbors to be classified as a cluster (θ_n), which are user-defined. Other clustering methods can be used as well. If such a method requires a k as an input, a similar approach can be followed as for the quantile strategy, starting with $k = 1$ and increasing k up until the parfactor size minus one. Note that both strategies use the mean as mapping target because the distance between numbers and their mean is short. An example for both strategies is given in Table 1, showing which cluster or quantile ($q = 4$, i.e., quartiles) an entry is mapped to. The quantile strategy maps to four numbers. Clustering makes use of the accumulation around the number five and maps to only two distinct numbers. In the implementation for the evaluation, CoFE actually chooses the result of the strategy that maps to fewer different numbers, breaking ties by lower distance.

Next, the *extraction* step follows: CoFE extracts logical formulas in the same way as a parfactor is transformed into an MLN, getting a list of formulas, each assigned with a weight. The third step is *minimization*, for which CoFE sorts the formulas sharing the same weight into buckets labeled with this weight. Then, the formulas of each bucket are set to be minimized into one minimal formula, for which CoFE uses the Quine-McCluskey algorithm [9]. The output for a parfactor is the set of minimized logical formulas, each assigned with a weight. Consider the smokers example again: When we use the parfactor ψ, as described above, as input for CoFE with parameters $\epsilon = 0.1, \theta_d = 0.1, \theta_n = 1$, CoFE correctly returns the two formulas given in Eqs. (1) and (2). We could also apply CoFE to answers to queries for (conditional) probability distributions over a set of randvars, turning answers into formulas as well.

On the ϵ and Its Effect on Error and Reduction. If applying CoFE to each parfactor in a parfactor model and unifying the outputs, we get an MLN representing the same full joint distribution as the set of reduced parfactors. If using this MLN (or the reduced parfactor model) for query answering, then the query results can diverge from the result of the original model. As mentioned before, CoFE relies on a user-defined ϵ. With a large ϵ, CoFE is able to reduce more potentials but we expect the divergence in query results to rise. With a small ϵ, CoFE most likely reduces fewer numbers while we expect query results to not diverge to a large extent. In a worst case scenario, CoFE is not able to reduce the number of formulas at all, i.e., there are r^n formulas for the r^n potentials the canonical table representation has, with r being the range cardinality of the n PRVs the parfactor is defined over. However, with a large enough ϵ and an optimal minimization result, we get k clusters or q quantiles leading to k or q formulas of length n, which is no longer exponential in n. The upcoming evaluation looks into both reduction and errors in query answering empirically.

4   Empirical Evaluation

In this section, we evaluate CoFE empirically. First, we describe the test setting in more detail. Second, we look at CoFE's capability of reconstructing a given formula, distorting potentials by adding noise. Third, we evaluate the number and length of formulas CoFE outputs as well as the error it incurs during query answering and briefly discuss the results in the light of readability.

4.1   Test Setting

The first part of the evaluation looks at CoFE's performance reconstructing latent formulas under noise: By applying CoFE to a dataset in which noise is added to potentials, we can show that the algorithm is robust against noise. In particular, we can simulate extracting latent formulas from a dataset by treating the original model as the latent one and the noisy model as the given input. We may not add too much noise, because otherwise the noisy model would lose information and CoFE could not extract anything useful.

The second part looks at the sparsity as well as the incurred error. A reduced number of formulas comes along with deviations in query answers if using the extracted formulas for inference. Thus, we take a look at the number of formulas and their length as well as the mean error for queries in the reduced model, which also indicates how much information encoded in a distribution we preserve. As queries, we use a set of representative queries where for each PRV in a model we pose a query with an arbitrary grounding. The error is the deviation of the query answer on the mapped model from the query answer on the noised model.

We perform two tests on the smokers example from [3], which we have used throughout this article as an example. The tests differ in the noise standard deviation σ. Moreover, we create an artificial dataset for investigating the effect of the ratio of the cluster sizes. We create a model with nine parfactors, each defined over three randvars. Parfactor $g_i, i = 1 \ldots 9$, has $i - 1$ ones and $9 - i$ twos in the potentials. We perform two tests with different standard deviations for noise on the artificial dataset. Table 2a shows the test parameters. We choose the parameters so that clustering is applicable and that clusters can span over a standard deviation of the added noise.

Specifically, we have the following steps for each test: First, we add a normally distributed noise with a mean of zero to the potentials in parfactors. Next, we apply CoFE to the noised model. For the first part, we calculate the Hellinger distances between the original model, the noised, and the extracted one. For the second part, we look at the formulas and the mean error for query answering.

4.2   Distance and Reconstruction

Due to adding noise to the potentials, the model used as input to CoFE has a certain Hellinger distance to the original model. Figure 1 shows the Hellinger distances from the original model to the noised and mapped ones. For Smokers1 and Art1, CoFE can effectively filter out the noise and reconstruct the original

Table 2. Evaluating CoFE: Number of formulas extracted per parfactor (#), number of atoms per formula (L), and the mean absolute error (E).

(a) Test parameters						(b) Test results			
test name	dataset	σ	ϵ	θ_d	θ_n	test name	#	L	E
Smokers1	smokers	0.5	0.3	2	2	Smokers1	2	3	0.004
Smokers2	smokers	1	0.3	2	2	Smokers2	2	4-7	0.31
Art1	artificial	0.1	0.05	0.2	2	Art1	1-2	1-4	0.01
Art2	artificial	0.2	0.1	0.4	2	Art2	1-2	1-4	0.021

distribution. For Smokers1, the mapped model has a Hellinger distance of 0.01 to the original model. For Art1, CoFE at least halves the Hellinger distance compared to the one of the noised model. When we treat the original distribution as the latent one underlying the noised model in this tests, we capture the latent formulas. Considering Smokers2, CoFE can no longer filter out the noise due to the high standard deviation compared to the absolute potentials. Moreover, CoFE not even approximately reconstructs the original distribution, but rather mixes the original clusters. For most parfactors in Art2, CoFE can drastically reduce the noise and reconstruct the original clusters. But, CoFE mixes the two clusters in two parfactors. Thus, CoFE only roughly captures the original model.

4.3 Sparsity and Error

Table 2b shows the number and length of formulas extracted as well as the mean absolute error. In all tests, we reduce the number of formulas exponentially compared to the canonical extraction. We extract two formulas per parfactor instead of the eight formulas we would get with the canonical transformation to an MLN. Moreover, all formulas, except for Smokers2, are only up to one atom longer than without simplification and minimization. For Smokers1, CoFE correctly returns the two formulas given in Eqs. (1) and (2). Because of the added noise, the weights are slightly different: 0.074 for Eq. (1) and 2.03 for Eq. (2).

For Smokers1 and Art1, the error is small and at most 0.01. Comparing Art2 to Art1, the error doubles as does the standard deviation of the noise added. For Smokers2, the mean absolute error is with 0.31 clearly higher than for Smokers1 due to the higher noise standard deviation.

In summary, we can increase the sparsity of the encoding by extracting significantly less formulas than without reduction. Moreover, we preserve core information and the user can control how much information loss is tolerable. Looking at the evaluation from a readability viewpoint, we hypothesize that a sparsely encoded distribution turned into an MLN formula is easier to understand or more readable as a human. Additionally, the fewer formulas we have, the better we can understand these formulas; and the shorter the formula is, the better we can understand this particular formula. Given this hypothesis, we can record

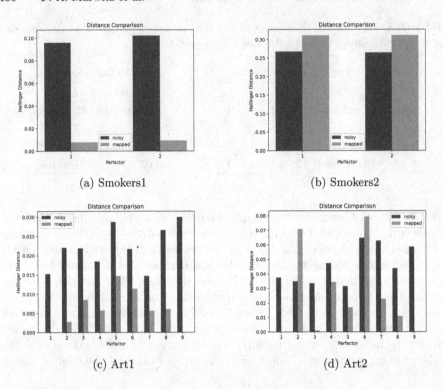

Fig. 1. Hellinger distances from the original to the noised and mapped models

that the formulas extracted with CoFE are at least as readable as the result of the canonical transformation from a parfactor to an MLN. In the worst case, our result would not differ in terms of readability from the one without reduction and minimization. With reduction, we may combine some formulas into one formula. Without minimization, this one formula is as long as the merged formulas together. With minimization, we can only shorten the formula or leaving it as it is. Under this hypothesis, using CoFE on query answers enables another form of interpretation of query answers. Future work includes to further investigate this avenue of readability, which also touches on ideas explored in transparent machine learning or explainable AI.

5   Conclusion

We present an algorithm to get an even more sparse encoding of a full joint distribution encoded in tabular-like parfactors. To this end, the algorithm reduces the number of different potentials in a parfactor before extracting formulas, up to a user-defined maximum distance ϵ between the original distribution and the reduced distribution in the parfactor. With the ϵ, the user can trade off the potential for reduction with the preservation (accuracy) of the original distribution. Specifically, we test out two different reduction strategies, based on clusters and quantiles respectively. After formula extraction, a minimization step ensures that formulas are as short as possible. Because of the reduction step, the algorithm can extract latent formulas hidden behind distorted potentials, while being able to preserve core information, with small errors observed in our evaluation with a small distance. Furthermore, we hypothesize that human understanding can improve greatly by extracting few and short formulas.

For future work, we look at testing out further reduction strategies, analyzing the relationship between the changes in the distribution and resulting reduction as well as error, and investigating the potential for increased readability and human understanding.

References

1. Ahmadi, B., Kersting, K., Mladenov, M., Natarajan, S.: Exploiting symmetries for scaling loopy belief propagation and relational training. Mach. Learn. **92**(1), 91–132 (2013)
2. Braun, T., Möller, R.: Lifted junction tree algorithm. In: Friedrich, G., Helmert, M., Wotawa, F. (eds.) KI 2016. LNCS (LNAI), vol. 9904, pp. 30–42. Springer, Cham (2016). https://doi.org/10.1007/978-3-319-46073-4_3
3. Van den Broeck, G., Taghipour, N., Meert, W., Davis, J., De Raedt, L.: Lifted probabilistic inference by first-order knowledge compilation. In: IJCAI 2011 Proceedings of the 22nd International Joint Conference on AI, pp. 2178–2185. IJCAI Organization (2011)
4. Chakraborty, S.: Generating discrete analogues of continuous probability distributions-a survey of methods and constructions. J. Stat. Distrib. Appl. **2**(1), 1–30 (2015)
5. Chavira, M., Darwiche, A.: Compiling Bayesian networks using variable elimination. In: IJCAI 2007 Proceedings of the 20th International Joint Conference on AI, pp. 2443–2449. IJCAI Organization (2007)
6. De Raedt, L., Kimmig, A., Toivonen, H.: ProbLog: a probabilistic prolog and its application in link discovery. In: IJCAI 2007 Proceedings of 20th International Joint Conference on AI, pp. 2062–2467. IJCAI Organization (2007)
7. Ester, M., Kriegel, H.P., Sander, J., Xu, X.: A density-based algorithm for discovering clusters in large spatial databases with noise. In: KDD 1996 Proceedings of the 2nd International Conference on Knowledge Discovery and Data Mining, pp. 226–231. AAAI Press (1996)
8. Gogate, V., Domingos, P.: Probabilistic theorem proving. In: UAI 2011 Proceedings of the 27th Conference on Uncertainty in AI, pp. 256–265. AUAI Press (2011)
9. McCluskey, E.J.: Minimization of Boolean functions. Bell Syst. Tech. J. **35**(6), 1417–1444 (1956)
10. Natarajan, S., Khot, T., Kersting, K., Gutmann, B., Shavlik, J.: Gradient-based boosting for statistical relational learning: the relational dependency network case. Mach. Learn. **86**, 25–56 (2012)
11. Poole, D.: First-order probabilistic inference. In: IJCAI 2003 Proceedings of the 18th International Joint Conference on AI, pp. 985–991. IJCAI Organization (2003)
12. Richardson, M., Domingos, P.: Markov logic networks. Mach. Learn. **62**(1–2), 107–136 (2006)

13. Schubert, E., Sander, J., Ester, M., Kriegel, H.P., Xu, X.: DBSCAN revisited, revisited: why and how you should (still) use DBSCAN. ACM Trans. Database Syst. (TODS) **42**(3), 19 (2017)
14. Taghipour, N., Fierens, D., Davis, J., Blockeel, H.: Lifted variable elimination: decoupling the operators from the constraint language. J. Artif. Intell. Res. **47**, 393–439 (2013)
15. Van den Broeck, G.: Lifted inference and learning in statistical relational models. Ph.D. thesis, KU Leuven (2013)

Feature Learning by Least Generalization

Hien D. Nguyen[1,2(✉)] and Chiaki Sakama[3]

[1] University of Information Technology, Ho Chi Minh City, Vietnam
hiennd@uit.edu.vn
[2] Vietnam National University, Ho Chi Minh City, Vietnam
[3] Wakayama University, Wakayama, Japan
sakama@wakayama-u.ac.jp

Abstract. This paper provides an empirical study for feature learning based on induction. We encode image data into first-order expressions and compute their *least generalization*. An interesting question is whether the least generalization can extract a common pattern of input data. We introduce three different methods for feature extraction based on symbolic manipulation. We perform experiments using the MNIST datasets and show that the proposed methods successfully capture features from training data and classify test data in around 90% accuracies. The results of this paper show potentials of induction and symbolic reasoning to feature learning or pattern recognition from raw data.

Keywords: Feature learning · Least generalization · Interpretable machine learning

1 Introduction

Feature learning or *representation learning* is the technique to discover the necessary representations for feature detection or classification from data [3]. In machine learning, neural networks (NN) and *deep learning* [9] are widely used for this purpose. Deep learning has powerful capability in feature learning, while it does neither show what is learned nor explain why an output is obtained. This raises the need of *interpretable machine learning* [12] or *explainable AI* (XAI) [1] that aims to make AI systems results more understandable to humans.

Inductive logic programming (ILP) [6, 11] realizes machine learning based on symbolic reasoning. In contrast to the NN approaches, ILP can learn human-readable hypotheses from small amounts of data, which enables to accumulate learned results as knowledge and to share them by humans. One of the challenging issues of ILP is learning from raw data. In [5], the authors say:

> Most ILP systems require data in perfect symbolic form. However, much real-world data, such as images and speech, cannot easily be translated into a symbolic form. Perhaps the biggest challenge in ILP is to learn how to both perceive sensory input and learn a symbolic logic program to explain the input.

N. Katzouris and A. Artikis (Eds.): ILP 2021, LNAI 13191, pp. 193–202, 2022.
https://doi.org/10.1007/978-3-030-97454-1_14

The goal of this study is to realize feature learning from raw data using ILP techniques. To this end, we first encode image data into first-order atoms by representing pixel information in terms. Next we compute *least generalization* of those atoms. Least generalization [14, 15] is a technique of inductive generalization and extracts a common pattern among expressions. Then, an interesting question is whether least generalization can extract a common pattern of input data as features. We also introduce two different methods for feature extraction based on symbolic manipulation. We implement the proposed methods and test on the MNIST datasets. Experimental results show that some of the methods successfully extract features of handwritten digits and fashion figures in a human-readable manner. The extracted features are used for classification and their accuracy, precision and recall are evaluated.

The rest of this paper is organized as follows. Section 2 describes the proposed method, and Sect. 3 presents experimental results. Section 4 discusses related issues, and Sect. 5 summarizes the paper.

2 Feature Learning by Least Generalization

2.1 Least Generalization

A *first-order language* consists of an alphabet and all formulas defined over it. The definition is the standard one in the literature [4, 6]. A *term* is either (i) a constant, (ii) a variable, or (iii) $f(t_1, \ldots, t_m)$ where f is an m-ary ($m \geq 1$) function symbol and $t_1, \ldots, t_m$ are terms. An *atom* is a formula $P(t_1, \ldots, t_n)$ ($n \geq 1$) where P is an n-ary predicate and t_i's are terms. An *expression* is either a term or an atom. Two atoms are *compatible* if they have the same n-ary predicate. The set of all variables (resp. terms, atoms) in the language is denoted by Var (resp. $Term$, $Atom$). The set of all expressions is defined as $Exp = Term \cup Atom$. A *substitution* is a mapping σ from Var into $Term$ such that the set $\Gamma = \{\langle x, \sigma(x) \rangle \mid x \neq \sigma(x) \text{ and } x \in Var\}$ is finite. When $\sigma(x_i) = t_i$ for $i = 1, \ldots, n$, it is also written as $\sigma = \{t_1/x_1, \ldots, t_n/x_n\}$. The set of all substitutions in the language is denoted by Sub. The identity mapping ε over Var is the *empty substitution*.

Let $\sigma \in Sub$ and $E \in Exp$. Then $E\sigma$ is defined as follows:

$$E\sigma = \begin{cases} \sigma(x) & \text{if } E = x \text{ for } x \in Var, \\ a & \text{if } E = a \text{ for a constant } a, \\ f(t_1\sigma, \ldots, t_m\sigma) & \text{if } E = f(t_1, \ldots, t_m) \in Term, \\ P(t_1\sigma, \ldots, t_n\sigma) & \text{if } E = P(t_1, \ldots, t_n) \in Atom. \end{cases}$$

A preorder relation $\leq$ over $Atom$ is defined as follows. For any $A, B \in Atom$, $A \leq B$ if $A = B\theta$ for some $\theta \in Sub$. Then, B is a *generalization* of A if $A \leq B$.

Definition 1 (least generalization). ([14, 15]) Let $A_1, A_2 \in Atom$. An atom $A \in Atom$ is a *common generalization* of A_1 and A_2 if $A_i \leq A$ for $i = 1, 2$. In particular, A is a *least common generalization* of A_1 and A_2 if A is a common generalization of A_1 and A_2, and $A \leq A'$ for any common generalization A' of A_1 and A_2. Least common generalization is simply called *least generalization*. The least generalization of A_1 and A_2 is written as $lg(\{A_1, A_2\})$.

An algorithm for computing least generalization is introduced by [14,15]. Here we refer the one from [6] (Fig. 1).[1]

Input : Two compatible atoms A_1 and A_2
Output : $G = lg(\{A_1, A_2\})$

1. Set $A_1' = A_1$ and $A_2' = A_2$, $\theta_1 = \theta_2 = \varepsilon$, and $i = 0$.
   Let $z_1, z_2, \ldots$ be a sequence of variables not appearing in A_1 or A_2.
2. If $A_1' = A_2'$, then output $G := A_1'$ and stop.
3. Let p be the leftmost symbol position where A_1' and A_2' differ. Let s and t be the terms occurring at this position in A_1' and A_2', respectively.
4. If, for some j with $1 \leq j \leq i$, $z_j\theta_1 = s$ and $z_j\theta_2 = t$, then replace s at the position p in A_1' by z_j, replace t at the position p in A_2' by z_j, and go to 2.
5. Otherwise set i to $i+1$, replace s at the position p in A_1' by z_i, and replace t at the position p in A_2' by z_i. Set θ_1 to $\theta_1 \cup \{s/z_i\}$, θ_2 to $\theta_2 \cup \{t/z_i\}$, and go to 2.

Fig. 1. Algorithm for Least Generalization [6]

2.2 Encoding Image Data into First-Order Expressions

We encode image data into first-order expressions and compute their least generalization. We first describe a method of encoding image data into terms. An image (in black, white or grayscale) is presented by $28 \times 28 = 784$ pixels where each pixel is an integer value from 0 to 255.[2] An image is then represented as a vector $v \in \mathbb{R}^{784}$ that contains pixel values as elements. Each pixel x ($0 \leq x \leq 255$) is transformed to the term $f^k(z)$ with a variable z where

$$k = \left\lfloor \frac{x}{64} \right\rfloor + 1,$$
$$f^1(z) = f(z) \text{ and } f^{k+1}(z) = f(f^k(z)) \ (1 \leq k \leq 3).$$

where $\lfloor \ \rfloor$ is the floor function of a real argument x which returns the greatest integer less than or equal to x. The function symbol f is used to represent "closeness" of pixels. For instance, when $0 \leq x_1, x_2 \leq 63$, both x_1 and x_2 are represented as $f(z)$. When $x_1 = 80$ and $x_2 = 200$, for instance, x_1 is represented as $f^2(z)$ and x_2 is represented as $f^4(z)$. This representation helps to keep information of the range of shades in computing least generalization.

With this encoding, a vector v is encoded into an atom having 784 arities:

$$P(t_{1.1}, \ldots, t_{1.28}, t_{2.1}, \ldots, t_{2.28}, \ldots, t_{28.1}, \ldots, t_{28.28}).$$

---

[1] It is also called *anti-unification*.
[2] 0 means black and 255 means white. In between, every other number is a shade of gray ranging from black to white.

Fig. 2. An example of a 28×28 image.

In this paper, the existence of a predicate is unimportant, so hereafter we identify the above atom with the tuple $(t_{1.1}, \ldots, t_{1.28}, t_{2.1}, \ldots, t_{2.28}, \ldots, t_{28.1}, \ldots, t_{28.28})$.

Example 1. The image of Fig. 2 is encoded into a tuple of terms as follows:

$(\underbrace{f(z), \ldots, f(z)}_{28 \times 6 \text{ values}}, \quad \%\text{1st to 6th rows}$

$\underbrace{f(z), \ldots, f(z)}_{16 \text{ values}}, f^3(z), f^4(z), f^4(z), f^3(z), \underbrace{f(z), \ldots, f(z)}_{8 \text{ values}}, \quad \%\text{7th row}$

$\underbrace{f(z), \ldots, f(z)}_{14 \text{ values}}, f^2(z), f^4(z), f^4(z), f^2(z), f^2(z), f^4(z), \underbrace{f(z), \ldots, f(z)}_{8 \text{ values}}, \quad \%\text{8th row}$

$\ldots, \underbrace{f(z), \ldots, f(z)}_{28 \text{ values}}) \quad \%\text{28th row}$

2.3 Extracting Features

Training data is classified by their labels. Suppose a set of training data $C_l = \{A_1, \ldots, A_n\}$ (called a *class*) where l is a label and A_i $(1 \leq i \leq n)$ is a first-order atom (or a tuple) representing an image. The least generalization of C_l is then computed as follows.

Algorithm 2: Least generalization of training data

Input : a set of training data $C_l = \{A_1, \ldots, A_n\}$ where A_i $(1 \leq i \leq n)$ is a first-order atom (tuple) representing an image and l is a label.
Output : least generalization of C_l (written $lg(C_l)$).

1. Put $A_0 := A_1$.
2. For i from 2 to n do:
   Compute $A_0 := lg(\{A_0, A_i\})$ by the algorithm of least generalization (Fig. 1).
3. Return A_0.

The output of Algorithm 2 is decoded into pixel data by the converse transformation of the encoding presented in Sect. 2.2: a term $f^k(z)$ $(1 \leq k \leq 4)$ in a tuple is converted into the pixel with the value $(k - 1) \times 64$. The obtained vector $u \in \mathbb{R}^{784}$ is viewed as features extracted by least generalization. We refer this way of extracting features by **GEN** and call u a *feature vector* by **GEN**.

Next we introduce two different methods for feature extraction. Suppose a set of training data $D_l = \{v_1, \ldots, v_n\}$ where l is a label and $v_k \in \mathbb{R}^{784}$ $(1 \leq k \leq n)$ is a vector representing an image. Put

$$v_k = (x^k_{1.1}, \ldots, x^k_{1.28}, x^k_{2.1}, \ldots, x^k_{2.28}, \ldots, x^k_{28.1}, \ldots, x^k_{28.28}) \qquad (1 \leq k \leq n)$$

where x^k_{ij} is a pixel value. Then, define

$$S_{ij} = \{ x^k_{ij} \mid 1 \leq k \leq n \} \quad (1 \leq i, j \leq 28).$$

S_{ij} is a collection of pixel values at the location (i, j) from training data. Then, **FRQ** and **AVE** are defined as follows.

FRQ: Select the integer value u_{ij} that appears most frequently in S_{ij}.
AVE: Compute the average value v_{ij} of elements in S_{ij} and put $w_{ij} = \lfloor v_{ij} \rfloor$.

Put $u = (u_{1.1}, \ldots, u_{1.28}, u_{2.1}, \ldots, u_{2.28}, \ldots, u_{28.1}, \ldots, u_{28.28})$ and $w = (w_{1.1}, \ldots, w_{1.28}, w_{2.1}, \ldots, w_{2.28}, \ldots, w_{28.1}, \ldots, w_{28.28})$. Then u and w are viewed as vectors that represent features extracted by **FRQ** and **AVE**, respectively. We call u (resp. w) *a feature vector* by **FRQ** (resp. **AVE**).

2.4   Classification of Images

We next use the result of extracted features for classifying unlabelled test data. When there are m classes, the classification is done using the following algorithm.

Algorithm 3: Classification of test data

Input : a vector v representing an unlabelled 28×28 image, and the set of feature
   vectors of training data: $S = \{ u_k \mid k = 1, \ldots, m \}$.
Output : the label of v.

1. For each class k $(1 \leq k \leq m)$, compute

$$D_k = \sum_{ij} \mid u_{ij} - v_{ij} \mid \qquad (1 \leq i, j \leq 28)$$

   where u_{ij} is an element in u_k and v_{ij} is an element in v.
2. Return $l = k$ as the label of v where D_l is minimal among $D_1, \ldots, D_m$.

The set S of feature vectors is obtained by one of **GEN**, **FRQ**, and **AVE**. The label of a testing data is determined in a way that the sum of differences between pixel values in each location is minimal. [3]

---

[3] If D_l is not unique, the one with the minimum index l is selected.

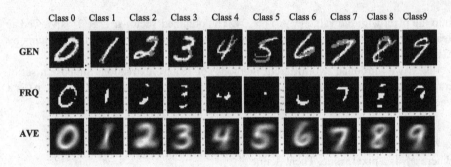

Fig. 3. Features of the MNIST dataset obtained by **GEN**, **FRQ**, and **AVE**

3 Experimental Results

We conduct experiments using two datasets, MINST hand-written digits and Fashion MNIST,[4] which are widely used as benchmark for feature learning. Each dataset is split into two parts: the training set (60,000 images) and the test set (10,000 images). The experimental testing is done by two stages: (i) extracting features from training data using **GEN**, **FRQ**, and **AVE**; and (ii) classifying test data and computing their *Precision*, *Recall*, and *Accuracy* to evaluate the methods. Precision, recall, and accuracy, which are widely used measures in machine learning, are defined as:

$$Precision := \frac{TP}{TP + FP} \quad Recall := \frac{TP}{TP + FN} \quad Accuracy := \frac{TP + TN}{TP + TN + FP + FN}$$

where TP, TN, FP, and FN mean *True Positive* (correctly predicted as positive), *True Negative* (correctly predicted as negative), *False Positive* (incorrectly predicted as positive), and *False Negative* (incorrectly predicted as negative), respectively.[5]

3.1 Testing on MNIST Dataset

The MNIST data are classified into 10 classes (0–9). Then features are extracted in each class using **GEN**, **FRQ**, and **AVE**. The results of feature extraction is shown in Fig. 3. By the figure, we observe that most digits produced by **GEN** and **AVE** are readable, while those produced by **FRQ** are less readable. The precision, recall and accuracy of three methods are summarized in Table 1. By the table, we can see that **AVE** shows the maximum average of 94% in accuracy, 80% in precision and 66% in recall. The accuracy of **GEN** and **FRQ** are around 90%. The 93% accuracy of **FRQ** is a bit surprise because the output of feature extraction is less readable. The result indicates that classification does not necessarily require the whole image of a digit.

---

[4] http://yann.lecun.com/exdb/mnist/, https://www.kaggle.com/zalando-research/fashionmnist.

[5] Dataset, code, and results of testing are available at https://drive.google.com/drive/folders/1Zno76nKDhENor-lEt9sQW7dYzPlyT4JQ?usp=sharing.

Table 1. The precision, recall and accuracy on the MNIST dataset

Class	GEN			FRQ			AVE		
	Precision	Recall	Accuracy	Precision	Recall	Accuracy	Precision	Recall	Accuracy
0	0.42	0.91	0.94	0.75	0.65	0.94	0.82	0.94	0.98
1	0.93	0.49	0.88	0.92	0.80	0.96	0.99	0.35	0.79
2	0.19	0.86	0.91	0.39	0.65	0.92	0.42	0.97	0.94
3	0.61	0.50	0.90	0.70	0.61	0.92	0.62	0.72	0.94
4	0.80	0.34	0.83	0.79	0.71	0.95	0.67	0.83	0.96
5	0.51	0.38	0.88	0.24	0.34	0.89	0.33	0.87	0.94
6	0.44	0.60	0.92	0.72	0.67	0.94	0.79	0.86	0.97
7	0.17	0.61	0.90	0.70	0.62	0.92	0.77	0.86	0.96
8	0.22	0.66	0.91	0.59	0.59	0.92	0.44	0.86	0.94
9	0.33	0.32	0.86	0.52	0.58	0.91	0.78	0.69	0.94
Average	**0.46**	**0.57**	**0.89**	**0.63**	**0.62**	**0.93**	**0.66**	**0.80**	**0.94**

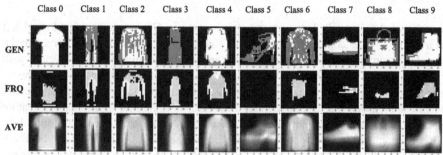

Fig. 4. Features of the Fashion-MNIST dataset obtained by **GEN**, **FRQ**, and **AVE**

3.2 Testing on Fashion-MNIST Dataset

The Fashion-MNIST data is classified into 10 classes (Class 0: T-shirt/top, Class 1: Trouser, Class 2: Pullover, Class 3: Dress, Class 4: Coat, Class 5: Sandal, Class 6: Shirt, Class 7: Sneaker, Class 8: Bag, Class 9: Ankle boot). Figure 4 shows the results of feature extraction using three methods. By the figure, we can observe that **GEN** and **AVE** capture the shape of each class with a few exceptions. Again, the output of **FRQ** is less clearer than the others. The precision, recall and accuracy of each method are computed using test data as in Table 2. As before, **AVE** outputs the highest values among three methods. It is known that Fashion-MNIST is significantly harder than MNIST, while the proposed three methods still keeps around the 90% accuracy.

4   Discussion

Feature learning from labelled data has been done using neural networks (NN). In deep leaning models, features are extracted in hidden layers and then represented by the

Table 2. The precision, recall and accuracy on the Fashion-MNIST dataset

Class	GEN			FRQ			AVE		
	Precision	Recall	Accuracy	Precision	Recall	Accuracy	Precision	Recall	Accuracy
0	0.61	0.48	0.90	0.16	0.23	0.86	0.62	0.76	0.94
1	0.87	0.72	0.95	0.83	0.97	0.98	0.94	0.76	0.96
2	0.21	0.47	0.90	0.44	0.40	0.88	0.25	0.64	0.91
3	0.25	0.22	0.84	0.48	0.82	0.94	0.69	0.55	0.91
4	0.68	0.37	0.85	0.63	0.27	0.80	0.66	0.43	0.88
5	0.43	0.73	0.93	0.56	0.32	0.84	0.53	0.42	0.88
6	0.14	0.35	0.89	0.01	0.06	0.89	0.17	0.37	0.89
7	0.89	0.54	0.91	0.37	0.74	0.92	0.89	0.57	0.92
8	0.47	0.96	0.95	0.046	0.155	0.88	0.56	0.96	0.95
9	0.80	0.80	0.96	0.93	0.52	0.91	0.79	0.85	0.97
Average	**0.54**	**0.56**	**0.91**	**0.45**	**0.45**	**0.89**	**0.61**	**0.63**	**0.92**

neurons of the network. However, what is learned in NN is uninterpretable and left as a black box. In contrast to the NN approaches, our approach based on symbolic reasoning is interpretable and transparent. Representing an image data as a vector with pixel values, **GEN**, **FRQ**, and **AVE** compute feature vectors that represent features of training data. Functions computing those features are explicitly given, then one can understand reasons why test data is classified into some classes. In this respect, feature learning in this paper realizes *interpretable machine learning*. Given n training data, **GEN** is computed in $O(n \times \log^2 m)$ using m processors [13], and **FRQ** and **AVE** are computed in $O(n)$. Classification of a test data is done in $O(l \times k^2)$ where l is the number of elements in a vector v and k is the number of classes.

There are few studies on encoding image data into first-order formulas except [2], which introduces an NN architecture called the *first-order state autoencoder* (FOSAE). Given the feature vectors of objects in the environment, FOSAE automatically learns to identify a set of predicates (relations) as well as to select appropriate objects as arguments for the predicates. The resulting representation is used for classical planning. The goal of [2] is not feature learning but predicate symbol grounding. It does not use induction but uses NN to detect common pattern between objects that define a relation.

There are some approaches for integrating low-level perception in NN with high-level reasoning in LP. *Differentiable ILP* (∂ILP) [8] combines ILP and NN and learns symbolic rules that are robust to noisy and ambiguous data. In the MNIST classification task, a convolutional NN (ConvNet) is connected to ∂ILP. When an image is fed into the pretrained ConvNet, it predicts a probability distribution for the target variable. The image is then converted to the most probable atom and is merged to ILP. *DeepProbLog* [10] integrates NN and probabilistic LP in a way that the output of NN is encapsulated in the form of *neural predicates*. In *abductive learning* [7], NN is used for obtaining pseudo-labels from training data, which are then treated as groundings of the primitive concepts for abductive reasoning in LP. These studies combine background knowledge represented as LP with the output of NN, while raw data is processed using NN.

5 Concluding Remarks

This paper introduced new methods that learn features of labelled images by symbolic reasoning, then classify unlabelled images by comparing them with learned feature vectors. Our approach is purely symbolic and does not use NN for learning from image data. To the best of our knowledge, this is the first attempt that realizes feature learning using symbolic reasoning without relying on NN. Although the classification accuracy achieved in this paper is still inferior to the state of the art of NN technologies,[6] the current paper shows potentials of symbolic reasoning for feature learning from raw data.

For efficient implementation, an algorithm proposed in [13] realizes parallel computation of least generalization. In this paper, a pixel x is transformed to a term $f^k(z)$ in a way that black is represented by $f(z)$ and white is represented by $f^4(z)$. This means that least generalization of black and white becomes black, while one may argue that the result should be gray. It would be interesting to realize an alternative transformation from pixel values to terms and compare their effects. We continue to investigate more robust and effective representation of raw data in terms of symbolic expressions, and its application to data other than images.

References

1. Adadi, A., Berrada, M.: Peeking inside the black-box: a survey on explainable artificial intelligence (XAI). IEEE Access **6**, 52138–52160 (2018)
2. Asai, M.: Unsupervised grounding of plannable first-order logic representation from images. In: Proceedings of the 21th International Conference on Automated Planning and Scheduling, pp. 583–591 (2019)
3. Bengio, Y., Courville, A.: Representation learning: a review and new perspectives. IEEE Trans. Pattern Anal. Mach. Intell. **35**(8), 1798–1828 (2013)
4. Chang, C.L., Lee, R.T.C.: Symbolic Logic and Mechanical Theorem Proving. Academic Press, New York (1973)
5. Cropper, A., Dumancic, S., Evans, R., et al.: Inductive logic programming at 30. Mach. Learn. **111**, 147–172 (2022)
6. Nienhuys-Cheng, S.-H., de Wolf, R.: Foundations of Inductive Logic Programming. LNCS, vol. 1228. Springer, Heidelberg (1997). https://doi.org/10.1007/3-540-62927-0
7. Dai, W., Xu, Q., Yu, Y., Zhou, Z.: Bridging machine learning and logical reasoning by abductive learning. In: Advances in Neural Information Processing Systems 32, pp. 2811–2822 (2019)
8. Evans, R., Grefenstette, E.: Learning explanatory rules from noisy data. J. AI Res. **61**, 1–64 (2018)
9. LeCun, Y., Bengio, Y., Hinton, G.: Deep learning. Nature **521**, 436–444 (2015)
10. Manhaeve, R., Dumancic, S., Kimmig, A., Demeester, T., De Raedt, L.: DeepProbLog: neural probabilistic logic programming. In: Advances in Neural Information Processing Systems 31, pp. 3753–3763 (2018)
11. Muggleton, S. (ed.): Inductive Logic Programming. Academic Press, Cambridge (1992)
12. Molnar, C.: Interpretable Machine Learning: A Guide for Making Black Box Models Explainable, Lulu.com (2020)

---

[6] 99.87% accuracy (9.2021). https://paperswithcode.com/sota/image-classification-on-mnist.

13. Nguyen, H.D., Sakama, C.: A new algorithm for computing least generalization of a set of atoms. In: Kazakov, D., Erten, C. (eds.) ILP 2019. LNCS (LNAI), vol. 11770, pp. 81–97. Springer, Cham (2020). https://doi.org/10.1007/978-3-030-49210-6_8
14. Plotkin, G.D.: A note on inductive generalization. In: Machine Intelligence, vol. 5, pp. 153–163. Edinburgh University Press (1970)
15. Reynolds, J.C.: Transformational systems and the algebraic structure of atomic formulas. In: Machine Intelligence, vol. 5, pp. 135–151. Edinburgh University Press (1970)

Learning Logic Programs Using Neural Networks by Exploiting Symbolic Invariance

Yin Jun Phua[1,2]([⊠]) and Katsumi Inoue[1,2]

[1] The Graduate University for Advanced Studies, SOKENDAI, Tokyo, Japan
[2] National Institute of Informatics, Tokyo, Japan
{phuayj,inoue}@nii.ac.jp

Abstract. Learning from Interpretation Transition (LFIT) is an unsupervised learning algorithm which learns the dynamics just by observing state transitions. LFIT algorithms have mainly been implemented in the symbolic method, but they are not robust to noisy or missing data. Recently, research works combining logical operations with neural networks are receiving a lot of attention, with most works taking an extraction based approach where a single neural network model is trained to solve the problem, followed by extracting a logic model from the neural network model. However most research work suffer from the combinatorial explosion problem when trying to scale up to solve larger problems. In particular a lot of the invariance that hold in the symbolic world are not getting utilized in the neural network field. In this work, we present a model that exploits symbolic invariance in our problem. We show that our model is able to scale up to larger tasks than previous work.

Keywords: Neural network · LFIT · Interpretability · Neural-Symbolic AI

1 Introduction

We interact with various different complex dynamic systems in our everyday lives. These systems with various components evolve over time in a manner that we can observe. Understanding the influences between these components within these dynamic systems provide valuable insights. With the knowledge of the influences and relationships between the components, it becomes possible to manipulate the dynamic system for a desired outcome or to plan for certain events. In most real world systems however, we do not have direct access to the underlying rules that govern them. Most of the time though, we are able to obtain observations of the systems. Learning from Interpretation Transition (LFIT) [12] is an unsupervised learning algorithm which learns the dynamics just by observing state transitions. Under the LFIT framework, the dynamics of the system is represented as normal logic programs (NLP). LFIT can be

© Springer Nature Switzerland AG 2022
N. Katzouris and A. Artikis (Eds.): ILP 2021, LNAI 13191, pp. 203–218, 2022.
https://doi.org/10.1007/978-3-030-97454-1_15

applied to multi-agent systems, where learning other agents' behavior can be crucial for decision making, or even to biological systems [19], where knowing the interaction between genes can lead to huge breakthrough in developing drugs to cure illnesses.

LFIT algorithms have mainly been implemented in two different methods, the symbolic method and the neural network method. The symbolic method utilizes logical operations to learn and induce logic programs [18]. This family of algorithms have been well-developed and has the nice property of being interpretable. It is also known to scale well to larger systems. However, it is not without its downsides. For example, it only learns what it can see, i.e. the prediction for data not in the training set will always be incorrect. In real world applications this is a particularly huge problem because we cannot always obtain perfect observations of a system. Another shortcoming is that logical operations employed by this family of algorithms lack ambiguous notations. This means that any error or noise present within the data will be reflected directly in the learned model.

In recent years, research works combining logical operations with neural networks have gained a lot of attention [3]. Whilst the motivation for most of these research lie in the interpretability of neural networks, the ability to introduce ambiguity to the input data is also perceived as one of their strengths. As such, most of the work has been focused on inspecting trainable parameters and extracting rules from it. In a similar spirit applying LFIT to neural networks, there is NN-LFIT [9], where a neural network is trained to model the system and a logic program is extracted based on the weights of the trained neural network. NN-LFIT has been demonstrated to be able to generalize from small amount of training data, and it is also robust against noisy or erroneous data. There is also an extension of this work by [20] where instead of brute forcing all values to construct a truth table, the authors used heuristics to derive the logical rules from the trained neural network.

One of the big problems that leads to the scalability problem in methods combining neural networks with symbolic is the combinatorial explosion problem. While symbolic methods also suffer from the combinatorial explosion problem, the application of neural networks towards symbolic problems have multiple different ways of blowing up combinatorially. In δILP [6], the scalability problem is so severe that each predicate has to be limited to only 2 clauses whereas symbolic methods have no such limits. In δLFIT, the number of variables were limited to 5 variables due to memory constraint, where real world application often require thousands of variables. We observe that several invariances that hold in symbolic space are not considered in neural network methods. We refer to these invariances as *symbolic invariance*. One such invariance is the order of inputs. In LFIT, inputs are represented as a set of state transitions. The ordering of the states within each transition are significant given the ordering conveys the meaning of time, but the ordering for the transitions as an input doesn't matter to the algorithm. Whereas in neural network methods, different ordering of the transitions are presented as different inputs, and thus all permutation of the input transitions are treated as different points in the learning space.

This data inefficiency combined with memory space explosion, seems to lead to most work in the neural symbolic field to be currently impractical for real world application. We speculate that being much more data efficient and reducing memory usage could lead to a much more practical application. In this work we hope to demonstrate a method to exploit this invariance, although it is not a generally applicable method, we hope that this will inspire other works as well.

In this paper, we propose the δLFIT+ model which aim to solve the scalability problem, building on top of δLFIT. This paper is structured as follows, we will first cover some necessary background on LFIT and some preliminary for δLFIT in Sect. 2. Next we will present our methods of δLFIT+ in Sect. 3. Following that, we will show our experimental results in Sect. 4. In Sect. 5, we will discuss some of our observations. Next, we will describe some related works in Sect. 6. Finally, we will be summarizing our work and discussing some further research that are possible in Sect. 7.

2   Background

2.1   LFIT

The LFIT algorithm strives to learn an NLP that explains the observation obtained from a dynamic system. The dynamics of a changing system with respect to time can be represented by introducing time as an argument. Therefore we can consider the state of an atom A at time t as $A(t)$. A dynamic rule can then be described as follows:

$$A(t + 1) \leftarrow A_1(t) \wedge \cdots \wedge A_m(t) \wedge \neg A_{m+1}(t) \wedge \cdots \wedge \neg A_n(t) \tag{1}$$

this rule means that, if all of $A_1, A_2, \ldots, A_m$ is true at time t, and all of A_{m+1}, $A_{m+2}, \ldots, A_n$ is false at time t, then the head A will be true at time $t + 1$. $A_1, A_2, \ldots, A_m$ can be denoted as b^+ representing the positive literals that appear in the rule while $A_{m+1}, A_{m+2}, \ldots, A_n$ can be denoted as b^- representing the negative literals that appear in the rule. However, noting that even though rule (1) has time arguments in each of the atoms, t and $t + 1$ only appear in the right hand side and left handside respectively, and thus can be omitted [11]. Therefore rule (1) can be equally expressed as the following propositional rule:

$$A \leftarrow A_1 \wedge \cdots \wedge A_m \wedge \neg A_{m+1} \wedge \cdots \wedge \neg A_n$$

A can be any one of $A_1, \ldots, A_n$ and this will not be considered a cyclic rule, due to the implicit time parameter they will be considered as separate literals. However, in the paper, we would like to treat A on the left and on the right equally, therefore we will be referring to A and any other literals as a variable, which is different from the propositional variable.

Given a set P of such propositional rules, we can simulate the state transition of a dynamical system with the T_P operator.

An Herbrand interpretation I is a subset of the Herbrand base $\mathcal{B}$. For a logic program P and an Herbrand interpretation I, the immediate consequence operator (or T_P operator) is the mapping $T_P : 2^{\mathcal{B}} \to 2^{\mathcal{B}}$:

$$T_P(I) = \{h(R) \mid R \in P, b^+(R) \subseteq I, b^-(R) \cap I = \emptyset\}. \tag{2}$$

Given a set of Herbrand interpretations E and $\{T_P(I) \mid I \in E\}$, the LFIT algorithm outputs a logic program P which completely represents the dynamics of E.

The LFIT algorithm, in its simplest form, can be described as an algorithm that requires an input of a set of state transitions $S = \{(I, T_P(I)) \mid I \in E\}$ and an initial NLP P_0, then outputs an NLP P such that P is consistent with the input S.

2.2   Rule Classification

To build a classifier, all the possible rules that a system can have given the Herbrand base $\mathcal{B}$ have to be known and enumerated. If there are no restrictions, the number of rules that are valid is infinite. Therefore some restrictions have to be placed.

First consider the following operation.

Definition 1 (Simplification of Rules). *A rule can be simplified according to the following operations:*

- *$a \wedge a$ is simplified to a*
- *$\neg a \wedge \neg a$ is simplified to $\neg a$*
- *$a \wedge \neg a$ and $\neg a \wedge a$ is simplified to $\bot$*

where a is an atom.

Since we are only considering a non-cyclic NLP, a body that has been simplified to $\bot$ is considered to be equivalent of having an empty body $a \leftarrow$.

With such operation, the following can now be considered.

Definition 2 (Minimal Rule). *A rule is considered to be minimal, if its logical formula cannot be simplified further.*

For every Herbrand base $\mathcal{B}$, a finite ordered set of rules $\tau(\mathcal{B})$ that contains all minimal rules for any system that has Herbrand base $\mathcal{B}$ can be generated. In a classification scenario, each rule needs to be assigned to a class. To ease this, a deterministic approach of mapping each rule to an index, which corresponds to a class, is defined.

Definition 3 (Length of a rule). *The length of a rule $R \in \tau(\mathcal{B})$ is defined as $\|b(R)\|$.*

Definition 4 (Index of element in ordered set). *Let S be an ordered set, the index of element $e \in S$, is defined as $\sigma_S(e) = \|S_{<e}\|$, where $\sigma_S : S \mapsto \mathbb{N}$ and $S_{<e} = \{x \mid x < e, x \in S\}$.*

Definition 5 (Ordered Herbrand Base). *The ordered Herbrand base $\mathcal{B}_o$ contains the same elements as $\mathcal{B}$ except each element has an ordered relation $<$.*

The relation $<$ on $\mathcal{B}_o$ can be defined arbitrarily, but in most cases, the lexicographical ordering is the most convenient. Now, consider a set of rules $\tau_l(\mathcal{B}_o)$, where $\tau_l(\mathcal{B}_o) = \{R \mid \|b(R)\| \leq l, R \in \tau(\mathcal{B}_o)\} \subseteq \tau(\mathcal{B}_o)$ which contains all rules that are less than or equal to length l. The number of rules in $\tau_l(\mathcal{B}_o)$ can be given by the following formula:

$$\|\tau_l(\mathcal{B}_o)\| = \begin{cases} 1 & \text{if } l = 0, \\ \|\tau_{l-1}(\mathcal{B}_o)\| + \binom{n}{l} \times 2^l & \text{if } l > 0. \end{cases} \tag{3}$$

where $n = \|\mathcal{B}_o\|$ is the number of elements in the Herbrand base and $\binom{n}{k}$ represents the binomial coefficient.

Also consider the ordered set $\tilde{\tau}_l(\mathcal{B}_o) = \{R \mid \|b(R)\| = l, R \in \tau(\mathcal{B}_o)\}$ containing all the rules R that are exactly of length l. The ordered relation for $\tilde{\tau}_l$ is defined by first ordering the negation by marking the negative literals as 1s and positive literals as 0s. With that, the position of negations in the literals can be mapped into a binary number. Note that there is no information loss here, as the binary number mapping is only used for ordering. Next, we look at each atom in the rule and order them according to $\mathcal{B}_o$. In this relation, $\{a, b\} < \{a, c\} < \{\neg a, b\} < \{\neg b, c\} < \{\neg a, \neg c\}$.

The index of a rule R $\sigma_{\tau(\mathcal{B}_o)}(R)$ can be obtained by performing the following calculation:

$$\sigma_{\tau(\mathcal{B}_o)}(R) = \|\tau_{l-1}(\mathcal{B}_o)\| + \sigma_{\tilde{\tau}_l(\mathcal{B}_o)}(R)$$

where $l = \|b(R)\|$ is the length of the rule R.

Recall that in a rule, an atom can be present as either positive, negative, or not be present at all. Therefore the number of possible rules for an n-variable system ($n = \|\mathcal{B}\|$) is $\|\tau_n(\mathcal{B}_o)\| = 3^n$. Thus, for an n-variable system, the total number of classes the to be classified is $3^n \times n$, with each variable in the system taking the head of the rules.

2.3   δLFIT

δLFIT [16] is composed of an LSTM and a feed forward layer. The input for δLFIT L is a continuous sequence of state transitions, in which starting from an initial state I_0, the T_P operator is applied repeatedly to get the entire sequence $L = (I_0, T_P(I_0), T_P(T_P(I_0)), \dots)$. The hidden state from the LSTM is then fed into the feed forward layer. The output of the feed forward layer is then fed to a sigmoid layer, from which the probability for each rules can be obtained. δLFIT assigns each rule, in combination of each head, to 1 output node. Therefore the number of output nodes in δLFIT for a given n variable system is $3^n \times n$.

3 δLFIT+

Several techniques have been applied to the original δLFIT model to make it much more memory efficient and data efficient. These techniques are described in the following sub sections.

3.1 Input Sequence Invariance

In the original δLFIT model, changing the order of the input sequence changes the output. To mitigate this issue, the dataset needs to be augmented with various permutation of the ordering, however this makes the dataset really big. A similar problem existed in the image processing community, whereby each permutation of the image has to be augmented into the dataset. This was the case until a pooling operation in the form of convolution came along.

Conventionally, recurrent neural networks (RNN) are used in order to process sequences. Each element in the sequence takes different amount of operations to reach the output, therefore the semantic of a sequence is inherently reflected in the RNN structure. The LSTM architecture used in δLFIT is an example of an RNN. Recent state of the art however, heavily preferences transformer [21] and the attention mechanism to process sequence. Compared to RNN, transformer is relatively flat with no inherent structure for representing order of sequences. A positional encoding which is directly added to the input value is provided as a means of indicating each elements' positions. There might be an inclination to just remove the positional encoding and expect that the resulting architecture to be sequence invariant. However due to the mathematical operations performed, changing the ordering of the sequence will result in different calculations. To achieve true sequence invariance, we look to the set transformer architecture.

The set transformer architecture [14] is introduced here to make the network invariant to the input sequence. This drastically improves data efficiency and generalization. Set transformer is a variance of the original transformer architecture, but with sequence invariance. In the set transformer architecture, the multi head attention is used as the pooling operation. To ensure that the result of the pooling operation does not change with respect to the order of the input, self-attention is applied to the input. Recall that the multi head attention is a query-key-value operation described as follows [21]:

$$\text{Attention}(Q, K, V) = \text{softmax}(\frac{QK^T}{\sqrt{d_k}})V$$

the authors of the set transformer architecture observed that if $K = V$, different ordering of elements in K or V results in the same formula. Further, since QK^T is the pairwise relationship between the elements of both matrix, it is thus possible to get the relationship between each of the elements of the input. In the natural language processing world, this is usually equated to how each word in a sentence relates to each other. In the LFIT literature, this can be thought of as the relationship between each state.

3.2   Rule Length Sharing

The original δLFIT assigned each output node to each possible rule. This is obviously problematic as the number of outputs scale by $3 \times n^3$. The reality is much worse as the number of outputs is multiplied by the number of possible heads, which is the number of elements in the Herbrand base. So the first most obvious thing that can lead to reducing the number of outputs, is by reusing the same output node for different heads. This can be accomplished by having an extra input that indicates the head of the rule.

However, this still leaves us with the number of outputs scaling by n^3, which is still exponentially explosive. Here, another reuse strategy can be applied. Namely, the outputs can be reused for rules with different lengths. Each output, depending on the input, represents a different set of rules that is predicted by the neural network. So if the input indicates rule length of 1, then each of the output are rules of length 1.

Therefore, the number of output required now is just the maximum number of rules in one of the lengths. Consider the set $\widetilde{\tau}_l(H) = \{R \mid \|b(R)\| = l\}$ that contains all rules R of length l. From Eq. (3), the cardinality of this set at l is the following:

$$\|\widetilde{\tau}_l(H)\| = \binom{n}{l} \times 2^l$$

Given that $\lim_{n \to \infty} \frac{2^l}{\binom{n}{l}} = 0$, the maximum number of outputs scale to $O(\binom{n}{l})$. It is clear that $\arg\max_l \binom{n}{l} = \frac{n}{2}$, therefore the maximum number of outputs for any given n, is expected to be $\binom{n}{n/2} \times 2^{n/2}$. This is much less than the original $n \times 3^n$.

3.3   Subsumed Label Smoothing

We apply label smoothing by setting to a value μ in labels which are not the actual rules, but rules that are subsumed by actual rules. With the splitting of the length of the rules, the labels will be largely 0 for the majority of the dataset if only minimal logic programs are considered. For example, consider a logic program consisting of only rules with a maximum of 3 literals in the body. The labels for this logic program at length 4 and beyond will be 0. Since the majority of the dataset is 0, this will encourage the neural network to shortcut and output 0 all the time to minimize the objective. In natual language processing, it is a standard procedure to apply label smoothing to words unrelated as a form of regularization. This technique is applied here in a slightly different way, to help aid in training and not to penalize when the network gets too confident. Each rule that is subsumed in the logic program is set to μ. This avoids scenario where the label is just 0.

3.4   Label Imbalance

Due to the rule length sharing technique described in Sect. 3.2, there is a huge imbalance in the number of positive labels in the dataset. As shown in Fig. 1, the number of positive labels for the first few classes are much larger. This is due to them being reused in a greater number of rule lengths. Comparing to the last few classes at the right edge, which are only used when $l = n/2$. To counteract this imbalance, a positive example weight is calculated based on the positive: negative example ratio, and then applied to the loss function.

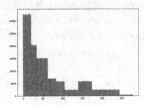

Fig. 1. The amount of positive labels for each class in the dataset.

3.5   Network Architecture

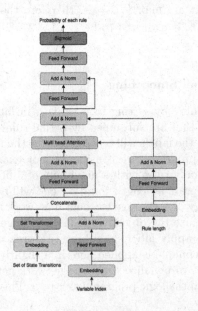

Fig. 2. The network architecture of δLFIT+

The network architecture is designed such that it predicts logical rules for each variable and rule length separately. Each variable and rule length reuse the same parameters and are differentiated through input.

The neural network receives a set of state transitions as input, the variable index and the length of the rule to produce predictions for. The set of state transitions is a set $S_x = \{(I, \theta_x) \mid I \in E\}$ where E is a set of Herbrand interpretations. θ_x denotes a boolean value of whether the atom x belongs in the interpretation of the next state $T_P(I)$. Since in LFIT, rules are learned by categorizing interpretations in positive examples and negative examples, a similar approach is taken here as well. $(I, 1)$ denote all positive examples while $(I, 0)$ denote all negative examples. More concretely, I is represented as a vector $v \in \{0, 1\}^n$, where n is the size of the Herbrand base. Each element in vector v is set to 0 if it is not in the interpretation and 1 if it is. Note that the index position of each atom in v is order-dependent. This vector v can then be interpreted into a binary number. For an Herbrand base of size n, v can range from 0 to 2^n. To consider whether a given state is a positive example or negative example, 0 to 2^n denotes negative example and $2^n + 1$ to $2^{(n+1)}$ denotes positive example.

The two other inputs, variable index and length of the rule are provided to the network as integers. The network will then learn an approriate embedding for these features to produce a prediction.

The entire neural network architecture is depicted in Fig. 2. Each input is fed into an embedding layer. The embedding layer contains learnable weights, followed by a GELU activation [10], and a LayerNorm [1].

The state transition features are then fed into the set transformer described in Sect. 3.1. The other inputs are fed through a feed forward residual layer. The feed forward residual layer typically consist of two affine transformations and a GELU activation. The output of this feed forward layer is then added to the output of the embedding layer followed by a LayerNorm.

The output from the state transitions and variable index layers are then concatenated into a single vector, representing the state transitions and the respective variable to learn from. The result of the concatenation is then fed through another feed forward residual layer.

A multi head attention is then applied, with the key and value both being the features from state transitions and variable. The query being the rule length. The intuition for this is to allow the network to focus on features that are relevant on the rule length it is being asked to predict. The output from the multi head attention layer is then added with the query of rule length, followed by a LayerNorm. This result is then fed through another feed forward layer.

A final feed forward layer is applied, and the output is an element-wise sigmoid. The result represents the probability of each rule described in Sect. 2.2, with respect to the input rule length l and the head of the rule x, for it to be included in the logic program. A threshold δ_t is used to determine the rules to include, note that more than 1 rule can be simultaneously chosen for the same head x.

Algorithm 1: The δLFIT+ algorithm

Input : Set of transitions $S = \{(I, T_P(I) \mid I \in E\}$, Herbrand base $\mathcal{B}$
Output: Logic program P
$n := \|\mathcal{B}\|$;
$P := \{\}$;
foreach $x \in \mathcal{B}$ **do**
  Encode each element $s \in S$ into binary numbers S_x;
  $R_x := \{\}$;
  for $l = 0$ **to** n **do**
    $R_{xl} := \delta\text{LFIT+} (S_x, x, l)$;
    `/* `R_{xl}` contains all rules of the form `$x \leftarrow \beta$` where `β` is a`
      `conjuction of literals and `$\|\beta\| = l$ `*/`
    Simplify R_{xl};
    $R_x = R_x \cup R_{xl}$;
  end
  Simplify R_x ;   `// `R_x` contains all rules of the form `$x \leftarrow \beta$
  `/* After simplification `R_x` will contain one or more rules that`
    `are not subsumed by each other`   `*/`
  $P = P \cup R_x$;
end
return P

3.6   Training Methods

Training is performed by generating artificial training data. Each data point corresponds to a randomly generated normal logic program. A random sequence of state transitions that conforms to the deterministic semantics is first generated. In deterministic semantics, a single state only transitions to another particular state. The symbolic bottom-up LFIT algorithm is then applied to this random sequence to learn a minimal logic program. The data point is then the sequence of state transitions, and the minimal logic program as the label. For each data point, the full initial states (all 2^n states) are generated. However during training, only 80% of the data point is selected to improve the generalizability of the network.

Subsumed label smoothing is applied randomly to 20% of the rules each batch. For each subsumed rule, the label gets 0.25 added to its value. It is possible for a single rule to be subsumed by multiple rules, therefore a maximum of 0.75 is also applied, to not let the network confuse with the true label.

3.7 δLFIT+ Algorithm

The δLFIT+ algorithm is described in Algorithm 1. The resulting logic program is produced by iterating through every variable in the Herbrand base, and every length up to the number of variables. Simplification of the rules is performed at each step to eliminate rules such as $a \leftarrow b$ and $a \leftarrow \neg b$. Only the top 10 rules that exceeds 0.97 probability is selected into R_{xl}.

Table 1. The MSE for the state transitions generated by the predicted logic programs compared to δLFIT.

Boolean network	δLFIT	δLFIT+^{3}	δLFIT+^{5}	δLFIT+^{7}
3-node (a)	0.095	0.271	0.271	0.271
3-node (b)	0.054	0.188	0.208	0.208
Raf	0.253	0.188	0.208	0.208
5-node	0.142	–	0.278	0.325
7-node	–	–	–	0.223
WNT5A [22]	–	–	–	0.194

4   Experiments

To evaluate our methods, we perform several experiments comparing the performance with and without our improvements. The network is implemented in PyTorch [15]. We also perform comparisons with the original δLFIT model. Evaluations are performed on boolean networks taken from the PyBoolNet [13] repository, which are commonly used for such methods.

4.1   Experimental Methods

The network was trained with the Adadelta [23] optimizer. After training for 10 epochs, the network is evaluated by feeding data from the boolean networks. We then produce state transitions from the predicted logic program, and calculated the mean squared error between the state transitions from the predicted logic program and the boolean network.

During training, we only focus on one of the variables and one particular rule length for each data point. The selection for the variable is randomized within each batch, but the selection for the rule length is fixed for each batch, instead randomizing between different batches. This is done primarily for computational efficiency reasons. For each data point, we pick 80% of the states from all possible states for training. E.g., for 5 variables there are $2^5 = 32$ possible states, thus we pick 25 state transitions for training. These 25 states are picked randomly each epoch. Validation is performed on data point withheld from the training process. The results are taken only from 1 run of the experiment, due to the lengthiness in the process of training, and also when we did multiple runs on the smaller systems, we did not observe significant variance in the results.

4.2   Baseline

Baseline results are shown in Table 1. δLFIT wasn't able to deal with more than 5 variables therefore the results are omitted for 7 variable networks. The top number next to δLFIT+ represents the number of variables that was trained on. δLFIT+^{3} means that the specific network was trained with 3 variables, and thus

Table 2. The MSE for the state transitions generated by the predicted logic programs with and without set transformers, and with and without label smoothing

Boolean network	δLFIT+^{5}	δLFIT+$^5_{\neg T}$	δLFIT+$^5_{\neg S}$
3-node (a)	0.271	0.313	0.271
3-node (b)	0.208	0.292	0.208
Raf	0.208	0.271	0.208
5-node	0.278	0.375	0.378

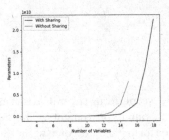

Fig. 3. Number of parameters in 10 billions, of the network with rule length sharing compared to without rule length sharing

have 12 output nodes. Networks trained with more variables have more output nodes and thus can deal with larger boolean networks, together with smaller networks.

4.3   Regular Transformer

In this experiment, we replaced the set transformer in the network architecture to a regular transformer. The results are shown in Table 2. Results are taken by randomizing the order of the state transitions and taking the average.

4.4   Rule Length Sharing

We show the difference in number of parameters with rule length sharing compared to without rule length sharing in Fig. 3. Without this, the number of parameters start exploding from 14 variables. However, with rule length sharing this effect is delayed until 16 variables. Contrasting with the state of the art natural language processing model like GPT-3, which has 175 billion parameters [2], there are still some leeway in terms of network architecture, however it will require state of the art hardware and large amount of computational time to actually train it. We did not perform any experiments to validate the difference in terms of accuracy because it will require a significant restructuring in the training process. We think that the restructuring is sufficiently impactful that the difference in accuracy that we will be measuring will not just be the effect of sharing rule lengths, but also the difference in the entire training process.

4.5 Without Label Smoothing

In this experiment, we trained the network without applying subsumed label smoothing. The results are shown in Table 2 with the results for $\delta\text{LFIT}+^5_{\neg S}$ being one without label smoothing applied. No clear performance difference was found with the 3 variable networks, but the network that trained without label smoothing performed significantly worse with the 5 node boolean network.

5 Discussion

In general, we observed that there is a drop in accuracy across the board as the outputs get reused. $\delta\text{LFIT}+$ performed poorer on the other networks, except in the boolean network Raf, where δLFIT struggled because the same state was repeated. We also observed that $\delta\text{LFIT}+^3$ performing better than $\delta\text{LFIT}+^5$ for 3 variable networks. Memory efficiency has also improved from δLFIT, which allowed us to easily train a network with 7 variables. However, generating training data for 8 variables and beyond required too much time with the amount of computational resource that we had, therefore we were unable to train the networks.

With the rule length sharing method proposed, we were able to cut the number of parameters in the model by half. This allowed us to use larger number of batch size during training to increase training speed. However with the reduced number of output nodes, this might have led to a potential loss in terms of accuracy, as now each output node represents multiple rules, compared to one output node one rule in δLFIT.

Subsumed label smoothing did not have any visible impact on smaller networks with 3 variables, but with 5 variables the effects were visible. In particular, with the same hyperparameter, we observed that $\delta\text{LFIT}+^5_{\neg S}$ was overfitting, meaning training loss decreased very rapidly while validation loss remained high. Adding subsumed label smoothing helped apply some regularization to $\delta\text{LFIT}+^5$.

$\delta\text{LFIT}+$ took 1 day to generate and train for 3 variable systems, while it took 5 days to generate and train for 7 variable systems. Compared to other LFIT methods, the runtime for $\delta\text{LFIT}+$ is significantly higher. However, most methods only focus on learning a single system whereas $\delta\text{LFIT}+$ learns a general n-variable system. The advantage for this is that, in real world applications, novel systems that are being investigated often have only small amount of observation data available. A technique that only works with the obtained observation data will overfit, whereas $\delta\text{LFIT}+$ can avoid the overfitting problem.

6 Related Work

The combination of symbolic methods and neural networks, recently also referred to as Neural-Symbolic AI (NSAI), has been an active area of research for several years [8], but has recently gained attention. Much of the attention stems from the lack of interpretability in deep learning, where there have been so much success in various different fields. In the work done by Garcez and Zaverucha [7], the authors proposed an algorithm that first translates a logic program that is provided as background knowledge into a neural network. The neural network is then trained with examples, then a logic program is extracted based on the weights of the neural network. In another work done by Garcez et al. [4], the authors proposed a method to extract logic program from a neural network that was trained from scratch. However, these methods place severe constraints on the architecture of the neural network and a heavy assumption on the neural network model itself. Thus they are unable to capitalize on the recent advancements in neural network and a new method of extraction needs to be devised before they can be applied to new architectures.

In δILP [6], the authors introduced an algorithm that incorporates differentiable machine learning and ILP. Again, the basic idea here is that given an ILP task, the algorithm learns differentiable parameters that allow it to solve the ILP task. A logic program is then subsequently extracted from the learned parameters. While this method suffers from an exponential dependency on the number of allowed predicates, and thus has scalability problems, the main difference with our approach is that we do not perform extraction to obtain logic programs.

More recently, Dong et al. [5] proposed Neural Logic Machines (NLM) that solved to a certain extent the scalability problem that δILP faced. This work joins a different class of family like Neural Programmer-Interpreters [17], in which neural networks are used to approximate the semantics of a program. Our work differs in that we use neural networks to classify different semantics for different programs, where as NLM is learning to emulate the semantics of a program.

7   Conclusion

In this work, we have shown a method to exploit symbolic invariance with neural network. We described several other improvement techniques to help achieve better data efficiency and memory efficiency. We then performed several experiments and contrast it with δLFIT. We also showed the effectiveness of several of our techniques.

There are several more improvements that can be made to further increase data efficiency, like attempting to exploit invariance in the ordering of the variables. The ordering of variables are invariant as a whole, but has to be dependent on each other which makes it non-trivial to exploit, therefore further research needs to be done in order to achieve this. We can also apply this technique to other semantics, such as systems that have delays, or are asynchronous.

References

1. Ba, J.L., Kiros, J.R., Hinton, G.E.: Layer normalization (2016)
2. Brown, T.B., Mann, B., et al.: Language models are few-shot learners. CoRR, abs/2005.14165 (2020)
3. d'Avila Garcez, A.S., Gori, M., Lamb, L.C., Serafini, L., Spranger, M., Tran, S.N.: Neural-symbolic computing: an effective methodology for principled integration of machine learning and reasoning. CoRR, abs/1905.06088 (2019)
4. Garcez, A.D.A., Broda, K., Gabbay, D.M.: Symbolic knowledge extraction from trained neural networks: a sound approach. Artif. Intell. **125**(1), 155–207 (2001)
5. Dong, H., Mao, J., Lin, T., Wang, C., Li, L., Zhou, D.: Neural logic machines. CoRR, abs/1904.11694 (2019)
6. Evans, R., Grefenstette, E.: Learning explanatory rules from noisy data. CoRR, abs/1711.04574 (2017)
7. Avila Garcez, A.S., Zaverucha, G.: The connectionist inductive learning and logic programming system. Appl. Intell. **11**(1), 59–77 (1999)
8. d'Avila Garcez, A.S., Gabbay, D.M., Broda, K.B.: Neural-symbolic learning system: foundations and applications. Springer, Heidelberg (2002). https://doi.org/10.1007/978-1-4471-0211-3
9. Gentet, E., Tourret, S., Inoue, K.: Learning from interpretation transition using feed-forward neural network. In: Proceedings of ILP 2016, CEUR Proceedings 1865, pp. 27–33 (2016)
10. Hendrycks, D., Gimpel, K.: Bridging nonlinearities and stochastic regularizers with gaussian error linear units. CoRR, abs/1606.08415 (2016)
11. Inoue, K.: Logic programming for boolean networks. In: Walsh, T. (ed.) IJCAI 2011, Proceedings of the 22nd International Joint Conference on Artificial Intelligence, Barcelona, Catalonia, Spain, 16–22 July 2011, pp. 924–930. IJCAI/AAAI (2011)
12. Inoue, K., Ribeiro, T., Sakama, C.: Learning from interpretation transition. Mach. Learn. **94**(1), 51–79 (2013). https://doi.org/10.1007/s10994-013-5353-8
13. Klarner, H., Streck, A., Siebert, H.: PyBoolNet: a python package for the generation, analysis and visualization of boolean networks. Bioinformatics **33**(5), 770–772 (2016)
14. Lee, J., Lee, Y., Kim, J., Kosiorek, A., Choi, S., Teh, Y.W.: Set transformer. CoRR, abs/1810.00825 (2018)
15. Paszke, A., et al.: Pytorch: an imperative style, high-performance deep learning library. In: Wallach, H., Larochelle, H., Beygelzimer, A., d' Alché-Buc, F., Fox, E., Garnett, R. (eds.) Advances in Neural Information Processing Systems, vol. 32, pp. 8024–8035. Curran Associates Inc (2019)
16. Phua, Y.J., Inoue, K.: Learning logic programs from noisy state transition data. In: Kazakov, D., Erten, C. (eds.) ILP 2019. LNCS (LNAI), vol. 11770, pp. 72–80. Springer, Cham (2020). https://doi.org/10.1007/978-3-030-49210-6_7
17. Reed, S., De Freitas, N.: Neural programmer-interpreters. arXiv preprint arXiv:1511.06279 (2015)
18. Ribeiro, T., Inoue, K.: Learning prime implicant conditions from interpretation transition. In: Davis, J., Ramon, J. (eds.) ILP 2014. LNCS (LNAI), vol. 9046, pp. 108–125. Springer, Cham (2015). https://doi.org/10.1007/978-3-319-23708-4_8
19. Ribeiro, T., Magnin, M., Inoue, K., Sakama, C.: Learning delayed influences of biological systems. Front. Bioeng. Biotechnol. **2**, 81 (2015)

20. Rintala, T., et al.: Using boolean network extraction of trained neural networks to reverse-engineer gene-regulatory networks from time-series data (2019)
21. Vaswani, A., et al.: Attention is all you need. CoRR, abs/1706.03762 (2017)
22. Xiao, Y., Dougherty, E.R.: The impact of function perturbations in Boolean networks. Bioinformatics **23**(10), 1265–1273 (2007)
23. Zeiler, M.D.: ADADELTA: an adaptive learning rate method. CoRR, abs/1212.5701 (2012)

Learning and Revising Dynamic Temporal Theories in the Full Discrete Event Calculus

Oliver Ray[✉]

Department of Computer Science, University of Bristol, Bristol, UK
csxor@bristol.ac.uk

Abstract. This paper presents the first automatic method for learning and revising dynamic temporal theories in the full-fledged Discrete Event Calculus (DEC), where fluents may be temporarily released from the law of inertia and subject to qualitative or quantitative domain laws. This is done by proposing a reformulation of the DEC, called the eXploratory Event Calculus (XEC), which can be more efficiently handled by state-of-the-art answer set solvers, and which supports a range of different logical semantics and policy options for resolving conflicts relating to the truth value or release status of fluents. The paper shows how XEC outperforms DEC on standard reasoning benchmarks, and how it can be used with an ILP system XHAIL to provide the first proof-of-principle demonstration of theory learning and revision in the full-featured DEC.

Keywords: Theory revision · Answer set programming · Event calculus

1 Introduction

This paper presents the first automatic method for learning and revising dynamic temporal theories in the full-fledged Discrete Event Calculus (DEC) widely seen as the de-facto standard in modern logic-based reasoning about action and change [25]. Unlike prior work on the induction of event calculi theories, which is limited to fragments of DEC with static fluents, positive/negative effects, fluent/action preconditions and trigger axioms, the proposed method supports all standard DEC constructs, including concurrent/disjunctive events, cumulative/cancelling effects, causal/effect constraints as well as dynamic fluents which can be temporarily released from the law of inertia and subject instead to qualitative constraints or quantitative trajectories. To make these advanced modelling features amenable to ILP techniques, this paper proposes a novel reformulation of the DEC, called the eXploratory Event Calculus (XEC), which tackles the following four key limitations of existing axiomatisations:

– Existing encodings contain trajectory axioms with triply nested temporal quantifiers that are known to cause poor scalability of answer set solvers used in contemporary DEC reasoning tools;

© Springer Nature Switzerland AG 2022
N. Katzouris and A. Artikis (Eds.): ILP 2021, LNAI 13191, pp. 219–233, 2022.
https://doi.org/10.1007/978-3-030-97454-1_16

- Existing encodings are written for 2nd-order circumscriptive logics that allow potentially unstable models and enforce a strict view of inertial integrity that is often not desirable from a logic programming point of view;
- Existing encodings offer no support for different policies used elsewhere in the literature to resolve conflicts between concurrent events competing to determine the truth value or release status of fluents;
- Existing encodings have only been applied to domain theories carefully crafted by human experts and there is no known prior work on automatic learning or revision of theories with dynamic fluents.

To tackle these issues, the XEC provides a native answer set encoding of the DEC whose trajectory axioms contain just two temporal quantifiers, and which also provides a set of optional clauses to support a range of logical semantics and conflict policies from the literature [19]. The main contributions are to show how XEC outperforms DEC on standard benchmarks using state-of-the-art reasoners [17], and to show how XEC can be used with an ILP system XHAIL [28] in a proof-of-principle case study to incrementally learn and revise dynamic domain theories under different conflict resolution policies, all for the first time.

2   Background and Related Work

The Event Calculus (EC) is a logical formalism for commonsense reasoning about events (actions) and fluents (properties) in temporal domains [25]. It emerged in 1980s as a way of using logic programming to formalise the behaviour of simple (static) fluents subject to the so-called frame law of inertia - which dictates that properties should persist unchanged in the absence of modifying actions [16]. It was extended in the 1990s using mainly 2nd-order circumscription to address further aspects of the qualification and ramification problems, and to model more complex (dynamic) fluents, which can be temporarily released from the inertial frame in order to follow qualitative domain laws or quantitative gradual change trajectories [30]. This allows the modelling of temporal domains that integrate logical and numerical features: like the classic textbook example of an object whose height is initially fixed prior to it being released by an event which sets it on a trajectory defined by the equations of gravity, until it is brought to a stop by another event caused by it finally hitting the ground [25].

The Discrete Event Calculus (DEC) emerged in the 2000s from applications of SAT solving to event calculus model computation [24]. This was done by rewriting eight core axioms of the continuous EC, all triply quantified in time, with eight equivalent discrete axioms, all linear in time – and retaining just two cubic trajectory axioms. The success of tools like DEC-Reasoner [23] prompted a shift in focus away from infinite continuous timelines towards their projection onto finite discrete timelines which could be efficiently grounded and solved. While SAT was superseded by ASP in the 2010s, the original DEC encoding remains at the heart of modern reasoners, which now use a translation from 2nd-order circumscription into ASP using a method called F2LP [17], whose current superiority was established on a standard suite of deductive temporal benchmarks [17, Fig.5]. For a formal introduction to the DEC, the reader is referred to the textbook [25] (but an informal understanding of some key ideas may also be gleaned from the case study presented later in Sect. 4).

While the DEC axioms have dominated logical-based temporal reasoning for nearly two decades, they also impose several limitations this paper seeks to avoid. Aside from the inefficiency of the trajectory axioms with their triply nested temporal quantifiers, they also make several assumptions which are not universally accepted. On one hand, there are differences between the early logic programming semantics (which take a relaxed approach to inertial integrity but only allow stable models) and the later circumscriptive semantics (which enforce a strict view of inertial integrity but may admit unsupported models). This can result in subtle differences in the behaviour of EC benchmarks. On another hand, various conflict resolution policies have been proposed in the literature which differ from the rather naive standard approach used in the DEC.

For example, while DEC insists *"initiating and terminating a fluent at the same time causes inconsistency"* [24, Sec. 2], other work argues for an alternative view where *"simultaneously initiating and terminating a fluent simply gives rise to two sets of models (one in which the fluent is true immediately afterwards and one in which it is false)"* [19, Sec. 2.4] resulting in a non-deterministic choice. And the EC examples packaged with XHAIL [6] adopt another approach where conflicting initiation and termination of a fluent results in its state flipping. It is easy to envisage situations where other choices are appropriate, but these have not been studied until now. And nor has the possibility of other types of conflict: such as when concurrent events compete to bind/free a dynamic fluent to/from the inertial frame; or when two trajectories try to control the same fluent.

It is perhaps not surprising EC conflict policies have been given such short shrift when it is realised that all DEC benchmarks to date have been carefully hand-crafted by experts to avoid any inadvertent possibility to simultaneously stop/start or bind/free a fluent, and to ensure trajectories don't interfere with each other or attempt to control fluents which have not been properly released. But these formalities cannot be taken for granted when domain axioms are learnt and revised by machines. If such choices are left implicit and arbitrary (as they often are) then theories may not respect the intended assumptions and behave incorrectly on different DEC variants or reasoning toolchains.

ILP has roots in temporal induction going back over 15 years to work on theory completion in action languages [9,15,18,26] and basic fragments of EC using Clint [29], Progol [22], Alecto [21] and XHAIL [27]. Further development of XHAIL [28] paved the way for the first real-world applications of EC in software engineering [3,7] which evolved into two substantial lines of work on temporal learning [1,2] and theory revision [5,8]. XHAIL also inspired many other systems optimised for temporal reasoning: e.g. ILED [13], OLED [11], INSPIRE [14] and I2XHAIL [20]. While additional enhancements have since been made to these methods [4,10,12,31], there has yet to be any work on the induction of theories with dynamic fluents and trajectories or the analysis of different conflict policies and logical semantics. Most recently, [32] developed belief revision methods for a doxastic extension of a static DEC fragment, but this formalism excludes state-constraints, trigger axioms, non-determinism, dynamic fluents, gradual change trajectories, and a host of other standard features of the full-fledged DEC.

3   The eXploratory Event Calculus (XEC)

To begin tackling these issues, this section introduces a reformulation of the DEC, called the eXploratory Event Calculus (XEC), whose key benefits are that it includes a more efficient encoding of trajectories (whose axioms have at most two temporal quantifiers) and it provides a set of optional clauses (which can simply be un-commented) to support a range of logical semantics and conflict policies from the literature [19]. This is achieved by the answer set program in Listing 1, which consists of four key parts:

i. axioms for *(non)inertial* fluents and their optional Stop-Start policies;
ii. axioms for *dynamic* fluents and their optional Bind-Free policies;
iii. axioms for *(anti)trajectories* that scale quadratically with time;
iv. optional axioms to simulate circumscriptive semantics (if needed to strictly enforce inertial integrity and generate potentially unsupported models).

As shown by the domain declarations, XEC recognises several different types of fluent: Intuitively, *inertial* (aka. *primitive* or *frame*) fluents, F, are properties that are normally subject to the commonsense law of inertia. Conversely, *non-inertial* (aka. *derived* or *nonframe*) fluents, N, are properties whose truth is solely determined by qualitative state constraints or quantitative trajectories. Although inertial and noninertial fluents are mutually exclusive, the former can be made to behave like the latter by declaring them as *dynamic* fluents, D, and allowing them to be explicitly *released* from the inertial frame for certain periods of time. Finally, *monitored* fluents, M, are inertial fluents that may be used to sustain trajectories, and *controlled* fluents, C, are dynamic or noninertial fluents that may be determined by trajectories. The core XEC axioms which define these behaviours are superficially similar to existing translations of DEC into ASP such as those obtained from F2LP or given in [25, Fig.15], but there are three key conceptual differences that should be kept in mind:

First, XEC is written in a native logic programming style with core rules that only need to formalise when `holdsAt` and `releasedAt` are true (and not when they are false). This avoids the need for several choice literals and integrity constraints that arise when DEC is translated from circumscriptive extensions of classical logic into answer set programs. Although a classical semantics be emulated, if required, by un-commenting the optional clauses in the last section of the listing, by default they are omitted from the XEC as they are arguably inefficient, unnecessary, and undesirable from a logic programming point of view.

Second, XEC is written so that the core axioms only fire in the absence of conflicts. This results in conservative default policies of stopping fluents in case of start-stop conflicts (SSCs) and binding fluents in case of bind-free conflicts

```
1   %%%%%%%%%%%%%%% i. INERTIAL (& NONINERTIAL) FLUENTS %%%%%%%%%%%%%%%%
2
3     #domain inertial(F). #domain noninertial(N). #domain event(E).
4     #domain time(T;T1;T2). #domain succ(R,S). succ(T1,T2):-T2=T1+1.
5
6     % STOP-START CONFLICT (SSC) RESOLUTION POLICY OPTIONS        %
7     % (uncomment default* and another option to override):        %
8     %------------------------------------------------------------%
9     % ssc(F,T) :- stops(F,T), starts(F,T).                      %   STOP*
10    % holdsAt(F,S) :- ssc(F,R), not releasedAt(F,S).            %   START
11    % {holdsAt(F,S)} :- ssc(F,R), not releasedAt(F,S).         %   PICK
12    % holdsAt(F,S) :- ssc(F,R), holdsAt(F,R), not releasedAt(F,S).   % HOLD
13    % holdsAt(F,S) :- ssc(F,R), not holdsAt(F,R), not releasedAt(F,S).%   FLIP
14    % :- ssc(F,T).                                               %   FAIL
15
16    holdsAt(F,S)  :-  starts(F,R), not stops(F,R), not releasedAt(F,S).
17    holdsAt(F,S)  :-  holdsAt(F,R), not stops(F,R), not releasedAt(F,S).
18    starts(F,T)  :-  happens(E,T), initiates(E,F,T).
19    stops(F,T)  :-  happens(E,T), terminates(E,F,T).
20
21  %%%%%%%%%%%%%%%%%%%%%%%% ii.DYNAMIC FLUENTS %%%%%%%%%%%%%%%%%%%%%%%%
22
23    #domain dynamic(D).
24
25    % BIND-FREE CONFLICT (BFC) RESOLUTION POLICY OPTIONS        %
26    % (uncomment default* and another option to override):        %
27    %------------------------------------------------------------%
28    % bfc(D,T) :- binds(D,T), frees(D,T).                       %   BIND*
29    % releasedAt(D,S) :- bfc(D,R).                              %   FREE
30    % {releasedAt(D,S)} :- bfc(D,R).                           %   PICK
31    % releasedAt(D,S) :- bfc(D,R), releasedAt(D,R).            % HOLD
32    % releasedAt(D,S) :- bfc(D,R), not releasedAt(D,R),        %   FLIP
33    % :- bfc(D,T).                                              %   FAIL
34
35    releasedAt(D,S)  :-  frees(D,R), not binds(D,R).
36    releasedAt(D,S)  :-  releasedAt(D,R), not binds(D,R).
37    frees(D,T)  :-  happens(E,T), releases(E,D,T).
38    binds(D,T)  :-  starts(D,T).
39    binds(D,T)  :-  stops(D,T).
40
41  %%%%%%%%%%%%% iii. TRAJECTORY (& ANTITRAJECTORY) AXIOMS %%%%%%%%%%%%
42
43    #domain monitored(M). #domain controlled(C).
44
45    holdsAt(C,T1+T2) :- followT(M,T1,T2), trajectory(M,T1-1,C,T2+1).
46    followT(M,S,0) :- starts(M,R), holdsAt(M,S), not releasedAt(M,S).
47    followT(M,T,S) :- followT(M,T,R), not stops(M,T+R), time(T+S).
48
49    holdsAt(C,T1+T2) :- followA(M,T1,T2), antiTrajectory(M,T1-1,C,T2+1).
50    followA(M,S,0) :- stops(M,R), not holdsAt(M,S), not releasedAt(M,S).
51    followA(M,T,S) :- followA(M,T,R), not starts(M,T+R), time(T+S).
52
53  %%%%%%%%%%%%%%%%%%%%%%% iv. CLASSICAL SEMANTICS %%%%%%%%%%%%%%%%%%%%%%%
54
55    % {holdsAt(F,T)}. {holdsAt(N,T)}.
56    % :- holdsAt(F,S), {holdsAt(F,R), starts(F,R), releasedAt(F,S)}0.
57    % :- holdsAt(F,R), {holdsAt(F,S), stops(F,R), releasedAt(F,S)}0.
58    % :- holdsAt(F,S), holdsAt(F,R), stops(F,R), {starts(F,R), releasedAt(F,S)}0.
59    % :- starts(F,R), {holdsAt(F,S), holdsAt(F,R), stops(F,R), releasedAt(F,S)}0.
60
61    % {releasedAt(D,T)}.
62    % :- releasedAt(F,S), {releasedAt(F,R), frees(F,R)}0.
63    % :- releasedAt(F,R), {releasedAt(F,S), binds(F,R)}0.
64    % :- releasedAt(F,S), releasedAt(F,R), binds(F,R), {frees(F,R)}0.
65    % :- frees(F,R), {releasedAt(F,S), releasedAt(F,R), binds(F,R)}0.
66
```

Listing 1. eXploratory Event Calculus (XEC) with optional policies.

(BFCs). But those policies can be overridden by simply un-commenting the first optional policy clause (representing a conflict detection rule that replaces the default starred option) along with one of the following clauses in order to invoke one of five substitute policies that either: apply the converse of the default policy (Start/Free); make a non-deterministic choice (Pick); maintain the status quo (Hold); change the status quo (Flip); or declare a logical inconsistency (Fail).

Note that, if more than one optional policy is un-commented, then the label positions depict a partial order in which any lower option will take priority over any other options vertically above them; and where the combination of Hold and Flip is equivalent to Fail. Note also that it is possible to customise any of these policies and/or add new ones which might be appropriate in a specific modelling task. Note also that the conflict detection rules for `ssc` and `bsc` can be treated as definitional abbreviations which can be trivially unfolded from the program. They are included here only to make the code slight easier to read and to make the optional policy definitions slightly more compact.

Third, XEC introduces a new encoding of (anti)trajectories whose rules (in contrast to prior work) are quantified over at most two timepoints[1]. This is done by introducing the predicates `followT` and `followA` to recast (anti)trajectory definitions into a successor state form in the same way `holdsAt` and `releasedAt` were first recast in the DEC by eliminating `clipped` and `declipped` from the continuous EC. Intuitively an atom of the form `followT(f,t,k)` means that, at time `t+k`, we are `k` time steps into a trajectory we have been following since the fluent `f` was turned on at time `t`. Thus trajectory axioms in XEC are quadratic in time, as opposed to cubic, and all other core axioms remain linear.

This version of XEC faithfully emulates canonical DEC behaviour by only allowing trajectories to be cancelled by an explicit terminating event on the monitored fluent. Since the SSC and BFC policies may both override the effect an initiating event may have in the next time, the trajectory axioms check to ensure the monitored fluent did actually hold at the time after the initiating event (so the initiation was not overruled by a competing termination) and the monitored fluent was not released (so the initiation was not overruled by a competing release - which would then have meant state constraints must have activated the fluent instead of the initiating event)!

To show the benefits of XEC over DEC in terms of reduced grounding size and solving time, tests were run on nine deductive benchmarks previously used to show the superiority of F2LP over the prior state-of-the-art DEC-Reasoner [24]. All benchmarks were tested on the same timeline 0..50. All fluents were assumed to be inertial and dynamic. Model correctness was verified by hand. As shown in Table 1, the optional classical XEC axioms were used in three tasks to emulate unsupported DEC models (resulting from an apparent oversight in the original benchmark definition) where an object can arbitrarily change height due to a lack of trajectory offsets resulting from the large value of maxstep=50. A set

---

[1] Although the last rules for `followT` and `followA` do syntactically mention three timepoints R, S and T, domain declarations mean that S is merely an abbreviation for R+1, and so the rule is only actually quantified over two times: R and T.

Table 1. Comparison of execution time and grounding size of XEC (right) and DEC (centre) on 9 standard benchmarks from [17, Fig.5] (left). Grounding size (number of rules; number of atoms) computed by Gringo 3.0.5 with timeline 0..50 in all tasks. Execution time (grounding time; solving time of first model) computed by Clasp 3.1.0 (averaged over 5 trials) on a Windows 10 i64 command shell running on a Dell Lattitude 5480 with Intel Core i7 2.6 GHz CPU and 16 Gb RAM. Note that F2LP runtimes are not included in this table.

Task [maxstep=50]	DEC (F2LP+ASP)	XEC (ASP)
Bus Ride (disjunctive event)	**144** ms (gnd:86±11; slv:58±4) **47** kb (rul:2,618; atm:157)	**112** ms (gnd:56±4; slv:56±2) **12** kb (rul:603; atm:123)
Commuter [c] (compound event)	**1,736** ms (gnd:946±4; slv:790±7) **8,590** kb (rul:436,497; atm:7,237)	**140** ms (gnd:74±4; slv:66±2) **28** kb (rul:1,470; atm:203)
Kitchen Sink (trajectory+trigger)	**1,694** ms (gnd:940±16; slv:754±11) **8,713** kb (rul:404,507; atm:970)	**242** ms (gnd:136±9; slv:106±4) **383** kb (rul:19,664; atm:728)
Thielscher Circuit [b] (causal constraint)	**374** ms (gnd:210±9; slv:164±7) **1,084** kb (rul:66,901; atm:409)	**140** ms (gnd:78±13; slv:62±7) **58** kb (rul:2,688; atm:394)
Walking Turkey (effect constraint)	**148** ms (gnd:82±7; slv:66±7) **29** kb (rul:1,576; atm:154)	**140** ms (gnd:70±9; slv:70±7) **11** kb (rul:424; atm:155)
Falling w/AntiTraj [a] (traj.+antitraj.)	**346** ms (gnd:218±7; slv:128±2) **799** kb (rul:43,919; atm:664)	**258** ms (gnd:152±2; slv:106±2) **491** kb (rul:26,165; atm:664)
Falling w/Events [a] (traj.+rebind.)	**1,898** ms (gnd:1,056±13; slv:812±7) **9,907** kb (rul:454,657; atm:1,072)	**332** ms (gnd:190±7; slv:142±2) **884** kb (rul:44,726; atm:1,072)
Hot Air Balloon [a] (traj.+antitraj.)	**158** ms (gnd:90±0; slv:68±2) **104** kb (rul:5,790; atm:410)	**160** ms (gnd:86±2; slv:74±7) **115** kb (rul:6,602; atm:410)
Telephone1 (direct effects)	**264** ms (gnd:158±2; slv:106±2) **350** kb (rul:17,950; atm:819)	**158** ms (gnd:88±4; slv:70±0) **68** kb (rul:3,309; atm:275)

a {XEC run with optional classical axioms.
b {DEC and XEC both run with (identical) additional causal axioms.
c {DEC and XEC both replaced by (independent) durative variants.

of additional causal definitions [25, CC1-4, Sec.6.5.0] were added to both DEC and XEC in one task involving the use of causal constraints. In one task involving compound events, DEC was replaced by a standard durative extension of the (continuous) EC [25, EC1-19,Appndx.C] while a bespoke durative variant of the (discrete) XEC was developed by adapting the method introduced above for formalising trajectories (but whose details are beyond the scope of this paper).

4   XEC Theory Learning and Revision with XHAIL

XHAIL [28] is a nonmonotonic ILP system based on the credulous answer set semantics. It allows the annotation of answer set programs with *examples* (which are positive/negative ground literals representing goals or properties that a user desires to be true/false in some model of the program) and *mode declarations* (which specify syntactic constraints on the heads/bodies of clauses that may be potentially added to program in order to achieve those goals). Integer weights and priorities may be attached to examples or mode declarations in order to modulate the built-in compression heuristics and semantic biases that are provided as a means of pragmatically identifying extensions or revisions of a knowledge base to ensure the existence of models with the required properties [6].

The running example in this section shows how XHAIL can perform multiple rounds of theory learning and revision in the full-featured XEC under different conflict resolution policies. This is done by cumulatively adding fragments of code (comprising the facts, rules, examples and mode declarations contained in the text boxes below identified by red labels) to an input file that initially contains just the bare XEC axioms in Listing 1. Summaries of XHAIL's response are also given at key points (denoted by the output messages in the text boxes below identified by blue chevrons). In the absence of any optional axioms initially being asserted, the XEC initially implements the default (Stop/Bind) polices to resolve SSC/BFC conflicts respectively.

The first fragment 01 of additional code declares 11 timepoints 0,1,..,10, along with an inertial fluent (f) that is known to hold in the initial state, and an event e that is known to occur on all of the timepoints defined so far. The #example directive (which can also be thought of as a goal) tells XHAIL to try and construct models where f holds at time 2. The #display directive tells XHAIL to print out true instances of holdsAt/2 (when it is called with the -f option for displaying full output). As expected, given this input file, XHAIL will simply return the one and only trivial model of the code defined thus far:

```
01:   %%% Start with default policies: SSC=Stop; BFC=Bind
      time(0..10). inertial(f). holdsAt(f,0). event(e). happens(e,0..10).
      #example holdsAt(f,2). #display holdsAt/2.
```

```
>>>   model: holdsAt(f,0) holdsAt(f,1) holdsAt(f,2)...holdsAt(f,9) holdsAt(f,10)
```

The second fragment 02 of additional code then adds another goal stating that f should in fact be false at time 1. Now XHAIL will have to infer a hypothesis in order to make both existing goals true (as the only model currently has f true always). The head declarations allow XHAIL to infer atoms of the form initiates(e,f,T) and terminates(e,f,T) where e is a specific event, f is a specific fluent, and T is a variable representing a timepoint.

```
02:   #example not holdsAt(f,1).
      #modeh initiates($event, $inertial, +time).
      #modeh terminates($event, $inertial, +time).
```

If the variable placemarker denoted "+" had been replaced by a constant placemarker denoted "$", then XHAIL would have returned a ground abductive hypothesis consisting of the facts `terminates(e,f,0)` and `initiates(e,f,1)`. But as the "+" in the third argument must be replaced by a variable, there is no solution to this problem under the default (Stop) SSC policy. This is because event e would end up simultaneously initiating and terminating f at every time point. And since the termination would always take priority, there would be no way for f to become true again at time 2 once it had been false at 1.

```
>>> no meaningful answers, ...
```

But if we now switch to a nondeterministic SSC policy by un-commenting the conflict detection rule (line 9) and the alternative Pick option rule (line 11) as shown in fragment 03, then XHAIL is able to return a hypothesis. This is because the competition between the initiating and terminating effect of e on f allows a nondeterministic choice on every time point, so the goals can now be correctly satisfied according to the (seemingly over-general) hypothesis below:

```
03:  %%% Switch to secondary SSC policy: SSC=Pick; BFC=Bind
     ssc(F,T) :- stops(F,T), starts(F,T).
     {holdsAt(F,S)} :- ssc(F,R), not releasedAt(F,S).
```

```
>>> hypothesis: initiates(e,f,V1). terminates(e,f,V1).
```

On the other hand, if we override the SSC policy again, using the Fail option in fragment 04, then the previous hypothesis is no longer a correct solution:

```
04:  %%% Switch to tertiary SSC policy: SSC=Fail; BFC=Bind
     :- ssc(F,T).
```

```
>>> no meaningful answers, ...
```

However, if the body declarations in fragment 05 are also added, then XHAIL is able to qualify the earlier hypothesis by restricting the conditions under which initiation and termination may occur, so an SSC may be avoided:

```
05:  #modeb holdsAt($inertial,+time). #modeb not holdsAt($inertial,+time).
```

```
>>> hypothesis:
      terminates(e,f,V1) :- holdsAt(f,V1), time(V1).
      initiates(e,f,V1) :- not holdsAt(f,V1), time(V1).
```

The hypothesis returned above implies that the state of f will constantly alternate: being true at even times and false at odd times. As f is known to be initially true at 0, the occurrence of e at 0 will result in the termination of f at the next timepoint 1. In turn, this will allow the occurrence of e at 1 to re-initiate f at 2; and so on up to the last timepoint 10.

However, if we are given the extra observations in fragment 06 that f does not actually hold at 4, even though it does at 6, then it is no longer possible find a correct hypothesis:

06:
```
#example not holdsAt(f,4). #example holdsAt(f,6).
```

>>>
```
no meaningful answers, ...
```

But a more complex hypothesis can be found if we supply the additional code in fragment 07 which introduces an integer type (potentially distinct from timepoints) and adds a body declaration for a newly defined predicate which indicates when one integer is a multiple of another. This results in a hypothesis stating that each occurrence of e will try to initiate f whenever f is false; but will try to terminate f on any time point that is a multiple of 3. The means that after time 0, when f is defined as initially true, it will repeatedly turn off for one time point before turning on for the next two.

07:
```
int(0..9). multiple(T1,T2) :- T2>1, T1 #mod T2==0.
#modeb multiple(+time, $int).
```

>>>
```
hypothesis:
   terminates(e,f,V1) :- multiple(V1,3),time(V1).
   initiates(e,f,V1) :- not holdsAt(f,V1), time(V1).
```

But if, as shown in fragment 08, f is made dynamic and an event d is added that releases f at time 5, then XHAIL must infer an additional hypothesis clause under the default BFC policy (Bind). This is because, if left uncontested, the release at 5 would push f to be false at 6, which would violate a goal (in fragment 06). This can be avoided by generating a conflict at 5 such that the initiation of f by d will take priority over the release of f by d, thereby keeping f true at 6 (note that e does not attempt to initiate f at 5 because f is true at 5).

08:
```
dynamic(f). event(d). releases(d,f,T). happens(d,5).
```

>>>
```
hypothesis:
   terminates(e,f,V1) :- multiple(V1,3), time(V1).
   initiates(e,f,V1) :- not holdsAt(f,V1), time(V1).
   initiates(d,f,V1).
```

Yet, if we now switch to the converse BFC policy (Free), by un-commenting the conflict detection rule (line 28) along with the alternative Free option rule (line 29) as shown in fragment 09, then the release of fluents would be favoured instead, and the previous escape is no longer possible:

09:
```
%%% Switch to secondary BFC policy: SSC=Fail; BFC=Free
bfc(D,T) :- binds(D,T), frees(D,T).
releasedAt(D,S) :- bfc(D,R).
```

>>>
```
no meaningful answers, ...
```

Given that f must now be released at 6, we can instead allow XHAIL to infer a state law in order to justify its truth at 6. This can be done by writing the mode declaration shown in fragment 10 allowing the abduction of ground instances of holdsAt/2. But, since we don't want to trivialise the whole learning task by simply letting XHAIL directly abduce each and every example given thus far, we attach a cost of 10 (or any other high number) on this mode declaration in order to make its use ten times less preferable than other head and body declarations (which all inherit a default cost of 1).

```
10 :   #modeh holdsAt($dynamic,$time)=10.
```

```
       hypothesis:
>>>        terminates(e,f,V1) :- multiple(V1,3), time(V1).
           initiates(e,f,V1) :- not holdsAt(f,V1), time(V1).
           holdsAt(f,6).
```

At this point we may decide we want to accept the clauses learnt so far into the knowledge base. But as we are not yet sure if they are fully trustworthy, we can use a method originally proposed in [28, p.338] to add the clauses in a way that allows them to be subsequently revised as follows: (i) we wrap each (revisable) body literal b in the clause in an atom of the form $try(n, m, b)$ – where each (revisable) clause is assigned a unique identifier m and each literal within that clause is assigned a unique identifier n; and (ii) we add a literal $not\ exception(m, h)$ – where h is the atom in the head of the clause. Then two rules for each try atom are added: one representing the possibility of deleting the literal form the clause, and one representing the possibility of keeping it. The language bias is then set to allow literals to be deleted or exceptions to be inserted as shown in the following code fragment 11:

```
       holdsAt(f,6) :- not exception(0,holdsAt(f,6)).

       terminates(e,f,T) :-
           try(1,1,multiple(T,3)), not exception(1,terminates(e,f,T)).
       try(1,1,multiple(T,3)) :- del(1,1).
       try(1,1,multiple(T,3)) :- not del(1,1), multiple(T,3).

       initiates(e,f,T) :-
11 :       try(1,2,not_holdsAt(f,T)), not exception(2,initiates(e,f,T)).
       try(1,2,not_holdsAt(f,T)) :- del(1,2).
       try(1,2,not_holdsAt(f,T)) :- not del(1,2), not holdsAt(f,T).

       literal(1..1). clause(0..2).

       #modeh del($literal,$clause).
       #modeh exception($clause,holdsAt(f,six)). six(6).
       #modeh exception($clause,terminates(e,f,+time)).
       #modeh exception($clause,initiates(e,f,+time)).
```

With all of the previous code fragments included in the input file, XHAIL now returns an empty hypothesis, confirming that the provisional knowledge we just added does satisfy indeed satisfy all of the required goals. But if any further goals are added, then XHAIL would have the ability to infer hypotheses containing rules for del or exception, which would be interpreted as instructions for revising these clauses (through a post-processing step that would explicitly add or remove the indicated literals or clauses).

Adding the extra information in fragment 11, that d happens at 8 but f is false at 9, introduces an inconsistency that can only be removed by tightening the definition of terminates. This is because, according to our current code, once d causes f to be released (and thus false) at 9, then e will try to both initiate f (because f is false at 9) and to also terminate f (because 9 is a multiple of 3) - which is not allowed under the current (Fail) SSC policy.

11:
```
happens(d,8).
:- holdsAt(f,9).
```

In this case, one of the (now many) hypotheses returned by XHAIL is shown below, which is viewed as an instruction to modify the revisable clause with ID 1 for the termination of f by adding the complements of any literals in the body of the learnt exception clause into the body of original clause.

>>>
```
hypothesis: exception(1,terminates(e,f,V1)) :- not holdsAt(f,V1).
```

After conveniently renaming variables to reflect their types, we are left with a revised version of the previously learnt clauses as shown in fragment 12, which we now decide to assert, exactly as given, into our knowledge base:

12:
```
terminates(e,f,T) :- multiple(T,3), holdsAt(f,T).
initiates(e,f,T) :- not holdsAt(f,T).
holdsAt(f,6).
```

The final part of the example now shows how trajectories can be learnt on top of all the information we just asserted. The method shown below works by fitting a polynomial of some chosen degree to a set of observations in order to define a domain specific trajectory. To keep things simple we will stick to a linear regression using a polynomial of degree 1. First the timeline is extended by 5 more points 11..15 and new types are introduced to represent equation coefficients and values. Atoms of the form $linear(x_0, x_1, t, v)$ facilitate linear regression by essentially pre-computing mappings from a timepoint t to a value v using coefficients x_0 and x_1 to define a linear equation $v = x_1.t + x_0$. We define the trajectory parameter types beginning and elapsed as synonyms for time and we specify the monitored fluent f and the controlled fluents g(V). There is also an integrity constraint stating that fluent g can only have at most one value V at any given time T. The mode declarations in fragment 13 then allow XHAIL to learn the definition of a trajectory in terms of a linear equation:

```
     #domain time(T). time(11..15).
     #domain coeff(X0;X1;X2). coeff(0..2).
     #domain value(V;V1;V2). value(0..15).

     linear(X0,X1,T,V) :- V==X1*T+X0.
     beginning(T). elapsed(T).
13:  noninertial(g(V)). controlled(g(V)). monitored(f).
     :- holdsAt(g(V1),T), holdsAt(g(V2),T), V1!=V2.

     #example holdsAt(g(5),11).
     #example holdsAt(g(11),14).

     #modeh trajectory(f, +beginning, g(+value), +elapsed).
     #modeb linear($coeff, $coeff, +time, +value).
```

When run on this task, XHAIL produces the following hypothesis, which can be more simply written `trajectory(f,T1,g(2*T1+1)):-multiple(T1,3)`.

```
     hypothesis:
       trajectory(f,V1,g(V2),V3) :-
>>>        multiple(V1,3),linear(1,2,V3,V2),
           beginning(V1),elapsed(V3),value(V2).
```

The method used in this initial demonstration of trajectory learning can be generalised to higher order polynomials. For example, in theory the rule `quadratic(X0,X1,X2,T,V):-V==X2*T*T+X1*T+X0` could be used to implement quadratic regression. But, in practice, this method does not scale very in ASP. In contrast to the previous learning tasks which were all solved in an instant, this task (which remember is still conjoined with the 12 previous code snippets) took about 20 s to solve. Given the general-purpose nature of the revisions being performed by XHAIL it should be clear this example can easily be extended to learn antitrajectories, triggers, causal constants, or any other standard (or even non-standard) types of DEC domain axiom.

5   Conclusion

This first contribution of this paper was to introduce the eXploratory Event Calculus (XEC) as a pragmatic framework for commonsense temporal reasoning under a set of various conflict policies and semantic options. This work has begun to allow the systematic comparison of existing work in terms of the explicit or implicit choices they have made and how those choices impact upon theory learning and revision. In contrast to the prevailing trend of translating DEC theories from 2nd order circumscriptive logic into ASP, the work presented here suggests that the use of native ASP programs may have significant conceptual and practical advantages.

The second contribution of this paper was to present the first axiomatisation of EC trajectories that does not rely upon any rules quantified over more than two timepoints. This technique offers significant efficiency benefits for any work involving reasoning with EC trajectories using ASP systems on fully materialised timelines. This reformulation may be exploited by EC researchers wishing to use the newly proposed XEC or the canonical DEC from which it was derived.

The third contribution of this paper was to show how the ILP system XHAIL can be applied to the tasks of theory completion and theory revision in a fully featured XEC under different reasoning policies. This work provides the first known demonstration of learning and revision of full-fledged temporal theories with dynamic fluents and trajectories. While this is a significant step forwards, future work is needed to develop more efficient regression techniques in order to make trajectory learning sufficiently scalable in real-world applications.

References

1. Alrajeh, D., Kramer, J., Russo, A., Uchitel, S.: Learning operational requirements from goal models. In: Proceedings of the 31st International Conference on Software Engineering, pp. 265–275 (2009)
2. Alrajeh, D., Kramer, J., Russo, A., Uchitel, S.: An inductive approach for modal transition system refinement. In: Technical Communications of the International Conference of Logic Programming ICLP, pp. 106–116 (2011)
3. Alrajeh, D., Ray, O., Russo, A., Uchitel, S.: Using abduction and induction for operational requirements elaboration. J. Appl. Logic 7(3), 275–288 (2009)
4. Artikis, A., Sergot, M., Paliouras, G.: An event calculus for event recognition. IEEE Trans. Knowl. Data Eng. 27(4), 895–908 (2015)
5. Athakravi, D., Corapi, D., Russo, A., De Vos, M., Padget, J., Satoh, K.: Handling change in normative specifications. In: Baldoni, M., Dennis, L., Mascardi, V., Vasconcelos, W. (eds.) Declarative Agent Languages and Technologies X, Proceeding of the 10th International Workshop (DALT 2012), Revised Selected Papers. Lecture Notes in Artificial Intelligence, vol. 7784, pp. 1–19. Springer, Heidelberg (2013)
6. Bragaglia, S., Ray, O.: Nonmonotonic learning in large biological networks. In: Inductive Logic Programming, pp. 33–48 (2015)
7. Corapi, D., Ray, O., Russo, A., Bandara, A., Lupu, E.: Learning rules from user behaviour. In: in Proceedings of the 5th International Conference on Artificial Intelligence Applications and Innovations (AIAI 2009), pp. 459–468 (2009)
8. Corapi, D., Russo, A., De Vos, M., Padget, J., Satoh, K.: Normative design using inductive learning. Theory Pract. Logic Prog. 11(4–5), 783–799 (2011)
9. Fern, A., Givan, R., Siskind, J.M.: Specific-to-general learning for temporal events with application to learning event definitions from video. J. AI Res. 17, 379–449 (2002)
10. Katzouris, N., Artikis, A.: WOLED: a tool for online learning weighted answer set rules for temporal reasoning under uncertainty. In: Proceedings of the 17th International Conference on Principles of Knowledge Representation and Reasoning, KR 2020, Rhodes, Greece, 12–18 September 2020, pp. 790–799 (2020)
11. Katzouris, N., Artikis, A., Paliouras, G.: Online learning of event definitions. Theory Pract. Logic Program. 16(5–6), 817–833 (2016)
12. Katzouris, N., Artikis, A., Paliouras, G.: Parallel online event calculus learning for complex event recognition. Future Gener. Comput. Syst. 94, 468–478 (2019)
13. Katzouris, N., Paliouras, G., Artikis, A.: Incremental learning of event definitions with inductive logic programming. Mach. Learn. 100, 555–585 (2015)

14. Kazmi, M., Schuller, P., Saygin, Y.: Improving scalability of inductive logic programming via pruning and best-effort optimisation. Expert Syst. Appl. **87**, 291–303 (2017)
15. Klingspor, V., Morik, K.J., Rieger, A.D.: Learning concepts from sensor data of a mobile robot. Mach. Learn. **23**(2), 305–332 (1996)
16. Kowalski, R., Sergot, M.: A logic-based calculus of events. New Gener. Comput. **4**(1), 67–95 (1986)
17. Lee, J., Palla, R.: Reformulating the situation calculus and the event calculus in the general theory of stable models and in answer set programming. J. Artif. Intell. Res. **43**, 571–620 (2012)
18. Lorenzo, D., Otero, R.P.: Learning to reason about actions. In: Proceedings 14th European Conference on AI (ECAI 2000), pp. 316–320 (2000)
19. Miller, R., Shanahan, M.: Some alternative formulations of the event calculus. In: Kakas, A.C., Sadri, F. (eds.) Computational Logic: Logic Programming and Beyond. LNCS (LNAI), vol. 2408, pp. 452–490. Springer, Heidelberg (2002). https://doi.org/10.1007/3-540-45632-5_17
20. Mitra, A., Baral, C.: Incremental and iterative learning of answer set programs from mutually distinct examples. Theory Pract. Logic Program. **18**(3–4), 623–637 (2018)
21. Moyle, S.: Using theory completion to learn a robot navigation control program. In: Matwin, S., Sammut, C. (eds.) ILP 2002. LNCS (LNAI), vol. 2583, pp. 182–197. Springer, Heidelberg (2003). https://doi.org/10.1007/3-540-36468-4_12
22. Moyle, S., Muggleton, S.: Learning programs in the event calculus. In: Lavrač, N., Džeroski, S. (eds.) ILP 1997. LNCS, vol. 1297, pp. 205–212. Springer, Heidelberg (1997). https://doi.org/10.1007/3540635149_49
23. Mueller, E.: A tool for satisfiability-based commonsense reasoning in the event calculus. In: Proceedings of 7th International Florida AI Research Society Conference, pp. 147–152 (2004)
24. Mueller, E.T.: Event calculus reasoning through satisfiability. J. Logic Comput. **14**(5), 703–730 (2004)
25. Mueller, E.T.: Commonsense Reasoning: An Event Calculus Based Approach, 2nd edn. Morgan Kaufmann Publishers Inc., San Francisco (2014)
26. Needham, C.J., Santos, P.E., Magee, D.R., Devin, V., Hogg, D.C., Cohn, A.G.: Protocols from perceptual observations. Artif. Intell **167**(1), 103–136 (2005)
27. Ray, O.: Using abduction for induction of normal logic programs. In: Proceedings of the ECAI'06 Workshop on Abduction and Induction in Artificial Intelligence and Scientific Modelling (AIAI 2007), pp. 28–31 (2006), http://people.cs.bris.ac.uk/~oray/AIAI06/AIAI06.pdf
28. Ray, O.: Nonmonotonic abductive inductive learning. J. Appl. Logic **7**(3), 329–340 (2009)
29. Sablon, G., Bruynooghe, M.: Using the event calculus to integrate planning and learning in an intelligent autonomous agent. In: Proceedings of 2nd European Workshop on Planning (EWS 1993), pp. 254–265 (1994)
30. Shanahan, M.: The Event Calculus Explained, pp. 409–430 (1999)
31. Skarlatidis, A., Paliouras, G., Artikis, A., Vouros, G.A.: Probabilistic event calculus for event recognition. ACM Trans. Comput. Logic (TOCL) **16**(02, Article 11), 1–37 (2015)
32. Tsampanaki, N., Patkos, T., Flouris, G., Plexousakis, D.: Revising event calculus theories to recover from unexpected observations. Ann. Math. Artif. Intell. **89**, 209–236 (2021)

Human-Like Rule Learning from Images Using One-Shot Hypothesis Derivation

Dany Varghese[1][(✉)], Roman Bauer[1], Daniel Baxter-Beard[2],
Stephen Muggleton[3], and Alireza Tamaddoni-Nezhad[1]

[1] Department of Computer Science, University of Surrey, Guildford, UK
{dany.varghese,r.bauer,a.tamaddoni-nezhad}@surrey.ac.uk
[2] School of Computing, Newcastle University, Newcastle upon Tyne, UK
[3] Department of Computing, Imperial College London, London, UK
s.muggleton@imperial.ac.uk

Abstract. Unlike most computer vision approaches, which depend on hundreds or thousands of training images, humans can typically learn from a single visual example. Humans achieve this ability using background knowledge. Rule-based machine learning approaches such as Inductive Logic Programming (ILP) provide a framework for incorporating domain specific background knowledge. These approaches have the potential for human-like learning from small data or even one-shot learning, i.e. learning from a single positive example. By contrast, statistics based computer vision algorithms, including Deep Learning, have no general mechanisms for incorporating background knowledge. This paper presents an approach for one-shot rule learning called One-Shot Hypothesis Derivation (OSHD) based on using a logic program declarative bias. We apply this approach to two challenging human-like computer vision tasks: 1) Malayalam character recognition and 2) neurological diagnosis using retinal images. We compare our results with a state-of-the-art Deep Learning approach, called Siamese Network, developed for one-shot learning. The results suggest that our approach can generate human-understandable rules and outperforms the deep learning approach with a significantly higher average predictive accuracy.

1 Introduction

Deep Neural Networks (DNNs) [2,10,19] have demonstrated state-of-the-art results on many pattern recognition tasks, especially in image classification problems [6,12]. However, recent studies [27] revealed major differences between human visual cognition and DNNs. For example, it is easy to produce images that are completely unrecognizable to humans, though DNN visual learning algorithms believe them to be recognizable objects with over 99% confidence [27]. Another major difference is related to the number of required training examples. Humans can typically learn from a single visual example [15], unlike statistical learning which depends on hundreds or thousands of images. Humans achieve

N. Katzouris and A. Artikis (Eds.): ILP 2021, LNAI 13191, pp. 234–250, 2022.
https://doi.org/10.1007/978-3-030-97454-1_17

this ability using background knowledge, which plays a critical role. By contrast, statistics based computer vision algorithms have no general mechanisms for incorporating background knowledge.

The performance of DNNs in medical imaging analysis and clinical risk prediction has been exceptionally promising. For example, recent evidence suggests that certain neurological pathologies such as Alzheimer's and Parkinson's disease can be associated with retinal abnormalities [5, 21]. Nevertheless, despite the many opportunities DNNs present for healthcare, their clinical use remains limited as they suffer from the black-box situation. This constitutes a significant problem for clinicians: a lack of understanding of the inner workings of such methods renders it problematic to explain the diagnosis and treatment process to their patients. Moreover, DNNs usually require large training data which are not always available, for example in the diagnosis of neurological conditions, which are highly heterogeneous and often involve comorbidities.

In this paper, we present an approach for one-shot rule learning called One-Shot Hypothesis Derivation (OSHD) based on logic program declarative bias which is first introduced in [31]. We apply this approach to two different the challenging tasks; Malayalam character recognition & neurological diagnosis using retinal images. We have created a dataset for Malayalam hand-written characters which includes high level properties of the language based on the 'Omniglot' dataset designed for developing human-level concept learning algorithms [16]. We present character recognition as an extended work of [31]. For neurological diagnosis, we have collected the images from the UK Biobank [28] and extracted retinal vascular features (RVFs). We compare our results with a state-of-the-art Deep Learning approach, called Siamese Network [14], which is popular for one-shot learning.

2   One-Shot Hypothesis Derivation (OSHD)

In this paper we adopt a form of ILP which is suitable for one-shot learning and is based on using a logic program declarative bias, i.e. using a logic program to represent the declarative bias over the hypothesis space. Using a logic program, declarative bias has several advantages. Firstly, a declarative bias logic program allows us to easily port bias from one problem to another similar problem (e.g. for transfer learning). Secondly, it is possible to reason about the bias at the meta-level. Declarative bias will also help to reduce the size of the search space for the target concept or hypothesis derivation [1, 26]. We refer to this approach as One-Shot Hypothesis Derivation (OSHD) which is a special case of Top-Directed Hypothesis Derivation (TDHD) as described in [23].

Definition 1 (One-Shot Hypothesis Derivation). *The input to an OSHD system is the vector $S_{TDHD} = \langle NT, \top, B, E, e \rangle$ where NT is a set of "non-terminal" predicate symbols, $\top$ is a logic program representing the declarative bias over the hypothesis space, B is a logic program representing the background knowledge and E is a set of examples and e is a positive example in E. The following three conditions hold for clauses in $\top$: (a) each clause in $\top$ must contain* at least one occurrence of an element of NT while clauses in B and E must not contain any occurrences of elements of NT, (b) any predicate appearing in the head of some clause in ⊤ must not occur in the body of any clause in B and (c) the head of the first clause in ⊤ is the target predicate and the head predicates for other clauses in ⊤ must be in NT. The aim of an OSHD learning system is to find a set of consistent hypothesised clauses H, containing no occurrence of NT, such that for each clause $h \in H$ the following two conditions hold:

$$\top \models h \tag{1}$$
$$B, h \models e \tag{2}$$

The following theorem is a special case of Theorem 1 in [23].

Theorem 1. *Given $S_{OSHD} = \langle NT, \top, B, E, e \rangle$ assumptions (1) and (2) hold only if there exists an SLD refutation R of ¬e from ⊤, B, such that R can be re-ordered to give $R' = D_h R_e$ where D_h is an SLD derivation of a hypothesis h for which (1) and (2) hold.*

According to Theorem 1, implicit hypotheses can be extracted from the refutations of e. Let us now consider a simple example on learning a rule describing the properties of a concept (alphabet).

Example 1. Let $S_{OSHD} = \langle NT, \top, B, E, e \rangle$ where NT, B, e and ⊤ are as follows:

$$NT = \{\$body\}$$
$$B = b_1 = \text{property1(a)} \leftarrow \qquad \top = \begin{cases} \top_1 : \text{alphabet}(X) \leftarrow \$body(X) \\ \top_2 : \$body(X) \leftarrow \text{property1}(X) \\ \top_3 : \$body(X) \leftarrow \text{property2}(X) \end{cases}$$
$$e = \text{alphabet(a)} \leftarrow$$

Given the linear refutation, $R = \langle \neg e, \top_1, \top_2, b_1 \rangle$, we now construct the re-ordered refutation $R' = D_h R_e$ where $D_h = \langle \top_1, \top_2 \rangle$ derives the clause $h = \text{alphabet}(X) \leftarrow \text{property1}(X)$ for which (1) and (2) hold.

The user of OSHD can specify a declarative bias ⊤ in the form of a logic program. A general ⊤ theory can be also generated from user specified mode declarations. Figure 1 represents a simplified example of user specified mode declarations and the automatically constructed ⊤ theory.

The OSHD Learning algorithm can be described in 3 main steps:

1. Generate all hypotheses, H_e that are generalizations of e
2. Compute the coverage of each hypothesis in H_e
3. Build final theory, T, by choosing a subset of hypotheses in H_e that maximises a given score function (e.g. compression).

In step 1, H_e is generated using the OSHD hypothesis derivation described earlier in this section.

The second step of the algorithm, computing the coverage of each hypothesis, is not needed if the user program is a pure logic program (i.e. all relationships in the background knowledge are self contained and do not rely on Prolog built-in predicates). This is because, by construction, the OSHD hypothesis derivation modeh(alphabet(+image)).

modeb(has_prop1(+image)).

modeb(has_prop2(+image)).

$$T = \begin{cases} \mathsf{T}_1 : \text{alphabet}(X) \leftarrow \$body(X). \\ \mathsf{T}_2 : \$body(X) \leftarrow \\ \mathsf{T}_3 : \$body(X) \leftarrow \text{has\_prop1}(X), \$body(X). \\ \mathsf{T}_4 : \$body(X) \leftarrow \text{has\_prop2}(X), \$body(X). \end{cases}$$

Fig. 1. Mode declarations and a T theory automatically constructed from it

generates all hypotheses that entail a given example with respect to the user supplied mode declarations. This implies that the coverage of a hypothesis is exactly the set of examples that have it as their generalization. However, this coverage computation step is needed for the negative examples, as they were not used to build the hypothesis set.

For step 3, the compression-based evaluation function used for the experiments in this paper is:

$$\sum Covered\_Examples\_Weight - Total\_Literals \qquad (3)$$

The weight associated to an example may be defined by the user but by default, positive examples have weight 1 and negative examples weight -1. In general, negative examples are defined with a weight smaller than 0 and positive examples with a weight greater than 0.

3 Siamese Neural Networks

In this paper, we use a state-of-the-art Deep Learning approach, called Siamese Network [14], which has been developed for one-shot learning. The original Siamese Networks were first introduced in the early 1990s by Bromley and LeCun to solve signature verification as an image matching problem [4]. A Siamese network is a Deep Learning architecture with two parallel neural networks with the same properties in terms of weight, layers etc. Each network takes a different input, and their outputs are combined using an energy function at the top to provide some prediction. The energy function computes a metric between the highest level feature representation on each side (Fig. 2). Weight tying guarantees that two extremely similar images could not possibly be mapped by their respective networks to very different locations in feature space because each network computes the same function. Also, the network is symmetric, so that whenever we present two distinct images to the twin networks, the top conjoining layer will compute the same metric as if we were to present the same two images but to the opposite twin.

A Siamese network model is defined using a convolutional neural network (CNN), mainly developed to work with image data. CNNs can be considered as regularized versions of multilayer perceptrons. Multilayer perceptrons usually mean fully connected networks; each neuron in one layer is connected to all neurons in the next layer. We stack three layers: the convolutional Layer, pooling Layer, and fully connected layer to form CNN.

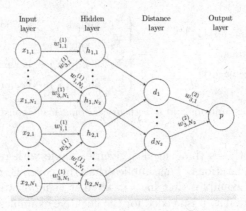

Fig. 2. A simple 2 hidden layer Siamese Neural Network [14]

- **Convolutional layers** apply a convolution operation to the input, passing the result to the next layer. A convolution converts all the pixels in its receptive field into a single value. For example, if one apply a convolution to an image, the image size is decreased as well as information in individual fields are brought together into a single pixel. The final output of the convolutional layer is a vector.
- **Pooling layers** reduce the dimensions of data by combining the outputs of neuron clusters at one layer into a single neuron in the next layer. Local pooling combines small clusters. There are two common types of pooling in popular use: max and average. Max pooling uses the maximum value of each local cluster of neurons in the feature map, while average pooling takes the average value.
- **Fully connected layers** connect every neuron in one layer to every neuron in another layer. It is the same as a traditional multi-layer perceptron neural network (MLP). The flattened matrix goes through a fully connected layer to classify the images.

Koch et al. [14] use a convolutional neural siamese architecture to classify pairs of omniglot images. In the experiments of this paper, we have adopted the same model as defined in [14]. Our standard model is a Siamese neural network with L fully-connected layers each with N_l units, where $h_{1,l}$ represents the hidden vector in layer l for the first twin, and $h_{2,l}$ denotes the same for the second twin. We use exclusively rectified linear (ReLU) units in the first $L-1$ layers. After the $(L-1)^{th}$ feed-forward layer, we compare the features computed by each twin via a fixed distance function.

4 One-Shot Learning for Malayalam Character Recognition

We apply OSHD as well as Deep Learning (i.e. Siamese Network) to the challenging task of one-shot Malayalam character recognition. This is a challenging task due to spherical and complex structure of Malayalam hand-written language.

4.1 Character Recognition and Human-Like Background Knowledge

Malayalam is one of the four major languages of the Dravidian language family and originated from the ancient Brahmi script. Malayalam is the official language of Kerala, a state of India with roughly forty-five million people. Unlike for other languages, there is currently no efficient algorithm for Malayalam handwritten recognition. The handwriting recognition for Malayalam script is a major challenge compared to the recognition of other scripts because of the following reasons: presence of large number of alphabets, different writing styles, spherical features of alphabets, and similarity in character shapes. We selected the handwritten characters from the 'Omniglot' dataset [16]. Sample Malayalam alphabets from our dataset are shown in Fig. 3 (characters 'Aha' and 'Tha'). Feature extraction is conducted utilizing a set of advanced geometrical features [30] and directional features.

Geometrical Features. Every character may be identified by its geometric designations such as loops, junctions, arcs, and terminals. Geometrically, a loop means a closed path. Malayalam characters contain more intricate loops which may contain some up and downs within the loops itself. So we follow a concept as shown in Fig. 3(b). If the figure has a continuous closed curve then we will identify it as a loop. Junctions may be defined as a meeting point of two or more curves or line. It is easy for human to identify the junction from an image as shown in Fig. 3(c). As per dictionary definitions, an arc is a component of a curve. So in our case, a path with semi opening will be considered as an arc. Please refer to Fig. 3(d) for more details. Terminals may be classified as points where the character stroke ends, i.e. no more connection beyond that point. Figure 3(e) is a self-explanatory example for the definition.

We have included the visual explanation for the geometrical feature extraction in Fig. 3. We have selected two characters to explicate the features as shown in Fig. 3 and marked each geometrical features as we discussed. Table 1 will give an abstract conception about the dataset we have developed for the experiments from the 'Omniglot' dataset.

Directional Features. Every character may be identified by its directional specifications such as starting and ending points of the stroke. There are certain unwritten rules for Malayalam characters, e.g. the writing always commences from left and moves towards the right direction. Native Malayalam users can

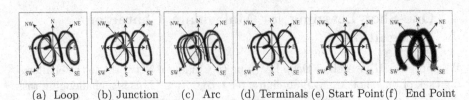

(a) Loop   (b) Junction   (c) Arc   (d) Terminals (e) Start Point (f) End Point

Fig. 3. Human-like feature extraction criteria

easily identify the starting and ending point. However, we will need to consider the starting and ending point as features so that these can be easily identified without semantic knowledge of a character. The starting and ending points are determined by standard direction properties. Figure 3(f) will give you an idea about developing the directional features from an alphabet. As we discussed, a user can identify both starting and ending point of the character displayed in Fig. 3(f) easily whereas the terminus point of Fig. 3(e) is arduous to determine.

4.2   Mode Declarations

In this section, we define the OSHD specific details of the declarative bias, defined by mode declaration and background knowledge representation used in our experiments. The first step was to develop and represent the background knowledge based on the concepts described in Sect. 4.1. Table 1 shows the geometrical and directional features of 5 different alphabets. Here, we use the same notations used in Progol [22] and Toplog [23].

For example, in our first experiment, *alphabet(+character)* is the head of the hypothesis, where *+character* defines the character identifier *character* as an input argument. We are using four predicates in the body part of the hypothesis as shown in the Listing 1.1. Note that $+$, $-$, $\#$ indicate input, output or a constant value arguments.

Listing 1.1. Mode declarations

```
:- modeh(1,alphabet(+character)).
:- modeb(*,has_gemproperties(+character,-properties)).
:- modeb(*,has_gemproperties_count(+properties,
                        #geo_feature_name,#int)).
:- modeb(*,has_dirproperties(+character,-properties)).
:- modeb(*,has_dirproperties_feature(+properties,
                    #dir_feature_name,#featurevalue)).
```

The meaning of each *modeb* condition is defined as follows:

has_gemproperties/2 predicate was used to represent the geometrical features as defined in Table 1. The input argument *character* is the unique identifier for an alphabet, *properties* refers to the property names.

has_gemproperties_count/3 predicate outlines the count of the particular feature associated with the alphabet. The *properties* indicate unique identifiers for a

Table 1. Geometrical and directional properties

Character ID	Geometrical properties				Directional properties	
	No. loops	No. junctions	No. arcs	No. terminals	Starting point	Ending point
1	2	4	3	2	sw	null
2	3	4	3	2	sw	null
3	3	4	3	2	sw	null
4	1	2	3	2	null	se
5	1	3	3	2	nw	se

particular geometrical property of a particular alphabet, *geo_feature_name* refers to the property name and *int* stands for the feature count.

has_dirproperties/2 predicate used to represent the directional features mentioned in Table 1. The *character* is the unique identifier for the alphabet, *properties* refers to the property names.

has_dirproperties_count/3 predicate outlines the count of a particular directional feature associated with the alphabet. The *properties* is a unique identifier for a particular property of a particular alphabet, *dir_feature_name* refers to the property name and *featurevalue* stands for the feature vale.

5   One-Shot Learning for Neurological Diagnosis Using Retinal Images

Recent evidence suggests that certain neurological pathologies such as Alzheimer's and Parkinson's disease can be associated with retinal abnormalities [5, 21]. Retinal fundus imaging and optical coherence tomography (OCT), powerful techniques for imaging the retina and highly informative from a clinical perspective [32], could therefore potentially be used for the early detection and diagnosis of these diseases. This is interesting also from a practical perspective, because retinal fundus photography and OCT are non-invasive, cheap, quick to perform, highly sensitive and specific. Moreover, these methods provide digital outputs that can be easily stored and analysed with modern AI tools. Indeed, a recent study shows relatively high accuracy in the usage of AI for the diagnosis of Alzheimer's disease from retinal fundus images [29]. However, numerous challenges remain to be addressed, such as regarding the capability for humans to understand the model, as well as the significant requirements for large amounts of data.

Here, we use our proposed OSHD approach for model construction and revision in retinal fundus image analysis. This approach has several benefits: it provides human-understandable reasoning that enable the medical practitioner to explain to the patient the computational diagnosis. Moreover, the OSHD approach allows for the incorporation of patient-specific information (e.g. age, weight, lifestyle, etc.) and so supports personalised treatments. Furthermore, the OSHD approach requires much fewer samples for training than state-of-the-art

DNN techniques. This is a highly valuable feature particularly for the diagnosis of neurological conditions, which are highly heterogeneous and often involve comorbidities. Hence, the most relevant and well-suited datasets are usually of limited size. The capability to make efficient use of limited datasets is therefore paramount for such computational methods. We here present a preliminary demonstration for this proposed approach.

5.1   Retinal Vasculature Features

Table 2. Retinal Vascular Features (RVFs) with the retinal zone of interest

Parameter	Description	Retinal zone
CRAE	Central Retinal Arteriolar Equivalent	B
CRVE	Central Retinal Venular Equivalent	B
AVR	Arteriole-Venular ratio	B
FDa	Fractal Dimension arteriole	C
FDv	Fractal Dimension venular	C
BSTDa	Zone B Standard Deviation arteriole	B
BSTDv	Zone B Standard Deviation venular	B
TORTa	Tortuosity arteriole	C
TORTv	Tortuosity venular	C

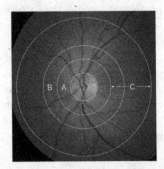

Fig. 4. Retinal zones considered in this study. Three concentric zones were introduced for the computation of retinal fundus image features, i.e. zones A, B and C [7].

Our selection of retinal vascular features (RVFs) for the analysis of the retinal images is based on the study by Frost et al. [7] where significant differences were found in specific RVFs between healthy controls and subjects with Alzheimer's disease. To simplify the derivation of a diagnostic algorithm, we decided to use only a subset of these features in our experiments. In particular, Frost et al. mentioned 13 RVF's in their experiment, while we selected 9 relevant and well-established features for our experiments. These selected RVFs are listed in Table 2. Briefly, the RVFs were measured based on the width and branching geometry of retinal vessels. In accordance with [7], we introduced concentric zones of interest A, B and C to compute the RVFs. Notably, the feature analysis did not incorporate information from zone A (region from 0 to 0.5 disc diameters away from the disc margin). The analysed two zones were 0.5-1.0 disc diameters away from the disc margin (zone B, Fig. 4) and 0.5-2.0 disc diameters away from the disc margin (zone C, Fig. 4). Restricting the measurements to these two zones ensured that the vessels had attained arteriolar status. The measured zone for each feature is listed in Table 2.

5.2   Retinal Fundus Image Dataset

The participants for this study were selected from the UK Biobank resource [28]. The UK Biobank recruited 500,000 people of ages between 40 and 69 to undergo a variety of tests and have their health followed throughout their lives. Notably, only a subset of these participants had their retinas imaged (in total 84,767). Retinal imaging was conducted using the TOPCON 3D OCT 1000 Mk2 which simultaneously performs OCT and takes a fundus photograph. The images produced are centred on the macula, have a 45° field of view and have the dimensions 2,048 by 1,536.

5.3   Extraction of Subject Data and Background Knowledge (BK) Preparation

Fig. 5. Demonstration of processing steps for vessel segmentation and artery *vs.* vein classification (Color figure online)

Extraction of Subject-Specific Clinical Information. The vast majority of the information about the participants was collated in the form of a large CSV (Comma Separated Values) file, where each row represents a participant and each column represents a data point. The UK Biobank online system provides explanations for the codes used for the column names and the associated data. Diagnoses in the dataset were encoded according to the International Classification of Diseases, Tenth Revision (ICD-10). A detailed analysis of the participant data file yielded 18 Alzheimer's, 133 Parkinson's and 54 vascular dementia sufferers who satisfied these two conditions: they had (1) fundus images taken, and (2) were diagnosed with exactly one of these three conditions. In addition to images from these diseased subjects, we used images of 528 subjects that were healthy with respect to these three conditions. Notably, we used only fundus images of the left eye.

Optic Disc Localisation. We followed an approach that uses pyramidal decomposition based on the Haar-discrete wavelet transform in order to localize the optic disc to certain regions. Template matching is then employed to further localize the optic disc. This particular approach is detailed by Lalonde et al. [17].

Artery/Vein Classification. The method we have used for artery/vein classification was developed by Galdran et al. [8]. In particular, we use a fully CNN to classify pixels into four separate categories: background, vein, artery or uncertain. Figure 5 shows the segmentation and artery/vein classification steps applied to a sample image. In the image, arteries are shown in red, veins in blue, and areas of uncertainty are coloured in green.

Vascular Feature Extraction. Retinal vascular features mentioned in Table 2 were extracted. To this end, vascular calibres were calculated for the six most extensive arterioles and six largest venules. The standard deviation of the width in zone B (BSTD) was calculated for the arteriolar and venular networks. Summary measures of vascular equivalent calibre were also calculated (central retinal arterial (CRAE) and venular (CRVE) equivalent calibre), based on the improved Knudston-Parr-Hubbard formula [11,13]. CRAE and CRVE represent the equivalent single-vessel parent calibre (width) for the six arterioles and venules, respectively. From these indices, the arteriole-to-venule ratio (AVR) was calculated (AVR = CRAE/CRVE). Natural patterns such as vessel networks often exhibit fractal properties, whereby they appear the same when viewed over a range of magnifications. The fractal dimension (FD) describes the range of scales over which this self-similarity is observed. In this study, the fractal dimension of the retinal vascular network was calculated using the box-counting method [20]. Larger values reflect a more complex branching pattern. Retinal vascular tortuosity is defined as the integral of the curvature squared along the path of the vessel, normalized by the total path length [9]. All vessels in the zone of interest with a width > 40 µm were measured. The estimates were summarized as the average tortuosity of the measured vessels. A smaller tortuosity value indicates straighter vessels.

Data Encoding and Background Knowledge Preparation. The RVF's from the measurement extraction step will be stored. During the data labelling step, the distribution of each RVF is analysed and classified into three categories: low, medium, and high. The next step is to prepare background knowledge from these labelled data and will be done according to the *mode* definitions. Sample background knowledge for a patient is displayed in Listing 1.2.

Listing 1.2. Sample BK for a retinal image using labelled RVF's

```
cr_arteriolar_equivalent(patientid_0,high).
cr_venular_equivalent(patientid_0,low).
av_ratio(patientid_0,high).
sd_arteriole(patientid_0,medium).
sd_venular(patientid_0,low).
fd_arteriole(patientid_0,low).
fd_venular(patientid_0,medium).
tortuosity_arteriole(patientid_0,low).
tortuosity_venular(patientid_0,low).
```

6 Experiments

In this section we evaluate the OSHD approach on two different applications. The first application is complex character recognition, which is the extension of an initial study presented in [31]. We have used 46 alphabets (46 classes) from the Malayalam language, and for each alphabet, 20 different handwritten images are selected and divided equally into training and test sets.

The second application is a novel diagnosis approach for three neurodegenerative diseases, namely vascular dementia, Parkinson's disease and Alzheimer's disease. We have used four different classes, as mentioned in Sect. 5.3, and each class contains 18 images, divided equally as training and test sets. Notably, this study is highly innovative as it investigates the usage of modern machine learning based analysis of retinal images for the classification of neurodegenerative diseases. In this section we test the following null hypotheses:

Null Hypothesis 1 OSHD cannot outperform Siamese Networks in one-shot learning for complex character recognition.

Null Hypothesis 2 OSHD cannot outperform Siamese Networks in one-shot learning for neurodegenerative disease identification.

Null Hypothesis 3 OSHD cannot learn human comprehensible rules for either of applications in Null Hypotheses 1 and 2.

6.1 Materials and Methods

The OSHD algorithm in this experiment is based on Top-Directed Hypothesis Derivation implemented in Toplog [23], and uses mode declarations and background knowledge which defined earlier in this paper. The Siamese Network used in the experiment is based on the implementation described in [14].

The data, codes and configuration input files used in the experiments in this section are available from: https://github.com/danyvarghese/One-Shot-ILP.

We endeavoured to reiterate the same concept of working with both architectures and repeated the experiments for different numbers of folds. Each fold consists of a single positive example and n negative examples. In our experiments, we use the term 'number of classes' to indicate the total number of negative examples (in addition to the one positive example) used for the cross-validation.

In order to reject the Null Hypotheses 1 and 2, we adapted an experimental setting used for one-shot learning by Siamese Networks as in [14]. We follow a '20-way N-class' experimental setting for each dataset. In this setting, 20 is the number of runs and N is the number of classes (N varies from 2 to 7 for character recognition and 2 to 4 for neurodegenerative diseases). As we are doing one-shot learning, we use one positive example at each run with negative examples which are from the other classes (the X axis in the learning curves of Fig. 6). In the following, we define specific parameter settings for each algorithm.

OSHD Parameter Settings. The following Toplog parameter settings were used in this experiment: *clause_length* (value = 15) defines the maximum number of literals (including the head) of a hypothesis, *evalfn* (Value = compression) defines which function to use when scoring a clause. The default scoring function is compression. *positive_example_inflation* multiplies the weights of all positive examples by this factor. This parameter is set to 10 and 5 for character recognition and the neurodegenerative dataset, respectively, and negative example inflation multiplies the weights of all negative examples by this factor. This parameter is set to 5 for both datasets.

Siamese Networks Parameter Settings. For the implementation of the Siamese Network, we followed the same setups used by Koch et al. [14]. Koch et al. use a convolutional Siamese network to classify pairs of 'Omniglot' images, so the twin networks are both CNNs. The twins each have the following architecture: convolution with 64 (10×10) filters, 'max_pooling' convolution 128 (7×7), 'max_pooling' convolution 128 (4×4) filters and 'max_pooling' convolution 256 (4×4) filters, all with 'relu' activation functions. The twin networks reduce their inputs down to smaller and smaller 3D tensors. Finally, there is a fully connected layer with 4096 units.

In most implementations of Siamese Networks, the training model is developed using a large amount of data. Also, particularly in the case of character recognition, characters from one language are usually compared against the characters from other languages [3,18]. In contrast, in our experiments we only consider alphabets from a single language. This is advantageous because it renders the training process less data-demanding, as well as requires less expertise in choosing suitable comparison languages.

6.2   Results and Discussions

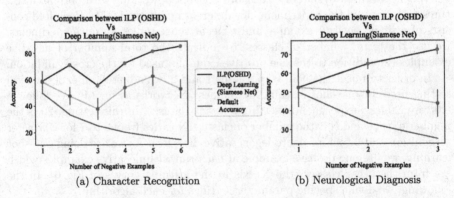

(a) Character Recognition   (b) Neurological Diagnosis

Fig. 6. Average Predictive accuracy of ILP (OSHD) vs Deep Learning (Siamese Net)

Figure 6(a) shows the average predictive accuracy of ILP (OSHD) vs Deep Learning (Siamese Net) in One-shot character recognition with increasing number of negative examples (number of different classes). As shown in this figure, Siamese Net and OSHD have almost same accuracy for class 2. In all other cases, OSHD outperforms Siamese Net with significant difference. Figure 6(b) shows the average predictive accuracy of ILP (OSHD) vs Deep Learning (Siamese Net) in the neurodegenerative diseases with increasing numbers of negative examples. As in the character recognition dataset, Siamese net and OSHD have a similar accuracy for class 2. In all other cases, OSHD outperforms Siamese net with a significant difference. We have also used a T-test to check the validity of the null hypothesis. For the CR experiment, we obtained 2.813 as the t-value and 0.008 as the p-value, whereas we obtained 3.658 and 0.001 for the neurodegenerative dataset experiment, respectively. The T-test as well as the predictive accuracy reject the null hypotheses 1 and 2.

Due to the involved quantities and complexities, recording and displaying all the learned rules is beyond the scope of this work. However, we have shown some random learned rules generated during the experiments in Table 3, which allows to assess hypothesis 3. The rules from Table 3 suggest that OSHD can lean rules which are human comprehensible and can be easily communicated with domain experts, so null hypothesis 3 is also rejected.

Table 3. Example of learned rules

Character recognition	Neurological diagnosis
alphabet(A) :-	
has_gemproperties(A, B),	diagnosis(A,parkinson) :-
has_gemproperties(A, C),	fd_venular(A,medium),
has_gemproperties_count(B, junctions, 4),	cr_arteriolar_equivalent(A,medium),
has_gemproperties(A, D)	tortuosity_arteriole(A,low)

7   Conclusion

In this paper, we presented a novel approach for one-shot rule learning called One-Shot Hypothesis Derivation (OSHD) [31] that is based on using a logic program declarative bias. We applied this approach to two challenging computer vision tasks: 1) Malayalam character recognition and 2) neurological diagnosis from retinal images. The features used to express the background knowledge for character recognition were developed in such a way that it is well-suited for human visual cognition also. We demonstrated the learning of rules for each character which is more natural and in accordance with human visual understanding. For neurological diagnosis, we collected and quantified several retinal vascular features. We compared our results with a state-of-the-art Deep Learning approach, called Siamese Network, which has been developed for one-shot learning.

The results suggest that our approach can generate human-understandable rules and also outperforms the deep learning approach with a significantly higher average predictive accuracy. Its was clear from the results that deep learning paradigm needs more data and its efficiency is decreased when dealing with a small amount of data. As future work we would like to further extend the background knowledge for the nueurological diagnosis problem to include more semantic information and also explore the framework of Meta-Interpretive Learning (MIL) [24] for the purpose of one-shot learning from images [25].

Acknowledgements. Dany Varghese was supported by Vice Chancellor's PhD Scholarship Award at the University of Surrey. Roman Bauer was supported by the Engineering and Physical Sciences Research Council of the United Kingdom (EP/S001433/1). The authors also thankfully acknowledge that the retinal images were obtained using UK Biobank application number 1969. Alireza Tamaddoni-Nezhad and Stephen Muggleton were supported by the EPSRC Network Plus grant on Human-Like Computing (HLC).

References

1. Adé, H., Raedt, L.D., Bruynooghe, M.: Declarative bias for specific-to-general ILP systems. Mach. Learn. **20**, 119–154 (1995)
2. Bennett, C.H., et al.: Contrasting advantages of learning with random weights and backpropagation in non-volatile memory neural networks. IEEE Access **7**, 73938–73953 (2019)
3. Bouma, S.: One shot learning and Siamese networks in Keras (2017). https://sorenbouma.github.io/blog/oneshot/
4. Bromley, J., Guyon, I., LeCun, Y., Säckinger, E., Shah, R.: Signature verification using a "Siamese" time delay neural network. In: Proceedings of the 6th International Conference on Neural Information Processing Systems, pp. 737–744 (1993)
5. Cheung, C.Y.l., Ikram, M.K., Chen, C., Wong, T.Y.: Imaging retina to study dementia and stroke. Progr. Retinal Eye Res. **57**, 89–107 (2017)
6. Varghese, D., Shankar, V.: A novel approach for single image super resolution using statistical mathematical model. IJAER **10**(44) (2015)
7. Frost, S., Kanagasingam, Y., Sohrabi, H., Vignarajan, J., Bourgeat, P., et al.: Retinal vascular biomarkers for early detection and monitoring of Alzheimer's disease. Transl. Psychiatry **3**, e233 (2013)
8. Galdran, A., Meyer, M., Costa, P., MendonÇa, Campilho, A.: Uncertainty-aware artery/vein classification on retinal images. In: 2019 IEEE 16th International Symposium on Biomedical Imaging (ISBI 2019), pp. 556–560 (2019)
9. Hart, W.E., Goldbaum, M., Côté, B., Kube, P., Nelson, M.R.: Measurement and classification of retinal vascular tortuosity. Int. J. Med. Inform. **53**(2), 239–252 (1999)
10. Hinton, G.: Learning multiple layers of representation. Trends Cogn. Sci. **11**, 428–434 (2007)
11. Hubbard, L.D., Brothers, R.J., King, W.N., et al.: Methods for evaluation of retinal microvascular abnormalities associated with hypertension/sclerosis in the atherosclerosis risk in communities study. Ophthalmology **106**(12), 2269–2280 (1999)

12. Neethu, K.S., Varghese, D.: An incremental semi-supervised approach for visual domain adaptation. In: 2017 International Conference on Communication and Signal Processing (ICCSP), pp. 1343–1346 (2017)
13. Knudtson, M., Lee, K.E., Hubbard, L., Wong, T., et al.: Revised formulas for summarizing retinal vessel diameters. Curr. Eye Res. **27**, 143–149 (2003)
14. Koch, G., Zemel, R., Salakhutdinov, R.: Siamese neural networks for one-shot image recognition. In: Proeedings of International Conference on Machine Learning, vol. 37 (2015)
15. Lake, B., Salakhutdinov, R., Gross, J., Tenenbaum, J.: One shot learning of simple visual concepts. In: Proceedings of the 33rd Annual Conference of the Cognitive Science Society, pp. 2568–2573 (2011)
16. Lake, B.M., Salakhutdinov, R., Tenenbaum, J.B.: Human-level concept learning through probabilistic program induction. Science **350**(6266), 1332–1338 (2015)
17. Lalonde, M., Beaulieu, M., Gagnon, L.: Fast and robust optic disc detection using pyramidal decomposition and Hausdorff-based template matching. IEEE Trans. Med. Imaging **20**, 1193–200 (2001)
18. Lamba, H.: One shot learning with Siamese networks using Keras (2019). https://towardsdatascience.com/one-shot-learning-with-siamese-networks-using-keras-17f34e75bb3d
19. Liu, X., He, P., Chen, W., Gao, J.: Multi-task deep neural networks for natural language understanding. CoRR 1901.11504 (2019)
20. Mainster, M.: The fractal properties of retinal vessels: embryological and clinical implications. Eye **4**, 235–241 (1990)
21. McGrory, S., Taylor, A.M., Kirin, M., et al.: Retinal microvascular network geometry and cognitive abilities in community-dwelling older people: the Lothian birth cohort 1936 study. Ophthalmology **101**(7), 993–998 (2017)
22. Muggleton, S.: Inverse entailment and Progol. N. Gener. Comput. **13**, 245–286 (1995)
23. Muggleton, S.H., Santos, J.C.A., Tamaddoni-Nezhad, A.: TopLog: ILP using a logic program declarative bias. In: Garcia de la Banda, M., Pontelli, E. (eds.) ICLP 2008. LNCS, vol. 5366, pp. 687–692. Springer, Heidelberg (2008). https://doi.org/10.1007/978-3-540-89982-2_58
24. Muggleton, S., Lin, D., Tamaddoni-Nezhad, A.: Meta-interpretive learning of higher-order dyadic datalog: predicate invention revisited. Mach. Learn. **100**(1), 49–73 (2015)
25. Muggleton, S., Dai, W.Z., Sammut, C., Tamaddoni-Nezhad, A.: Meta-interpretive learning from noisy images. Mach. Learn. **107** (2018)
26. Nedellec, C.: Declarative bias in ILP (1996)
27. Nguyen, A., Yosinski, J., Clune, J.: Deep neural networks are easily fooled: high confidence predictions for unrecognizable images. In: 2015 IEEE Conference on Computer Vision and Pattern Recognition (CVPR), pp. 427–436 (2015)
28. Sudlow, C., et al.: UK biobank: an open access resource for identifying the causes of a wide range of complex diseases of middle and old age. PloS Med. (2015)
29. Tian, J., Smith, G., Guo, H., Liu, B., Pan, Z., et al.: Modular machine learning for Alzheimer's disease classification from retinal vasculature. Sci. Rep. **11**(1), 1–11 (2021)
30. Usman Akram, M., et al.: Geometric feature points based optical character recognition. In: 2013 IEEE Symposium on Industrial Electronics Applications, pp. 86–89 (2013)

31. Varghese, D., Tamaddoni-Nezhad, A.: One-shot rule learning for challenging character recognition. In: Proceedings of the 14th International Rule Challenge, CEUR, 2020, vol. 2644, pp. 10–27 (2020)
32. Zapata, M.A., Royo-Fibla, D., Font, O., Vela, J.I., et al.: Artificial intelligence to identify retinal fundus images, quality validation, laterality evaluation, macular degeneration, and suspected glaucoma. Clin. Ophthalmol. **14**, 419 (2020)

Generative Clausal Networks: Relational Decision Trees as Probabilistic Circuits

Fabrizio Ventola[1(✉)], Devendra Singh Dhami[1], and Kristian Kersting[1,2]

[1] Department of Computer Science, TU Darmstadt, Darmstadt, Germany
{ventola,devendra.dhami,kersting}@cs.tu-darmstadt.de
[2] Hessian Center for AI and Centre for Cognitive Science, Darmstadt, Germany

Abstract. In many real-world applications, the i.i.d. assumption does not hold and thus capturing the interactions between instances is essential for the task at hand. Recently, a clear connection between predictive modelling such as decision trees and probabilistic circuits, a form of deep probabilistic model, has been established although it is limited to propositional data. We introduce the first connection between relational rule models and probabilistic circuits, obtaining tractable inference from discriminative rule models while operating on the relational domain. Specifically, given a relational rule model, we make use of Mixed Sum-Product Networks (MSPNs)—a deep probabilistic architecture for hybrid domains—to equip them with a full joint distribution over the class and how (often) the rules fire. Our empirical evaluation shows that we can answer a wide range of probabilistic queries on relational data while being robust to missing, out-of-domain data and partial counts. We show that our method generalizes to different distributions outperforming strong baselines. Moreover, due to the clear probabilistic semantics of MSPNs we have informative model interpretations.

Keywords: Statistical relational learning · Tractable probabilistic models · Rule learning

1 Introduction

Relational decision trees (RDTs) [3] have been the workhorse in modern inductive logic programming for many years and form the backbone of several relational machine learning models. Recent work on the interpretation of Decision Trees as generative models [9] shed light on the surprising yet intuitive tight connection between robust discriminative models and powerful tractable generative models. This paves the way for the application of several methods and techniques designed for Decision Trees to the world of Probabilistic Circuits and vice-versa. However, in many real-world applications, the i.i.d. assumption does not hold and capturing the interactions between instances is fundamental for an arbitrary task such as classification or generation of new samples. Inspired by this, we aim to revisit RDTs using the techniques of principled propositionalization and a probabilistic interpretation.

F. Ventola and D. S. Dhami—Equal contribution.

N. Katzouris and A. Artikis (Eds.): ILP 2021, LNAI 13191, pp. 251–265, 2022.
https://doi.org/10.1007/978-3-030-97454-1_18

Statistical Relational Learning [11,17] models have been proposed to overcome the rigidity of well-known first-order rule learners such as TILDE [3] since they cannot naturally deal with uncertainty. However, most of these models such as Markov Logic Networks [34] and Relational Dependency Networks [29] are difficult to scale and their inference process is generally intractable. Recent approaches have tried to tackle intractability by taking advantage of Arithmetic Circuits [10] representations that, under certain conditions, especially by imposing particular constraints on their structure, can guarantee to provide tractable inference for a set of probabilistic queries. Nevertheless, these models have been mostly designed for propositional data and contributions for relational domain [14,21,28] are rather limited since they need specific input representation and make strong assumptions on the type of data distributions.

Specifically, inspired by [9] and considering the aforementioned limitations of SRL models, we introduce the first connection from relational rule models, specifically relational decision trees, to probabilistic circuits, precisely Sum-Product Networks (SPNs). With this aim, we present *Generative Clausal Networks (GCLNs)* as tractable generative models that can model the joint distribution of counts of the firing of rules (clauses) and can be powerful discriminators at the same time. As a discriminator, GCLNs are both accurate and robust to missing data. As probabilistic generators, they can be used for accurate data imputation, out-of-domain (OOD) detection, sample new data and predicate invention. Moreover, thanks to the probabilistic semantics, GCLNs are easy to interpret. GCLNs can also be seen as alternatives to relational Naive Bayes [14,22] since instead of learning a naive Bayes over clauses as features, we first learn all rules using an RDT and then turn it into joint distribution.

We make the following contributions: 1. We propose the first set of models that take advantage of RDT structure to learn powerful probabilistic circuits. 2. We take advantage of SPNs to learn both conditionals (discriminative) and joint (generative) models. 3. We show that our model is robust to noise, OOD data and missing values and takes advantage of both worlds of relational models and probabilistic circuits. 4. We show that our model is interpretable due to the use of first-order logic and SPNs.

2   Background and Related Work

Probabilistic Circuits: Sum-Product Networks (SPNs) are tractable deep density estimators [33] and they are part of the family of Probabilistic Circuits. SPNs can be seen as a deep extension of a particular class of Arithmetic Circuits [10] that encode probability distributions. They have been successfully applied on domains such as computer vision [41], natural language processing [7] and speech recognition [31].

Definition of SPNs. An SPN S, see Fig. 1, is a computational graph defined by a rooted DAG, encoding a probability distribution[1] P_X over a set of RVs $X = \{X_1, \ldots, X_n\}$, where inner nodes can be either weighted sum or product nodes over their children (graphically denoted respectively as $\oplus$ and $\otimes$), and leaves are valid distributions defined on a subset of the RVs $Z \subseteq X$. Each node $n \in S$ has a *scope* $\mathsf{scope}(n) \subseteq X$, defined as the set of RVs appearing in its descendant leaves. The subnetwork S_i, rooted

---

[1] We are not strict on "density" vs. "distribution".

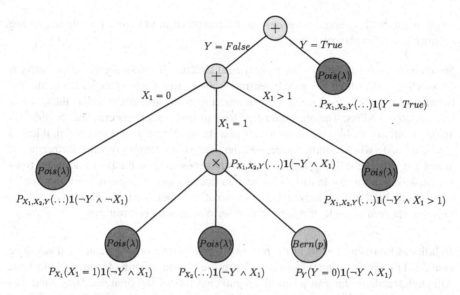

Fig. 1. A graphical interpretation of Generative Clausal Networks (GCLN). They are Sum-Product Networks (SPNs), where sum nodes (in yellow, weights are omitted here for simplicity) act on the number of true ground instances of clauses, while product nodes (in blue) can be view as realizing predicate conjunctions. Leaves consist of two types. Poisson distributions (in pink) encode exchangeable distribution templates and Bernoulli (in green) models the target class (some are omitted for simplicity). The symbol $\mathbf{1}()$ represents an indicator function. The root node and its children model the joint distribution $P(\boldsymbol{X}, Y)$ where $\boldsymbol{X}$ is the set of features and Y is the target variable. In this example, the root node introduces a latent variable that can be interpreted as a binary literal (best viewed in color). (Color figure online)

at node i, encodes a distribution over its scope i.e. $S_i(\boldsymbol{x}) = P_{\boldsymbol{X}_{|scope(i)}}(\boldsymbol{x})$ for each $\boldsymbol{x} \sim \boldsymbol{X}_{|scope(i)}$. Each edge (i, j) emanating from a sum node i to one of its children j has a non-negative weight w_{ij}, with $\sum_j w_{ij} = 1$. Weighted sum nodes represent a mixture over the probability distributions encoded by their children, while product nodes represent factorizations over contextually independent distributions. Thus, an SPN can be viewed as a deep hierarchical mixture model, where the hierarchy is based on the scope of the nodes w.r.t. the whole set of RVs $\boldsymbol{X}$. In a valid SPN, the probability assigned to a given state $\boldsymbol{x}$ of the RVs $\boldsymbol{X}$ can be read out at the root node, and will be denoted $S(\boldsymbol{x}) = P_{\boldsymbol{X}}(\boldsymbol{X} = \boldsymbol{x})$.

Inference Using SPNs. Given an SPN S, $S(\boldsymbol{x})$ can be computed by evaluating the network bottom-up. When evaluating a leaf node i concerning variable X_j, $S_i(x_j)$ corresponds to the probability of that state $P_i(X_j = x_j)$. The value of a product node corresponds to the product of its children's values: $S_i(\boldsymbol{x}_{|scope(i)}) = \prod_{i \rightarrow j \in S} S_j(\boldsymbol{x}_{|scope(j)})$; while, for a sum node, its value corresponds to the weighted sum of its children's values: $S_i(\boldsymbol{x}_{|scope(i)}) = \sum_{i \rightarrow j \in S} w_{ij} S_j(\boldsymbol{x}_{|scope(j)})$. All the exact marginal and conditional probabilities (with different amount of evidence), the exact partition function, and even approximate MPE queries and states can be computed in time linear in the *size* of the network i.e. its number of edges [30].

Structure Learning of SPNs. The prototypical structure learning algorithm for SPNs is LEARNSPN [16] which is a greedy learning schema to infer both the structure and the parameters of an SPN from data by executing a top-down structure search in the space of *tree-structured* SPNs. The algorithm first tries to find context-specific independencies among random variables (RVs) by means of a statistical test. When successful, it learns a product node where children represent the discovered context-specific factorization. When the variable splitting fails, the algorithm tries to slice the data matrix by rows i.e. clustering instances. In this case, the sum node weights represent the proportion of instances that fall in the relative cluster. Termination happens when a data slice contains only one random variable or when the number of instances is lower than a threshold μ.

Relational Learning: Most of the real-world data is relational in nature and has to be converted to a propositional form in order to use classic machine learning algorithms. Although standard, this can result in a significant loss of information. Thus, there has been a lot of research in developing methods that can handle relational data. TILDE [3] are logical decision trees based on the divide-and-conquer strategy and can be used to obtain relational clauses from the learned trees. Various methods [19,27] that propose relational learning and inference by using ensembles of these TILDE trees were also proposed. SPNs are inherently propositional, and model examples with an independent and identically distributed (i.i.d) assumption. Learning SPNs for relational domains [28] relaxed the i.i.d assumption by defining a set of object classes to model the relationship among various instances, along with learning a probability distribution over the features themselves. The key idea behind learning a relational SPN is the use of an aggregation statistic over variables to take advantage of symmetries existing in relational data.

Probabilistic Circuits for Count Data: Sum-Product Networks were originally proposed for univariate parametric distributions either in the form of Bernoulli or Gaussian distributions at leaves [33]. The state-of-the-art structure learning algorithm LEARN-SPN and part of its variants have been developed with the assumption that the data originated from a specific form of a multivariate distribution. Since a considerable amount of real-world data follows the Poisson distribution, recent developments have been focused on learning the structure of an SPN by assuming count data such as Poisson SPNs [25]. Several other models [13,39] have also been proposed that pertain specifically to count data.

3   Probabilistic Circuits over Logical Clauses

Using the expressive power of first-order logic, ILP systems can learn complex programs and discover relations between data instances. This is useful in many domains and real-world applications where i.i.d. assumption does not hold. Despite the expressive power and clear formalism, ILP systems cannot deal with uncertainty and, in general, do not provide tractable inference and learning. SRL models, such as MLNs, have

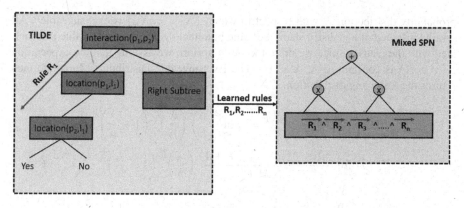

Fig. 2. An overview of learning the GCLN model (TILDE tree → rules → Mixed SPN on a conjunction of rules). The learned GCLN model is discriminative, generative and interpretable.

been devised to enhance first-order logic learners with probability in order to deal with uncertainty and be more flexible. Still, the major part of SRL models do not allow for out-of-the-box tractable inference and tractable approximations have limited expressive power and generalize poorly. Thus, we draw a connection from logical clauses and their counts to Tractable Probabilistic Models [8] that allows, given an arbitrary first-order learner, to:

- Answer in *linear time* a wide range of probabilistic queries e.g. how likely one or more rules can fire together and how many times do the rules fire.
- Learn a powerful Tractable Probabilistic Discriminator that expresses *confidence* about its predictions and that is also *robust to missing and out-of-domain data*.
- *Generate* samples and new predicates.

Generative Clausal Networks. The generative clausal networks (GCLNs) capture the correlations among non mutually exclusive rules which can also share predicates and fire simultaneously. To learn the GCLNs, we start by learning a set of first-order rules by employing TILDE, a well-known top-down inducer of logical decision trees and we keep the counts on how many times a clause fires given a certain data sample. To obtain the counts, for every rule the first and last entity are instantiated and then all the predicates that completely satisfy the partially grounded rules are obtained. Then, we learn a joint distribution over these counts together with the target by encoding such distribution by means of a prominent deep tractable density estimator tailored for hybrid domains i.e. MSPNs [26]. Figure 2 shows the overview to learn the GCLN model.

To model the class, we make use of a Bernoulli distribution; it is either true or false with some probability p. For the clausal features, however, we have to be a bit more careful. They are Exchangeable Distribution Templates [28]. That is, each clausal feature is a function that takes all the ground instances of the clause as a set of random variables $\{X_1, \ldots, X_n\}$ as input (n is unknown a priori), and returns a joint probability distribution P with respect to which $\{X_1, \ldots, X_n\}$ is exchangeable[2]. All ground instance of a clause c share the same binomial distribution with value p associated with the clause. Since we do not know n apriori, we assume that the expectation $p \cdot n =: \lambda$ is constant, $0 < \lambda < \infty$. The Exchangeable Distribution Template then returns the following distribution:

$$\lim_{n \to \infty} \binom{n}{k} p^k (1-p)^{n-k} = \lim_{n \to \infty} \binom{n}{k} \left(\frac{\lambda}{n}\right)^k \left(1 - \frac{\lambda}{n}\right)^{n-k}$$

$$= \lim_{n \to \infty} \frac{n(n-1)\ldots(n-k+1)}{k!} \left(\frac{\lambda}{n}\right)^k \left(1 - \frac{\lambda}{n}\right)^{n-k}$$

$$= \lim_{n \to \infty} \frac{\lambda^k}{k!} \left(1 - \frac{\lambda}{n}\right)^{n-k} = \frac{\lambda^k e^{-\lambda}}{k!}.$$

In other words, the expected rate of a rule firing equals λ, and we get overall a Poisson distribution. Although here we assume that domain elements are exchangeable, our method is rather flexible and it works also when the logical rules contain constants.

Actually, MSPNs allow one to abstract from parametric forms and combine SPNs and piecewise polynomial distributions to learn probabilistic circuits that provide exact and tractable inference without making specific distributional assumptions. In fact, to learn the SPN structure and parameters, MSPNs make use of nonparametric decomposition and conditioning steps using the Renyi Maximum Correlation Coefficient. Taking into account that in our setting we deal mostly with count data i.e. how many times a rule fires– and binary targets, we learn an MSPN by adopting the splitting test tailored for Poisson distributions from PSPNs [25]. In other words, we employ a clustering strategy based on the Renyi Maximum Correlation Coefficient and a variable independence test designed for Poisson distributions. We assume that the independence test is performed between Poisson RVs while clustering can include the target modeled as Bernoulli and therefore, it is better for the latter to be able to deal with arbitrary distributions. Thus, our variant can be seen as a generalization of PSPNs and it could be easily adapted and applied on other types of data distributions.

Interpreting GCLNs. Sum-Product Networks have been shown able to learn a useful representation of the data [38]. Thanks to the clear probabilistic semantics of probabilistic circuits such as SPNs we can easily interpret the learned model in different ways. First, considering that learning the MSPN splits the data matrix by rows and by columns, one could easily check these slicing operations performed during structure learning. By analyzing the learned SPN structure the propositional probabilistic interpretations can be extended for relational data. For example, sum nodes create clusters of instances that fire rules similarly while product nodes work similarly to a logical and. Second, an interpretation can be obtained by checking the samples the learned SPN generates at the sub-trees rooted at different inner nodes.

---

[2] A set of random variables is finitely exchangeable with respect to a joint distribution P, if all permutations of the variables result in the same joint probabilities. Note that finite exchangeable does not require independence; the random variables can have strong dependencies.

Consider a simple sub-tree rooted to a product node S_i having two Poisson distributions (with different scope) as children. This product node models how likely and how many times these two rules fire together "locally" in a specific context shaped by the sum nodes present along the path from the root node to S_i. Additionally, sum nodes introduce latent variables [30] that can be seen as introducing literals in the relational domain. Meanwhile, product nodes are defining new predicates by conjunction of other predicates i.e. given the conditioning done by sum nodes and splitting performed by product nodes one can interpret these operations as manipulating and creating new predicates. A graphical representation of this interpretation is depicted in Fig. 1.[3] For example, the density encoded by the product node $\otimes$ (in blue in the computation graph) is: $P_{X_1,X_2,Y}(X_1, X_2, Y) =$

$$P_{X_1}(X_1 = 1) \cdot P_{X_2}(X_2 = x_2) \cdot P_Y(Y = 0) \cdot \mathbf{1}(\neg Y \wedge X_1)$$

And for its two siblings, from left to right:

$$P_{X_1,X_2,Y}(X_1, X_2, Y) = P_{X_1}(X_1 = 0) \cdot P_{X_2}(X_2 = x_2) \cdot$$
$$P_Y(Y = 0) \cdot \mathbf{1}(\neg Y \wedge \neg X_1)$$
$$P_{X_1,X_2,Y}(X_1, X_2, Y) = P_{X_1}(X_1 > 1) \cdot P_{X_2}(X_2 = x_2) \cdot$$
$$P_Y(Y = 0) \cdot \mathbf{1}(\neg Y \wedge X_1 > 1)$$

While the right branch of the root node $\oplus$ encodes:

$$P_{X_1,X_2,Y}(X_1, X_2, Y) = P_{X_1}(X_1 = x_1) \cdot P_{X_2}(X_2 = x_2) \cdot$$
$$P_Y(Y = 1) \cdot \mathbf{1}(Y = \textit{True})$$

The weights of the sum nodes are proportional to the training instances that fall in the contexts they define e.g. regarding the root node, the weights are proportional to the amount of negative instances for the left branch and to the amount of positive instances for the right branch. They indicate how the two main populations of the distribution i.e. the negative and the positive samples, are distributed and encoded down the tree. On a perfectly balanced data set with a binary target the weight of each root sum node branch would be 0.5 (see Fig. 3).

As mentioned before, an interpretation can be obtained by generating samples from sub-trees rooted at the nodes that one would like to inspect. Therefore, considering the ability to generate samples in linear time, together with the clear semantics, GCLN is able to provide clear interpretations of the learned models w.r.t. the well-known counterparts like Relational Decision Trees or boosting methods where one could end up with very large models that are hard to interpret and thus are limited to compute predictions.

Missing Data Prediction. Dealing with missing data is a crucial and active area of research for both Machine Learning and Data Science with several open questions [2]. When dealing with missing values, task-specific methods such as MICE [4] or KNN [1] are generally used. Despite their popularity, these methods are not easily scalable,

---

[3] In the figure and in the following text $\mathbf{1}()$ represents an indicator function.

can be time-consuming and difficult to tune. Furthermore, often they do not provide confidence of their predictions, they could ignore the interactions with target variables and, mostly, they are able to perform only a single task. To overcome these shortcomings, probabilistic approaches that make use of tractable density estimators for handling missing data have been recently proposed [9,18] and can handle missing data "for free" without being trained specifically for that task but are restricted to propositional data. With GCLN one can gain these benefits in the relational domain. Our model can classify a sample having partial observation regarding the rule that it fires and for a given sample predict the rule counts that are not available i.e. *missing data imputation*. In general, being able to accurately classify samples with missing predicates or also predicting the counts is not a trivial task. Recently, this is getting a lot of attention in practical applications e.g. in case of *privileged features* [37], fairness or privacy issues one can access a set of predicates only at training time and access them at test time could be too expensive or even not allowed. For example, one can classify with a certain confidence if two drugs interact given the rule:

TargetAntagonist(B, C) ∧ EnzymeSubstrate(A, C) $\implies$ Interacts(A, B)

even if EnzymeSubstrate(A, C) is not available or one can predict a disease if

PositiveBloodCheck(A) ∧ HasDiabetes(A) ∧ HighBloodPressure(A) ∧ Tomography(A, T) ∧ PositiveManualCheck(T) $\implies$ HasDisease(A)

even if Tomography(A, T) and PositiveManualCheck(T) are too expensive to obtain.

Out-of-Domain Detection.   Another relevant task in machine learning is out-of-domain detection. This task is useful in many real-world applications such as computer vision [6] and NLP [15,35]. The goal is to distinguish between in-domain and out-of-domain data and this could be useful e.g. for being robust to adversarial attacks, another relevant application [23]. Within a probabilistic framework, one can consider the likelihood values to discriminate between in-domain and OOD data [32,40]. With GCLNs, this question can be answered by considering the likelihoods of data. Similar to missing data prediction, this comes "for free" i.e. without training the model explicitly for the task. Thus, GCLNs are powerful and flexible models that can perform several relevant tasks in the relational domain by answering a wide range of probabilistic queries.

4 Experiments

We aim to show our connection from Relational Decision Trees to Tractable Statistical Relational Inference and show that this leads to generative models that can act also as more accurate classifiers and are easier to interpret. We aim to answer the following questions: **(Q1)** Are GCLNs accurate discriminators? **(Q2)** Can GCLNs deal with missing data i.e. can they compute accurate predictions with missing data? Are GCLNs accurate probabilistic predictors for missing data imputation? **(Q3)** Are GCLNs able to perform out-of-domain detection? **(Q4)** Can GCLNs provide easy interpretations by means of their clear probabilistic semantics? **(Q5)** Can GCLNs take the best out of both propositional and relational worlds i.e. can GCLNs perform better than propositional and relational models being tractable?

All results are cross-validated with 5 folds and averaged over 5 different seeds to mitigate randomness. Since we are dealing with rule counts, there can be spurious rule firings that we can capture as well which leads to outliers, so we identify and move them to the training folds so the model is more robust. In fact, keeping them in the test set results in an "optimistic" bias in performance evaluation [5].

Datasets. We use 4 balanced relational data sets. **Drug-Drug Interaction (DDI)** [12]: consists of 78 drugs obtained from DrugBank[4]. The data set has 15 relations and the target is Interactions between drug entities. **Protein-Protein Interaction (PPI)** [20]: has 7 relations and is obtained from Alchemy. The target is the interaction relation between two protein entities. **NELL Sports** [24]: consists of information about players and teams and obtained from Never Ending Language Learner. It has 6 relations and the task is to predict whether a team plays a particular sport. **CiteSeer** [20]: consists of publication citations for Alchemy. It has 17 relations and the task is to predict the author of a citation.

(Q1) Probabilistic Classification. After splitting the data into training and test set, we use the default hyper-parameters of MSPNs[5] except $\mu = 100$. We compute the predictions i.e. ground target atoms as results of MPE queries, observing the counts of test samples. We compared GCLN (denoted as GCLN-P for clarity) and its binary variant GCLN-B that considers only if a rule fires or not, with several well-known high-performance propositional (Logistic Regression (LR), Gradient Boosting (GB), Neural Networks with 3 hidden layers (NN), Decision Trees (DT)), relational (TILDE) and statistical-relational (RDN-Boost and MLN-Boost) models. The results are shown in Table 1. GCLNs outperform the other models in the majority of data sets and have comparable performance on CiteSeer. This is due to the particular shape of the data set which consists of 15K instances and 9 features and is more likely to have spurious instances harder to discriminate. It is important to remark that, compared to the statistical-relational baselines, GCLNs provide general tractable—and exact in most of the common cases—inference. While compared to non-statistical models, GCLNs can provide also meaningful probabilities and interpretations, and they can be employed for several tasks as shown in the rest of the section. Thus, we can answer **(Q1)** affirmatively, GCLNs are accurate discriminators.

(Q2) Inference with Partial Clausal Counts. We want to test whether GCLNs are robust to missing data by: 1) predict the class of test instances with a variable amount of missing features, 2) missing data imputation, and 3) predict the class of test instances with partially observed counts i.e. during testing the clause might not fire always and thus we do not have the true counts.

For 1), we compute the class prediction accuracy with GCLNs removing a varying percentage of features at random at test time. Figure 4 shows that GCLNs are accurate even with a considerable amount of missing features and it degrades gracefully on CiteSeer. The improvement on PPI is probably due to the presence of noisy/redundant

---

[4] www.drugbank.ca.
[5] https://github.com/SPFlow/SPFlow.

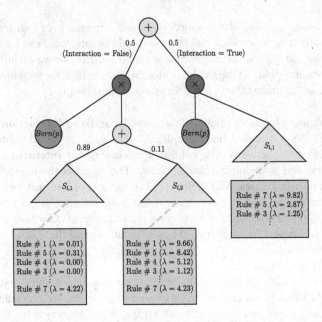

Fig. 3. Top levels of GCLN learned on DDI. GCLNs have clear semantics, the root sum node is clustering by label (balanced dataset) while the rest of the computation graph is encoding the different aspects of the distribution e.g. Rule #7 distributes differently basing on the label (i.e. the root node branch) while Rule #1 and #5 could fire many times for a small population of negative samples (consider the sum node weights along the path that brings to the sub-tree rooted at $S_{l,2}$ and the corresponding parameters λ).

features, considering no data preprocessing was done. Table 2 shows that, when the 30% of features are missing, GCLNs still perform strongly.

Regarding 2), we compared GCLNs with two standard data imputation methods: MICE and kNN[6]. Table 3 shows the accuracy as Mean Squared Error for the imputation of 30% of missing features chosen at random. The results show that GCLNs are competitive with task-specific state-of-the-art methods without being trained specifically for the task.

For 3), since GCLNs employ Poisson distributions, we can answer queries such as $P(X > k)$ i.e. how likely can a rule fire more times additionally to the observed count. To answer such queries, we propagate the computed probabilities

$$P(X > k) = 1 - \sum_{i=0}^{k} P(X = i)$$

from the leaves to the root, given the Poisson leaf parameters. This way, GCLNs can also compute predictions and perform classification with partial knowledge. To see how accurate are GCLNs in these cases, we picked two of the most discriminative rules (e.g. rule #1 and #7 for DDI, see Fig. 5) and reduced the values of the counts by 20%. Table 4 shows that GCLNs can be accurate discriminators even when the most discriminative

---

[6] Both Scikit-learn implementation with default hyperparameters.

Table 1. Classification results of baselines compared to GCLN. The 1st 4 classifiers are propositional, the next 3 are purely relational and the last 2 are our models. In most of the cases GCLN outperforms the baselines. Furthermore, in the same cases, this happens also when employing Bernoulli distributions (GCLN-B). When comparing GCLN-P and GCLN-B one can clearly see that modelling counts with Poisson distributions indeed improves performances (denoted ↑).

Data	Methods	Accuracy	AUC-ROC	AUC-PR	Data	Methods	Accuracy	AUC-ROC	AUC-PR
DDI	LR	**93.79**	**87.62**	83.64	*NELL*	LR	83.96	58.90	28.27
	GB	86.77	86.17	67.95		GB	87.69	75.28	48.07
	NN	87.54	85.03	69.21		NN	88.26	74.42	48.35
	DT	85.52	83.22	65.12		DT	87.27	71.77	45.71
	TILDE	72.52	73.43	70.79		TILDE	81.48	86.27	78.23
	RDN-B	75.54	82.87	83.13		RDN-B	81.26	88.47	83.41
	MLN-B	63.80	79.83	78.40		MLN-B	60.54	**89.44**	**85.30**
	GCLN-B	85.05	70.57	70.84		GCLN-B	80.74	38.72	23.15
	GCLN-P	92.22 ↑	87.53 ↑	**83.81** ↑		GCLN-P	89.83 ↑	89.44 ↑	56.39 ↑
PPI	LR	78.13	81.54	52.44	*CiteSeer*	LR	76.33	83.78	53.30
	GB	77.21	78.25	49.54		GB	96.05	**97.21**	87.24
	NN	76.94	75.75	47.49		NN	**96.50**	96.88	88.10
	DT	76.47	77.52	48.71		DT	95.33	96.79	85.38
	TILDE	62.20	62.87	58.27		TILDE	91.47	83.33	73.45
	RDN-B	67.15	72.84	74.02		RDN-B	94.72	97.11	**89.23**
	MLN-B	54.87	74.39	73.34		MLN-B	81.98	94.67	80.54
	GCLN-B	79.72	82.75	59.43		GCLN-B	77.18	71.34	41.20
	GCLN-P	**81.56** ↑	**91.16** ↑	**80.08** ↑		GCLN-P	86.42 ↑	71.57 ↑	42.57 ↑

Table 2. Class prediction performance with 30% missing clauses.

Data	Accuracy	AUC-ROC	AUC-PR
DDI	89.90 ± 0.035	79.23 ± 0.036	75.00 ± 0.040
PPI	84.77 ± 0.025	89.18 ± 0.024	79.83 ± 0.040
NELL	86.06 ± 0.054	79.96 ± 0.063	47.30 ± 0.092
CiteSeer	68.09 ± 0.103	50.69 ± 0.016	32.51 ± 0.013

rules have underestimated counts and we can answer (**Q2**) affirmatively. GCLNs are not only robust in case of noisy or redundant features but are also beneficial with partial knowledge.

(Q3) Out-of-Domain Detection. We want to test whether GCLNs are robust to and can detect out-of-domain data. To this aim, we take the regular (in-domain) test data instances and we flip the binary target variable value of those to generate out-of-domain test data sets. Then, we compute the average log-likelihoods of these sets. For in-domain data the higher the log-likelihood the better, while for out-of-domain data the lower the better. We run a comparison with Discrete Flows, a state-of-the-art neural density estimator [36]. As one can clearly see in Table 5, GCLNs assign, on average, remarkably lower log-likelihood to out-of-domain data compared to the one for in-domain test data,

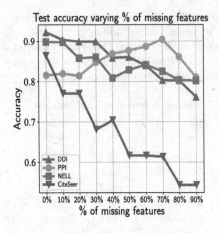

Fig. 4. Average test accuracy varying the amount of missing features. GCLNs are accurate also when a considerable amount of features is missing.

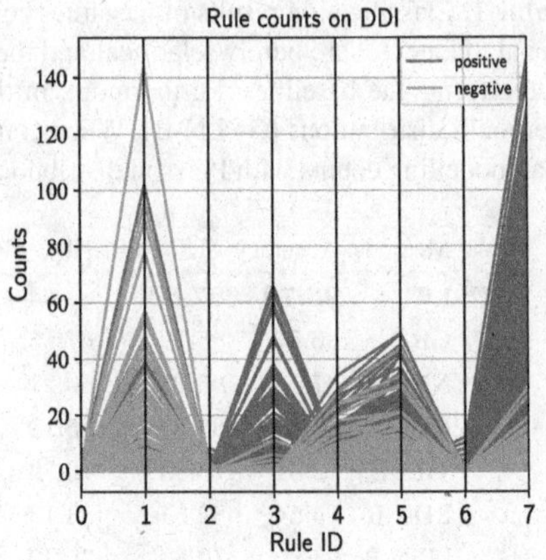

Fig. 5. Rule counts on DDI for each label i.e. no interaction and interaction between drugs.

Table 3. Missing data imputation MSE with 30% missing clauses.

Data	kNN	MICE	GCLN
DDI	37.41 ± 3.751	37.25 ± 3.451	40.72 ± 3.794
PPI	2.40 ± 3.451	1.44 ± 1.748	3.22 ± 4.320
NELL	18.53 ± 28.900	10.80 ± 16.644	42.58 ± 40.612
CiteSeer	0.76 ± 0.090	0.65 ± 0.011	1.02 ± 0.039

and lower than the one which Discrete Flows assign to out-of-domain data. This strong signal shows that GCLNs are effective in detecting out-of-domain data. Being able to perform out-of-domain detection also makes GCLNs more robust to potential adversarial attacks. Thus, we can answer (**Q3**) positively.

(Q4) Model Interpretation. We inspect the model interpretability by looking at the structural characteristics of the learned models and their parameters. We discovered that the root sum node of the SPNs does a high-level discrimination between instances, and respectively sub-populations of the distribution and thus discriminates between negative and positive examples. This is also consistent with the interpretation of deep models where the upper layers encode more abstract concepts. Similar observations can be done for the following layers where common patterns on how the counts distribute "locally" for both negative and positive samples are encoded down the SPN tree. For example, on DDI, a considerable group of positive instances has all the features equal to 0 (no rules fired) while several negative instances have all the features equal to 0 except the last one. This is a common pattern for negative samples i.e. when only the last rule fires one or more times. Figure 3 shows the top levels of the GCLN that performs the best on the training set. Some example rules learned for DDI are:

Table 4. Prediction with partially observed counts.

Data	Accuracy	AUC-ROC	AUC-PR
DDI	85.93 ± 0.042	94.11 ± 0.020	90.83 ± 0.015
PPI	42.65 ± 0.025	87.70 ± 0.063	83.09 ± 0.074
NELL	85.76 ± 0.058	63.02 ± 24.26	30.32 ± 0.092
CiteSeer	72.96 ± 0.014	50.00 ± 0.000	27.04 ± 0.089

Table 5. Average test log-likelihoods for in-domain data (the higher the better) and OOD (the lower the better). To create test OOD data we flip the target value of the test instances. One can see that GCLNs are also good OOD detectors, in fact, the log-likelihood of OOD data is much lower compared to the log-likelihood of in-domain instances, and also lower than the one which Discrete Flows assign to OOD data.

	GCLN		Discrete Flows	
Data	In-domain	OOD	In-domain	OOD
DDI	-9.02 ± 0.431	-21.55 ± 6.124	-6.92 ± 0.194	-6.95 ± 0.194
PPI	-7.91 ± 2.056	-8.61 ± 0.956	-6.98 ± 0.409	-6.93 ± 0.415
NELL	-21.37 ± 4.969	-23.02 ± 3.131	-11.81 ± 0.775	-12.24 ± 0.750
CiteSeer	-5.17 ± 0.122	-124.42 ± 23.824	-4.26 ± 0.200	-4.36 ± 0.200

Rule #1: Transporter(C, A) $\wedge$ Transporter(C, B) $\implies$ Interacts(A,B)
Rule #3: Transporter(C, A) $\wedge$ EnzymeInhibitor(A, D) $\wedge$ EnzymeSubstrate(B, D) $\wedge$ TransporterSubstrate(A, C) $\wedge$ TransporterInducer(A, E) $\implies$ Interacts(A,B)
Rule #7: TargetAntagonist(B, C) $\wedge$ EnzymeSubstrate(A, C) $\implies$ Interacts(A,B)

One can see that the top levels are capturing the high-level concepts in data where e.g. Rule #7 is likely to fire more many times for positive samples. The explanation is that the rule fires when the same protein acts as an antagonist for one drug and as a substrate for another i.e. they are more likely to interact. This is also confirmed by looking globally at how the rule counts distribute for different labels in Fig. 5. For example, one can see that the rules #7, #5 and #3 are very discriminative. Such interpretations can be provided also when computing predictions (see Q1) and used as explanations for XAI. Therefore, we can answer (**Q4**) positively.

(Q5) Ablation Study. We compare GCLNs with TILDE and GCLN-Bernoulli to check whether considering the rule counts is beneficial instead of the binary counterpart where we consider only if a rule fires or not and we model this by means of Bernoulli distributions. In this context, for clarity, GCLN-Poisson is an alias of GCLN. Looking at Table 1 we can see that GCLN-Poisson outperforms TILDE in all cases (up to 31% relative increase on PPI) except for CiteSeer. GCLN-Bernoulli has competitive accuracy performance when compared with the other methods and it outperforms them on PPI. However, GCLN-Poisson outperforms GCLN-Bernoulli in all the cases. This means that *GCLNs can take the best out of the two worlds* by improving upon the relational

model and when considering only when a rule fires or not. Moreover, in most of the cases, it outperforms all the propositional models and answers **(Q5)** affirmatively.

5 Conclusion

We introduce GCLNs and have drawn a connection from relational models to tractable probabilistic models that allow to compute general tractable inference, provide meaningful probabilities and have clear semantics that foster interpretability. Besides, GCLNs can act as both deep tractable generative model and accurate discriminator that is robust to missing and partially observed features, and can be used conveniently also for out-of-domain detection. Future work includes extending our model to the open-world domain and make use of multiple distributions. Encoding more relational models as probabilistic models thereby providing tractability is an important future direction.

Acknowledgments. This work was supported by the ICT-48 Network of AI Research Excellence Center "TAILOR" (EU Horizon 2020, GA No 952215), the Federal Ministry of Education and Research (BMBF; Competence Center for AI and Labour; "kompAKI", FKZ 02L19C150), the German Science Foundation (DFG, German Research Foundation; GRK 1994/1 "AIPHES"), the Hessian Ministry of Higher Education, Research, Science and the Arts (HMWK; projects "The Third Wave of AI" and "The Adaptive Mind"), the Hessian research priority programme LOEWE within the project "WhiteBox", and the Collaboration Lab "AI in Construction" (AICO).

References

1. Altman, N.S.: An introduction to kernel and nearest-neighbor nonparametric regression. The Am. Stat. (1992)
2. Austin, P.C., White, I.R., Lee, D.S., van Buuren, S.: Missing data in clinical research: a tutorial on multiple imputation. Can. J. Cardiol. (2020)
3. Blockeel, H., de Raedt, L.: Top-down induction of first-order logical decision trees. AI (1998)
4. van Buuren, S., Groothuis-Oudshoorn, K.: mice: Multivariate imputation by chained equations in r. J. Stat. Softw. (2011)
5. Cawley, G.C., Talbot, N.L.: On over-fitting in model selection and subsequent selection bias in performance evaluation. JMLR (2010)
6. Chattopadhyay, P., Balaji, Y., Hoffman, J.: Learning to balance specificity and invariance for in and out of domain generalization. In: Vedaldi, A., Bischof, H., Brox, T., Frahm, J.-M. (eds.) ECCV 2020. LNCS, vol. 12354, pp. 301–318. Springer, Cham (2020). https://doi.org/10.1007/978-3-030-58545-7_18
7. Cheng, W., Kok, S., Pham, H.V., Chieu, H.L., Chai, K.M.A.: Language modeling with sum-product networks. In: INTERSPEECH (2014)
8. Choi, Y., Vergari, A., Van den Broeck, G.: Probabilistic circuits: a unifying framework for tractable probabilistic models (2020)
9. Correia, A.H.C., Peharz, R., de Campos, C.P.: Joints in random forests. In: NeurIPS (2020)
10. Darwiche, A.: A differential approach to inference in Bayesian networks. JACM (2003)
11. De Raedt, L., Kersting, K., Natarajan, S., Poole, D.: Statistical relational artificial intelligence: logic, probability, and computation (2016)
12. Dhami, D.S., Kunapuli, G., Das, M., Page, D., Natarajan, S.: Drug-drug interaction discovery: kernel learning from heterogeneous similarities. Smart Health (2018)

13. Dhami, D.S., Yen, S., Kunapuli, G., Natarajan, S.: Non-parametric learning of Gaifman models. arXiv preprint arXiv:2001.00528 (2020)
14. Flach, P.A., Lachiche, N.: Naive Bayesian classification of structured data. Mach. Learn. (2004)
15. Gangal, V., Arora, A., Einolghozati, A., Gupta, S.: Likelihood ratios and generative classifiers for unsupervised out-of-domain detection in task oriented dialog. In: AAAI (2020)
16. Gens, R., Domingos, P.: Learning the structure of sum-product networks. In: ICML (2013)
17. Getoor, L., Taskar, B.: Statistical relational learning (2007)
18. Khosravi, P., Vergari, A., Choi, Y., Liang, Y., den Broeck, G.V.: Handling missing data in decision trees: a probabilistic approach. arXiv preprint arXiv:2006.16341 (2020)
19. Khot, T., Natarajan, S., Kersting, K., Shavlik, J.: Learning Markov logic networks via functional gradient boosting. In: ICDM (2011)
20. Kok, S., et al.: The alchemy system for statistical relational AI (2005)
21. Landwehr, N., Kersting, K., De Raedt, L.: nfoil: Integrating Naïve Bayes and foil. In: AAAI (2005)
22. Landwehr, N., Kersting, K., De Raedt, L.: Integrating Naive Bayes and foil. JMLR (2007)
23. Lee, K., Lee, K., Lee, H., Shin, J.: A simple unified framework for detecting out-of-distribution samples and adversarial attacks. In: NeurIPS (2018)
24. Mitchell, T., et al.: Never-ending learning. Commun. ACM (2018)
25. Molina, A., Natarajan, S., Kersting, K.: Poisson sum-product networks: a deep architecture for tractable multivariate Poisson distributions. In: AAAI (2017)
26. Molina, A., Vergari, A., Mauro, N.D., Natarajan, S., Esposito, F., Kersting, K.: Mixed sum-product networks: a deep architecture for hybrid domains. In: AAAI (2018)
27. Natarajan, S., Khot, T., Kersting, K., Gutmann, B., Shavlik, J.: Gradient-based boosting for statistical relational learning: the relational dependency network case. Mach. Learn. (2012)
28. Nath, A., Domingos, P.: Learning relational sum-product networks. In: AAAI (2015)
29. Neville, J., Jensen, D.: Relational dependency networks. JMLR (2007)
30. Peharz, R., Gens, R., Pernkopf, F., Domingos, P.M.: On the latent variable interpretation in sum-product networks. TPAMI (2017)
31. Peharz, R., Kapeller, G., Mowlaee, P., Pernkopf, F.: Modeling speech with sum-product networks: application to bandwidth extension. In: ICASSP (2014)
32. Peharz, R., et al.: Random sum-product networks: a simple and effective approach to probabilistic deep learning. In: UAI (2019)
33. Poon, H., Domingos, P.M.: Sum-product networks: a new deep architecture. In: UAI (2011)
34. Richardson, M., Domingos, P.: Markov logic networks. Mach. Learn. (2006)
35. Tan, M., et al.: Out-of-domain detection for low-resource text classification tasks. In: EMNLP-IJCNLP (2019)
36. Tran, D., Vafa, K., Agrawal, K.K., Dinh, L., Poole, B.: Discrete flows: invertible generative models of discrete data. In: NeurIPS 2019 (2019)
37. Vapnik, V., Vashist, A.: A new learning paradigm: learning using privileged information. Neural Netw. (2009)
38. Vergari, A., Di Mauro, N., Esposito, F.: Visualizing and understanding sum-product networks. Mach. Learn. (2019)
39. Yang, E., Ravikumar, P.K., Allen, G.I., Liu, Z.: On Poisson graphical models. In: NIPS (2013)
40. Yu, Z., Ventola, F., Kersting, K.: Whittle networks: a deep likelihood model for time series. In: ICML (2021)
41. Yuan, Z., Wang, H., Wang, L., Lu, T., Palaiahnakote, S., Tan, C.L.: Modeling spatial layout for scene image understanding via a novel multiscale sum-product network. Expert Syst. Appl. (2016)

A Simulated Annealing Meta-heuristic for Concept Learning in Description Logics

Patrick Westphal[1,2]([⊠]) [iD], Sahar Vahdati[2,3] [iD], and Jens Lehmann[1,3] [iD]

[1] Fraunhofer Institute for Intelligent Analysis and Information Systems, Dresden, Germany
patrick.westphal@iais.fraunhofer.de
[2] Institute for Applied Informatics, Leipzig, Germany
[3] University of Bonn, Bonn, Germany

Abstract. Ontologies – providing an explicit schema for underlying data – often serve as background knowledge for machine learning approaches. Similar to ILP methods, concept learning utilizes such ontologies to learn concept expressions from examples in a supervised manner. This learning process is usually cast as a search process through the space of ontologically valid concept expressions, guided by heuristics. Such heuristics usually try to balance *explorative* and *exploitative* behaviors of the learning algorithms. While exploration ensures a good coverage of the search space, exploitation focuses on those parts of the search space likely to contain accurate concept expressions. However, at their extreme ends, both paradigms are impractical: A totally random explorative approach will only find good solutions by chance, whereas a greedy but myopic, exploitative attempt might easily get trapped in local optima. To combine the advantages of both paradigms, different meta-heuristics have been proposed. In this paper, we examine the Simulated Annealing meta-heuristic and how it can be used to balance the exploration-exploitation trade-off in concept learning. In different experimental settings, we analyse how and where existing concept learning algorithms can benefit from the Simulated Annealing meta-heuristic.

Keywords: Inductive Logic Programming (ILP) · Description Logic (DL) · Concept Learning (CL) · Meta-heuristics

1 Introduction

The availability of vast amounts of structured data with explicit semantics offers great opportunities for analytics in downstream AI tasks. One such data source is the Linked Open Data cloud[1] which is a distributed and interlinked collection of knowledge bases expressed by means of ontologies covering many different domains. Ontologies provide means for a logic-based description of a domain of interest and allow to express *terminological* knowledge such as hierarchies

---

[1] https://lod-cloud.net/.

© Springer Nature Switzerland AG 2022
N. Katzouris and A. Artikis (Eds.): ILP 2021, LNAI 13191, pp. 266–281, 2022.
https://doi.org/10.1007/978-3-030-97454-1_19

of relations and *concepts* i.e. categories to classify individuals with common relevant features [1]. Further, knowledge bases also provide *assertional* knowledge, i.e. statements about individuals of the domain and how they relate to each other. An established formalism to express such background knowledge are Description Logics (DL) [1] which allow to formulate statements about the domain of interest in the form of axioms. One way to gain insights from such relational data is to inductively learn from positive and negative examples. Starting with a set of example individuals for a target concept, a concept description is learned s.t. it accurately covers positive examples while not covering negative examples [12]. Such concept descriptions can then serve as human and machine readable binary classifiers to classify unseen individuals w.r.t. the target concept. The idea of *concept learning* (CL) is often cast as a systematic search in the space of possible concept descriptions which is mainly aiming to maximize the example classification accuracy.

A common approach for exploring the search space is to follow a refinement-based approach which is guided by a heuristic [12]. Such approaches often take advantage of iteratively improving intermediate concept descriptions based on a given quality measure e.g. accuracy. This procedure can be seen as *Hill Climbing* where the whole refinement process is understood as a sequence of incremental changes to a candidate concept expression [16]. As many Hill Climbing methods, a concept learning algorithm might be prone to get stuck in a local optimum, which renders the algorithm *myopic*. In CL, this occurs when an intermediate candidate concept description scores too low with respect to the employed quality measure. Such concept descriptions are then ignored in further refinement iterations, but may be essential steps on the refinement path towards the optimal solution which is then never found by the algorithm. Such myopic behavior is usually caused by applying a heuristic which is greedily guiding the search process to achieve sensible solutions, while being incapable of leaving local optima or plateaus. To remedy this, different solutions have been explored in the field of mathematical optimization, however, only very few of them have been applied to CL. As one promising attempt to tackle myopia in CL, we extend existing algorithms with the established Simulated Annealing meta-heuristic. As our main contribution of this article, we propose a formalism to integrate Simulated Annealing into concept learning. Furthermore, we provide an evaluation of the resulting algorithm showing that we are able to tackle the myopia problem and achieve competitive results on synthetic and real world learning problems.

2   Related Work

Inductive Learning Systems. Different research fields have addressed *inductive* inference of general principles or patterns from specific facts considering background knowledge. Most prominently *Inductive Logic Programming* (ILP) contributes several systems implementing different strategies [14]. In CL the goals of ILP are adapted and extended using a different family of knowledge representation languages, namely Description Logics. Here, a common task is to learn concept descriptions from individuals serving as positive and negative examples. Such concept descriptions should cover the positive examples while not covering the negative ones. Several concept learning systems have been developed in this regard namely YINGYANG [9], DL-FOIL [5,8] and the DL-Learner [2].

YINGYANG is one of the early systems with the main strategy of applying the *counterfactual* method, i.e. finding concepts that cover negative examples and conjunctively add the negations of such concepts to the overall solution to rule out the wrongly covered negative examples.

DL-FOIL is a 'FOIL-like' algorithm that applies a sequential covering approach to concept learning. It partly reuses other CL techniques but extends the binary setting of evaluating the covered positive and negative examples to a three-valued setting, also considering examples of uncertain membership when evaluating a concept description.

The DL-Learner framework is a collection of learning algorithms and strategies for CL. The most prominent algorithms are the *OWL Class Expression Learner* (OCEL) [11] and the *Class Expression Learner for Ontology Engineering* (CELOE) [10]. Inspired by OCEL and CELOE, the authors of [18] proposed the ParCEL algorithm which was subsequently implemented in the DL-Learner framework. ParCEL tries to compute multiple partial concept descriptions in parallel which are eventually combined to form the target concept. This idea is further extended, in a way similar to the counterfactuals idea, by the same authors which lead to the SPaCEL algorithm [19].

Extended Meta-heuristics Approaches. Each of the aforementioned systems employs refinement strategies to systematically explore the space of ontologically valid concept descriptions. Similar to the findings made for refinement operators in the ILP domain [17], certain properties of upward and downward refinement operators in Description Logics were investigated [4,6,12]. Starting with an initial concept description, new concepts are derived by applying refinement rules through a downward (upward) refinement operator. Usually, the refined concepts are evaluated based on a *heuristic* which guides the search process by picking promising concepts for the next refinement iteration.

This basic paradigm lends itself for comparison with the *Hill Climbing* optimization techniques. In [3] the authors relate refinement-based ILP methods to Hill Climbing and propose to apply certain meta-heuristics, namely *Beam Search*, *Look-Ahead* methods, and the introduction of *Determinate Literals*, to overcome the Hill Climbing search-inherent myopia problem. Similarly, in [17] the authors introduce *Simulated Annealing* for non-myopic ILP. However, this approach cannot be applied to concept learning without modifications. A more general investigation about the introduction of randomized restarts into the search process was performed in [20]. Whereas the core idea of randomly picking a clause from an active set of considered clauses is similar to the random choice from the built search tree in CL as proposed here, many details differ.

Also motivated by the Hill Climbing analogy, in [15,16] DL-FOCL is proposed, which extends DL-FOIL by meta-heuristic strategies such as *Repeated Hill*

Table 1. Terms and Notations in Description Logics (summarized from [1]).

Notation	Description
N_C, N_R, N_I	Set of all concept names, role names, and individual names respectively
A, B, C, D	Concepts (or "classes") denoting sets of individuals where A, B are atomic concepts
$\top, \bot$	Concept denoting the complete domain Δ, and the empty concept, respectively
r, s	Roles (or "object properties")
$\sqcap, \sqcup, \neg$	Concept/role constructors allowing to define the concept/role *intersection*, *union*, and *negation*, respectively
$\exists r.C, \forall r.C$	Existential and universal restriction on the role r, respectively
$C \sqsubseteq D$	Inclusion axiom, meaning that C is a sub-concept/subclass of D
a, b	Individuals of a considered domain Δ
$C(a), r(a, b)$	Class assertion stating that individual a is an instance of concept C, and role assertion stating that individuals a and b are related via role R
$\mathcal{K} \models \alpha$	Entailment of axiom α from knowledge base $\mathcal{K}$

Climbing, *Look-Ahead* mechanisms, and *Tabu Search*. In this paper we extend the research on meta-heuristics in CL learning by considering the Simulated Annealing technique to systematically adjust explorative and exploitative traits of a learning algorithm.

3 Approach

Balancing exploration and exploitation when searching solutions is one of the key aspects in designing CL algorithms. Heuristics guiding an algorithm's behavior in this respect can follow established patterns published in the meta-heuristics literature [3,16,17], or combine different, more specific strategies as in [10,11]. Especially for refinement-based CL approaches, many meta-heuristics from combinatorial optimization theory are applicable. We concentrate on the Simulated Annealing meta-heuristic and its application to concept learning using the OCEL [11] and CELOE [10] algorithms. We further introduce the notion of *Adaptive Simulated Annealing* for concept learning and provide the details about the respective Simluated Annealing extensions for OCEL and CELOE.

3.1 Notation and Preliminaries

To express knowledge of a certain domain of discourse Δ we distinguish *individuals* being elements of the domain, and concepts, or "classes", representing sets of individuals. The relations between individuals are expressed by *roles*. An overview of the basic notations is given in Table 1. We also refer to candidate solutions, or hypotheses, as well as their refinements (in an abstract or more concrete sense). For notational clarity, a single candidate solution is denoted by the Greek letter σ, whereas sets of candidate solutions are represented by the uppercase Greek letter Σ (both optionally with indexes).

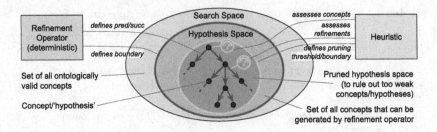

Fig. 1. Terms and Spaces in Concept Learning.

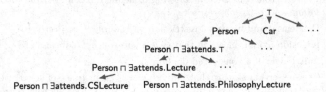

Fig. 2. Search tree of an example refinement

3.2 Concept Learning in Description Logics

We focus on the problem of inductively learning a (usually complex) concept describing a set of observed individuals from N_I. Given the set $N^+ = \{a_1^+, a_2^+, \ldots\} \subseteq N_I$ of *positive examples*, and the set $N^- = \{a_1^-, a_2^-, \ldots\} \subseteq N_I$ of *negative examples* a target concept C_t shall be learned, such that $\mathcal{K} \models C_t(a_i^+)$ for all $a_i^+ \in N^+$, and $\mathcal{K} \not\models C_t(a_i^-)$ for all $a_i^- \in N^-$, i.e. positive examples are entailed by the complex concept (not the negative examples). *Refinement-based* CL approaches achieve this by traversing the space of all ontologically valid concept descriptions, i.e. the *search space*. This is done in a systematic manner, e.g. by applying concept constructors and introducing existential/universal restrictions [12]. In this context, such generated concept descriptions are often called *hypotheses*. Given a *quasi-ordered* space $(\Sigma, \leq)$, a downward (upward) refinement operator ρ is a mapping from Σ to 2^Σ such that for any $\sigma \in \Sigma$ we have that $\sigma' \in \rho(\sigma)$ implies $\sigma' \leq \sigma$ ($\sigma \leq \sigma'$) [10]. Depending on the properties of the refinement operator this spans a certain *hypothesis space*. Since we are extending the OCEL and CELOE algorithms we are assuming a downward refinement operator ρ which is complete and proper, as reported in [12]. Moreover, as in [12], we restrict the concept length of the hypotheses generated in each refinement step to achieve finiteness. Further, we consider downward refinement operators over the quasi-ordered space $(\mathcal{L}, \sqsubseteq)$, i.e. over concept descriptions $\mathcal{L}$ and the subsumption relation $\sqsubseteq$ s.t. for each refinement $C' \in \rho(C)$ of an input concept C it holds that $C' \sqsubseteq C$. ρ, in general, is capable of generating concepts in the DL language $\mathcal{ALCHOQ}$ with concrete roles. An example refinement process is shown in Fig. 2. The set of nodes in this refinement graph can be seen as a sub-space of the hypothesis space which is dynamically extended per iteration. Moreover, the refinement operator ρ, in combination with the learning algorithm (OCEL or CELOE), eliminate

---

Algorithm 1: Basic concept learning algorithm

    Result: Best hypothesis σ_{best}
1   SearchTree $\leftarrow$ initial empty search tree
2   $\sigma_{best} \leftarrow$ initial candidate expression
3   SearchTree.add(σ_{best})
4   **repeat**
5   # *Find hypothesis in the whole search tree with highest score according to heuristc* χ
6   **for** σ_{tmp} in SearchTree **do**
7   **if** $\chi(\sigma_{tmp}) > \chi(\sigma_{best})$ **then**
8            $\sigma_{best} \leftarrow \sigma_{tmp}$

9      $\Sigma_{\rho,\sigma_{best}} \leftarrow \rho(\sigma_{best})$
10   **for** σ_{new} in $\Sigma_{\rho,\sigma_{best}}$ **do**
11   **if** σ_{new} *is not too weak* **then**
12   SearchTree.add(σ_{new})

13 **until** *stop criterion is satisfied*;

---

redundancies up to weak equality [10,12]. Hence, the refinement graph forms a tree known as *search tree* in the literature [10,12].

This example also illustrates the problem of myopia. Imagine we have a set of individuals representing CS students as positive examples, and another set of individuals representing philosophy students as negative examples. The background knowledge base contains information about the students' courses and the course taxonomy (with the axioms CSLecture $\sqsubseteq$ Lecture and PhilosophyLecture $\sqsubseteq$ Lecture). Now, if we want to learn a concept description for CS students, a valid hypothesis telling CS students apart from philosophy students would be Person $\sqcap$ $\exists$attends.CSLecture. However, during the refinement process, the hypotheses that are generated in all but the last iteration cover positive and negative examples to the same extent. Thus, a greedy and myopic learning algorithm could prune the refinement chain in earlier iterations, e.g. after refining to Person $\sqcap$ $\exists$attends.⊤ as it does not bring any quality improvements in terms of the concept description's classification accuracy.

A *heuristic*, being the component in a CL setting that takes care of the assessment of generated hypotheses, assigns numeric quality scores. Thus, it makes two hypotheses comparable, and imposes an order on the elements of the hypothesis space. Moreover, a heuristic may mark certain refinements as 'too weak' for further consideration, thus 'cutting' refinement edges in the search tree which will then never be followed. This quality-based pruning further restricts the considered part of the hypothesis space as sketched in Fig. 1. There are several actual quality metrics proposed for the binary [10] and three-valued [16] CL settings. Further, a heuristic might as well consider structural properties of a concept, e.g. penalizing overly complex hypotheses. In essence, the heuristic of a CL algorithm defines the exploitation strategy. However, it may also contain explorative traits, e.g. when penalizing hypotheses that were refined already too often, thus forcing the algorithm to explore other regions of the hypothesis space. In the CL model we introduced here, the heuristic is the core component to balance the exploration vs. exploitation trade-off. It will be denoted as a function $\chi : \Sigma \mapsto \mathbb{R}$ mapping hypotheses to real numbers in the following.

Having the notions of a refinement and a quality score in place, the analogies to the Hill Climbing strategy can be illustrated. In essence, Hill Climbing can be explained as iteratively assessing new candidate solutions retrieved by refining a given candidate and adopt new candidates if the quality score improved [13] (cf. Algorithm 2). To compare this with concept learning, a basic algorithm description abstracted from OCEL and CELOE is provided in Algorithm 1. One difference between refinement-based CL and Hill Climbing is that the refinement operator in concept learning, ρ, is defined to return a set of candidates, whereas the refinement in Hill Climbing, ρ_{hc}, returns just one refined hypothesis per invocation. Another difference is that a Hill Climbing algorithm would just keep track of the current best candidate hypothesis, whereas the CL algorithm presented here keeps track of the whole pruned sub space of the hypothesis space, explored so far. It is stored in the form of a search tree making use of the predecessor/successor relations imposed by the refinement operator. While this comes with a certain memory overhead, the search tree approach is more flexible, especially when the assessment scores of hypotheses may be dynamic. Also, since this allows to get a good overview of how well a certain region of the hypothesis space is explored (e.g. in terms of the number of the child nodes, tree depth etc.) this is of particular use for a balanced exploration strategy. In this regard, even though we kept the variable name $\sigma_{\mathbf{best}}$ to ease the comparison with Algorithm 2, the hypothesis refined in a certain iteration does not have to be the *best*, e.g. in terms of its classification quality, but should rather be understood as the best choice in terms of the "exploration-exploitation" strategy of the applied heuristic. Accordingly, neither OCEL nor CELOE strictly follow a greedy (and thus myopic) Hill Climbing approach but apply such balancing strategies. In their default settings both algorithms have built-in measures to escape local optima. However, the presented concept learning model can still be used to implement a pure greedy Hill Climbing-based approach by defining the heuristic accordingly. To do so, in Sect. 4 we configure the OCEL and CELOE algorithm in the most greedy way to show the potentials of a more balanced heuristic in terms of exploration. In the following, we will introduce the established Simulated Annealing meta-heuristic which dynamically adjusts the explorative and exploitative traits of a learning algorithm.

3.3 Simulated Annealing

When applying a Hill Climbing strategy, a refinement will only be applied if it improves the quality of the hypothesis w.r.t. a heuristc χ. Then every move will go 'uphill' which makes Hill Climbing a purely exploitative approach leading to myopia in case of local optima. The Simulated Annealing meta-heuristic dynamically adds explorative facets to the Hill Climbing procedure in a controlled way. This means, that with some probability, a move might go 'downhill', irrespective of the check whether the quality of a refined hypothesis $\rho_{hc}(\sigma)$ improved over the initial hypothesis σ. The probability of allowing such downhill moves is given by $p = e^{\frac{\chi(\rho_{hc}(\sigma)) - \chi(\sigma)}{t}}$. This probability depends on the magnitude of the quality degradation of $\rho_{hc}(\sigma)$ over σ, where greater degradations make it less

Algorithm 2: Hill Climbing

Result: The best solution σ
$\sigma \leftarrow$ initial candidate solution
repeat

    $\sigma_{new} \leftarrow \rho_{hc}(\sigma)$;
    if $\chi(\sigma_{new}) > \chi(\sigma)$ **then**
        $\sigma \leftarrow \sigma_{new}$

until σ *is the ideal solution or we run out of time;*

Algorithm 3: Simulated Annealing

Result: The best solution σ_{best}
$t \leftarrow$ high initial temperature
$\sigma \leftarrow$ initial candidate solution
$\sigma_{best} \leftarrow \sigma$
repeat

    $\sigma_{new} \leftarrow \rho_{hc}(\sigma))$;
    $p \leftarrow e^{\frac{\chi(\sigma_{new}) - \chi(\sigma)}{t}}$
    if $\chi(\sigma_{new}) > \chi(\sigma)$ *or* $rand(0,1) < p$ **then**
        $\sigma \leftarrow \sigma_{new}$
    $t \leftarrow t - 1$
    if $\chi(\sigma) > \chi(\sigma_{best})$ **then**
        $\sigma_{best} \leftarrow \sigma$

until σ_{best} *is the ideal solution, we run out of time, or* $t = 0$;

likely to take a downhill move. On the other hand, p depends on the parameter t which is usually interpreted as the *temperature* of the Simulated Annealing process. Higher temperatures increase the probability of taking downhill steps (which favors exploration), whereas lower temperatures decrease the probability p making the process more Hill Climbing-like. Simulated Annealing starts with a high temperature and cools down during the execution, turning the initially fully explorative strategy into a fully exploitative one. A sketch of the whole procedure is given in Algorithm 3. Besides cooling down one 'degree' at each iteration (as shown in Algorithm 3), other cooling schedules are possible, too.

If we relax the stop criterion of t being equal to 0, it might be the case that, after being cooled down, the algorithm gets stuck in a local optimum. To remedy this, the Simulated Annealing approach can be extended to 'heat up' again, whenever there are no improvements. We will call this *Adaptive Simulated Annealing* and will investigate its performance impact in Sect. 4. For this adaptive attempt further parameters need to be adjusted. First, analogous to the cooling schedule, there should be a strategy how fast to heat up again. Besides this, one needs to declare when to heat up, i.e. after how many iterations without improvement the cooling process will be reverted to a more explorative strategy.

3.4 Simulated Annealing in Concept Learning

The application of Simulated Annealing to concept learning follows the same goal of balancing exploration and exploitation during the learning process in a systematic way. The core intuition is to be more explorative when the hypotheses are of lower quality and gradually switch to a more greedy strategy when the quality of the learned concepts increases. Other than the aforementioned Hill Climbing approach, the refinement operator we consider in our CL setting returns a *set* of hypotheses, not just a single refinement. Therefore, introducing explorative behavior goes beyond probabilistically accepting or rejecting a single refinement. Instead, we refer to the search tree to introduce probabilistic, explorative moves. To pick a node from the search tree for applying the refinement operator, we usually choose the best one w.r.t. the algorithm's search heuristic (line 6–8 in Algorithm 1). In the proposed Simulated Annealing approach to concept learning, this is replaced by randomly choosing an arbitrary node with the probability p. The definition of p, however, also needs to be adjusted. Since we no longer have one hypothesis and just one refined version of it, we cannot refer to the quality improvement induced by the refinement step, anymore. To follow the intuition for introducing Simulated Annealing into the CL process, we base the value of p on the quality of the currently best hypothesis $\chi(\sigma_{best})$. Accordingly, p is adjusted to $p = e^{\frac{-\chi(\sigma_{best})}{t}}$. In its basic form, the proposed approach will decrease t after each iteration (i.e. the repeat loop in line 4–13 of Algorithm 1). The value of t is not considered as a stop criterion. To introduce an adaptive behavior for each iteration, we keep track whether the quality score of the best hypothesis, i.e. $\chi(\sigma_{best})$, improved. After a certain number of iterations without improvements, the temperature t is increased again, pushing the algorithm back to a more explorative behavior.

4   Empirical Evaluation

For empirical evaluations, we implemented our Simulated Annealing approach as part of the DL-Learner framework. In particular, we extended the OCEL and CELOE algorithms to investigate the potential of this meta-heuristic in CL. A new heuristic was designed realising the Simulated Annealing strategy as introduced in Subsect. 3.4. OCEL and CELOE can be run in a *pure* or *adaptive* Simulated Annealing setting. Both versions are evaluated in our experiments. The source code of the implemented algorithms is freely available in the *feature/extended-metaheuristics* branch of the DL-Learner GitHub project[2]. In the following, we explain the evaluation setting and discuss the results.

4.1   Evaluation Setup

Two types of evaluation setups have been considered: 1) a setting for evaluating an algorithm's capabilities of tackling the myopia problem, 2) a setting for providing insights into the performance of the CL approaches on real world learning problems. For the first part, we developed a dataset generator which can create knowledge bases in OWL of arbitrary size (in terms of the defined classes, object properties, datatype properties and individuals). For each dataset, a target concept description $C_{target} \equiv \exists r_1.(\cdots \exists r_n.C_+)\cdots)$ is generated, where all r_i (with $1 \le i \le n$) and $C_+ \in N_C$ are chosen randomly. The parameter n defines the *(nesting) depth* of the nested existential restriction. Further, the generator declares a defined number of positive and negative examples, as well as additional individuals being neither part of the positive nor part of the negative examples. The dataset generator takes care of creating axioms such that all positive examples will be instances of the target concept. Moreover, the atomic class filler concept C_+ has a sibling class C_-, such that all negative examples are instances of

---

[2] https://github.com/SmartDataAnalytics/DL-Learner/tree/feature/extended-metaheuristics.

$\exists r_1.(\cdots \exists r_n.C_-)\cdots)$. Accordingly, all hypotheses on the refinement chain up the second last step will cover positive and negative examples to the same extent. We generated three learning scenarios for each depth $n \in \{2, 3, 4\}$. The datasets are available for download on the dataset generator project page on GitHub[3]. All datasets have 50 classes, 20 object properties, 10 data properties, as well as 50 positive and 50 negative example individuals. Moreover, the total number of individuals is 300 per each dataset for depth 2, 400 for each dataset of depth '3, and 500 for each dataset of depth 4. The number of axioms for depth 2 datasets is 989, 985, and 986, respectively. For depth 3, the generated datasets have an axiom count of 1297, 1348, and 1371, respectively, and for depth 4 it is 1738, 1705, and 1694. We refer to this part of the evaluation as *synthetic datasets*. In the second part of our evaluation we used the datasets provided by the SML-Bench benchmarking system[4]. The properties of the respective datasets and learning problems are discussed in [21].

In the evaluation, we compare OCEL and CELOE with different configurations. As a baseline for both of the algorithms we configured OCEL and CELOE to be as greedy (and thus, myopic) as possible. Please note that the applied settings still will not make OCEL and CELOE purely greedy algorithms but still leave some measures against myopic behavior in place which cannot be disabled. We will refer to these baseline settings as OCEL (greedy) and CELOE (greedy).

We compare these two base line systems with their respective versions having the Simulated Annealing extensions in place. The start temperature for t is set to 2000 for each system. We configure them to be evaluated in two different settings: One configuration using the 'pure' Simulated Annealing method (OCEL SA, CELOE SA), and one version applying Adaptive Simulated Annealing (OCEL ASA, CELOE ASA). For OCEL ASA and CELOE ASA we set the *reHeatThreshold* to 2, which means that the temperature will be increased after two iterations without improvement.

For comparison against the algorithms in their default settings we also evaluated OCEL (default) and CELOE (default). For all OCEL versions we set the required *noisePercentage* parameter to 35, which makes OCEL accept a candidate expression even if 35% of the examples were misclassified. This parameter was set to a higher value to make OCEL accept and report hypotheses even if they are quite weak, instead of just returning an error message saying that no concept could be learned that complies with the (stricter) noise setting. We could not compare with other concept learning systems, e.g. those presented in [7,8,15], since, to the best of our knowledge, the respective implementations are tied to pre-defined evaluation scenarios and it would require a considerable refactoring effort to make them run standalone. All experiments were executed on a machine with 2 Intel Xeon 'Broadwell' CPUs with 8 cores running at 2.1 GHz with 128 GB of RAM using the SML-Bench benchmark executor.

---

[3] https://github.com/patrickwestphal/learning_scenario_generators/releases/tag/v0.1.0.

[4] https://github.com/SmartDataAnalytics/SML-Bench/tree/updates/learningtasks.

4.2 Results

Synthetic Datasets. The experiments performed on the synthetic datasets allow us to investigate the influence of the allotted execution time and the complexity of the target concept to learn. Whereas it is expected that a greater execution time will lead to better results, we are also interested in the learning behavior of the different algorithms having only a restricted time budget. We compared all OCEL and CELOE variants on the synthetic datasets with different nesting depths n. We chose nesting depths of 2, 3, and 4. With higher nesting depths the performance of all the evaluated learning algorithms dropped and rendered a comparison rather meaningless. We performed our evaluation in a 10-fold cross validation setting on each of three different random learning scenarios we generated per nesting depth and report the overall average accuracy and F_1-score of the best solutions found together with their standard deviations. We repeated the evaluation run with different allotted execution times ranging from 5 s to 60 s. The results are discussed for each nesting depth.

Table 2. Evaluation results on synthetic datasets with a **nesting depth of 2**. Reported are the average accuracy and its standard deviation (top), as well as average F_1-score and its standard deviation (bottom) of the 10-fold cross validation across all three datasets.

Runtime	OCEL (default)	OCEL (greedy)	OCEL SA	OCEL ASA	CELOE (default)	CELOE (greedy)	CELOE SA	CELOE ASA
5 s	0.76 ±0.17	0.76 ±0.17	0.71 ±0.17	0.71 ±0.17	1.00 ±0.00	0.50 ±0.00	0.50 ±0.00	0.50 ±0.00
10 s	0.76 ±0.17	0.76 ±0.17	0.71 ±0.17	0.71 ±0.17	1.00 ±0.00	0.50 ±0.00	0.67 ±0.24	0.67 ±0.24
30 s	0.76 ±0.17	0.76 ±0.17	0.73 ±0.17	0.73 ±0.18	1.00 ±0.00	0.50 ±0.00	0.68 ±0.24	0.68 ±0.24
60 s	0.76 ±0.17	0.73 ±0.16	0.73 ±0.18	0.70 ±0.16	1.00 ±0.00	0.50 ±0.00	1.00 ±0.00	1.00 ±0.00
Runtime	OCEL (default)	OCEL (greedy)	OCEL SA	OCEL ASA	CELOE (default)	CELOE (greedy)	CELOE SA	CELOE ASA
5 s	0.61 ±0.32	0.61 ±0.32	0.53 ±0.32	0.53 ±0.32	1.00 ±0.00	0.67 ±0.00	0.67 ±0.00	0.67 ±0.00
10 s	0.61 ±0.32	0.61 ±0.32	0.52 ±0.32	0.52 ±0.32	1.00 ±0.00	0.67 ±0.00	0.78 ±0.16	0.78 ±0.16
30 s	0.61 ±0.32	0.61 ±0.32	0.56 ±0.32	0.56 ±0.33	1.00 ±0.00	0.67 ±0.00	0.79 ±0.16	0.79 ±0.16
60 s	0.61 ±0.32	0.56 ±0.33	0.55 ±0.34	0.52 ±0.31	1.00 ±0.00	0.67 ±0.00	1.00 ±0.00	1.00 ±0.00

Nesting depth = 2 (Table 2). With a nesting depth of 2 the target concept description to learn has the shape of a doubly nested existential restriction $\exists r_1.(\exists r_2.C_+)$. This expression is still simple enough to favor CELOE's learning strategy of finding simple and human-readable concept descriptions. It can be seen that the explorative trait of the Simulated Annealing variants seemingly come as an overhead here, that does not pay off unless a long enough execution time is granted. The OCEL variants perform worse than CELOE (default) and establish a middle ground with accuracies around 75%. It can be seen that especially OCEL (default) and OCEL (greedy) behave very similar in terms of the susceptibility to execution time constraints. This also suggests that, other than CELOE (greedy), the OCEL (greedy) still has enough built-in explorative characteristics that allow it to overcome myopia irrespective of the settings we applied. This also holds for the following experiments which renders OCEL (greedy) rather unsuitable as a myopic base line for OCEL SA and OCEL ASA. However, we still kept it for reference.

Table 3. Evaluation results on synthetic datasets with a **nesting depth of 3**. Reported are the average accuracy and its standard deviation (top), as well as average F_1-score and its standard deviation (bottom) of the 10-fold cross validation across all three datasets.

Runtime	OCEL (default)	OCEL (greedy)	OCEL SA	OCEL ASA	CELOE (default)	CELOE (greedy)	CELOE SA	CELOE ASA
5 s	0.74 ±0.22	0.51 ±0.16	0.79 ±0.27	0.76 ±0.27	0.52 ±0.06	0.50 ±0.04	0.68 ±0.23	0.68 ±0.23
10 s	0.74 ±0.22	0.72 ±0.24	0.80 ±0.27	0.76 ±0.27	0.52 ±0.06	0.50 ±0.04	0.68 ±0.23	0.68 ±0.23
30 s	0.74 ±0.22	0.74 ±0.22	0.78 ±0.22	0.77 ±0.23	0.52 ±0.06	0.50 ±0.04	0.68 ±0.23	0.68 ±0.23
60 s	0.74 ±0.22	0.73 ±0.22	0.78 ±0.22	0.76 ±0.23	0.52 ±0.06	0.50 ±0.04	0.69 ±0.23	0.69 ±0.23
Runtime	OCEL (default)	OCEL (greedy)	OCEL SA	OCEL ASA	CELOE (default)	CELOE (greedy)	CELOE SA	CELOE ASA
5 s	0.63 ±0.31	0.36 ±0.17	0.73 ±0.32	0.71 ±0.32	0.67 ±0.03	0.66 ±0.03	0.78 ±0.16	0.78 ±0.16
10 s	0.63 ±0.31	0.62 ±0.32	0.74 ±0.32	0.71 ±0.32	0.67 ±0.03	0.66 ±0.03	0.78 ±0.16	0.78 ±0.16
30 s	0.63 ±0.31	0.63 ±0.31	0.70 ±0.31	0.73 ±0.28	0.67 ±0.04	0.66 ±0.03	0.78 ±0.16	0.78 ±0.16
60 s	0.63 ±0.31	0.61 ±0.31	0.69 ±0.31	0.70 ±0.30	0.67 ±0.04	0.66 ±0.03	0.78 ±0.16	0.78 ±0.16

Nesting depth = 3 (Table 3). With the more complex structure of the target concept description $\exists r_1.(\exists r_2.(\exists r_3.C_+))$ the CELOE variants fall behind in terms of accuracy, as expected due to their bias for simpler concepts. The numbers still show a considerable advantage of applying the Simulated Annealing meta-heuristic in terms of accuracy and give the overall best F_1-scores for this experiment which shows the potential of adding further explorative traits to CELOE's heuristic. However, it can be seen, that the adaptive setting seemingly hardly influences the outcomes of CELOE ASA in comparison with CELOE SA.

The OCEL variants in general perform better in terms of accuracy and provide a similar F_1-score compared to CELOE (default) and CELOE (greedy). The execution time constraints do not influence OCEL (default) but drastically do so in case of the other OCEL variants. Especially in case of very short execution times OCEL (greedy), OCEL SA, and OCEL ASA fail to find solutions for a considerable number of folds across all datasets. Accordingly, the numbers provided by SML-Bench might be misleading, as it only gives the averages of the folds where a solution was found. In Table 3 we marked these cases in brown. For the Simulated Annealing variants this shows that a sufficiently long runtime is needed to benefit from their explorative nature. With increased execution times, however, this 'exploration penalty' pays off and OCEL SA and OCEL ASA outperform the other OCEL variants both in terms of accuracy and F_1-score. Furthermore in case of OCEL we can see an influence of the adaptive setting of OCEL ASA which gives an improved F_1-score in our experiment.

Overall, this scenario seems to mark the sweet spot as the target concept description to learn is complex enough to gain advantage from additional explorative characteristics during the learning phase. Whereas runtime restrictions do not matter for the CELOE variants, OCEL's Simulated Annealing adaptions seem to need a certain amount of time to guarantee that an acceptable solution (w.r.t. to the configured noise setting mentioned above) can be found.

Nesting depth = 4 (Table 4). With a nesting depth of 4, i.e. the target concept structure $\exists r_1.(\exists r_2.(\exists r_3.(\exists r_4.C_+)))$, the performance of most of the examined algorithm decreased. The experiment seems to mark a tipping point especially for the OCEL variants as none of them managed to find acceptable solutions (given

Table 4. Evaluation results on synthetic datasets with a **nesting depth of 4**. Reported are the average accuracy and its standard deviation (top), as well as the average F_1-score and its standard deviation (bottom) of the 10-fold cross validation across all three datasets.

Runtime	OCEL (default)	OCEL (greedy)	OCEL SA	OCEL ASA	CELOE (default)	CELOE (greedy)	CELOE SA	CELOE ASA
5 s	0.61 ±0.18	0.60 ±0.18	0.59 ±0.19	0.62 ±0.13	0.54 ±0.11	0.49 ±0.03	0.53 ±0.10	0.53 ±0.10
10 s	0.65 ±0.14	0.65 ±0.10	0.60 ±0.13	0.60 ±0.13	0.54 ±0.11	0.49 ±0.03	0.53 ±0.10	0.53 ±0.10
30 s	0.61 ±0.18	0.62 ±0.18	0.62 ±0.13	0.60 ±0.13	0.53 ±0.11	0.49 ±0.03	0.53 ±0.11	0.53 ±0.11
60 s	0.61 ±0.18	0.60 ±0.18	0.59 ±0.19	0.62 ±0.13	0.53 ±0.11	0.49 ±0.03	0.53 ±0.11	0.53 ±0.11
Runtime	OCEL (default)	OCEL (greedy)	OCEL SA	OCEL ASA	CELOE (default)	CELOE (greedy)	CELOE SA	CELOE ASA
5 s	0.50 ±0.28	0.48 ±0.28	0.53 ±0.26	0.55 ±0.19	0.68 ±0.08	0.66 ±0.02	0.67 ±0.08	0.67 ±0.08
10 s	0.57 ±0.20	0.54 ±0.18	0.58 ±0.16	0.58 ±0.16	0.68 ±0.08	0.66 ±0.02	0.67 ±0.08	0.67 ±0.08
30 s	0.50 ±0.28	0.53 ±0.26	0.55 ±0.19	0.57 ±0.16	0.67 ±0.08	0.66 ±0.02	0.67 ±0.08	0.67 ±0.08
60 s	0.50 ±0.28	0.48 ±0.28	0.53 ±0.26	0.55 ±0.19	0.67 ±0.08	0.66 ±0.02	0.67 ±0.08	0.67 ±0.08

their configured noise settings) for all the folds across the datasets. Accordingly, the results should be interpreted with caution as they might relate to different subsets of the training and test folds. For CELOE in particular the accuracy and F_1-score of the Simulated Annealing variants dropped compared to the nesting depth of 3. This suggests that explorative behavior does not bring any advantages in a complex setting like this. Judging from the results of OCEL and CELOE in their default settings, this might be due to their exploitative strategies which are unfit for such a scenario, but which are essential for a balanced learning approach taking advantage of both exploration *and* exploitation. Accordingly, this suggests that a tailored heuristic would be needed to manage such scenarios, which is beyond the scope of this work.

Overall, however, in this experimentation setting we could show that the existing learning algorithms OCEL and CELOE can benefit from the Simulated Annealing meta-heuristic, especially in more complex cases which require a non-myopic search approach. In the following subsection we will examine the performance of the Simulated Annealing-based approaches on the real-world learning tasks provided by the SML-Bench framework.

SML-Bench. The experiments performed with the SML-Bench dataset library will give an overview of how well the proposed Simulated Annealing extensions work on real world problems. We chose all the datasets evaluated in [21] and granted a maximum execution time of 3 min. (Longer execution times gave no substantial improvements in terms of the results.) Overall it can be seen that the Simulated Annealing variants are competitive w.r.t. their base algorithms. In some cases, namely *carcinogenesis/1*, *mutagenesis/42* and *premierleague/1*, the time spent on exploration seems to cause that OCEL SA and OCEL ASA could not find acceptable solutions for all folds that comply with their noise settings. However, in case of *carcinogenesis/1* OCEL in its standard settings even failed on all but one fold which suggests that this not a problem inherent to the Simulated Annealing approach. We marked these cases in brown in Table 5. The only dataset where the Simulated Annealing variants did not provide any benefits is *mammographic/1*. Here, the base algorithms outperform the extensions in terms

Table 5. Average accuracy and its standard deviation (top), and average F_1-score and its standard deviation (bottom) of 10-fold cross validation run on SML-Bench datasets

Learning problem	OCEL (default)	OCEL (greedy)	OCEL SA	OCEL ASA	CELOE (default)	CELOE (greedy)	CELOE SA	CELOE ASA
carc./1	0.23 ±0.00	0.66 ±0.18	0.66 ±0.18	0.64 ±0.24	0.55 ±0.02	0.54 ±0.01	0.55 ±0.02	0.55 ±0.02
hepat./1	0.68 ±0.08	0.68 ±0.08	0.71 ±0.07	0.71 ±0.07	0.49 ±0.06	0.41 ±0.01	0.47 ±0.05	0.47 ±0.05
lymph./1	0.73 ±0.12	0.73 ±0.12	0.73 ±0.12	0.73 ±0.12	0.70 ±0.15	0.77 ±0.11	0.76 ±0.15	0.76 ±0.15
mam./1	0.82 ±0.05	0.82 ±0.05	0.77 ±0.08	0.77 ±0.08	0.49 ±0.02	0.46 ±0.00	0.46 ±0.00	0.46 ±0.00
mut./42	0.49 ±0.34	0.55 ±0.36	0.71 ±0.10	0.75 ±0.04	0.94 ±0.13	0.30 ±0.07	0.90 ±0.20	0.90 ±0.20
nctrer/1	0.80 ±0.09	0.80 ±0.09	0.82 ±0.11	0.82 ±0.11	0.59 ±0.03	0.59 ±0.01	0.61 ±0.04	0.61 ±0.04
prem./1	0.85 ±0.10	no results	0.83 ±0.15	0.83 ±0.15	0.98 ±0.05	0.49 ±0.02	0.64 ±0.25	0.64 ±0.25
pyrim./1	0.85 ±0.24	0.85 ±0.24	0.75 ±0.26	0.75 ±0.26	0.83 ±0.17	0.50 ±0.00	0.88 ±0.13	0.88 ±0.13
Learning problem	OCEL (default)	OCEL (greedy)	OCEL SA	OCEL ASA	CELOE (default)	CELOE (greedy)	CELOE SA	CELOE ASA
carc./1	0.15 ±0.00	0.65 ±0.20	0.65 ±0.20	0.62 ±0.27	0.71 ±0.01	0.70 ±0.01	0.71 ±0.01	0.71 ±0.01
hepat./1	0.53 ±0.14	0.53 ±0.13	0.58 ±0.26	0.58 ±0.26	0.61 ±0.03	0.58 ±0.01	0.61 ±0.02	0.61 ±0.02
lymph./1	0.76 ±0.10	0.76 ±0.10	0.76 ±0.10	0.76 ±0.10	0.78 ±0.10	0.82 ±0.00	0.81 ±0.11	0.81 ±0.11
mam./1	0.78 ±0.08	0.78 ±0.08	0.73 ±0.12	0.73 ±0.12	0.64 ±0.01	0.63 ±0.00	0.63 ±0.00	0.63 ±0.00
mut./42	0.25 ±0.42	0.32 ±0.43	0.10 ±0.25	0.17 ±0.31	0.93 ±0.14	0.46 ±0.08	0.90 ±0.16	0.90 ±0.16
nctrer/1	0.84 ±0.06	0.84 ±0.06	0.87 ±0.07	0.87 ±0.07	0.74 ±0.01	0.74 ±0.01	0.75 ±0.02	0.75 ±0.02
prem./1	0.81 ±0.13	no results	0.83 ±0.16	0.83 ±0.16	0.98 ±0.05	0.66 ±0.02	0.76 ±0.17	0.76 ±0.17
pyrim./1	0.84 ±0.22	0.84 ±0.22	0.67 ±0.38	0.67 ±0.38	0.84 ±0.15	0.67 ±0.00	0.89 ±0.13	0.89 ±0.13

of accuracy, as well as F_1-score. In all other cases we can see improvements, either for OCEL or CELOE. Except for the *premierleague/1* and *pyrimidine/1* datasets OCEL SA and OCEL ASA outperform OCEL (default). It seems, though, that the Adaptive Simulated Annealing approach provides very similar results to the 'pure' variant. This would suggest, that switching back to a more explorative strategy does not bring great advantages over keeping the exploitative strategy in OCEL. This picture is even more clear in case of CELOE SA and CELOE ASA which always provided the same numbers throughout all experiments (incl. those on the synthetic datasets). Nonetheless, CELOE's Simulated Annealing variants could prove better or equal to CELOE (default) in most of the cases. Overall, even though the Simulated Annealing variants proved to be better suited to learn the complex target expressions in the synthetic experiments this does not mean that they usually will produce more complex hypotheses. The results of the SML-Bench experiments rather show that while the learned expressions do differ, there are no such tendencies towards more complex class expressions.

5   Conclusions

In this paper we proposed an extension for two established concept learning algorithms from the DL-Learner framework based on the Simulated Annealing meta-heuristic. The design of the algorithm extensions is motivated by the goal to overcome the myopia problem by means of a systematic strategy for balancing the exploration and exploitation traits of a concept learning algorithm. On dedicated synthetic datasets we showed that our approach does indeed outperform OCEL and CELOE in more greedy, exploitation-oriented configurations, as well as in their default settings. We could further prove the competitiveness of our Simulated Annealing approach on real world concept learning problems provided by the SML-Bench benchmarking framework.

In future work, we will investigate settings for improving the Adaptive Simulated Annealing, especially for the CELOE algorithm where the 're-heat strategy' only had a minor impact. Further, we will examine other options to decide whether to focus more on explorative or exploitative search. Besides this, gained insights will also help to investigate related meta-heuristics not evaluated on the concept learning setting, yet.

References

1. Baader, F., Calvanese, D., McGuinness, D.L., Nardi, D., Patel-Schneider, P.F. (eds.): The Description Logic Handbook. Cambridge University Press, Cambridge (2007)
2. Bühmann, L., Lehmann, J., Westphal, P.: DL-learner - a framework for inductive learning on the semantic web. Web Seman. **39**, 15–24 (2016)
3. Castillo, L.P., Wrobel, S.: A comparative study on methods for reducing myopia of hill-climbing search in multirelational learning. In: ICML 2004. ACM (2004)
4. Esposito, F., Fanizzi, N., Iannone, L., Palmisano, I., Semeraro, G.: Knowledge-intensive induction of terminologies from metadata. In: McIlraith, S.A., Plexousakis, D., van Harmelen, F. (eds.) ISWC 2004. LNCS, vol. 3298, pp. 441–455. Springer, Heidelberg (2004). https://doi.org/10.1007/978-3-540-30475-3_31
5. Fanizzi, N., d'Amato, C., Esposito, F.: DL-FOIL - concept learning in description logics. In: ILP 2008, pp. 107–121 (2008)
6. Fanizzi, N., Ferilli, S., Iannone, L., Palmisano, I., Semeraro, G.: Downward refinement in the $\mathcal{ALN}$ description logic. In: HIS 2004, pp. 68–73. IEEE (2005)
7. Fanizzi, N., Rizzo, G., d'Amato, C.: Boosting DL concept learners. In: Hitzler, P., et al. (eds.) ESWC 2019. LNCS, vol. 11503, pp. 68–83. Springer, Cham (2019). https://doi.org/10.1007/978-3-030-21348-0_5
8. Fanizzi, N., Rizzo, G., d'Amato, C., Esposito, F.: DLFoil: class expression learning revisited. In: Faron Zucker, C., Ghidini, C., Napoli, A., Toussaint, Y. (eds.) EKAW 2018. LNCS (LNAI), vol. 11313, pp. 98–113. Springer, Cham (2018). https://doi.org/10.1007/978-3-030-03667-6_7
9. Iannone, L., Palmisano, I., Fanizzi, N.: An algorithm based on counterfactuals for concept learning in the semantic web. Appl. Intell. **26**(2), 139–159 (2007)
10. Lehmann, J., Auer, S., Bühmann, L., Tramp, S.: Class expression learning for ontology engineering. J. Web Semant. **9**(1), 71–81 (2011)
11. Lehmann, J., Hitzler, P.: A refinement operator based learning algorithm for the $\mathcal{ALC}$ description logic. In: Blockeel, H., Ramon, J., Shavlik, J., Tadepalli, P. (eds.) ILP 2007. LNCS (LNAI), vol. 4894, pp. 147–160. Springer, Heidelberg (2008). https://doi.org/10.1007/978-3-540-78469-2_17
12. Lehmann, J., Hitzler, P.: Concept learning in description logics using refinement operators. Mach. Learn. J. **78**(1–2), 203–250 (2010)
13. Luke, S.: Essentials of Metaheuristics, 2nd edn. Lulu, Abu Dhabi (2013)
14. Muggleton, S., Watanabe, H. (eds.): Latest Advances in Inductive Logic Programming. World Scientific, Singapore (2014)
15. Rizzo, G., Fanizzi, N., d'Amato, C.: Class expression induction as concept space exploration: from DL-Foil to DL-Focl. FGCS **180**, 256–272 (2020)
16. Rizzo, G., Fanizzi, N., d'Amato, C., Esposito, F.: A framework for tackling myopia in concept learning on the web of data. In: Faron Zucker, C., Ghidini, C., Napoli, A., Toussaint, Y. (eds.) EKAW 2018. LNCS (LNAI), vol. 11313, pp. 338–354. Springer, Cham (2018). https://doi.org/10.1007/978-3-030-03667-6_22

17. Serrurier, M., Prade, H.: Improving inductive logic programming by using simu-lated annealing. Inf. Sci. **178**(6), 1423–1441 (2008)
18. Tran, A.C., Dietrich, J., Guesgen, H.W., Marsland, S.: An approach to parallel class expression learning. In: Bikakis, A., Giurca, A. (eds.) RuleML 2012. LNCS, vol. 7438, pp. 302–316. Springer, Heidelberg (2012). https://doi.org/10.1007/978-3-642-32689-9_25
19. Tran, A.C., Dietrich, J., Guesgen, H.W., Marsland, S.: Parallel symmetric class expression learning. J. Mach. Learn. Res. **18**(1), 2145–2178 (2017)
20. Železný, F., Srinivasan, A., Page, C.D.: Randomised restarted search in ILP. Mach. Learn. **64**(1–3), 183–208 (2006)
21. Westphal, P., Bühmann, L., Bin, S., Jabeen, H., Lehmann, J.: SML-bench - a benchmarking framework for structured machine learning. SWJ **10**(2), 231–245 (2019)

Author Index

Printed in the United States
by Baker & Taylor Publisher Services